SCHAUM'S
OUTLINE OF

THEORY AND PROBLEMS OF

COMPUTER
GRAPHICS

ZHIGANG XIANG, Ph.D.

Associate Professor of Computer Science
Queens College of the City University of New York

ROY A. PLASTOCK, Ph.D.

Associate Professor of Mathematics
New Jersey Institute of Technology

SCHAUM'S OUTLINE SERIES

McGRAW-HILL
New York   St. Louis   San Francisco   Auckland   Bogotá   Caracas   Lisbon
London   Madrid   Mexico City   Milan   Montreal   New Delhi
San Juan   Singapore   Sydney   Tokyo   Toronto

Zhigang Xiang, is currently an associate professor of computer science at Queens College and the Graduate School and University Center of the City University of New York (CUNY). He received a BS degree in computer science and engineering from Beijing Polytechnic University, Beijing, China, in 1982, and the MS and Ph.D degrees in computer science from the State University of New York at Buffalo in 1984 and 1988, respectively. He has published numerous articles in well-respected computer graphics journals.

Roy A. Plastock, is an Associate Professor of Mathematics at New Jersey Institute of Technology. He is listed in *Who's Who in Frontier Science and Technology.* His special interests are computer graphics, computer vision, and artificial intelligence.

Schaum's Outline of Theory and Problems of
COMPUTER GRAPHICS

3 4 5 6 7 8 9 10 11 12 13 14 15 16 17 18 19 20   VFM   VFM   0 9 8 7 6 5 4

ISBN 0-07-135781-5

Sponsoring Editor: Barbara Gilson
Production Supervisor: Tina Cameron
Editing liaison: Maureen B. Walker
Project Supervision: Techset Composition Limited

Library of Congress Cataloging-in-Publication Data

McGraw-Hill
A Division of The McGraw·Hill Companies

To Qian, Wei, and my teachers

ZHIGANG XIANG

To Sharon, Adam, Sam, and the memory of Gordon S. Kalley

ROY PLASTOCK

PREFACE

We live in a world full of scientific and technological advances. In recent years it has become quite difficult not to notice the proliferation of something called computer graphics. Almost every computer system is set up to allow the user to interact with the system through a graphical user interface, where information on the display screen is conveyed in both textual and graphical forms. Movies and video games are popular showcases of the latest technology for people, both young and old. Watching the TV for a while, the likelihood is that you will see the magic touch of computer graphics in a commercial.

This book is both a self-contained text and a valuable study aid on the fundamental principles of computer graphics. It takes a goal-oriented approach to discuss the important concepts, the underlying mathematics, and the algorithmic aspects of the computerized image synthesis process. It contains hundreds of solved problems that help reinforce one's understanding of the field and exemplify effective problem-solving techniques.

Although the primary audience are college students taking a computer graphics course in a computer science or computer engineering program, any educated person with a desire to look into the inner workings of computer graphics should be able to learn from this concise introduction. The recommended prerequisites are some working knowledge of a computer system, the equivalent of one or two semesters of programming, a basic understanding of data structures and algorithms, and a basic knowledge of linear algebra and analytical geometry.

The field of computer graphics is characterized by rapid changes in how the technology is used in everyday applications and by constant evolution of graphics systems. The life span of graphics hardware seems to be getting shorter and shorter. An industry standard for computer graphics often becomes obsolete before it is finalized. A programming language that is a popular vehicle for graphics applications when a student begins his or her college study is likely to be on its way out by the time he or she graduates.

In this book we try to cover the key ingredients of computer graphics that tend to have a lasting value (only in relative terms, of course). Instead of compiling highly equipment-specific or computing environment-specific information, we strive to provide a good explanation of the fundamental concepts and the relationship between them. We discuss subject matters in the overall framework of computer graphics and emphasize mathematical and/or algorithmic solutions. Algorithms are presented in pseudo-code rather than a particular programming language. Examples are given with specifics to the extent that they can be easily made into working versions on a particular computer system.

We believe that this approach brings unique benefit to a diverse group of readers. First, the book can be read by itself as a general introduction to computer graphics for people who want technical substance but not the burden of implementational overhead. Second, it can be used by instructors and students as a resource book to supplement any comprehensive primary text. Third, it may serve as a stepping-stone for practitioners who want something that is more understandable than their graphics system's programmer's manuals.

The first edition of this book has served its audience well for over a decade. I would like to salute and thank my coauthors for their invaluable groundwork. The current version represents a significant revision to the original, with several chapters replaced to cover new topics, and the remaining material updated throughout the rest of the book. I hope that it can serve our future audience as well for years to come.

Thank you for choosing our book. May you find it stimulating and rewarding.

ZHIGANG XIANG

CONTENTS

Introduction

Computer graphics is generally regarded as a branch of computer science that deals with the theory and technology for computerized image synthesis. A computer-generated image can depict a scene as simple as the outline of a triangle on a uniform background and as complex as a magnificent dinosaur in a tropical forest. But how do these things become part of the picture? What makes drawing on a computer different from sketching with a pen or photographing with a camera? In this chapter we will introduce some important concepts and outline the relationship among these concepts. The goal of such a mini-survey of the field of computer graphics is to enable us to appreciate the various answers to these questions that we will detail in the rest of the book not only in their own right but also in the context of the overall framework.

1.1   A MINI-SURVEY

First let's consider drawing the outline of a triangle (see Fig. 1-1). In real life this would begin with a decision in our mind regarding such geometric characteristics as the type and size of the triangle, followed by our action to move a pen across a piece of paper. In computer graphics terminology, what we have envisioned is called the object definition, which defines the triangle in an abstract space of our choosing. This space is continuous and is called the *object space*. Our action to draw maps the imaginary object into a triangle on paper, which constitutes a continuous display surface in another space called the *image space*. This mapping action is further influenced by our choice regarding such factors as the location and orientation of the triangle. In other words, we may place the triangle in the middle of the paper, or we may draw it near the upper left corner. We may have the sharp corner of the triangle pointing to the right, or we may have it pointing to the left.

A comparable process takes place when a computer is used to produce the picture. The major computational steps involved in the process give rise to several important areas of computer graphics. The area that attends to the need to define objects, such as the triangle, in an efficient and effective manner is called geometric representation. In our example we can place a two-dimensional Cartesian coordinate system into the object space. The triangle can then be represented by the x and y coordinates of its three vertices, with the understanding that the computer system will connect the first and second vertices with a line segment, the second and third vertices with another line segment, and the third and first with yet another line segment.

The next area of computer graphics that deals with the placement of the triangle is called transformation. Here we use matrices to realize the mapping of the triangle to its final destination in the image space. We can set up the transformation matrix to control the location and orientation of the displayed triangle. We can even enlarge or reduce its size. Furthermore, by using multiple settings for the

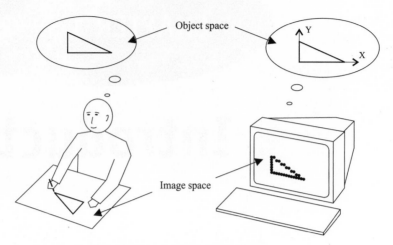

Fig. 1-1   Drawing a triangle.

transformation matrix, we can instruct the computer to display several triangles of varying size and orientation at different locations, all from the same model in the object space.

At this point most readers may have already been wondering about the crucial difference between the triangle drawn on paper and the triangle displayed on the computer monitor (an exaggerated version of what you would see on a real monitor). The former has its vertices connected by smooth edges, whereas the latter is not exactly a line-drawing. The fundamental reason here is that the image space in computer graphics is, generally speaking, not continuous. It consists of a set of discrete pixels, i.e., picture elements, that are arranged in a row-and-column fashion. Hence a horizontal or vertical line segment becomes a group of adjacent pixels in a row or column, respectively, and a slanted line segment becomes something that resembles a staircase. The area of computer graphics that is responsible for converting a continuous figure, such as a line segment, into its discrete approximation is called scan conversion.

The distortion introduced by the conversion from continuous space to discrete space is referred to as the aliasing effect of the conversion. While reducing the size of individual pixels should make the distortion less noticeable, we do so at a significant cost in terms of computational resources. For instance, if we cut each pixel by half in both the horizontal and the vertical direction we would need four times the number of pixels in order to keep the physical dimension of the picture constant. This would translate into, among other things, four times the memory requirement for storing the image. Exploring other ways to alleviate the negative impact of the aliasing effect is the focus of another area of computer graphics called anti-aliasing.

Putting together what we have so far leads to a simplified graphics pipeline (see Fig. 1-2), which exemplifies the architecture of a typical graphics system. At the start of the pipeline, we have primitive objects represented in some application-dependent data structures. For example, the coordinates of the vertices of a triangle, viz., (x_1, y_1), (x_2, y_2), and (x_3, y_3), can be easily stored in a 3×2 array. The graphics system first performs transformation on the original data according to user-specified parameters, and then carries out scan conversion with or without anti-aliasing to put the picture on the screen. The coordinate system in the middle box in Fig. 1-2 serves as an intermediary between the object coordinate system on the

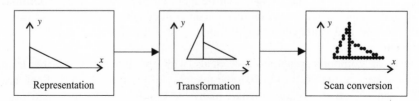

Fig. 1-2   A simple graphics pipeline.

left and the image or device coordinate system on the right. It is called the world coordinate system, representing where we place transformed objects to compose the picture we want to draw. The example in the box shows two triangles: the one on the right is a scaled copy of the original that is moved up and to the right, the one on the left is another scaled copy of the original that is rotated 90° counterclockwise around the origin of the coordinate system and then moved up and to the right in the same way.

In a typical implementation of the graphics pipeline we would write our application program in a host programming language and call library subroutines to perform graphics operations. Some subroutines are used to prescribe, among other things, transformation parameters. Others are used to draw, i.e., to feed original data into the pipeline so current system settings are automatically applied to shape the end product coming out of the pipeline, which is the picture on the screen.

Having looked at the key ingredients of what is called two-dimensional graphics, we now turn our attention to three-dimensional graphics. With the addition of a third dimension one should notice the profound distinction between an object and its picture. Figure 1-3 shows several possible ways to draw a cubic object, but none of the drawings even come close to being the object itself. The drawings simply represent projections of the three-dimensional object onto a two-dimensional display surface. This means that besides three-dimensional representation and transformation, we have an additional area of computer graphics that covers projection methods.

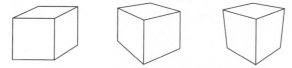

Fig. 1-3   Several ways to depict a cube.

Did you notice that each drawing in Fig. 1-3 shows only three sides of the cubic object? Being a solid three-dimensional object the cube has six plane surfaces. However, we depict it as if we were looking at it in real life. We only draw the surfaces that are visible to us. Surfaces that are obscured from our eyesight are not shown. The area of computer graphics that deals with this computational task is called hidden surface removal. Adding projection and hidden surface removal to our simple graphics pipeline, right after transformation but before scan conversion, results in a prototype for three-dimensional graphics.

Now let's follow up on the idea that we want to produce a picture of an object in real-life fashion. This presents a great challenge for computer graphics, since there is an extremely effective way to produce such a picture: photography. In order to generate a picture that is photo-realistic, i.e., that looks as good as a photograph, we need to explore how a camera and nature work together to produce a snapshot.

When a camera is used to photograph a real-life object illuminated by a light source, light energy coming out of the light source gets reflected from the object surface through the camera lens onto the negative, forming an image of the object. Generally, the part of the object that is closer to the light source should appear brighter in the picture than the part that is further away, and the part of the object that is facing away from the light source should appear relatively dark. Figure 1-4 shows a computer-generated

Fig. 1-4   Two shaded spheres.

image that depicts two spherical objects illuminated by a light source that is located somewhere between the spheres and the "camera" at about the ten to eleven o'clock position. Although both spheres have gradual shadings, the bright spot on the large sphere looks like a reflection of the light source and hence suggests a difference in their reflectance property (the large sphere being shinier than the small one). The mathematical formulae that mimic this type of optical phenomenon are referred to as local illumination models, for the energy coming directly from the light source to a particular object surface is not a full account of the energy arriving at that surface. Light energy is also reflected from one object surface to another, and it can go through a transparent or translucent object and continue on to other places. Computational methods that strive to provide a more accurate account of light transport than local illumination models are referred to as global illumination models.

Now take a closer look at Fig. 1-4. The two objects seem to have super-smooth surfaces. What are they made of? How can they be so perfect? Do you see many physical objects around you that exhibit such surface characteristics? Furthermore, it looks like the small sphere is positioned between the light source and the large sphere. Shouldn't we see its shadow on the large sphere? In computer graphics the surface shading variations that distinguish a wood surface from a marble surface or other types of surface are referred to as surface textures. There are various techniques to add surface textures to objects to make them look more realistic. On the other hand, the computational task to include shadows in a picture is called shadow generation.

Before moving on to prepare for a closer look at each of the subject areas we have introduced in this mini-survey, we want to briefly discuss a couple of allied fields of computer science that also deal with graphical information.

Image Processing

The key element that distinguishes image processing (or digital image processing) from computer graphics is that image processing generally begins with images in the image space and performs pixel-based operations on them to produce new images that exhibit certain desired features. For example, we may reset each pixel in the image displayed on the monitor screen in Fig. 1-1 to its complementary color (e.g., black to white and white to black), turning a dark triangle on a white background to a white triangle on a dark background, or vice versa. While each of these two fields has its own focus and strength, they also overlap and complement each other. In fact, stunning visual effects are often achieved by using a combination of computer graphics and image processing techniques.

Computer–Human Interaction

While the main focus of computer graphics is the production of images, the field of computer–human interaction promotes effective communication between man and machine. The two fields join forces when it comes to such areas as graphical user interfaces. There are many kinds of physical devices that can be attached to a computer for the purpose of interaction, starting with the keyboard and the mouse. Each physical device can often be programmed to deliver the function of various logical devices (e.g., Locator, Choice—see below). For example, a mouse can be used to specify locations in the image space (acting as a Locator device). In this case a cursor is often displayed as visual feedback to allow the user see the locations being specified. A mouse can also be used to select an item in a pull-down or pop-up manual (acting as a Choice device). In this case it is the identification of the selected manual item that counts and the item is often highlighted as a whole (the absolute location of the cursor is essentially irrelevant). From these we can see that a physical device may be used in different ways and information can be conveyed to the user in different graphical forms. The key challenge is to design interactive protocols that make effective use of devices and graphics in a way that is user-friendly—easy, intuitive, efficient, etc.

1.2 WHAT'S AHEAD

We hope that our brief flight over the landscape of the graphics kingdom has given you a good impression of some of the important landmarks and made you eager to further your exploration. The following chapters are dedicated to the various subject areas of computer graphics. Each chapter begins with the necessary background information (e.g., context and terminology) and a summary account of the material to be discussed in subsequent sections.

We strive to provide clear explanation and inter-subject continuity in our presentation. Illustrative examples are used freely to substantiate discussion on abstract concepts. While the primary mission of this book is to offer a relatively well-focused introduction to the fundamental theory and underlying technology, significant variations in such matters as basic definitions and implementation protocols are presented in order to have a reasonably broad coverage of the field. In addition, interesting applications are introduced as early as possible to highlight the usefulness of the graphics technology and to encourage those who are eager to engage in hands-on practice.

Algorithms and programming examples are given in pseudo-code that resembles the C programming language, which shares similar syntax and basic constructs with other widely used languages such as C++ and Java. We hope that the relative simplicity of the C-style code presents little grammatical difficulty and hence makes it easy for you to focus your attention on the technical substance of the code.

There are numerous solved problems at the end of each chapter to help reinforce the theoretical discussion. Some of the problems represent computation steps that are omitted in the text and are particularly valuable for those looking for further details and additional explanation. Other problems may provide new information that supplements the main discussion in the text.

Image Representation

A digital image, or image for short, is composed of discrete pixels or picture elements. These pixels are arranged in a row-and-column fashion to form a rectangular picture area, sometimes referred to as a raster. Clearly the total number of pixels in an image is a function of the size of the image and the number of pixels per unit length (e.g. inch) in the horizontal as well as the vertical direction. This number of pixels per unit length is referred to as the resolution of the image. Thus a 3×2 inch image at a resolution of 300 pixels per inch would have a total of 540,000 pixels.

Frequently image size is given as the total number of pixels in the horizontal direction times the total number of pixels in the vertical direction (e.g., 512×512, 640×480, or 1024×768). Although this convention makes it relatively straightforward to gauge the total number of pixels in an image, it does not specify the size of the image or its resolution, as defined in the paragraph above. A 640×480 image would measure $6\frac{2}{3}$ inches by 5 inches when presented (e.g., displayed or printed) at 96 pixels per inch. On the other hand, it would measure 1.6 inches by 1.2 inches at 400 pixels per inch.

The ratio of an image's width to its height, measured in unit length or number of pixels, is referred to as its aspect ratio. Both a 2×2 inch image and a 512×512 image have an aspect ratio of $1/1$, whereas both a $6 \times 4\frac{1}{2}$ inch image and a 1024×768 image have an aspect ratio of $4/3$.

Individual pixels in an image can be referenced by their coordinates. Typically the pixel at the lower left corner of an image is considered to be at the origin $(0, 0)$ of a pixel coordinate system. Thus the pixel at the lower right corner of a 640×480 image would have coordinates $(639, 0)$, whereas the pixel at the upper right corner would have coordinates $(639, 479)$.

The task of composing an image on a computer is essentially a matter of setting pixel values. The collective effects of the pixels taking on different color attributes give us what we see as a picture. In this chapter we first introduce the basics of the most prevailing color specification method in computer graphics (Sect. 2.1). We then discuss the representation of images using direct coding of pixel colors (Sect. 2.2) versus using the lookup-table approach (Sect. 2.3). Following a discussion of the working principles of two representative image presentation devices, the display monitor (Sect. 2.4) and the printer (Sect. 2.5), we examine image files as the primary means of image storage and transmission (Sect. 2.6). We then take a look at some of the most primitive graphics operations, which primarily deal with setting the color attributes of pixels (Sect. 2.7). Finally, to illustrate the construction of beautiful images directly in the discrete image space, we introduce the mathematical background and detail the algorithmic aspects of visualizing the Mandelbrot set (Sect. 2.8).

2.1   THE RGB COLOR MODEL

Color is a complex, interdisciplinary subject spanning from physics to psychology. In this section we only introduce the basics of the most widely used color representation method in computer graphics. We will have additional discussion later in another chapter.

Figure 2-1 shows a color coordinate system with three primary colors: R (red), G (green), and B (blue). Each primary color can take on an intensity value ranging from 0 (off—lowest) to 1 (on—highest). Mixing these three primary colors at different intensity levels produces a variety of colors. The collection of all the colors obtainable by such a linear combination of red, green, and blue forms the cube-shaped RGB color space. The corner of the RGB color cube that is at the origin of the coordinate system corresponds to black, whereas the corner of the cube that is diagonally opposite to the origin represents white. The diagonal line connecting black and white corresponds to all the gray colors between black and white. It is called the gray axis.

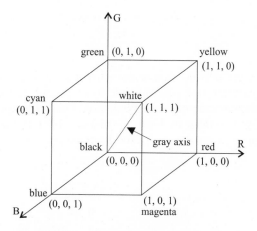

Fig. 2-1   The RGB color space.

Given this RGB color model an arbitrary color within the cubic color space can be specified by its color coordinates: (r, g, b). For example, we have $(0, 0, 0)$ for black, $(1, 1, 1)$ for white, $(1, 1, 0)$ for yellow, etc. A gray color at $(0.7, 0.7, 0.7)$ has an intensity halfway between one at $(0.9, 0.9, 0.9)$ and one at $(0.5, 0.5, 0.5)$.

Color specification using the RGB model is an additive process. We begin with black and add on the appropriate primary components to yield a desired color. This closely matches the working principles of the display monitor (see Sect. 2.4). On the other hand, there is a complementary color model, called the CMY color model, that defines colors using a subtractive process, which closely matches the working principles of the printer (see Sect. 2.5).

In the CMY model we begin with white and take away the appropriate primary components to yield a desired color. For example, if we subtract red from white, what remains consists of green and blue, which is cyan. Looking at this from another perspective, we can use the amount of cyan, the complementary color of red, to control the amount of red, which is equal to one minus the amount of cyan. Figure 2-2 shows a coordinate system using the three primaries' complementary colors: C (cyan), M (magenta), and Y (yellow). The corner of the CMY color cube that is at $(0, 0, 0)$ corresponds to white, whereas the corner of the cube that is at $(1, 1, 1)$ represents black (no red, no green, no blue). The following formulas summarize the conversion between the two color models:

$$\begin{pmatrix} R \\ G \\ B \end{pmatrix} = \begin{pmatrix} 1 \\ 1 \\ 1 \end{pmatrix} - \begin{pmatrix} C \\ M \\ Y \end{pmatrix} \qquad \begin{pmatrix} C \\ M \\ Y \end{pmatrix} = \begin{pmatrix} 1 \\ 1 \\ 1 \end{pmatrix} - \begin{pmatrix} R \\ G \\ B \end{pmatrix}$$

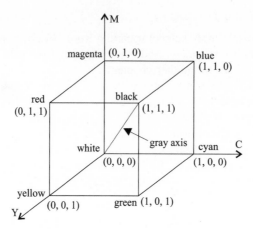

Fig. 2-2   The CMY color space.

2.2   DIRECT CODING

Image representation is essentially the representation of pixel colors. Using direct coding we allocate a certain amount of storage space for each pixel to code its color. For example, we may allocate 3 bits for each pixel, with one bit for each primary color (see Fig. 2-3). This 3-bit representation allows each primary to vary independently between two intensity levels: 0 (off) or 1 (on). Hence each pixel can take on one of the eight colors that correspond to the corners of the RGB color cube.

bit 1: r	bit 2: g	bit 3: b	color name
0	0	0	black
0	0	1	blue
0	1	0	green
0	1	1	cyan
1	0	0	red
1	0	1	magenta
1	1	0	yellow
1	1	1	white

Fig. 2-3   Direct coding of colors using 3 bits.

A widely accepted industry standard uses 3 bytes, or 24 bits, per pixel, with one byte for each primary color. This way we allow each primary color to have 256 different intensity levels, corresponding to binary values from 00000000 to 11111111. Thus a pixel can take on a color from $256 \times 256 \times 256$ or 16.7 million possible choices. This 24-bit format is commonly referred to as the true color representation, for the difference between two colors that differ by one intensity level in one or more of the primaries is virtually undetectable under normal viewing conditions. Hence a more precise representation involving more bits is of little use in terms of perceived color accuracy.

A notable special case of direct coding is the representation of black-and-white (bilevel) and gray-scale images, where the three primaries always have the same value and hence need not be coded separately. A black-and-white image requires only one bit per pixel, with bit value 0 representing black and 1 representing white. A gray-scale image is typically coded with 8 bits per pixel to allow a total of 256 intensity or gray levels.

Although this direct coding method features simplicity and has supported a variety of applications, we can see a relatively high demand for storage space when it comes to the 24-bit standard. For example, a 1000×1000 true color image would take up three million bytes. Furthermore, even if every pixel in that image had a different color, there would only be one million colors in the image. In many applications the number of colors that appear in any one particular image is much less. Therefore the 24-bit representation's ability to have 16.7 million different colors appear simultaneously in a single image seems to be somewhat overkill.

2.3 LOOKUP TABLE

Image representation using a lookup table can be viewed as a compromise between our desire to have a lower storage requirement and our need to support a reasonably sufficient number of simultaneous colors. In this approach pixel values do not code colors directly. Instead, they are addresses or indices into a table of color values. The color of a particular pixel is determined by the color value in the table entry that the value of the pixel references.

Figure 2-4 shows a lookup table with 256 entries. The entries have addresses 0 through 255. Each entry contains a 24-bit RGB color value. Pixel values are now 1-byte, or 8-bit, quantities. The color of a pixel whose value is i, where $0 \leq i \leq 255$, is determined by the color value in the table entry whose address is i. This 24-bit 256-entry lookup table representation is often referred to as the 8-bit format. It reduces the storage requirement of a 1000×1000 image to one million bytes plus 768 bytes for the color values in the lookup table. It allows 256 simultaneous colors that are chosen from 16.7 million possible colors.

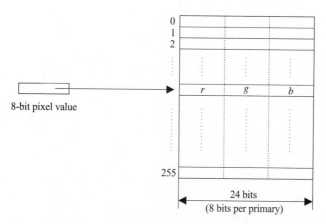

Fig. 2-4   A 24-bit 256-entry lookup table.

It is important to remember that, using the lookup table representation, an image is defined not only by its pixel values but also by the color values in the corresponding lookup table. Those color values form a *color map* for the image.

2.4 DISPLAY MONITOR

Among the numerous types of image presentation or output devices that convert digitally represented images into visually perceivable pictures is the display or video monitor.

We first take a look at the working principle of a monochromatic display monitor, which consists mainly of a cathode ray tube (CRT) along with related control circuits. The CRT is a vacuum glass tube with the display screen at one end and connectors to the control circuits at the other (see Fig. 2-5). Coated on the inside of the display screen is a special material, called phosphor, which emits light for a period of time when hit by a beam of electrons. The color of the light and the time period vary from one type of

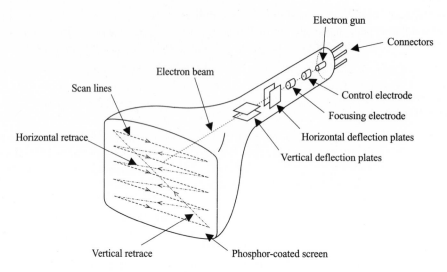

Fig. 2-5   Anatomy of a monochromatic CRT.

phosphor to another. The light given off by the phosphor during exposure to the electron beam is known as fluorescence, the continuing glow given off after the beam is removed is known as phosphorescence, and the duration of phosphorescence is known as the phosphor's persistence.

Opposite to the phosphor-coated screen is an electron gun that is heated to send out electrons. The electrons are regulated by the control electrode and forced by the focusing electrode into a narrow beam striking the phosphor coating at small spots. When this electron beam passes through the horizontal and vertical deflection plates, it is bent or deflected by the electric fields between the plates. The horizontal plates control the beam to scan from left to right and retrace from right to left. The vertical plates control the beam to go from the first scan line at the top to the last scan line at the bottom and retrace from the bottom back to the top. These actions are synchronized by the control circuits so that the electron beam strikes each and every pixel position in a scan line by scan line fashion. As an alternative to this electrostatic deflection method, some CRTs use magnetic deflection coils mounted on the outside of the glass envelope to bend the electron beam with magnetic fields.

The intensity of the light emitted by the phosphor coating is a function of the intensity of the electron beam. The control circuits shut off the electron beam during horizontal and vertical retraces. The intensity of the beam at a particular pixel position is determined by the intensity value of the corresponding pixel in the image being displayed.

The image being displayed is stored in a dedicated system memory area that is often referred to as the frame buffer or refresh buffer. The control circuits associated with the frame buffer generate proper video signals for the display monitor. The frequency at which the content of the frame buffer is sent to the display monitor is called the refreshing rate, which is typically 60 times or frames per second (60 Hz) or higher. A determining factor here is the need to avoid flicker, which occurs at lower refreshing rates when our visual system is unable to integrate the light impulses from the phosphor dots into a steady picture. The persistence of the monitor's phosphor, on the other hand, needs to be long enough for a frame to remain visible but short enough for it to fade before the next frame is displayed.

Some monitors use a technique called interlacing to "double" their refreshing rate. In this case only half of the scan lines in a frame is refreshed at a time, first the odd numbered lines, then the even numbered lines. Thus the screen is refreshed from top to bottom in half the time it would have taken to sweep across all the scan lines. Although this approach does not really increase the rate at which the entire screen is refreshed, it is quite effective in reducing flicker.

Color Display

Moving on to color displays there are now three electron guns instead of one inside the CRT (see Fig. 2-6), with one electron gun for each primary color. The phosphor coating on the inside of the display screen consists of dot patterns of three different types of phosphors. These phosphors are capable of emitting red, green, and blue light, respectively. The distance between the center of the dot patterns is called the pitch of the color CRT. It places an upper limit on the number of addressable positions on the display area. A thin metal screen called a shadow mask is placed between the phosphor coating and the electron guns. The tiny holes on the shadow mask constrain each electron beam to hit its corresponding phosphor dots. When viewed at a certain distance, light emitted by the three types of phosphors blends together to give us a broad range of colors.

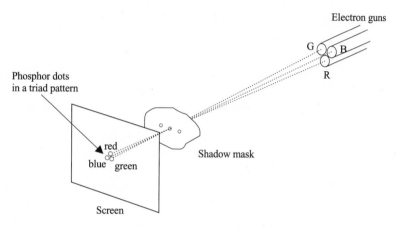

Fig. 2-6   Color CRT using a shadow mask.

2.5   PRINTER

Another typical image presentation device is the printer. A printer deposits color pigments onto a print media, changing the light reflected from its surface and making it possible for us to see the print result.

Given the fact that the most commonly used print media is a piece of white paper, we can in principle utilize three types of pigments (cyan, magenta, and yellow) to regulate the amount of red, green, and blue light reflected to yield all RGB colors (see Sect. 2.1). However, in practice, an additional black pigment is often used due to the relatively high cost of color pigments and the technical difficulty associated with producing high-quality black from several color pigments.

While some printing methods allow color pigments to blend together, in many cases the various color pigments remain separate in the form of tiny dots on the print media. Furthermore, the pigments are often deposited with a limited number of intensity levels. There are various techniques to achieve the effect of multiple intensity levels beyond what the pigment deposits can offer. Most of these techniques can also be adapted by the display devices that we have just discussed in the previous section.

Halftoning

Let's first take a look at a traditional technique called halftoning from the printing industry for bilevel devices. This technique uses variably sized pigment dots that, when viewed from a certain distance, blend with the white background to give us the sensation of varying intensity levels. These dots are arranged in a pattern that forms a 45° screen angle with the horizon (see Fig. 2-7 where the dots are enlarged for illustration). The size of the dots is inversely proportional to the intended intensity level. When viewed at a far enough distance, the stripe in Fig. 2-7 exhibits a gradual shading from white (high intensity) on the left to black (low intensity) on the right. An image produced using this technique is called a halftone. In practice, newspaper halftones use 60 to 80 dots per inch, whereas book and magazine halftones use 120 to 200 dots per inch.

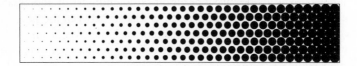

Fig. 2-7   A halftone stripe.

Halftone Approximation

Instead of changing dot size we can approximate the halftone technique using pixel-grid patterns. For example, with a 2 × 2 bilevel pixel grid we can construct five grid patterns to produce five overall intensity levels (see Fig. 2-8). We can increase the number of overall intensity levels by increasing the size of the pixel grid (see the following paragraphs for an example). On the other hand, if the pixels can be set to multiple intensity levels, even a 2 × 2 grid can produce a relatively high number of overall intensity levels. For example, if the pixels can be intensified to four different levels, we can follow the pattern sequence in Fig. 2-8 to bring each pixel from one intensity level to the next to approximate a total of thirteen overall intensity levels (one for all pixels off and four for each of the three non-zero intensities, see Fig. 2-9).

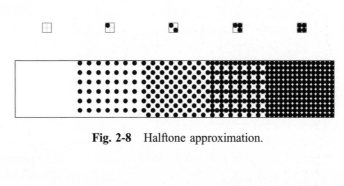

Fig. 2-8   Halftone approximation.

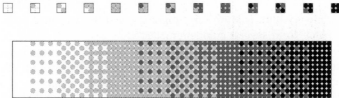

Fig. 2-9   Halftone approximation with 13 intensity levels.

These halftone grid patterns are sometimes referred to as dither patterns. There are several considerations in the design of dither patterns. First, the pixels should be intensified in a growth-from-the-grid-center fashion in order to mimic the growth of dot size. Second, a pixel that is intensified to a certain level to approximate a particular overall intensity should remain at least at that level for all subsequent overall intensity levels. In other words, the patterns should evolve from one to the next in order to minimize the differences in the patterns for successive overall intensity levels. Third, symmetry should be avoided in order to minimize visual artifacts such as streaks that would show up in image areas of uniform intensity. Fourth, isolated "on" pixels should be avoided since they are sometimes hard to reproduce.

We can use a dither matrix to represent a series of dither patterns. For example, the following 3×3 matrix:

$$\begin{pmatrix} 5 & 2 & 7 \\ 1 & 0 & 3 \\ 6 & 8 & 4 \end{pmatrix}$$

represents the order in which pixels in a 3×3 grid are to be intensified. For bilevel reproduction, this gives us ten intensity levels from level 0 to level 9, and intensity level I is achieved by turning on all pixels that correspond to values in the dither matrix that are less than I. If each pixel can be intensified to three different levels, we follow the order defined by the matrix to set the pixels to their middle intensity level and then to their high intensity level to approximate a total of nineteen overall intensity levels.

This halftone approximation technique is readily applicable to the reproduction of color images. All we need is to replace the dot at each pixel position with an RGB or CMY dot pattern (e.g., the triad pattern shown in Fig. 2-6). If we use a 2×2 pixel grid and each primary or its complement can take on two intensity levels, we achieve a total of $5 \times 5 \times 5 = 125$ color combinations.

At this point we can turn to the fact that halftone approximation is a technique that trades spatial resolution for more colors/intensity levels. For a device that is capable of producing images at a resolution of 400×400 pixels per inch, halftone approximation using 2×2 dither patterns would mean lowering its resolution effectively to 200×200 pixels per inch.

Dithering

A technique called dithering can be used to approximate halftones without reducing spatial resolution. In this approach the dither matrix is treated very much like a floor tile that can be repeatedly positioned one copy next to another to cover the entire floor, i.e., the image. A pixel at (x, y) is intensified if the intensity level of the image at that position is greater than the corresponding value in the dither matrix. Mathematically, if D_n stands for an $n \times n$ dither matrix, the element $D_n(i, j)$ that corresponds to pixel position (x, y) can be found by $i = x \bmod n$ and $j = y \bmod n$. For example, if we use the 3×3 matrix given earlier for a bilevel reproduction and the pixel of the image at position (2, 19) has intensity level 5, then the corresponding matrix element is $D_3(2, 1) = 3$, and hence a dot should be printed or displayed at that location.

It should be noted that, for image areas that have constant intensity, the results of dithering are exactly the same as the results of halftone approximation. Reproduction differences between these two methods occur only when intensity varies.

Error Diffusion

Another technique for continuous-tone reproduction without sacrificing spatial resolution is called the Floyd–Steinberg error diffusion. Here a pixel is printed using the closest intensity the device can deliver. The error term, i.e., the difference between the exact pixel value and the approximated value in the reproduction, is then propagated to several yet-to-be-processed neighboring pixels for compensation. More specifically, let S be the source image that is processed in a left-to-right and top-to-bottom pixel order, $S(x, y)$ be the pixel value at location (x, y), and e be $S(x, y)$ minus the approximated value. We update the value of the pixel's four neighbors (one to its right and three in the next scan line) as follows:

$$S(x + 1, y) = S(x + 1, y) + ae$$
$$S(x - 1, y - 1) = S(x - 1, y - 1) + be$$
$$S(x, y - 1) = S(x, y - 1) + ce$$
$$S(x + 1, y - 1) = S(x + 1, y - 1) + de$$

where parameters a through d often take values $\frac{7}{16}$, $\frac{3}{16}$, $\frac{5}{16}$, and $\frac{1}{16}$, respectively. These modifications are for the purpose of using the neighboring pixels to offset the reproduction error at the current pixel location. They are not permanent changes made to the original image.

Consider, for example, the reproduction of a gray scale image (0: black, 255: white) on a bilevel device (level 0: black, level 1: white), if a pixel whose current value is 96 has just been mapped to level 0, we have $e = 96$ for this pixel location. The value of the pixel to its right is now increased by $96 \times \frac{7}{16} = 42$ in order to determine the appropriate reproduction level. This increment tends to cause such neighboring pixel to be reproduced at a higher intensity level, partially compensating the discrepancy brought on by mapping value 96 to level 0 (which is lower than the actual pixel value) at the current location. The other three neighboring pixels (one below and to the left, one immediately below, and one below and to the right) receive 18, 30, and 6 as their share of the reproduction error at the current location, respectively.

Results produced by this error diffusion algorithm are generally satisfactory, with occasional introduction of slight echoing of certain image parts. Improved performance can sometimes be obtained by alternating scanning direction between left-to-right and right-to-left (minor modifications need to be made to the above formulas).

2.6   IMAGE FILES

A digital image is often encoded in the form of a binary file for the purpose of storage and transmission. Among the numerous encoding formats are BMP (Windows Bitmap), JPEG (Joint Photographic Experts Group File Interchange Format), and TIFF (Tagged Image File Format). Although these formats differ in technical details, they share structural similarities.

Figure 2-10 shows the typical organization of information encoded in an image file. The file consists largely of two parts: header and image data. In the beginning of the file header a binary code or ASCII string identifies the format being used, possibly along with the version number. The width and height of the image are given in numbers of pixels. Common image types include black and white (1 bit per pixel), 8-bit gray scale (256 levels along the gray axis), 8-bit color (lookup table), and 24-bit color. Image data format specifies the order in which pixel values are stored in the image data section. A commonly used order is left to right and top to bottom. Another possible order is left to right and bottom to top. Image data format also specifies if the RGB values in the color map or in the image are interlaced. When the values are given in an interlaced fashion, the three primary color components for a particular lookup table entry or a particular pixel stay together consecutively, followed by the three color components for the next entry or pixel. Thus the color values in the image data section are a sequence of red, green, blue, red, green, blue, etc. When the values are given in a non-interlaced fashion, the values of one primary for all table entries or pixels appear

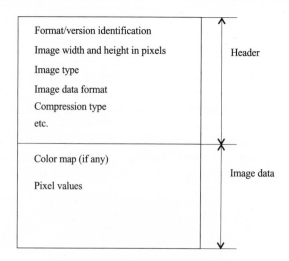

Fig. 2-10   Typical image file format.

first, then the values of another primary, followed by the values of the third primary. Thus the image data are in the form of red, red, ..., green, green, ..., blue, blue, ...

The values in the image data section may be compressed, using such compression algorithms as run-length encoding (RLE). The basic idea behind RLE can be illustrated with a character string "xxxxxxyyzzzz", which takes 12 bytes of storage. Now if we scan the string from left to right for segments of repeating characters and replace each segment by a 1-byte repeat count followed by the character being repeated, we convert or compress the given string to "6x2y4z", which takes only 6 bytes. This compressed version can be expanded or decompressed by repeating the character following each repeat count to recover the original string.

The length of the file header is often fixed, for otherwise it would be necessary to include length information in the header to indicate where image data starts (some formats include header length anyway). The length of each individual component in the image data section is, on the other hand, dependent on such factors as image type and compression type. Such information, along with additional format-specific information, can also be found in the header.

2.7   SETTING THE COLOR ATTRIBUTES OF PIXELS

Setting the color attributes of individual pixels is arguably the most primitive graphics operation. It is typically done by making system library calls to write the respective values into the frame buffer. An aggregate data structure, such as a three-element array, is often used to represent the three primary color components. Regardless of image type (direct coding versus lookup table), there are two possible protocols for the specification of pixel coordinates and color values.

In one protocol the application provides both coordinate information and color information simultaneously. Thus a call to set the pixel at location (x, y) in a 24-bit image to color (r, g, b) would look like

setPixel(x, y, rgb)

where rgb is a three-element array with $rgb[0] = r$, $rgb[1] = g$, and $rgb[2] = b$. On the other hand, if the image uses a lookup table then, assuming that the color is defined in the table, the call would look like

setPixel(x, y, i)

where i is the address of the entry containing (r, g, b).

Another protocol is based on the existence of a current color, which is maintained by the system and can be set by calls that look like

setColor(rgb)

for direct coding, or

setColor(i)

for the lookup table representation. Calls to set pixels now need only to provide coordinate information and would look like

setPixel(x, y)

for both image types. The graphics system will automatically use the most recently specified current color to carry out the operation.

Lookup table entries can be set from the application by a call that looks like

setEntry(i, rgb)

which puts color (r, g, b) in the entry whose address is i. Conversely, values in the lookup table can be read back to the application with a call that looks like

getEntry(i, rgb)

which returns the color value in entry i through array parameter rgb.

There are sometimes two versions of the calls that specify RGB values. One takes RGB values as floating point numbers in the range of [0.0, 1.0], whereas the other takes them as integers in the range of [0, 255]. Although the floating point version is handy when the color values come from some continuous formula, the floating point values are mapped by the graphics system into integer values before being written into the frame buffer.

In order to provide basic support for pixel-based image-processing operations there are calls that look like

getPixel(x, y, rgb)

for direct coding or

getPixel(x, y, i)

for the lookup table representation to return the color or index value of the pixel at (x, y) back to the application.

There are also calls that read and write rectangular blocks of pixels. A useful example would be a call to set all pixels to a certain background color. Assuming that the system uses a current color we would first set the current color to be the desired background color, and then make a call that looks like:

clear()

to achieve the goal.

2.8   EXAMPLE: VISUALIZING THE MANDELBROT SET

An elegant and illustrative example showing the construction of beautiful images by setting the color attributes of individual pixels directly from the application is the visualization of the Mandelbrot set. This remarkable set is based on the following transformation:

$$x_{n+1} = x_n^2 + z$$

where both x and z represent complex numbers. For readers who are unfamiliar with complex numbers it suffices to know that a complex number is defined in the form of $a + bi$. Here both a and b are real numbers; a is called the real part of the complex number and b the imaginary part (identified by the special symbol i). The magnitude of $a + bi$, denoted by $|a + bi|$, is equal to the square root of $a^2 + b^2$. The sum of two complex numbers $a + bi$ and $c + di$ is defined to be $(a + c) + (b + d)i$. The product of $a + bi$ and $c + di$ is defined to be $(ac - bd) + (ad + bc)i$. Thus the square of $a + bi$ is equal to $(a^2 - b^2) + 2abi$. For example, the sum of $0.5 + 2.0i$ and $1.0 - 1.0i$ is $1.5 + 1.0i$. The product of the two is $2.5 + 1.5i$. The square of $0.5 + 2.0i$ is $-3.75 + 2.0i$ and the square of $1.0 - 1.0i$ is $0.0 - 2.0i$.

The Mandelbrot set is the set of complex numbers z that do not diverge under the above transformation with $x_0 = 0$ (both the real and imaginary parts of x_0 are 0). In other words, to determine if a particular complex number z is a member of the set, we begin with $x_0 = 0$, followed by $x_1 = x_0^2 + z$, $x_2 = x_1^2 + z, \ldots, x_{n+1} = x_n^2 + z, \ldots$. If $|x|$ goes towards infinity when n increases, then z is not a member. Otherwise, z belongs to the Mandelbrot set.

Figure 2-11 shows how to produce a discrete snapshot of the Mandelbrot set. On the left hand side is the complex plane where the horizontal axis Re measures the real part of complex numbers and the vertical axis Im measures the imaginary part. Hence an arbitrary complex number z corresponds to a point in the complex plane. Our goal is to produce an image of width by height (in numbers of pixels) that depicts the z values in a rectangular area defined by (Re_min, Im_min) and (Re_max, Im_max). This rectangular area has the same aspect ratio as the image so as not to introduce geometric distortion. We subdivide the area to match the pixel grid in the image. The color of a pixel, shown as a little square in the pixel grid, is determined by the complex number z that corresponds to the lower left corner of the little square. Although only width × height points in the complex plane are used to compute the image, this relatively

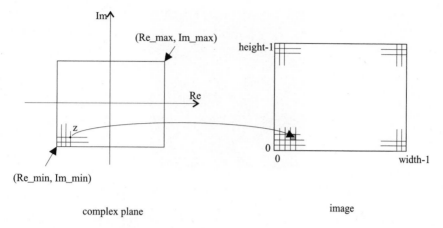

Fig. 2-11 Visualizing the Mandelbrot set.

straightforward approach to discrete sampling produces reasonably good approximations for the purpose of visualizing the set.

There are many ways to decide the color of a pixel based on the corresponding complex number z. What we do here is to produce a gray scale image where the gray level of a non-black pixel represents proportionally the number of iterations it takes for $|x|$ to be greater than 2. We use 2 as a threshold for divergence because x diverges quickly under the given transformation once $|x|$ becomes greater than 2. If $|x|$ remains less than or equal to 2 after a preset maximum number of iterations, we simply set the pixel value to 0 (black).

The following pseudo-code implements what we have discussed in the above paragraphs. We use N to represent the maximum number of iterations, z.real the real part of z, and z.imag the imaginary part of z. We also assume a 256-entry gray scale lookup table where the color value in entry i is (i, i, i). The formula in the second call to setColor is to obtain a proportional mapping from $[0, N]$ to $[1, 255]$:

```
int i, j, count;
float delta = (Re_max − Re_min)/width;

for (i = 0, z.real = Re_min; i < width; i ++ , z.real+ = delta)
  for ( j = 0, z.imag = Im_min; j < height; j++, z.imag+ = delta) {
    count = 0;
    complex number x = 0;
    while (|x| <= 2.0 && count < N) {
      compute x = x² + z;
      count++;
    }
    if (|x| <= 2.0) setColor(0);
    else setColor(1 + 254*count/N);
    setPixel(i, j);
  }
```

The image in Fig. 2-12 shows what is nicknamed the Mandelbrot bug. It visualizes an area where $-2.0 \leq z.$ real ≤ 0.5 and $-1.25 \leq z.$ imag ≤ 1.25 with $N = 64$. Most z values that are outside the area lead x to diverge quickly, whereas the z values in the black region belong to the Mandelbrot set. It is along the contour of the bug-like figure that we see the most dynamic alterations between divergence and non-divergence, together with the most significant variations in the number of iterations used in the divergence test. The brighter a pixel, the longer it took to conclude divergence for the corresponding z. In principle the rectangular area can be reduced indefinitely to zoom in on any active region to show more intricate details.

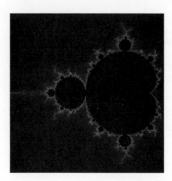

Fig. 2-12   The Mandelbrot set

Julia Sets

Now if we set z to some fixed non-zero value and vary x_0 across the complex plane, we obtain a set of non-divergence numbers (values of x_0 that do not diverge under the given transformation) that form a Julia set. Different z values lead to different Julia sets. The image in Fig. 2-13 is produced by making slight modifications to the pseudo-code for the Mandelbrot set. It shows the Julia set defined by $z = -0.74543 + 0.11301i$ with $-1.2 \le x_0.\text{real} \le 1.2$, $-1.2 \le x_0.\text{imag} \le 1.2$, and $N = 128$.

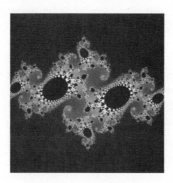

Fig. 2-13   A Julia set.

Solved Problems

2.1   What is the resolution of an image?

SOLUTION

The number of pixels (i.e., picture elements) per unit length (e.g., inch) in the horizontal as well as vertical direction.

2.2   Compute the size of a 640×480 image at 240 pixels per inch.

SOLUTION

$640/240$ by $480/240$ or $2\frac{2}{3}$ by 2 inches.

2.3   Compute the resolution of a 2×2 inch image that has 512×512 pixels.

SOLUTION

512/2 or 256 pixels per inch.

2.4   What is an image's aspect ratio?

SOLUTION

The ratio of its width to its height, measured in unit length or number of pixels.

2.5   If an image has a height of 2 inches and an aspect ratio of 1.5, what is its width?

SOLUTION

width $= 1.5 \times$ height $= 1.5 \times 2 = 3$ inches.

2.6   If we want to resize a 1024×768 image to one that is 640 pixels wide with the same aspect ratio, what would be the height of the resized image?

SOLUTION

height $= 640 \times 768/1024 = 480$.

2.7   If we want to cut a 512×512 sub-image out from the center of an 800×600 image, what are the coordinates of the pixel in the large image that is at the lower left corner of the small image?

SOLUTION

$[(800 - 512)/2, (600 - 512)/2] = (144, 44)$.

2.8   Sometimes the pixel at the upper left corner of an image is considered to be at the origin of the pixel coordinate system (a left-handed system). How to convert the coordinates of a pixel at (x, y) in this coordinate system into its coordinates (x', y') in the lower-left-corner-as-origin coordinate system (a right-handed system)?

SOLUTION

$(x', y') = (x, m - y - 1)$ where m is the number of pixels in the vertical direction.

2.9   Find the CMY coordinates of a color at $(0.2, 1, 0.5)$ in the RGB space.

SOLUTION

$(1 - 0.2, 1 - 1, 1 - 0.5) = (0.8, 0, 0.5)$.

2.10   Find the RGB coordinates of a color at $(0.15, 0.75, 0)$ in the CMY space.

SOLUTION

$(1 - 0.15, 1 - 0.75, 1 - 0) = (0.85, 0.25, 1)$.

2.11   If we use direct coding of RGB values with 2 bits per primary color, how many possible colors do we have for each pixel?

SOLUTION

$2^2 \times 2^2 \times 2^2 = 4 \times 4 \times 4 = 64.$

2.12 If we use direct coding of RGB values with 10 bits per primary color, how many possible colors do we have for each pixel?

SOLUTION

$2^{10} \times 2^{10} \times 2^{10} = 1024^3 = 1,073,741,824 > 1$ billion.

2.13 The direct coding method is flexible in that it allows the allocation of a different number of bits to each primary color. If we use 5 bits each for red and blue and 6 bits for green for a total of 16 bits per pixel, how many possible simultaneous colors do we have?

SOLUTION

$2^5 \times 2^5 \times 2^6 = 2^{16} = 65,536.$

2.14 If we use 12-bit pixel values in a lookup table representation, how many entries does the lookup table have?

SOLUTION

$2^{12} = 4096.$

2.15 If we use 2-byte pixel values in a 24-bit lookup table representation, how many bytes does the lookup table occupy?

SOLUTION

$2^{16} \times 24/8 = 65,536 \times 3 = 196,608.$

2.16 True or false: fluorescence is the term used to describe the light given off by a phosphor after it has been exposed to an electron beam. Explain your answer.

SOLUTION

False. Phosphorescence is the correct term. Fluorescence refers to the light given off by a phosphor while it is being exposed to an electron beam.

2.17 What is persistence?

SOLUTION

The duration of phosphorescence exhibited by a phosphor.

2.18 What is the function of the control electrode in a CRT?

SOLUTION

Regulate the intensity of the electron beam.

2.19 Name the two methods by which an electron beam can be bent?

SOLUTION

Electrostatic deflection and magnetic deflection.

2.20   What do you call the path the electron beam takes when returning to the left side of the CRT screen?

SOLUTION

Horizontal retrace.

2.21   What do you call the path the electron beam takes at the end of each refresh cycle?

SOLUTION

Vertical retrace.

2.22   What is the pitch of a color CRT?

SOLUTION

The distance between the center of the phosphor dot patterns on the inside of the display screen.

2.23   Why do many color printers use black pigment?

SOLUTION

Color pigments (cyan, magenta, and yellow) are relatively more expensive and it is technically difficult to produce high-quality black using several color pigments.

2.24   Show that with an $n \times n$ pixel grid, where each pixel can take on m intensity levels, we can approximate $n \times n \times (m - 1) + 1$ overall intensity levels.

SOLUTION

Since the $n \times n$ pixels can be set to a non-zero intensity value one after another to produce $n \times n$ overall intensity levels, and there are $m - 1$ non-zero intensity levels for the individual pixels, we can approximate a total of $n \times n \times (m - 1)$ non-zero overall intensity levels. Finally we need to add one more overall intensity level that corresponds to zero intensity (all pixels off).

2.25   Represent the grid patterns in Fig. 2-8 with a dither matrix.

SOLUTION

$$\begin{pmatrix} 0 & 2 \\ 3 & 1 \end{pmatrix}$$

2.26   What are the error propagation formulas for a top-to-bottom and right-to-left scanning order in the Floyd–Steinberg error diffusion algorithm?

SOLUTION

$$S(x - 1, y) = S(x - 1, y) + ae$$
$$S(x + 1, y - 1) = S(x + 1, y - 1) + be$$
$$S(x, y - 1) = S(x, y - 1) + ce$$
$$S(x - 1, y - 1) = S(x - 1, y - 1) + de$$

2.27   What is RLE?

SOLUTION

RLE stands for run-length encoding, a technique for image data compression.

2.28 Follow the illustrative example in the text to reconstruct the string that has been compressed to "981435" using RLE.

SOLUTION

"8888888884555"

2.29 If an 8-bit gray scale image is stored uncompressed in sequential memory or in an image file in left-to-right and bottom-to-top pixel order, what is the offset or displacement of the byte for the pixel at (x, y) from the beginning of the memory segment or the file's image data section?

SOLUTION

offset $= y \times n + x$ where n is the number of pixels in the horizontal direction.

2.30 What if the image in Prob. 2.29 is stored in left-to-right and top-to-bottom order?

SOLUTION

offset $= (m - y - 1)n + x$ where n and m are the number of pixels in the horizontal and vertical direction, respectively.

2.31 Develop a pseudo-code segment to initialize a 24-bit 256-entry lookup table with gray-scale values.

SOLUTION

```
int i, rgb[3];
for (i = 0; i < 256; i++) {
    rgb[0] = rgb[1] = rgb[2] = i;
    setEntry(i, rgb);
}
```

2.32 Develop a pseudo-code segment to swap the red and green components of all colors in a 256-entry lookup table.

SOLUTION

```
int i, x, rgb[3];
for (i = 0; i < 256; i++) {
    getEntry(i, rgb);
    x = rgb[0];
    rgb[0] = rgb[1];
    rgb[1] = x;
    setEntry(i, rgb);
}
```

2.33 Develop a pseudo-code segment to draw a rectangular area of $w \times h$ (in number of pixels) that starts at (x, y) using color rgb.

SOLUTION

```
int i, j;
setColor(rgb);
for (j = y; j < y + h; j++)
    for (i = x; i < x + w; i++) setPixel(i, j);
```

2.34   Develop a pseudo-code segment to draw a triangular area with the three vertices at (x, y), $(x, y + t)$, and $(x + t, y)$, where integer $t \geq 0$, using color *rgb*.

SOLUTION

```
int i, j;
setColor(rgb);
for ( j = y; j <= y + t; j++)
    for (i = x; i <= x + y + t − j; i++) setPixel(i, j);
```

2.35   Develop a pseudo-code segment to reset every pixel in an image that is in the 24-bit 256-entry lookup table representation to its complementary color.

SOLUTION

```
int i, rgb[3];
for (i = 0; i < 256; i++) {
    getEntry(i, rgb);
        rgb[0] = 255 − rgb[0];
        rgb[1] = 255 − rgb[1];
        rgb[2] = 255 − rgb[2];
    setEntry(i, rgb);
}
```

2.36   What if the image in Prob. 2.35 is in the 24-bit true color representation?

SOLUTION

```
int i, j, rgb[3];
for ( j = 0; j < height; j++)
    for (i = 0; i < width; i++) {
    getPixel(i, j, rgb);
        rgb[0] = 255 − rgb[0];
        rgb[1] = 255 − rgb[1];
        rgb[2] = 255 − rgb[2];
    setPixel(i, j, rgb);
}
```

2.37   Calculate the sum and product of $0.5 + 2.0i$ and $1.0 − 1.0i$.

SOLUTION

$$(0.5 + 1.0) + (2.0 + (−1.0))i = 1.5 + 1.0i$$
$$(0.5 \times 1.0 − 2.0 \times (−1.0)) + (0.5 \times (−1.0) + 2.0 \times 1.0)i = 2.5 + 1.5i$$

2.38   Calculate the square of the two complex numbers in Prob. 2.37.

SOLUTION

$$(0.5^2 − 2.0^2) + 2 \times 0.5 \times 2.0i = −3.75 + 2.0i$$
$$(1.0^2 − (−1.0)^2) + 2 \times 1.0 \times (−1.0)i = 0.0 − 2.0i$$

2.39   Show that $1 + 254 \times \text{count}/N$ provides a proportional mapping from count in $[0, N]$ to c in $[1, 255]$.

SOLUTION

Proportional mapping means that we want

$$(c - 1)/(255 - 1) = (\text{count} - 0)/(N - 0)$$

Hence $c = 1 + 254 \times \text{count}/N$.

2.40 Modify the pseudo code for visualizing the Mandelbrot set to visualize the Julia sets.

SOLUTION

```
int i, j, count;
float delta = (Re_max − Re_min)/width;
for (i = 0, x.real = Re_min; i < width; i++, x.real+ = delta)
    for ( j = 0, x.imag = Im_min; j < height; j++, x.imag+ = delta) {
        count = 0;
        while (|x| ≤ 2.0 && count < N) {
            compute x = x² + z;
            count++;
        }
        if (|x| ≤ 2.0) setColor(0);
        else setColor(1 + 254*count/N);
        setPixel(i, j);
    }
```

2.41 How to avoid the calculation of square root in an actual implementation of the algorithms for visualizing the Mandelbrot and Julia sets?

SOLUTION

Test for $|x|^2 \leq 4.0$ instead of $|x| \leq 2.0$.

Supplementary Problems

2.42 Can a 5 by $3\frac{1}{2}$ inch image be presented at 6 by 4 inch without introducing geometric distortion?

2.43 Refering to Prob. 2.42, what if the original is $5\frac{1}{4}$ by $3\frac{1}{2}$ inch?

2.44 Given the portrait image of a person, describe a simple way to make the person look more slender.

2.45 An RGB color image can be converted to a gray-scale image using the formula $0.299R + 0.587G + 0.114B$ for gray levels (see Chap. 11, Sec. 11.1 under "The NTSC YIQ Color Model"). Assuming that getPixel(x, y, rgb) now reads pixel values from a 24-bit input image and setPixel(x, y, i) assigns pixel values to an output image that uses a gray-scale lookup table, develop a pseudo-code segment to convert the input image to a gray-scale output image.

CHAPTER 3

Scan Conversion

Many pictures, from 2D drawings to projected views of 3D objects, consist of graphical primitives such as points, lines, circles, and filled polygons. These picture components are often defined in a continuous space at a higher level of abstraction than individual pixels in the discrete image space. For instance, a line is defined by its two endpoints and the line equation, whereas a circle is defined by its radius, center position, and the circle equation. It is the responsibility of the graphics system or the application program to convert each primitive from its geometric definition into a set of pixels that make up the primitive in the image space. This conversion task is generally referred to as scan conversion or rasterization.

The focus of this chapter is on the mathematical and algorithmic aspects of scan conversion. We discuss ways to handle several commonly encountered primitives including points, lines, circles, ellipses, characters, and filled regions in an efficient and effective manner. We also discuss techniques that help to "smooth out" the discrepancies between the original element and its discrete approximation. The implementation of these algorithms and mathematical solutions (and many others in subsequent chapters) varies from one system to another and can be in the form of various combinations of hardware, firmware, and software.

3.1 SCAN-CONVERTING A POINT

A mathematical point (x, y) where x and y are real numbers within an image area, needs to be scan-converted to a pixel at location (x', y'). This may be done by making x' to be the integer part of x, and y' the integer part of y. In other words, $x' = \text{Floor}(x)$ and $y' = \text{Floor}(y)$, where function Floor returns the largest integer that is less than or equal to the argument. Doing so in essence places the origin of a continuous coordinate system for (x, y) at the lower left corner of the pixel grid in the image space [see Fig. 3-1(a)]. All points that satisfy $x' \leq x < x' + 1$ and $y' \leq y < y' + 1$ are mapped to pixel (x', y'). For example, point P_1 (1.7, 0.8) is represented by pixel (1, 0). Points P_2 (2.2, 1.3) and P_3 (2.8, 1.9) are both represented by pixel (2, 1).

Another approach is to align the integer values in the coordinate system for (x, y) with the pixel coordinates [see Fig. 3-1(b)]. Here we scan convert (x, y) by making $x' = \text{Floor}(x + 0.5)$ and $y' = \text{Floor}(y + 0.5)$. This essentially places the origin of the coordinate system for (x, y) at the center of pixel (0, 0). All points that satisfy $x' - 0.5 \leq x < x' + 0.5$ and $y' - 0.5 \leq y < y' + 0.5$ are mapped to pixel (x', y'). This means that points P_1 and P_2 are now both represented by pixel (2, 1), whereas point P_3 is represented by pixel (3, 2).

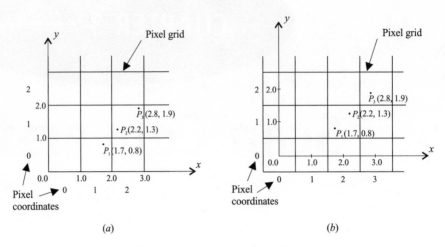

Fig. 3-1   Scan-converting points.

We will assume, in the following sections, that this second approach to coordinate system alignment is used. Thus all pixels are centered at the integer values of a continuous coordinate system where abstract graphical primitives are defined.

3.2   SCAN-CONVERTING A LINE

A line in computer graphics typically refers to a line segment, which is a portion of a straight line that extends indefinitely in opposite directions. It is defined by its two endpoints and the line equation $y = mx + b$, where m is called the slope and b the y intercept of the line. In Fig. 3-2 the two endpoints are described by $P_1(x_1, y_1)$ and $P_2(x_2, y_2)$. The line equation describes the coordinates of all the points that lie between the two endpoints.

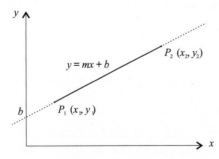

Fig. 3-2   Defining a line.

A note of caution: this slope–intercept equation is not suitable for vertical lines. Horizontal, vertical, and diagonal ($|m| = 1$) lines can, and often should, be handled as special cases without going through the following scan-conversion algorithms. These commonly used lines can be mapped to the image space in a straightforward fashion for high execution efficiency.

Direct Use of the Line Equation

A simple approach to scan-converting a line is to first scan-convert P_1 and P_2 to pixel coordinates (x_1', y_1') and (x_2', y_2'), respectively; then set $m = (y_2' - y_1')/(x_2' - x_1')$ and $b = y_1' - mx_1'$. If $|m| \leq 1$, then for every integer value of x between and excluding x'_1 and x'_2, calculate the corresponding value of y using the equation and scan-convert (x, y). If $|m| > 1$, then for every integer value of y between and excluding y'_1 and y'_2, calculate the corresponding value of x using the equation and scan-convert (x, y).

While this approach is mathematically sound, it involves floating-point computation (multiplication and addition) in every step that uses the line equation since m and b are generally real numbers. The challenge is to find a way to achieve the same goal as quickly as possible.

DDA Algorithm

The digital differential analyzer (DDA) algorithm is an incremental scan-conversion method. Such an approach is characterized by performing calculations at each step using results from the preceding step. Suppose at step i we have calculated (x_i, y_i) to be a point on the line. Since the next point (x_{i+1}, y_{i+1}) should satisfy $\Delta y / \Delta x = m$ where $\Delta y = y_{i+1} - y_i$ and $\Delta x = x_{i+1} - x_i$, we have

$$y_{i+1} = y_i + m\Delta x$$

or

$$x_{i+1} = x_i + \Delta y/m$$

These formulas are used in the DDA algorithm as follows. When $|m| \leq 1$, we start with $x = x'_1$ (assuming that $x'_1 < x'_2$) and $y = y'_1$, and set $\Delta x = 1$ (i.e., unit increment in the x direction). The y coordinate of each successive point on the line is calculated using $y_{i+1} = y_i + m$. When $|m| > 1$, we start with $x = x'_1$ and $y = y'_1$ (assuming that $y'_1 < y'_2$), and set $\Delta y = 1$ (i.e., unit increment in the y direction). The x coordinate of each successive point on the line is calculated using $x_{i+1} = x_i + 1/m$. This process continues until x reaches x'_2 (for the $|m| \leq 1$ case) or y reaches y'_2 (for the $|m| > 1$ case) and all points found are scan-converted to pixel coordinates.

The DDA algorithm is faster than the direct use of the line equation since it calculates points on the line without any floating-point multiplication. However, a floating-point addition is still needed in determining each successive point. Furthermore, cumulative error due to limited precision in the floating-point representation may cause calculated points to drift away from their true position when the line is relatively long.

Bresenham's Line Algorithm

Bresenham's line algorithm is a highly efficient incremental method for scan-converting lines. It produces mathematically accurate results using only integer addition, subtraction, and multiplication by 2, which can be accomplished by a simple arithmetic shift operation.

The method works as follows. Assume that we want to scan-convert the line shown in Fig. 3-3 where $0 < m < 1$. We start with pixel $P'_1(x'_1, y'_1)$, then select subsequent pixels as we work our way to the right, one pixel position at a time in the horizontal direction towards $P'_2(x'_2, y'_2)$. Once a pixel is chosen at any step, the next pixel is either the one to its right (which constitutes a lower bound for the line) or the one to its right and up (which constitutes an upper bound for the line) due to the limit on m. The line is best approximated by those pixels that fall the least distance from its true path between P'_1 and P'_2.

Using the notation of Fig. 3-3, the coordinates of the last chosen pixel upon entering step i are (x_i, y_i). Our task is to choose the next one between the bottom pixel S and the top pixel T. If S is chosen, we have $x_{i+1} = x_i + 1$ and $y_{i+1} = y_i$. If T is chosen, we have $x_{i+1} = x_i + 1$ and $y_{i+1} = y_i + 1$. The actual y coordinate of the line at $x = x_{i+1}$ is $y = mx_{i+1} + b = m(x_i + 1) + b$. The distance from S to the actual line in the y direction is $s = y - y_i$. The distance from T to the actual line in the y direction is $t = (y_i + 1) - y$.

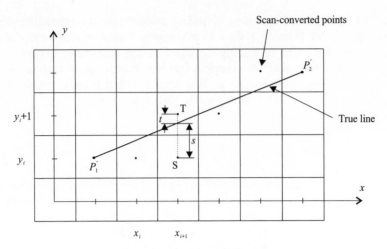

Fig. 3-3   Scan-converting a line.

Now consider the difference between these two distance values: $s - t$. When $s - t$ is less than zero, we have $s < t$ and the closest pixel is S. Conversely, when $s - t$ is greater than zero, we have $s > t$ and the closest pixel is T. We also choose T when $s - t$ is equal to zero. This difference is

$$s - t = (y - y_i) - [(y_i + 1) - y]$$
$$= 2y - 2y_i - 1 = 2m(x_i + 1) + 2b - 2y_i - 1$$

Substituting m by $\Delta y / \Delta x$ and introducing a decision variable $d_i = \Delta x(s - t)$, which has the same sign as $(s - t)$ since Δx is positive in our case, we have

$$d_i = 2\Delta y^* x_i - 2\Delta x^* y_i + C \qquad \text{where } C = 2\Delta y + \Delta x(2b - 1)$$

Similarly, we can write the decision variable d_{i+1} for the next step as

$$d_{i+1} = 2\Delta y^* x_{i+1} - 2\Delta x^* y_{i+1} + C$$

Then

$$d_{i+1} - d_i = 2\Delta y(x_{i+1} - x_i) - 2\Delta x(y_{i+1} - y_i)$$

Since $x_{i+1} = x_i + 1$, we have

$$d_{i+1} = d_i + 2\Delta y - 2\Delta x(y_{i+1} - y_i)$$

If the chosen pixel is the top pixel T (meaning that $d_i \geq 0$) then $y_{i+1} = y_i + 1$ and so

$$d_{i+1} = d_i + 2(\Delta y - \Delta x)$$

On the other hand, if the chosen pixel is the bottom pixel S (meaning that $d_i < 0$) then $y_{i+1} = y_i$ and so

$$d_{i+1} = d_i + 2\Delta y$$

Hence we have

$$d_{i+1} = \begin{cases} d_i + 2(\Delta y - \Delta x) & \text{if } d_i \geq 0 \\ d_i + 2\Delta y & \text{if } d_i < 0 \end{cases}$$

Finally, we calculate d_1, the base case value for this recursive formula, from the original definition of the decision variable d_i:

$$d_1 = \Delta x[2m(x_1 + 1) + 2b - 2y_1 - 1]$$
$$= \Delta x[2(mx_1 + b - y_1) + 2m - 1]$$

Since $mx_1 + b - y_1 = 0$, we have

$$d_1 = 2\Delta y - \Delta x$$

In summary, Bresenham's algorithm for scan-converting a line from $P'_1(x'_1, y'_1)$ to $P'_2(x'_2, y'_2)$ with $x'_1 < x'_2$ and $0 < m < 1$ can be stated as follows:

```
int x = x'_1, y = y'_1;
int dx = x'_2 - x'_1, dy = y'_2 - y'_1, dT = 2(dy - dx), dS = 2dy;
int d = 2dy - dx;
setPixel(x, y);
while (x < x'_2) {
    x++;
    if (d < 0)
        d = d + dS;
    else {
        y++;
        d = d + dT;
    }
    setPixel(x, y);
}
```

Here we first initialize decision variable d and set pixel P'_1. During each iteration of the while loop, we increment x to the next horizontal position, then use the current value of d to select the bottom or top (increment y) pixel and update d, and at the end set the chosen pixel.

As for lines that have other m values we can make use of the fact that they can be mirrored either horizontally, vertically, or diagonally into this $0°$ to $45°$ angle range. For example, a line from (x'_1, y'_1) to (x'_2, y'_2) with $-1 < m < 0$ has a horizontally mirrored counterpart from $(x'_1, -y'_1)$ to $(x'_2, -y'_2)$ with $0 < m < 1$. We can simply use the algorithm to scan-convert this counterpart, but negate the y coordinate at the end of each iteration to set the right pixel for the line. For a line whose slope is in the $45°$ to $90°$ range, we can obtain its mirrored counterpart by exchanging the x and y coordinates of its endpoints. We can then scan-convert this counterpart but we must exchange x and y in the call to setPixel.

3.3 SCAN-CONVERTING A CIRCLE

A circle is a symmetrical figure. Any circle-generating algorithm can take advantage of the circle's symmetry to plot eight points for each value that the algorithm calculates. Eight-way symmetry is used by reflecting each calculated point around each $45°$ axis. For example, if point 1 in Fig. 3-4 were calculated with a circle algorithm, seven more points could be found by reflection. The reflection is accomplished by reversing the x, y coordinates as in point 2, reversing the x, y coordinates and reflecting about the y axis as in point 3, reflecting about the y axis as in point 4, switching the signs of x and y as in point 5, reversing the x, y coordinates, reflecting about the y axis and reflecting about the x axis as in point 6, reversing the x, y coordinates and reflecting about the y axis as in point 7, and reflecting about the x axis as in point 8.

To summarize:

$$
\begin{array}{ll}
P_1 = (x, y) & P_5 = (-x, -y) \\
P_2 = (y, x) & P_6 = (-y, -x) \\
P_3 = (-y, x) & P_7 = (y, -x) \\
P_4 = (-x, y) & P_8 = (x, -y)
\end{array}
$$

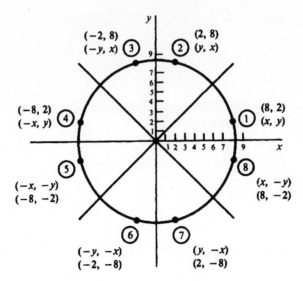

Fig. 3-4   Eight-way symmetry of a circle.

Defining a Circle

There are two standard methods of mathematically defining a circle centered at the origin. The first method defines a circle with the second-order polynomial equation (see Fig. 3-5)

$$y^2 = r^2 - x^3$$

where x = the x coordinate

y = the y coordinate

r = the circle radius

With this method, each x coordinate in the sector, from 90° to 45°, is found by stepping x from 0 to $r/\sqrt{2}$, and each y coordinate is found by evaluating $\sqrt{r^2 - x^2}$ for each step of x. This is a very inefficient method, however, because for each point both x and r must be squared and subtracted from each other; then the square root of the result must be found.

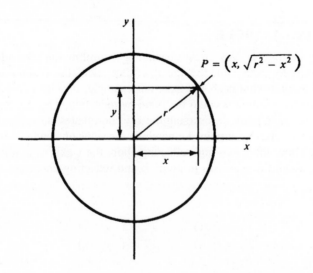

Fig. 3-5   Circle defined with a second-degree polynomial equation.

The second method of defining a circle makes use of trigonometric functios (see Fig. 3-6):

$$x = r \cos \theta \qquad y = r \sin \theta$$

where θ = current angle

r = circle radius

x = x coordinate

y = y coordinate

By this method, θ is stepped from θ to $\pi/4$, and each value of x and y is calculated. However, computation of the values of $\sin \theta$ and $\cos \theta$ is even more time-consuming than the calculations required by the first method.

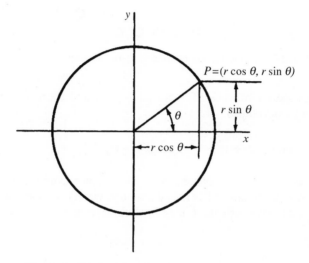

Fig. 3-6   Circle defined with trigonometric functions.

Bresenham's Circle Algorithm

If a circle is to be plotted efficiently, the use of trigonometric and power functions must be avoided. And, as with the generation of a straight line, it is also desirable to perform the calculations necessary to find the scan-converted points with only integer addition, subtraction, and multiplication by powers of 2. *Bresenham's circle algorithm* allows these goals to be met.

Scan-converting a circle using Bresenham's algorithm works as follows. If the eight-way symmetry of a circle is used to generate a circle, points will only have to be generated through a 45° angle. And, if points are generated from 90° to 45°, moves will be made only in the $+x$ and $-y$ directions (see Fig. 3-7).

The best approximation of the true circle will be described by those pixels in the raster that fall the least distance from the true circle. Examine Fig. 3-8. Notice that, if points are generated from 90° and 45°, each new point closest to the true circle can be found by taking either of two actions: (1) move in the x direction one unit or (2) move in the x direction one unit and move in the negative y direction one unit. Therefore, a method of selecting between these two choices is all that is necessary to find the points closest to the true circle.

Assume that (x_i, y_i) are the coordinates of the last scan-converted pixel upon entering step i (see Fig. 3-8). Let the distance from the origin to pixel T squared minus the distance to the true circle squared = $D(T)$. Then let the distance from the origin to pixel S squared minus the distance to the true

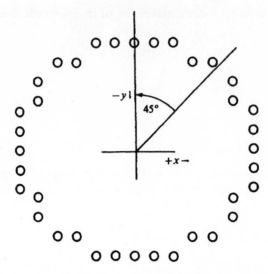

Fig. 3-7   Circle scan-converted with Bresenham's algorithm.

circle squared $= D(S)$. As the coordinates of T are $(x_i + 1, y_i)$ and those of S are $(x_i + 1, y_i - 1)$, the following expressions can be developed:

$$D(T) = (x_i + 1)^2 + y_i^2 - r^2 \qquad D(S) = (x_i + 1)^2 + (y_i - 1)^2 - r^2$$

This function D provides a relative measurement of the distance from the center of a pixel to the true circle. Since $D(T)$ will always be positive (T is outside the true circle) and $D(S)$ will always be negative (S is inside the true circle), a decision variable d_i may be defined as follows:

$$d_i = D(T) + D(S)$$

Therefore

$$d_i = 2(x_i + 1)^2 + y_i^2 + (y_i - 1)^2 - 2r^2$$

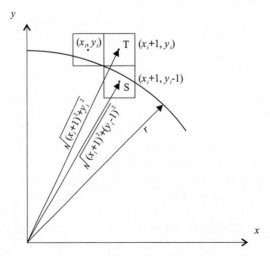

Fig. 3-8   Choosing pixels in Bresenham's circle algorithm.

When $d_i < 0$, we have $|D(T)| < |D(S)|$ and pixel T is chosen. When $d_i \geq 0$, we have $|D(T)| \geq |D(S)|$ and pixel S is selected. We can also write the decision variable d_{i+1} for the next step:

$$d_{i+1} = 2(x_{i+1} + 1)^2 + y_{i+1}^2 + (y_{i+1} - 1)^2 - 2r^2$$

Hence

$$d_{i+1} - d_i = 2(x_{i+1} + 1)^2 + y_{i+1}^2 + (y_{i+1} - 1)^2 - 2(x_i + 1)^2 - y_i^2 - (y_i - 1)^2$$

Since $x_{i+1} = x_i + 1$, we have

$$d_{i+1} = d_i + 4x_i + 2(y_{i+1}^2 - y_i^2) - 2(y_{i+1} - y_i) + 6$$

If T is the chosen pixel (meaning that $d_i < 0$) then $y_{i+1} = y_i$ and so

$$d_{i+1} = d_i + 4x_i + 6$$

On the other hand, if S is the chosen pixel (meaning that $d_i \geq 0$) then $y_{i+1} = y_i - 1$ and so

$$d_{i+1} = d_i + 4(x_i - y_i) + 10$$

Hence we have

$$d_{i+1} = \begin{cases} d_i + 4x_i + 6 & \text{if } d_i < 0 \\ d_i + 4(x_i - y_i) + 10 & \text{if } d_i \geq 0 \end{cases}$$

Finally, we set $(0, r)$ to be the starting pixel coordinates and compute the base case value d_1 for this recursive formula from the original definition of d_i:

$$d_1 = 2(0 + 1)^2 + r^2 + (r - 1)^2 - 2r^2 = 3 - 2r$$

We can now summarize the algorithm for generating all the pixel coordinates in the 90° to 45° octant that are needed when scan-converting a circle of radius r:

```
int x = 0, y = r, d = 3 − 2r;
while (x <= y) {
  setPixel(x, y);
  if (d < 0)
    d = d + 4x + 6;
  else {
    d = d + 4(x − y) + 10;
    y−−;
  }
  x++;
}
```

Note that during each iteration of the while loop we first set a pixel whose position has already been determined, starting with $(0, r)$. We then test the current value of decision variable d in order to update d and determine the proper y coordinate of the next pixel. Finally we increment x.

Midpoint Circle Algorithm

We present another incremental circle algorithm that is very similar to Bresenham's approach. It is based on the following function for testing the spatial relationship between an arbitrary point (x, y) and a circle of radius r centered at the origin:

$$f(x, y) = x^2 + y^2 - r^2 \begin{cases} < 0 & (x, y) \text{ inside the circle} \\ = 0 & (x, y) \text{ on the circle} \\ > 0 & (x, y) \text{ outside the circle} \end{cases}$$

Now consider the coordinates of the point halfway between pixel T and pixel S in Fig. 3-8: $(x_i + 1, y_i - \frac{1}{2})$. This is called the midpoint and we use it to define a decision parameter:

$$p_i = f(x_i + 1, y_i - \tfrac{1}{2}) = (x_i + 1)^2 + (y_i - \tfrac{1}{2})^2 - r^2$$

If p_i is negative, the midpoint is inside the circle, and we choose pixel T. On the other hand, if p_i is positive (or equal to zero), the midpoint is outside the circle (or on the circle), and we choose pixel S. Similarly, the decision parameter for the next step is

$$p_{i+1} = (x_{i+1} + 1)^2 + (y_{i+1} - \tfrac{1}{2})^2 - r^2$$

Since $x_{i+1} = x_i + 1$, we have

$$p_{i+1} - p_i = [(x_i + 1) + 1]^2 - (x_i + 1)^2 + (y_{i+1} - \tfrac{1}{2})^2 - (y_i - \tfrac{1}{2})^2$$

Hence

$$p_{i+1} = p_i + 2(x_i + 1) + 1 + (y_{i+1}^2 - y_i^2) - (y_{i+1} - y_i)$$

If pixel T is chosen (meaning $p_i < 0$), we have $y_{i+1} = y_i$. On the other hand, if pixel S is chosen (meaning $p_i \geq 0$), we have $y_{i+1} = y_i - 1$. Thus

$$p_{i+1} = \begin{cases} p_i + 2(x_i + 1) + 1 & \text{if } p_i < 0 \\ p_i + 2(x_i + 1) + 1 - 2(y_i - 1) & \text{if } p_i \geq 0 \end{cases}$$

We can continue to simplify this in terms of (x_i, y_i) and get

$$p_{i+1} = \begin{cases} p_i + 2x_i + 3 & \text{if } p_i < 0 \\ p_i + 2(x_i - y_i) + 5 & \text{if } p_i \geq 0 \end{cases}$$

Or we can write it in terms of (x_{i+1}, y_{i+1}) and have

$$p_{i+1} = \begin{cases} p_i + 2x_{i+1} + 1 & \text{if } p_i < 0 \\ p_i + 2(x_{i+1} - y_{i+1}) + 1 & \text{if } p_i \geq 0 \end{cases}$$

Finally, we compute the initial value for the decision parameter using the original definition of p_i and $(0, r)$:

$$p_i = (0 + 1)^2 + (r - \tfrac{1}{2})^2 - r^2 = \tfrac{5}{4} - r$$

One can see that this is not really integer computation. However, when r is an integer we can simply set $p_1 = 1 - r$. The error of being $\frac{1}{4}$ less than the precise value does not prevent p_1 from getting the appropriate sign. It does not affect the rest of the scan-conversion process either, because the decision variable is only updated with integer increments in subsequent steps.

The following is a description of this midpoint circle algorithm that generates the pixel coordinates in the 90° to 45° octant:

```
int x = 0, y = r, p = 1 - r;
while (x <= y) {
    setPixel(x, y);
    if (p < 0)
        p = p + 2x + 3;
    else {
        p = p + 2(x - y) + 5;
        y--;
    }
    x++;
}
```

Arbitrarily Centered Circles

In the above discussion of the circle algorithms we have assumed that a circle is centered at the origin. To scan-convert a circle centered at (x_c, y_c), we can simply replace the setPixel(x, y) statement in the algorithm description with setPixel$(x + x_c, y + y_c)$. The reason for this to work is that a circle centered at (x_c, y_c) can be viewed as a circle centered at the origin that is moved by x_c and y_c in the x and y direction, respectively. We can achieve the effect of scan-converting this arbitrarily centered circle by relocating scan-converted pixels in the same way as moving the circle's center from the origin.

3.4 SCAN-CONVERTING AN ELLIPSE

The ellipse, like the circle, shows symmetry. In the case of an ellipse, however, symmetry is four- rather than eight-way. There are two methods of mathematically defining a ellipse.

Polynomial Method of Defining an Ellipse

The polynomial method of defining an ellipse (Fig. 3-9) is given by the expression

$$\frac{(x - h)^2}{a^2} + \frac{(y - k)^2}{b^2} = 1$$

where (h, k) = ellipse center

a = length of major axis

b = length of minor axis

When the polynomial method is used to define an ellipse, the value of x is incremented from h to a. For each step of x, each value of y is found by evaluating the expression

$$y = b\sqrt{1 - \frac{(x - h)^2}{a^2}} + k$$

This method is very inefficient, however, because the squares of a and $(x - h)$ must be found; then floating-point division of $(x - h)^2$ by a^2 and floating-point multiplication of the square root of $[1 - (x - h)^2/a^2]$ by b must be performed (see Prob. 3.20).

Routines have been found that will scan-convert general polynomial equations, including the ellipse. However, these routines are logic intensive and thus are very slow methods for scan-converting ellipses.

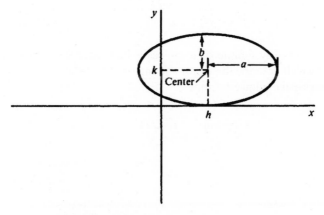

Fig. 3-9   Polynomial description of an ellipse.

Trigonometric Method of Defining an Ellipse

A second method of defining an ellipse makes use of trigonometric relationships (see Fig. 3-10). The following equations define an ellipse trigonometrically:

$$x = a\cos(\theta) + h \qquad \text{and} \qquad y = b\sin(\theta) + k$$

where (x, y) = the current coordinates
a = length of major axis
b = length of minor axis
θ = current angle
(h, k) = ellipse center

For generation of an ellipse using the trigonometric method, the value of θ is varied from 0 to $\pi/2$ radians (rad). The remaining points are found by symmetry. While this method is also inefficient and thus generally too slow for interactive applications, a lookup table containing the values for $\sin(\theta)$ and $\cos(\theta)$ with θ ranging from 0 to $\pi/2$ rad can be used. This method would have been considered unacceptable at one time because of the relatively high cost of the computer memory used to store the values of θ. However, because the cost of computer memory has plummeted in recent years, this method is now quite acceptable.

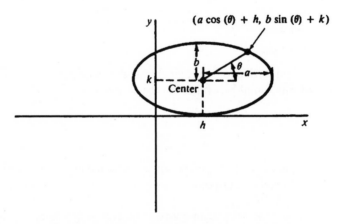

Fig. 3-10   Trigonometric description of an ellipse.

Ellipse Axis Rotation

Since the ellipse shows four-way symmetry, it can easily be rotated 90°. The new equation is found by trading a and b, the values which describe the major and minor axes. When the polynomial method is used, the equations used to describe the ellipse become

$$\frac{(x - h)^2}{b^2} + \frac{(y - k)^2}{a^2} = 1$$

where (h, k) = ellipse center
a = length of major axis
b = length of minor axis

When the trigonometric method is used, the equations used to describe the ellipse become

$$x = b\cos(\theta) + h \qquad \text{and} \qquad y = a\sin(\theta) + k$$

where (x, y) = current coordinates
$\qquad a$ = length of major axis
$\qquad b$ = length of minor axis
$\qquad \theta$ = current angle
$\qquad (h, k)$ = ellipse center

Assume that you would like to rotate the ellipse through an angle other than 90°. It can be seen from Fig. 3-11 that rotation of the ellipse may be accomplished by rotating the x and y axis α degrees. When this is done, the equations describing the x, y coordinates of each scan-converted point become

$$x = a\cos(\theta) - b\sin(\theta + \alpha) + h \qquad y = b\sin(\theta) + a\cos(\theta + \alpha) + k$$

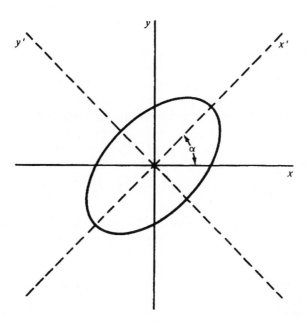

Fig. 3-11　Rotation of an ellipse.

Midpoint Ellipse Algorithm

This is an incremental method for scan-converting an ellipse that is centered at the origin in standard position (i.e., with its major and minor axes parallel to the coordinate system axes). It works in a way that is very similar to the midpoint circle algorithm. However, because of the four-way symmetry property we need to consider the entire elliptical curve in the first quadrant (see Fig. 3-12).

Let's first rewrite the ellipse equation and define function f that can be used to decide if the midpoint between two candidate pixels is inside or outside the ellipse:

$$f(x, y) = b^2x^2 + a^2y^2 - a^2b^2 \begin{cases} < 0 & (x, y) \text{ inside the ellipse} \\ = 0 & (x, y) \text{ on the ellipse} \\ > 0 & (x, y) \text{ outside the ellipse} \end{cases}$$

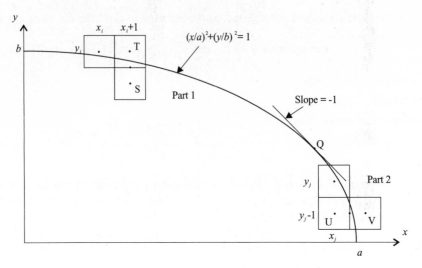

Fig. 3-12   Scan-converting an ellipse.

Now divide the elliptical curve from $(0, b)$ to $(a, 0)$ into two parts at point Q where the slope of the curve is -1. Recall that the slope of a curve defined by $f(x, y) = 0$ is $dy/dx = -fx/fy$, where fx and fy are partial derivatives of $f(x, y)$ with respect to x and y, respectively. We have $fx = 2b^2x$, $fy = 2a^2y$, and $dy/dx = -2b^2x/2a^2y$. This shows that the slope of the curve changes monotonically from one side of Q to the other. Hence we can monitor the slope value during the scan-conversion process to detect Q.

Our starting point is $(0, b)$. Suppose that the coordinates of the last scan-converted pixel upon entering step i are (x_i, y_i). We are to select either $T(x_i + 1, y_i)$ or $S(x_i + 1, y_i - 1)$ to be the next pixel. The midpoint of the vertical line connecting T and S is used to define the following decision parameter:

$$p_i = f(x_i + 1, y_i - \tfrac{1}{2}) = b^2(x_i + 1)^2 + a^2(y_i - \tfrac{1}{2})^2 - a^2b^2$$

If $p_i < 0$, the midpoint is inside the curve, and we choose pixel T. On the other hand, if $p_i \geq 0$, the midpoint is outside or on the curve, and we choose pixel S. Similarly, we can write the decision parameter for the next step:

$$p_{i+1} = f(x_{i+1} + 1, y_{i+1} - \tfrac{1}{2}) = b^2(x_{i+1} + 1)^2 + a^2(y_{i+1} - \tfrac{1}{2})^2 - a^2b^2$$

Since $x_{i+1} = x_i + 1$, we have

$$p_{i+1} - p_i = b^2[(x_{i+1} + 1)^2 - x_{i+1}^2] + a^2[(y_{i+1} - \tfrac{1}{2})^2 - (y_i - \tfrac{1}{2})^2]$$

Hence

$$p_{i+1} = p_i + 2b^2x_{i+1} + b^2 + a^2[(y_{i+1} - \tfrac{1}{2})^2 - (y_i - \tfrac{1}{2})^2]$$

If T is the chosen pixel (meaning $p_i < 0$), we have $y_{i+1} = y_i$. On the other hand, if pixel S is chosen (meaning $p_i \geq 0$), we have $y_{i+1} = y_i - 1$. Thus we can express p_{i+1} in terms of p_i and (x_{i+1}, y_{i+1}):

$$p_{i+1} = \begin{cases} p_i + 2b^2x_{i+1} + b^2 & \text{if } p_i < 0 \\ p_i + 2b^2x_{i+1} + b^2 - 2a^2y_{i+1} & \text{if } p_i \geq 0 \end{cases}$$

The initial value for this recursive expression can be obtained by evaluating the original definition of p_i with $(0, b)$:

$$p_1 = b^2 + a^2(b - \tfrac{1}{2})^2 - a^2b^2 = b^2 - a^2b + a^2/4$$

We now move on to derive a similar formula for part 2 of the curve. Suppose pixel (x_j, y_j) has just been scan-converted upon entering step j. The next pixel is either $U(x_j, y_j - 1)$ or $V(x_j + 1, y_j - 1)$. The midpoint of the horizontal line connecting U and V is used to define the decision parameter

$$q_j = f(x_j + \tfrac{1}{2}, y_j - 1) = b^2(x_j + \tfrac{1}{2})^2 + a^2(y_i - 1)^2 - a^2b^2$$

If $q_j < 0$, the midpoint is inside the curve and V is chosen. On the other hand, if $q_j \geq 0$, it is outside or on the curve and U is chosen. We also have

$$q_{j+1} = f(x_{j+1} + \tfrac{1}{2}, y_{j+1} - 1) = b^2(x_{j+1} + \tfrac{1}{2})^2 + a^2(y_{j+1} - 1)^2 - a^2b^2$$

Since $y_{j+1} = y_j - 1$, we have

$$q_{j+1} - q_j = b^2[(x_{j+1} + \tfrac{1}{2})^2 - (x_j + \tfrac{1}{2})^2] + a^2[(y_{j+1} - 1)^2 - y_{j+1}^2]$$

Hence

$$q_{j+1} = q_j + b^2[(x_{j+1} + \tfrac{1}{2})^2 - (x_j + \tfrac{1}{2})^2] - 2a^2y_{j+1} + a^2$$

If V is the chosen pixel (meaning $q_j < 0$), we have $x_{j+1} = x_j + 1$. On the other hand, if U is chosen (meaning $q_j \geq 0$), we have $x_{j+1} = x_j$. Thus we can express q_{j+1} in terms of q_j and (x_{j+1}, y_{j+1}):

$$q_{j+1} = \begin{cases} q_j + 2b^2x_{j+1} - 2a^2y_{j+1} + a^2 & \text{if } q_j < 0 \\ q_j - 2a^2y_{j+1} + a^2 & \text{if } q_j \geq 0 \end{cases}$$

The initial value for this recursive expression is computed using the original definition of q_j and the coordinates (x_k, y_k) of the last pixel chosen for part 1 of the curve:

$$q_1 = f(x_k + \tfrac{1}{2}, y_k - 1) = b^2(x_k + \tfrac{1}{2})^2 + a^2(y_k - 1)^2 - a^2b^2$$

We can now put together a pseudo-code description of the midpoint algorithm for scan-converting the elliptical curve in the first quadrant. There are a couple of technical details that are worth noting. First, we keep track of the slope of the curve by evaluating the partial derivatives fx and fy at each chosen pixel position. This means that $fx = 2b^2x_i$ and $fy = 2a^2y_i$ for position (x_i, y_i). Since we have $x_{i+1} = x_i + 1$ and $y_{i+1} = y_i$ or $y_i - 1$ for part 1, and $x_{j+1} = x_j$ or $x_j + 1$ and $y_{j+1} = y_j - 1$ for part 2, the partial derivatives can be updated incrementally using $2b^2$ and/or $-2a^2$. For example, if $x_{i+1} = x_i + 1$ and $y_{i+1} = y_i - 1$, the partial derivatives for position (x_{i+1}, y_{i+1}) are $2b^2x_{i+1} = 2b^2x_i + 2b^2$ and $2a^2y_{i+1} = 2a^2y_i - 2a^2$. Second, since $2b^2x_{i+1}$ and $2a^2y_{i+1}$ appear in the recursive expression for the decision parameters, we can use them to efficiently compute p_{i+1} as well as q_{j+1}:

```
int x = 0, y = b;      /* starting point */
int aa = a*a, bb = b*b, aa2 = aa*2, bb2 = bb*2;
int fx = 0, fy = aa2*b;      /* initial partial derivatives */
int p = bb − aa*b + 0.25*aa;      /* compute and round off p₁ */
while ( fx < fy) { /* |slope| < 1 */
  setPixel(x, y);
  x++;
  fx = fx + bb2;
  if (p < 0)
    p = p + fx + bb;
  else {
    y--;
    fy = fy − aa2;
    p = p + fx + bb − fy;
  }
}
setPixel(x, y);      /* set pixel at (xₖ, yₖ) */
```

```
p = bb(x + 0.5)(x + 0.5) + aa(y − 1)(y − 1) − aa*bb;       /* set q₁ */
while (y > 0) {
    y−−;
    fy = fy − aa2;
    if (p >= 0)
        p = p − fy + aa;
    else {
        x++;
        fx = fx + bb2;
        p = p + fx − fy + aa;
    }
    setPixel(x, y);
}
```

3.5   SCAN-CONVERTING ARCS AND SECTORS

Arcs

An arc [Fig. 3-13(a)] may be generated by using either the polynomial or the trigonometric method. When the trigonometric method is used, the starting value is set equal to θ_1 and the ending value is set equal to θ_2 [see Figs. 3-13(a) and 3-13(b)]. The rest of the steps are similar to those used when scan-converting a circle, except that symmetry is not used.

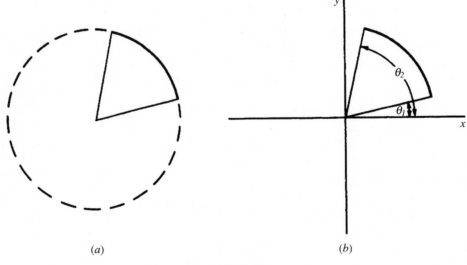

(a)   (b)

Fig. 3-13

When the polynomial method is used, the value of x is varied from x_1 to x_2 and the values of y are found by evaluating the expressio $\sqrt{r^2 − x^2}$ (Fig. 3-14).

From the graphics programmer's point of view, arcs would appear to be nothing more than portions of circles. However, problems occur if algorithms such as Bresenham's circle algorithm are used in drawing an arc. In the case of Bresenham's algorithm, the endpoints of an arc must be specified in terms of the x, y coordinates. The general formulation becomes inefficient when endpoints must be found (see Fig. 3-15). This occurs because the endpoints for each 45° increment of the arc must be found. Each of the eight points found by reflection must be tested to see if the point is between the specified endpoints of the arc. As a result, a routine to draw an arc based on Bresenham's algorithm must take the time to calculate and test

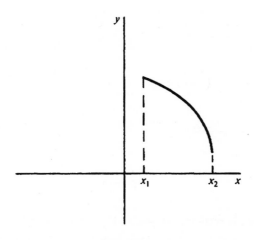

Fig. 3-14

every point on the circle's perimeter. There is always the danger that the endpoints will be missed when a method like this is used. If the endpoints are missed, the routine can become caught in an infinite loop.

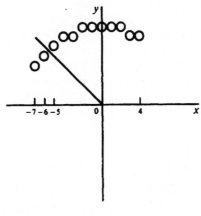

Fig. 3-15

Sectors

A sector is scan-converted by using any of the methods of scan-converting an arc and then scan-converting two lines from the center of the arc to the endpoints of the arc.

For example, assume that a sector whose center is at point (h, k) is to be scan-converted. First, scan-convert an arc from θ_1 to θ_2. Next, a line would be scan-converted from (h, k) to $(r\cos(\theta_1) + h, r\sin(\theta_1) + k)$. A second line would be scan-converted from (h, k) to $(r\cos(\theta_2) + h, r\sin(\theta_2) + k)$.

3.6   SCAN-CONVERTING A RECTANGLE

A rectangle whose sides are parallel to the coordinate axes may be constructed if the locations of two vertices are known [see Fig. 3-16(a)]. The remaining corner points are then derived [see Fig. 3-16(b)]. Once the vertices are known, the four sets of coordinates are sent to the line routine and the rectangle is

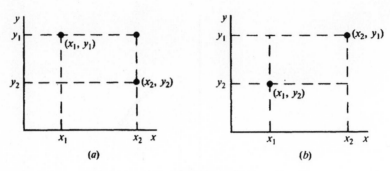

Fig. 3-16

scan-converted. In the case of the rectangle shown in Figs. 3-16(a) and 3-16(b), lines would be drawn as follows: line (x_1, y_1) to (x_1, y_2); line (x_1, y_2) to (x_2, y_2); line (x_2, y_2) to (x_2, y_1); and line (x_2, y_1) to (x_1, y_1).

3.7 REGION FILLING

Region filling is the process of "coloring in" a definite image area or region. Regions may be defined at the pixel or geometric level. At the pixel level, we describe a region either in terms of the bounding pixels that outline it or as the totality of pixels that comprise it (see Fig, 3-17). In the first case the region is called boundary-defined and the collection of algorithms used for filling such a region are collectively called boundary-fill algorithms. The other type of region is called an interior-defined region and the accompanying algorithms are called flood-fill algorithms. At the geometric level a region is defined or enclosed by such abstract contouring elements as connected lines and curves. For example, a polygonal region, or a filled polygon, is defined by a closed polyline, which is a polyline (i.e., a series of sequentially connected lines) that has the end of the last line connected to the beginning of the first line.

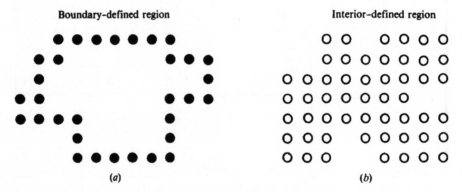

Fig. 3-17

4-Connected vs. 8-Connected

An interesting point here is that, while a geometrically defined contour clearly separates the interior of a region from the exterior, ambiguity may arise when an outline consists of discrete pixels in the image space. There are two ways in which pixels are considered connected to each other to form a "continuous" boundary. One method is called 4-connected, where a pixel may have up to four neighbors [see Fig. 3-18(a)]; the other is called 8-connected, where a pixel may have up to eight neighbors [see

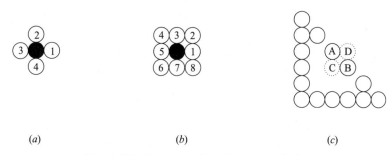

(a)   (b)   (c)

Fig. 3-18   4-connected vs. 8-connected pixels.

Fig. 3-18(*b*)]. Using the 4-connected approach, the pixels in Fig. 3-18(*c*) do not define a region since several pixels such as A and B are not connected. However using the 8-connected definition we identify a triangular region.

We can further apply the concept of connected pixels to decide if a region is connected to another region. For example, using the 8-connected approach, we do not have an enclosed region in Fig. 3-18(*c*) since "interior" pixel C is connected to "exterior" pixel D. On the other hand, if we use the 4-connected definition we have a triangular region since no interior pixel is connected to the outside.

Note that it is not a mere coincidence that the figure in Fig. 3-18(*c*) is a boundary-defined region when we use the 8-connected definition for the boundary pixels and the 4-connected definition for the interior pixels. In fact, using the same definition for both boundary and interior pixels would simply result in contradiction. For example, if we use the 8-connected approach we would have pixel A connected to pixel B (continuous boundary) and at the same time pixel C connected to pixel D (discontinuous boundary). On the other hand, if we use the 4-connectd definition we would have pixel A disconnected from pixel B (discontinuous boundary) and at the same time pixel C disconnected from pixel D (continuous boundary).

A Boundary-fill Algorithm

This is a recursive algorithm that begins with a starting pixel, called a seed, inside the region. The algorithm checks to see if this pixel is a boundary pixel or has already been filled. If the answer is no, it fills the pixel and makes a recursive call to itself using each and every neighboring pixel as a new seed. If the answer is yes, the algorithm simply returns to its caller.

This algorithm works elegantly on an arbitrarily shaped region by chasing and filling all non-boundary pixels that are connected to the seed, either directly or indirectly through a chain of neighboring relations. However, a straightforward implementation can take time and memory to execute due to the potentially high number of recursive calls, especially when the size of the region is relatively large.

Variations can be made to limit the number of recursive calls by structuring the order in which neighboring pixels are processed. For example, we can first fill pixels to the left and right of the seed on the same scan line until boundary pixels are hit (something that can be done using a loop control structure). We then inspect each pixel above and below the line just drawn (which can also be done with a loop) to see if it can be used as a new seed for the next horizontal line to fill. This way the number of recursive calls at any particular time is merely N when the current line is N scan lines away from the initial seed.

A Flood-fill Algorithm

This algorithm also begins with a seed (starting pixel) inside the region. It checks to see if the pixel has the region's original color. If the answer is yes, it fills the pixel with a new color and uses each of the pixel's neighbors as a new seed in a recursive call. If the answer is no, it returns to the caller.

This method shares great similarities in its operating principle with the boundary-fill algorithm. It is particularly useful when the region to be filled has no uniformly colored boundary. On the other hand, a region that has a well-defined boundary but is itself multiply colored would be better handled by the boundary-fill method.

The execution efficiency of this flood-fill algorithm can be improved in basically the same way as discussed above regarding the boundary-fill algorithm.

A Scan-line Algorithm

In contrast to the boundary-fill and flood-fill algorithms that fill regions defined at the pixel level in the image space, this algorithm handles polygonal regions that are geometrically defined by the coordinates of their vertices (along with the edges that connect the vertices). Although such regions can be filled by first scan-converting the edges to get the boundary pixels and then applying a boundary-fill algorithm to finish the job, the following is a much more efficient approach that makes use of the information regarding edges that are available during scan conversion to facilitate the filling of interior pixels.

We represent a polygonal region in terms of a sequence of vertices $V_1, V_2, V_3, \ldots$, that are connected by edges $E_1, E_2, E_3, \ldots$, (see Fig. 3-19). We assume that each vertex V_i has already been scan-converted to integer coordinates (x_i, y_i).

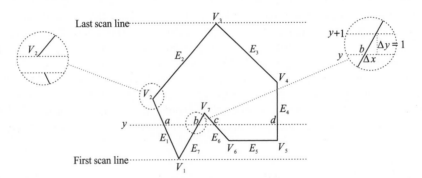

Fig. 3-19   Scan-converting a polygonal region.

The algorithm begins with the first scan line the polygon occupies and proceeds line by line towards the last scan line. For each scan line it finds all intersection points between the current scan line and the edges. For example, scan line y intersects edges E_1, E_7, E_6, and E_4 at points a, b, c, and b, respectively. The intersection points are sorted according to their x coordinates and grouped into pairs such as (a, b) and (c, d). A line is drawn from the first point to the second point in each pair.

Horizontal edges are ignored since the pixels that belong to them are automatically filled during scan conversion. For example, edge E_5 is drawn when the corresponding scan line is processed. The two intersection points between the scan line and edges E_6 and E_4 are connected by a line that equals exactly E_5.

Now we take a more careful look at cases when a scan line intersects a vertex. If the vertex is a local minimum or maximum such as V_1 and V_7, no special treatment is necessary. The two edges that join at the vertex will each yield an intersection point with the scan line. These two intersection points can be treated just like any other intersection points to produce pairs of points for the filling operation. As for vertices V_5 and V_6, they are simply local minimums, each with one joining edge that produces a single intersection point. On the other hand, if a scan line intersects a vertex (e.g., V_4) that is joined by two monotonically increasing or decreasing edges, getting two intersection points at that vertex location would lead to incorrect results (e.g., a total of three intersection points on the scan line that intersects V_4). The solution to this problem is to record only one intersection point at the vertex.

In order to support an efficient implementation of this scan line algorithm we create a data structure called an edge list (see Table 3-1). Each non-horizontal edge occupies one row/record. Information stored

Table 3-1　An edge list.

Edge	y_{min}	y_{max}	x coordinate of vertex with $y = y_{min}$	$1/m$
E_1	y_1	$y_2 - 1$	x_1	$1/m_1$
E_7	y_1	y_7	x_1	$1/m_7$
E_4	y_5	$y_4 - 1$	x_5	$1/m_4$
E_6	y_6	y_7	x_6	$1/m_6$
E_2	y_2	y_3	x_2	$1/m_2$
E_3	y_4	y_3	x_4	$1/m_3$

in each row includes the y coordinate of the edge's two endpoints, with y_{min} being the smaller value and y_{max} the larger value (may be decreased by 1 for reasons to be discussed below), the x coordinate of the endpoint whose y coordinate is y_{min}, and the inverse of the edge's slope m. The rows are sorted according to y_{min}. Going back to our example in Fig. 3-19, since edges E_1 and E_7 both originate from the lowest vertex V_1 at (x_1, y_1), they appear on top of the edge list, with m_1 and m_7 being their slope value, respectively.

Edges in the edge list become active when the y coordinate of the current scan line matches their y_{min} value. Only active edges are involved in the calculation of intersection points. The first intersection point between an active edge and a scan line is always the lower endpoint of the edge, whose coordinates are already stored in the edge's record. For example, when the algorithm begins at the first scan line, edges E_1 and E_7 become active. They intersect the scan line at (x_1, y_1).

Additional intersection points between an edge and successive scan lines can be calculated incrementally. If the edge intersects the current scan line at (x, y), it intersects the next scan line at $(x + 1/m, y + 1)$. For example, edge E_7 intersects scan line y at point b, and so the next intersection point on scan line $y + 1$ can be calculated by $\Delta x = 1/m_7$ since $\Delta y = 1$. This new x value can simply be kept in the x field of the edge's record.

An edge is deactivated or may even be removed from the edge list once the scan line whose y coordinate matches its y_{max} value has been processed, since all subsequent scan lines stay clear from it. The need that was mentioned early to give special treatment to a vertex where two monotonically increasing or decreasing edges meet is elegantly addressed by subtracting one from the y_{max} value of the lower edge. This means that the lower edge is deactivated one line before the scan line that intersects the vertex. Thus only the upper edge produces an intersection point with that scan line (see V_2 in Fig. 3-19). This explains why the initial y_{max} value for edges E_1 and E_4 has been decreased by one.

3.8　SCAN-CONVERTING A CHARACTER

Characters such as letters and digits are the building blocks of an image's textual contents. They can be presented in a variety of styles and sizes. The overall design style of a set of characters is referred to as its typeface or font. Commonly used fonts include Arial, Century Schoolbook, Courier, and Times New Roman. In addition, fonts can vary in appearance: **bold**, *italic*, and ***bold and italic***. Character size is typically measured in height in inches, points (approximately $\frac{1}{72}$ inch), and picas (12 points).

Bitmap Font

There are two basic approaches to character representation. The first is called a raster or bitmap font, where each character is represented by the on pixels in a bilevel pixel grid pattern called a bitmap (see Fig. 3-20). This approach is simple and effective since characters are defined in already-scan-converted form. Putting a character into an image basically entails a direct mapping or copying of its bitmap to a specific

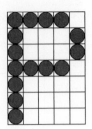

Fig. 3-20   Bitmap font.

location in the image space. On the other hand, a separate font consisting of scores of bitmaps for a set of characters is often needed for each combination of style, appearance, and size.

Although one might generate variations in appearance and size from one font, the overall results tends to be less than satisfactory. The example in Fig. 3-21 shows that we may overlay the bitmap in Fig. 3-20 onto itself with a horizontal offset of one pixel to produce (a) bold, and shift rows of pixels in Fig. 3-20 to produce (b) italic.

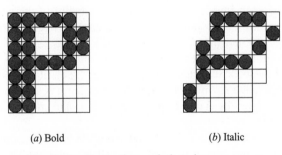

        (*a*) Bold   (*b*) Italic

Fig. 3-21   Generating variations in appearance.

Furthermore, the size of a bitmap font is dependent on image resolution. For example, a font using bitmaps that are 12 pixels high produces 12-point characters in an image with 72 pixels per inch. However, the same font will result in 9-point characters in an image with 96 pixels per inch, since 12 pixels now measure 0.125 inch, which is about 9 points. To get 12-point characters in the second image we would need a font with bitmaps that are 16 pixels high.

Outline Font

The second character representation method is called a vector or outline font, where graphical primitives such as lines and arcs are used to define the outline of each character (see Fig. 3-22). Although an outline definition tends to be less compact than a bitmap definition and requires relatively time-consuming scan-conversion operations, it can be used to produce characters of varying size, appearance, and even orientation. For example, the outline definition in Fig. 3-22 can be resized through a scaling transformation, made into italic through a shearing transformation, and turned around with respect to a reference point through a rotation transformation (see Chap. 4).

These transformed primitives can be scan-converted directly into characters in the form of filled regions in the target image area. Or they can be used to create the equivalent bitmaps that are then used to

Fig. 3-22   Outline font.

produce characters. This alternative is particularly effective in limiting scan-conversion time when the characters have repetitive occurrences in the image.

3.9 ANTI-ALIASING

Scan conversion is essentially a systematic approach to mapping objects that are defined in continuous space to their discrete approximation. The various forms of distortion that result from this operation are collectively referred to as the aliasing effects of scan conversion.

Staircase

A common example of aliasing effects is the staircase or jagged appearance we see when scan-converting a primitive such as a line or a circle. We also see the stair steps or "jaggies" along the border of a filled region.

Unequal Brightness

Another artifact that is less noticeable is the unequal brightness of lines of different orientation. A slanted line appears dimmer than a horizontal or vertical line, although all are presented at the same intensity level. The reason for this problem can be explained using Fig. 3-23, where the pixels on the horizontal line are placed one unit apart, whereas those on the diagonal line are approximately 1.414 units apart. This difference in density produces the perceived difference in brightness.

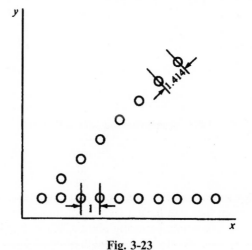

Fig. 3-23

The Picket Fence Problem

The picket fence problem occurs when an object is not aligned with, or does not fit into, the pixel grid properly. Figure 3-24(a) shows a picket fence where the distance between two adjacent pickets is not a multiple of the unit distance between pixels. Scan-converting it normally into the image space will result in uneven distances between pickets since the endpoints of the pickets will have to be snapped to pixel coordinates [see Fig. 3-24(b)]. This is sometimes called global aliasing, as the overall length of the picket fence is approximately correct. On the other hand, an attempt to maintain equal spacing will greatly distort the overall length of the fence [see Fig. 3-24(c)]. This is sometimes called local aliasing, as the distances between pickets are kept close to their true distances.

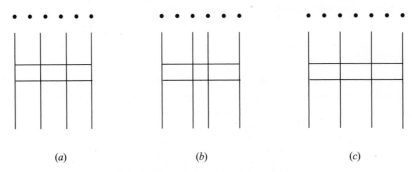

(a)   (b)   (c)

Fig. 3-24   The picket fence problem.

Another example of such a problem arises with the outline font. Suppose we want to scan-convert the uppercase character "E" in Fig. 3-25(a) from its outline description to a bitmap consisting of pixels inside the region defined by the outline. The result in Fig. 3-25(b) exhibits both asymmetry (the upper arm of the character is twice as thick as the other parts) and dropout (the middle arm is absent). A slight adjustment and/or realignment of the outline can lead to a reasonable outcome [see Fig. 3-25(c)].

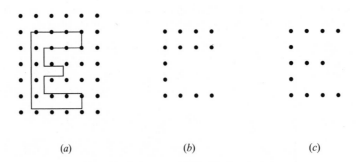

(a)   (b)   (c)

Fig. 3-25   Scan-converting an outline font.

Anti-aliasing

Most aliasing artifacts, when appear in a static image at a moderate resolution, are often tolerable, and in many cases, negligible. However, they can have a significant impact on our viewing experience when left untreated in a series of images that animate moving objects. For example, a line being rotated around one of its endpoints becomes a rotating escalator with length-altering steps. A moving object with small parts or surface details may have some of those features intermittently change shape or even disappear.

Although increasing image resolution is a straightforward way to decrease the size of many aliasing artifacts and alleviate their negative impact, we pay a heavy price in terms of system resource (going from $W \times H$ to $2W \times 2H$ means quadrupling the number of pixels) and the results are not always satisfactory. On the other hand, there are techniques that can greatly reduce aliasing artifacts and improve the appearance of images without increasing their resolution. These techniques are collectively referred to as anti-aliasing techniques.

Some anti-aliasing techniques are designed to treat a particular type of artifact. For instance, an outline font can be associated with a set of rules or hints to guide the adjustment and realignment that is necessary for its conversion into bitmaps of relatively low resolution. An example of such approach is called the TrueType font.

Pre-filtering and Post-filtering

Pre-filtering and post-filtering are two types of general-purpose anti-aliasing techniques. The concept of filtering originates from the field of signal processing, where true intensity values are continuous signals that consists of elements of various frequencies. Constant intensity values that correspond to a uniform region are at the low end of the frequency range. Intensity values that change abruptly and correspond to a sharp edge are at the high end of the spectrum. In order to lessen the jagged appearance of lines and other contours in the image space, we seek to smooth out sudden intensity changes, or in signal-processing terms, to filter out the high frequency components. A pre-filtering technique works on the true signal in the continuous space to derive proper values for individual pixels (filtering before sampling), whereas a post-filtering technique takes discrete samples of the continuous signal and uses the samples to compute pixel values (sampling before filtering).

Area Sampling

Area sampling is a pre-filtering technique in which we superimpose a pixel grid pattern onto the continuous object definition. For each pixel area that intersects the object, we calculate the percentage of overlap by the object. This percentage determines the proportion of the overall intensity value of the corresponding pixel that is due to the object's contribution. In other words, the higher the percentage of overlap, the greater influence the object has on the pixel's overall intensity value.

In Fig. 3-26(a) a mathematical line shown in dotted form is represented by a rectangular region that is one pixel wide. The percentage of overlap between the rectangle and each intersecting pixel is calculated analytically. Assuming that the background is black and the line is white, the percentage values can be used directly to set the intensity of the pixels [see Fig. 3-26(b)]. On the other hand, had the background been gray $(0.5, 0.5, 0.5)$ and the line green $(0, 1, 0)$, each blank pixel in the grid would have had the background gray value and each pixel filled with a fractional number f would have been assigned a value of $[0.5(1-f), 0.5(1-f)+f, 0.5(1-f)]$—a proportional blending of the background and object colors.

Although the resultant discrete approximation of the line in Fig. 3-26(b) takes on a blurry appearance, it no longer exhibits the sudden transition from an on pixel to an off pixel and vice versa, which is what we

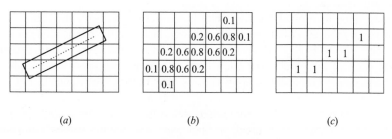

(a)   (b)   (c)

Fig. 3-26   Area sampling.

would get with an ordinary scan-conversion method [see Fig. 3-26(*c*)]. This tradeoff is characteristic of an anti-aliasing technique based on filtering.

Super Sampling

In this approach we subdivide each pixel into subpixels and check the position of each subpixel in relation to the object to be scan-converted. The object's contribution to a pixel's overall intensity value is proportional to the number of subpixels that are inside the area occupied by the object. Figure 3-27(*a*) shows an example where we have a white object that is bounded by two slanted lines on a black background. We subdivide each pixel into nine (3×3) subpixels. The scene is mapped to the pixel values in Fig. 3-27(*b*). The pixel at the upper right corner, for instance, is assigned $\frac{7}{9}$ since seven of its nine subpixels are inside the object area. Had the object been red $(1, 0, 0)$ and the background light yellow $(0.5, 0.5, 0)$, the pixel would have been assigned $(1 \times \frac{7}{9} + 0.5 \times \frac{2}{9}, 0.5 \times \frac{2}{9}, 0)$, which is $(\frac{8}{9}, \frac{1}{9}, 0)$.

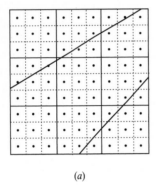

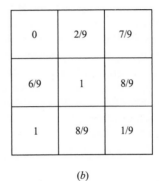

(*a*)   (*b*)

Fig. 3-27   Super sampling.

Super sampling is often regarded as a post-filtering technique since discrete samples are first taken and then used to calculate pixel values. On the other hand, it can be viewed as an approximation to the area sampling method since we are simply using a finite number of values in each pixel area to approximate the accurate analytical result.

Lowpass Filtering

This is a post-filtering technique in which we reassign each pixel a new value that is a weighted average of its original value and the original values of its neighbors. A lowpass filter in the form of a $(2n + 1) \times (2n + 1)$ grid, where $n \geq 1$, holds the weights for the computation. All weight values in a filter should sum to one. An example of a 3×3 filter is given in Fig. 3-28(*a*).

To compute a new value for a pixel, we align the filter with the pixel grid and center it at the pixel. The weighted average is simply the sum of products of each weight in the filter times the corresponding pixel's original value. The filter shown in Fig. 3-28(*a*) means that half of each pixel's original value is retained in its new value, while each of the pixel's four immediate neighbors contributes one eighth of its original value to the pixel's new value. The result of applying this filter to the pixel values in Fig. 3-26(*c*) is shown in Fig. 3-28(*b*).

A lowpass filter with equal weights, sometimes referred to as a box filter, is said to be doing neighborhood averaging. On the other hand, a filter with its weight values conforming to a two-dimensional Gaussian distribution is called a Gaussian filter.

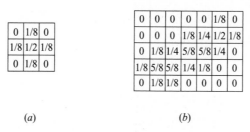

(a)   (b)

Fig. 3-28   Lowpass filtering.

Pixel Phasing

Pixel phasing is a hardware-based anti-aliasing technique. The graphics system in this case is capable of shifting individual pixels from their normal positions in the pixel grid by a fraction (typically $\frac{1}{4}$ and $\frac{1}{2}$) of the unit distance between pixels. By moving pixels closer to the true line or other contour, this technique is very effective in smoothing out the stair steps without reducing the sharpness of the edges.

3.10   EXAMPLE: RECURSIVELY DEFINED DRAWINGS

In this section we use two common graphical primitives to produce some interesting drawings. Each of these drawings is defined by applying a modification rule to a line or a filled triangle, breaking it into smaller pieces so the rule can be used to recursively modify each piece in the same manner. As the pieces become smaller and smaller, an intriguing picture emerges.

C Curve

A line by itself is a first-order C curve, denoted by C_0 (see Fig. 3-29). The modification rule for constructing successive generations of the C curve is to replace a line by two shorter, equal-length lines joining each other at a 90° angle, with the original line and the two new lines forming a right-angled triangle. See Fig. 3-29 for C_1, C_2, C_3, C_4, and C_5.

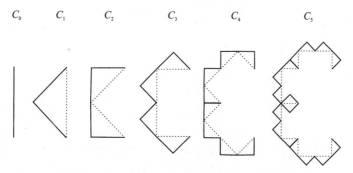

Fig. 3-29   Successive generations of the C curve.

Presume that the following call to the graphics library causes a line to be drawn from (x_1, y_1) to (x_2, y_2) using the system's current color:

line(x_1, y_1, x_2, y_2)

We can describe a pseudo-code procedure that generates C_n:

```
C-curve (float x, y, len, alpha; int n)
{
    if (n > 0) {
        len = len/sqrt(2.0);
        C-curve(x, y, len, alpha + 45, n - 1);
        x = x + len*cos(alpha + 45);
        y = y + len*sin(alpha + 45);
        C-curve(x, y, len, alpha - 45, n - 1);
    } else
        line(x, y, x + len*cos(alpha), y + len*sin(alpha));
}
```

where x and y are the coordinates of the starting point of a line, len the length of the line, alpha the angle (in degrees) between the line and the x axis, and n the number of recursive applications of the modification rule that is necessary to produce C_n. If $n = 0$, no modification is done and the line itself is drawn. Otherwise, two properly shortened lines, with one rotated counter-clockwise by 45° and the other clockwise by 45° from the current line position, are generated (representing one application of the modification rule), each of which is the basis of the remaining $n - 1$ steps of recursive construction.

The Koch Curve

As in the case of the C curve, a line by itself is a first-order Koch curve, denoted by K_0 (see Fig. 3-30). The modification rule for constructing successive generations of the Koch curve is to divide a line into three equal segments and replace the middle segment with two lines of the same length (the replaced segment and the two added lines form an equilateral triangle). See Fig. 3-30 for K_1, K_2, and K_3.

K_0 K_1 K_2 K_3

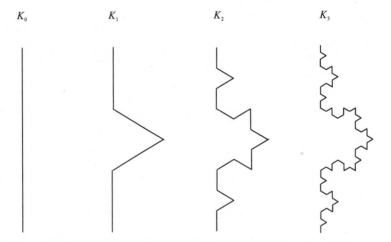

Fig. 3-30   Successive generations of the Koch curve.

The Sierpinski Gasket

This time our graphical primitive is a filled triangle, denoted by S_0 (see Fig. 3-31). The modification rule for constructing successive generations of the Sierpinski gasket is to take out the area defined by the lines connecting the midpoint of the edges of a filled triangle, resulting in three smaller ones that are similar to the original. See Fig. 3-31 for S_1, S_2, and S_3.

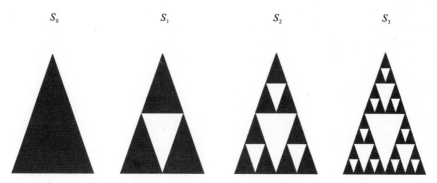

S_0 S_1 S_2 S_3

Fig. 3-31 Successive generations of the Sierpinski gasket.

Solved Problems

3.1 The endpoints of a given line are $(0,0)$ and $(6,18)$. Compute each value of y as x steps from 0 to 6 and plot the results.

SOLUTION

An equation for the line was not given. Therefore, the equation of the line must be found. The equation of the line ($y = mx + b$) is found as follows. First the slope is found:

$$m = \frac{\Delta y}{\Delta x} = \frac{y_2 - y_1}{x_2 - x_1} = \frac{18 - 0}{6 - 0} = \frac{18}{6} = 3$$

Next, the y intercept b is found by plugging y_1 and x_1 into the equation $y = 3x + b$: $0 = 3(0) + b$. Therefore, $b = 0$, so the equation for the line is $y = 3x$ (see Fig. 3-32).

3.2 What steps are required to plot a line whose slope is between $0°$ and $45°$ using the slope–intercept equation?

SOLUTION

1. Compute dx: $dx = x_2 - x_1$.
2. Compute dy: $dy = y_2 - y_1$.
3. Compute m: $m = dy/dx$.
4. Compute b: $b = y_1 - m \times x_1$.
5. Set (x, y) equal to the lower left-hand endpoint and set x_{end} equal to the largest value of x. If $dx < 0$, then $x = x_2$, $y = y_2$, and $x_{end} = x_1$. If $dx > 0$, then $x = x_1$, $y = y_1$, and $x_{end} = x_2$.
6. Test to determine whether the entire line has been drawn. If $x > x_{end}$, stop.
7. Plot a point at the current (x, y) coordinates.
8. Increment x: $x = x + 1$.
9. Compute the next value of y from the equation $y = mx + b$.
10. Go to step 6.

3.3 Use pseudo-code to describe the steps that are required to plot a line whose slope is between $45°$ and $-45°$ (i.e., $|m| > 1$) using the slope–intercept equation.

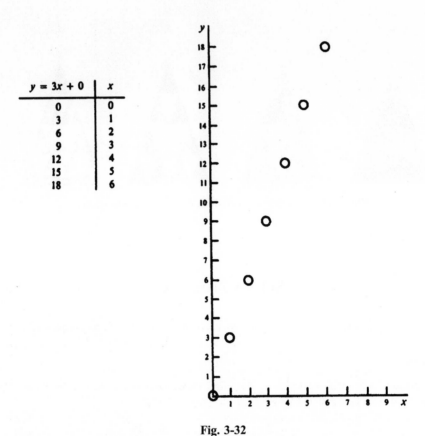

$y = 3x + 0$	x
0	0
3	1
6	2
9	3
12	4
15	5
18	6

Fig. 3-32

SOLUTION

Presume $y_1 < y_2$ for the two endpoints (x_1, y_1) and (x_2, y_2):

```
int x = x₁, y = y₁;
float xf, m = (y₂ − y₁)/(x₂ − x₁), b = y₁ − mx₁;
setPixel(x, y);
while (y < y₂) {
    y++;
    xf = (y − b)/m;
    x = Floor(xf + 0.5);
    setPixel(x, y);
}
```

3.4 Use pseudo-code to describe the DDA algorithm for scan-converting a line whose slope is between $-45°$ and $45°$ (i.e., $|m| \le 1$).

SOLUTION

Presume $x_1 < x_2$ for the two endpoints (x_1, y_1) and (x_2, y_2):

```
int x = x₁, y;
float yf = y₁, m = (y₂ − y₁)/(x₂ − x₁);
while (x <= x₂) {
    y = Floor(yf + 0.5);
    setPixel(x, y);
    x++;
    yf = yf + m;
}
```

3.5	Use pseudo-code to describe the DDA algorithm for scan-converting a line whose slope is between $45°$ and $-45°$ (i.e., $|m| > 1$).

SOLUTION

Presume $y_1 < y_2$ for the two endpoints (x_1, y_1) and (x_2, y_2):

```
int x, y = y₁;
float x_f = x₁, m_inv = (x₂ − x₁)/(y₂ − y₁);
while (y <= y₂) {
    x = Floor(x_f + 0.5);
    setPixel(x, y);
    x_f = x_f + m_inv;
    y++;
}
```

3.6	What steps are required to plot a line whose slope is between $0°$ and $45°$ using Bresenham's method?

SOLUTION

1.	Compute the initial values:

$$dx = x_2 - x_1 \qquad Inc_2 = 2(dy - dx)$$
$$dy = y_2 - y_1 \qquad d = Inc_1 - dx$$
$$Inc_1 = 2dy$$

2.	Set (x, y) equal to the lower left-hand endpoint and x_{end} equal to the largest value of x. If $dx < 0$, then $x = x_2$, $y = y_2$, $x_{end} = x_1$. If $dx > 0$, then $x = x_1$, $y = y_1$, $x_{end} = x_2$.
3.	Plot a point at the current (x, y) coordinates.
4.	Test to see whether the entire line has been drawn. If $x = x_{end}$, stop.
5.	Compute the location of the next pixel. If $d < 0$, then $d = d + Inc_1$. If $d \geq 0$, then $d = d + Inc_2$, and then $y = y + 1$.
6.	Increment x: $x = x + 1$.
7.	Plot a point at the current (x, y) coordinates.
8.	Go to step 4.

3.7	Indicate which raster locations would be chosen by Bresenham's algorithm when scan-converting a line from pixel coordinate $(1, 1)$ to pixel coordinate $(8, 5)$.

SOLUTION

First, the starting values must be found. In this case

$$dx = x_2 - x_1 = 8 - 1 = 7 \qquad dy = y_2 - y_1 = 5 - 1 = 4$$

Therefore:

$$Inc_1 = 2dy = 2 \times 4 = 8$$
$$Inc_2 = 2(dy - dx) = 2 \times (4 - 7) = -6$$
$$d = Inc_1 - dx = 8 - 7 = 1$$

The following table indicates the values computed by the algorithm (see also Fig. 3-33).

d	x	y
1	1	1
$1 + Inc_2 = -5$	2	2
$-5 + Inc_1 = 3$	3	2
$3 + Inc_2 = -3$	4	3
$-3 + Inc_1 = 5$	5	3
$5 + Inc_2 = -1$	6	4
$-1 + Inc_1 = 7$	7	4
$7 + Inc_2 = 1$	8	5

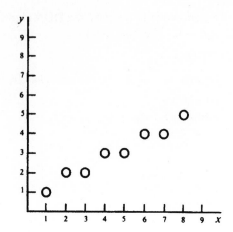

Fig. 3-33

3.8   In the derivation of Bresenham's line algorithm we have used s and t to measure the closeness of pixels S and T to the true line. However, s and t are only distances in the y direction. They are not really distances between a point to a line as defined in geometry. Can we be sure that, when $s = t$, the two pixels S and T are truly equally far away from the true line (hence we can choose either one to approximate the line)?

SOLUTION

As we can see in Fig. 3-34, when $s = t$ the true line intersects the vertical line connecting S and T at midpoint. The true distance from S to the line is dS and that from T to the line is dT. Since the two right-angled triangles are totally equal (they have equal angles and one pair of equal edges s and t), we get dS = dT.

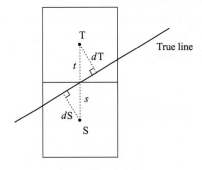

Fig. 3-34

3.9   Modify the description of Bresenham's line algorithm in the text to set all pixels from inside the loop structure.

SOLUTION 1

```
int x = x'_1, y = y'_1;
int dx = x'_2 - x'_1, dy = y'_2 - y'_1, dT = 2(dy - dx), dS = 2dy;
int d = 2dy - dx;
while (x <= x'_2) {
  setPixel(x, y);
  x++;
  if (d < 0)
    d = d + dS;
```

```
    else {
      y++;
      d = d + dT;
    }
  }
}
```

SOLUTION 2

```
int x = x₁′ − 1, y = y₁′;
int dx = x₂′ − x₁′, dy = y₂′ − y₁′, dT = 2(dy − dx), dS = 2dy;
int d = −dx;
while (x < x₂′) {
  x++;
  if (d < 0)
    d = d + dS;
  else {
    y++;
    d = d + dT;
  }
  setPixel(x, y);
}
```

3.10 What steps are required to generate a circle using the polynomial method?

SOLUTION

1. Set the initial variables: r = circle radius; (h, k) = coordinates of the circle center; $x = 0$; i = step size; $x_{end} = r/\sqrt{2}$.
2. Test to determine whether the entire circle has been scan-converted. If $x > x_{end}$, stop.
3. Compute the value of the y coordinate, where $y = \sqrt{r^2 - x^2}$.
4. Plot the eight points, found by symmetry with respect to the center (h, k), at the current (x, y) coordinates:

$$\begin{array}{ll}
\text{Plot}(x + h, y + k) & \text{Plot}(-x + h, -y + k) \\
\text{Plot}(y + h, x + k) & \text{Plot}(-y + h, -x + k) \\
\text{Plot}(-y + h, x + k) & \text{Plot}(y + h, -x + k) \\
\text{Plot}(-x + h, y + k) & \text{Plot}(x + h, -y + k)
\end{array}$$

5. Increment x: $x = x + i$.
6. Go to step 2.

3.11 What steps are required to scan-convert a circle using the trigonometric method?

SOLUTION

1. Set the initial variables: r = circle radius; (h, k) = coordinates of the circle center; i = step size; $\theta_{end} = \pi/4$ radians = $45°$; $\theta = 0$.
2. Test to determine whether the entire circle has been scan-converted. If $\theta > \theta_{end}$, stop.
3. Compute the value of the x and y coordinates:

$$x = r\cos(\theta) \qquad y = r\sin(\theta)$$

4. Plot the eight points, found by symmetry with respect to the center (h, k), at the current (x, y) coordinates:

$$\text{Plot}(x + h, y + k) \qquad \text{Plot}(-x + h, -y + k)$$
$$\text{Plot}(y + h, x + k) \qquad \text{Plot}(-y + h, -x + k)$$
$$\text{Plot}(-y + h, x + k) \qquad \text{Plot}(y + h, -x + k)$$
$$\text{Plot}(-x + h, y + k) \qquad \text{Plot}(x + h, -y + k)$$

5. Increment θ: $\theta = \theta + i$.
6. Go to step 2.

3.12 What steps are required to scan-convert a circle using Bresenham's algorithm?

SOLUTION

1. Set the initial values of the variables: $(h, k) =$ coordinates of circle center; $x = 0$; $y =$ circle radius r; and $d = 3 - 2r$.
2. Test to determine whether the entire circle has been scan-converted. If $x > y$, stop.
3. Plot the eight points, found by symmetry with respect to the center (h, k), at the current (x, y) coordinates:

$$\text{Plot}(x + h, y + k) \qquad \text{Plot}(-x + h, -y + k)$$
$$\text{Plot}(y + h, x + k) \qquad \text{Plot}(-y + h, -x + k)$$
$$\text{Plot}(-y + h, x + k) \qquad \text{Plot}(y + h, -x + k)$$
$$\text{Plot}(-x + h, y + k) \qquad \text{Plot}(x + h, -y + k)$$

4. Compute the location of the next pixel. If $d < 0$, then $d = d + 4x + 6$ and $x = x + 1$. If $d \geq 0$, then $d = d + 4(x - y) + 10$, $x = x + 1$, and $y = y - 1$.
5. Go to step 2.

3.13 When eight-way symmetry is used to obtain a full circle from pixel coordinates generated for the $0°$ to $45°$ or the $90°$ to $45°$ octant, certain pixels are set or plotted twice. This phenomenon is sometimes referred to as overstrike. Identify where overstrike occurs.

SOLUTION

At locations resulted from the initial coordinates $(r, 0)$ or $(0, r)$ since $(0, r) = (-0, r)$, $(0, -r) = (-0, -r)$, $(r, 0) = (r, -0)$, and $(-r, 0) = (-r, -0)$.

In addition, if the last generated pixel is on the diagonal line at $(\alpha r, \alpha r)$ where α approximates $1/\sqrt{(2.0)} = 0.7071$, then overstrike also occurs at $(\alpha r, \alpha r)$, $(-\alpha r, \alpha r)$, $(\alpha r, -\alpha r)$, and $(-\alpha r, -\alpha r)$.

3.14 Is overstrike harmful besides wasting time?

SOLUTION

It is often harmless since resetting a pixel with the same value does not really change the image in the frame buffer. However, if pixel values are sent out directly, for example, to control the exposure of a photographic medium, such as a slide or a negative, then overstrike amounts to double exposure at locations where it occurred.

Furthermore, if we set pixels using their complementary colors, then overstrike would leave them unchanged, since complementing a color twice simply yields the color itself.

3.15 When scan-converting a curve using the polynomial method (see Probs. 3.10, 3.20, and 3.25) or the trigonometric method (see Probs. 3.11, 3.21, and 3.24), a step size i is used to compute successive points on the true curve. These points are then mapped to the image space. What happens if i is too large? What happens if it is too small?

SOLUTION

If i is too large, the computed points will be relatively far from each other and the corresponding pixels will not form a continuous curve.

If i is too small, computed points will be so close to each other that two or more adjacent ones will be mapped to the same pixel, resulting in overstrike.

Note that it is not always possible to find a single step size for a specific scan-conversion task that yields a continuous curve without overstrike. In such cases we may take an adaptive approach in which adjustments are made to step size during scan-conversion based on points that have already been mapped to the image space. For example, if two consecutively computed points have been mapped to two pixels that are not connected to each other, then an additional point between the two points may be computed using half the step size.

3.16 Will the following description of Bresenham's circle algorithm and the one in the text produce the same results?

```
int x = 0, y = r, d = 3 − 2r;
setPixel(x, y);
while (x < y) {
   if (d < 0)
      d = d + 4x + 6;
   else {
      d = d + 4(x − y) + 10;
      y−−;
   }
   x++;
   setPixel(x, y);
}
```

SOLUTION

Let A be the correct set of pixels chosen by Bresenham's circle algorithm. Both versions produce A when the rightmost pixel in A is on the diagonal line $x = y$. However, when the coordinates of the rightmost pixel in A satisfies $x = y − 1$, only the version in the text stops properly. This version will produce one additional pixel beyond the 90° to 45° octant. This extra pixel mirrors the rightmost pixel in A with respect to the diagonal line.

3.17 In the derivation of Bresenham's circle algorithm we have used a decision variable $d_i = D(T) + D(S)$ to help choose between pixels S and T. However, function D as defined in the text is not a true measure of the distance from the center of a pixel to the true circle. Show that when $d_i = 0$ the two pixels S and T are not really equally far away from the true circle.

SOLUTION

Let dS be the actual distance from S to the true circle and dT be the actual distance from T to the true circle (see Fig. 3-35). Also substitute x for $x_i + 1$ and y for y_i in the formula for d_i to make the following proof easier to read:

$$d_i = 2x^2 + y^2 + (y − 1)^2 − 2r^2 = 0$$

Since $(r + dT)^2 = x^2 + y^2$ and $(r − dS)^2 = x^2 + (y − 1)^2$ we have

$$2r\,dT + dT^2 = x^2 + y^2 − r^2 \qquad \text{and} \qquad −2r\,dS + dS^2 = x^2 + (y − 1)^2 − r^2.$$

Hence

$$2r\,dT + dT^2 − 2r\,dS + dS^2 = 0$$
$$dT(2r + dT) = dS(2r − dS)$$

Since $dT/dS = (2r − dS)/(2r + dT) < 1$, we have $dT < dS$. This means that, when $d_i = 0$, pixel T is actually closer to the true circle than pixel S.

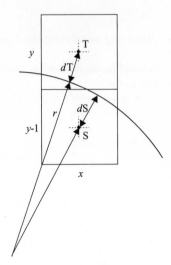

Fig. 3-35

3.18   Write a description of the midpoint circle algorithm in which decision parameter p is updated using x_{i+1} and y_{i+1} instead of x_i and y_i.

SOLUTION

```
int x = 0, y = r, p = 1 − r;
while (x <= y) {
   setPixel(x, y);
   x++;
   if (p < 0)
      p = p + 2x + 1;
   else {
      y−−;
      p = p + 2(x − y) + 1;
   }
}
```

3.19   Will the following description of the midpoint circle algorithm and the one in Prob. 3.18 produce the same results?

```
int x = 0, y = r, p = 1 − r;
setPixel(x, y);
while (x < y) {
   x++;
   if (p < 0)
      p = p + 2x + 1;
   else {
      y−−;
      p = p + 2(x − y) + 1;
   }
   setPixel(x, y);
}
```

SOLUTION

Similar to the solution for Prob. 3.16. Only the version in Prob. 3.18 produces the correct set of pixels under all circumstances.

3.20 What steps are required to generate an ellipse using the polynomial method?

SOLUTION

1. Set the initial variables: a = length of major axis; b = length of minor axis; (h, k) = coordinates of ellipse center; $x = 0$; i = step size; $x_{end} = a$.
2. Test to determine whether the entire ellipse has been scan-converted. If $x > x_{end}$, stop.
3. Compute the value of the y coordinate:

$$y = b\sqrt{1 - \frac{x^2}{a^2}}$$

4. Plot the four points, found by symmetry, at the current (x, y) coordinates:

$$\text{Plot}(x + h, y + k) \qquad \text{Plot}(-x + h, -y + k)$$
$$\text{Plot}(-x + h, y + k) \qquad \text{Plot}(x + h, -y + k)$$

5. Increment x: $x = x + i$.
6. Go to step 2.

3.21 What steps are required to scan-convert an ellipse using the trigonometric method?

SOLUTION

1. Set the initial variables: a = length of major axis; b = length of minor axis; (h, k) = coordinates of ellipse center; i = counter step size; $\theta_{end} = \pi/2$; $\theta = 0$.
2. Test to determine whether the entire ellipse has been scan-converted. If $\theta > \theta_{end}$, stop.
3. Compute the values of the x and y coordinates:

$$x = a\cos(\theta) \qquad y = b\sin(\theta)$$

4. Plot the four points, found by symmetry, at the current (x, y) coordinates:

$$\text{Plot}(x + h, y + k) \qquad \text{Plot}(-x + h, -y + k)$$
$$\text{Plot}(-x + h, y + k) \qquad \text{Plot}(x + h, -y + k)$$

5. Increment θ: $\theta = \theta + i$.
6. Go to step 2.

3.22 When four-way symmetry is used to obtain a full ellipse from pixel coordinates generated for the first quadrant, does overstrike occur? Where?

SOLUTION

Overstrike occurs at $(0, b)$, $(0, -b)$, $(a, 0)$, and $(-a, 0)$ since $(0, b) = (-0, b)$, $(0, -b) = (-0, -b)$, $(a, 0) = (a, -0)$, and $(-a, 0) = (-a, -0)$.

3.23 In the midpoint ellipse algorithm we have used only the coordinates (x_k, y_k) of the last pixel chosen for part 1 of the curve to compute the initial value q_1 of the decision parameter q_j for part 2. Can we also make use of the last value of the decision parameter p_i?

SOLUTION

The last computed value of the decision parameter p_i for part 1 of the curve is

$$p_k = f(x_k + 1, y_k - \tfrac{1}{2}) = b^2(x_k + 1)^2 + a^2(y_k - \tfrac{1}{2})^2 - a^2b^2$$
$$= b^2(x_k^2 + 2x_k + 1) + a^2(y_k^2 - y_k + \tfrac{1}{4}) - a^2b^2$$

Since

$$q_1 = f(x_k + \tfrac{1}{2}, y_k - 1) = b^2(x_k + \tfrac{1}{2})^2 + a^2(y_k - 1)^2 - a^2b^2$$
$$= b^2(x_k^2 + x_k + \tfrac{1}{4}) + a^2(y_k^2 - 2y_k + 1) - a^2b^2$$

We have

$$q_1 = p_k - b^2(x_k + \tfrac{3}{4}) - a^2(y_k - \tfrac{3}{4})$$

3.24   What steps are required to scan-convert an arc using the trigonometric method?

SOLUTION

1.   Set the initial variables: a = major axis; b = minor axis; (h, k) = coordinates of arc center; i = step size; θ = starting angle; θ_1 = ending angle.
2.   Test to determine whether the entire arc has been scan-converted. If $\theta > \theta_1$, stop.
3.   Compute the values of the x and y coordinates:

$$x = a\cos(\theta) + h \qquad y = a\sin(\theta) + k$$

4.   Plot the points at the current (x, y) coordinates: Plot(x, y).
5.   Increment θ: $\theta = \theta + i$.
6.   Go to step 2.

   (Note: for the arc of a circle $a = b$ = circle radius r.)

3.25   What steps are required to generate an arc of a circle using the polynomial method?

SOLUTION

1.   Set the initial variables: r = radius; (h, k) = coordinates of arc center; x = x coordinate of start of arc; x_1 = x coordinate of end of arc; i = counter step size.
2.   Test to determine whether the entire arc has been scan-converted. If $x > x_1$, stop.
3.   Compute the value of the y coordinate:

$$y = \sqrt{r^2 - x^2}$$

4.   Plot at the current (x, y) coordinates:

$$\text{Plot}(x + h, y + k)$$

5.   Increment x: $x = x + i$.
6.   Go to step 2.

3.26   What steps are required to scan-convert a rectangle whose sides are parallel to the coordinate axes?

SOLUTION

1.   Set initial variables: (x_1, y_1) = coordinates of first point specified; (x_2, y_2) = coordinates of second point specified.

2.   Plot the rectangle:

$$\text{Plot}(x_1, y_1) \quad \text{to} \quad (x_2, y_1) \qquad \text{Plot}(x_2, y_2) \quad \text{to} \quad (x_1, y_2)$$
$$\text{Plot}(x_2, y_1) \quad \text{to} \quad (x_2, y_2) \qquad \text{Plot}(x_1, y_2) \quad \text{to} \quad (x_1, y_1)$$

3.27   How would a flood-fill algorithm fill the region shown in Fig. 3-36, using the 8-connected definition for region pixels?

SOLUTION

1.   Assume that a seed is given at coordinate 3, 3. The flood-fill algorithm will inspect the eight points surrounding the seed (4, 4; 3, 4; 2, 4; 2, 3; 2, 2; 3, 2; 4, 2; 4, 3). Since all the points surrounding the seed have the region's original color, each point will be filled (see Fig. 3-37).

2.   Each of the eight points found in step 1 becomes a new seed, and the points surrounding each new seed are inspected and filled. This process continues until all the points surrounding all the seeds are rid of the region's original color (see Fig. 3-38).

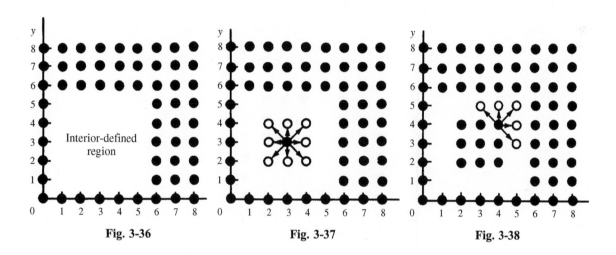

Fig. 3-36   Fig. 3-37   Fig. 3-38

3.28   Write a pseudo-code procedure to implement the boundary-fill algorithm in the text in its basic form, using the 4-connected definition for region pixels.

SOLUTION

```
BoundaryFill (int x, y, fill_color, boundary_color)
{
    int color;
    getPixel(x, y, color);
    if (color != boundary_color && color != fill_color) {
        setPixel(x, y, fill_color);
        BoundaryFill(x + 1, y, fill_color, boundary_color);
        BoundaryFill(x, y + 1, fill_color, boundary_color);
        BoundaryFill(x - 1, y, fill_color, boundary_color);
        BoundaryFill(x, y - 1, fill_color, boundary_color);
    }
}
```

3.29   Write a pseudo-code procedure to implement the flood-fill algorithm in the text in its basic form, using the 4-connected definition for region pixels.

SOLUTION

```
FloodFill (int x, y, fill_color, original_color)
{
    int color;
    getPixel(x, y, color);
    if (color == original_color) {
        setPixel(x, y, fill_color);
        FloodFill(x + 1, y, fill_color, original_color);
        FloodFill(x, y + 1, fill_color, original_color);
        FloodFill(x - 1, y, fill_color, original_color);
        FloodFill(x, y - 1, fill_color, original_color);
    }
}
```

3.30 The coordinates of the vertices of a polygon are shown in Fig. 3-39. (*a*) Write the initial edge list for the polygon. (*b*) State which edges will be active on scan lines $y = 6, 7, 8, 9$, and 10.

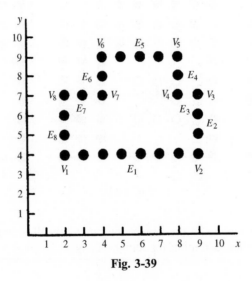

Fig. 3-39

SOLUTION

(*a*) Column x contains the x coordinate of the corresponding edge's lower endpoint. Horizontal edges are not included.

Edge	y_{min}	y_{max}	x	$1/m$
E_2	4	7	9	0
E_8	4	7	2	0
E_4	7	9	8	0
E_6	7	9	4	0

(b)   An edge becomes active when the scan line value y equals the edge's y_{min} value. The edge remains active until the scan line value y goes beyond the edge's y_{max} value. Therefore, the active edges for $y = 6, 7, 8,$ 9, and 10 appears as follows.

   At $y = 6$, E_2 and E_8.

   At $y = 7$, $y = y_{max}$ for both edges E_2 and E_8 so they remain active. Also at $y = 7$, edges E_4 and E_6 become active.

   At $y = 8$, E_2 and E_8 are removed from the edge list. E_4 and E_6 remain active.

   At $y = 9$, the active edges remain the same. At $y = 10$, edges E_2 and E_4 are removed from the edge list and the edge list becomes empty.

3.31   What are the three major adverse side effects of scan conversion?

SOLUTION

   The three major adverse effects of scan conversion are staircase appearance, unequal brightness of slanted lines, and the picket fence problem.

3.32   Suppose that in 3×3 super sampling a pixel has three of its subpixels in a red area, three in a green area, and three in a blue area, what is the pixel's overall color?

SOLUTION

   Each of the three areas is responsible for one third of the pixel's overall intensity value, which is $(\frac{1}{3}, \frac{1}{3}, \frac{1}{3})$.

3.33   Write a pseudo-code procedure for generating the Koch curve K_n (after the one in the text for generating C_n).

SOLUTION

```
Koch-curve (float x, y, len, alpha; int n)
{
  if (n > 0) {
    len = len/3;
    Koch-curve(x, y, len, alpha, n − 1);
    x = x + len*cos(alpha);
    y = y + len*sin(alpha);
    Koch-curve(x, y, len, alpha − 60, n − 1);
    x = x + len*cos(alpha − 60);
    y = y + len*sin(alpha − 60);
    Koch-curve(x, y, len, alpha + 60, n − 1);
    x = x + len*cos(alpha + 60);
    y = y + len*sin(alpha + 60);
    Koch-curve(x, y, len, alpha, n − 1);
  } else
    line(x, y, x + len*cos(alpha), y + len*sin(alpha));
}
```

3.34   Presume that the following statement produces a filled triangle with vertices at (x_1, y_1), (x_2, y_2), and (x_3, y_3):

   triangle$(x_1, y_1, x_2, y_2, x_3, y_3)$

Write a pseudo-code procedure for generating the Sierpinski gasket S_n (after the procedure in the text for generating C_n).

SOLUTION

```
S-Gasket (float x₁, y₁, x₂, y₂, x₃, y₃; int n)
{
    float x₁₂, y₁₂, x₁₃, y₁₃, x₂₃, y₂₃;
    if (n > 0) {
        x₁₂ = (x₁ + x₂)/2;
        y₁₂ = (y₁ + y₂)/2;
        x₁₃ = (x₁ + x₃)/2;
        y₁₃ = (y₁ + y₃)/2;
        x₂₃ = (x₂ + x₃)/2;
        y₂₃ = (y₂ + y₃)/2;
        S-Gasket(x₁, y₁, x₁₂, y₁₂, x₁₃, y₁₃, n − 1);
        S-Gasket(x₁₂, y₁₂, x₂, y₂, x₂₃, y₂₃, n − 1);
        S-Gasket(x₁₃, y₁₃, x₂₃, y₂₃, x₃, y₃, n − 1);
    } else
        triangle(x₁, y₁, x₂, y₂, x₃, y₃);
}
```

Supplementary Problems

3.35 Given the following equations, find the corresponding values of y for each value of x ($x = 2, 7, 1$): (a) $y = 4x + 3$, (b) $y = 1x + 0$, (c) $y = -3x - 4$, and (d) $y = -2x + 1$.

3.36 What steps are required to plot a line whose slope is between $45°$ and $90°$ using Bresenham's method?

3.37 What steps are required to plot a dashed line?

3.38 Show graphically that an ellipse has four-way symmetry by plotting four points on the ellipse:

$$x = a\cos(\theta) + h \qquad y = b\sin(\theta) + k$$

where $a = 2$
$\qquad b = 1$
$\qquad h = 0$
$\qquad k = 0$
$\qquad \theta = \pi/4,\ 3\pi/4,\ 5\pi/4,\ 7\pi/4$

3.39 How must Prob. 3.21 be modified if an ellipse is to be rotated (a) $\pi/4$, (b) $\pi/9$, and (c) $\pi/2$ radians?

3.40 What steps are required to scan-convert a sector using the trigonometric method?

3.41   What steps must be added to a fill algorithm if a region is to be filled with a pattern?

3.42   Why is it important for the designer to remain consistent when choosing either local or global aliasing?

3.43   What steps are required to scan-convert a polygonal area using the scan-line algorithm?

3.44   How can we eliminate overstrike?

CHAPTER 4

Two-Dimensional Transformations

Fundamental to all computer graphics system is the ability to simulate the manipulation of objects in space. This simulated spatial manipulation is referred to as *transformation*. The need for transformation arises when several objects, each of which is independently defined in its own coordinate system, need to be properly positioned into a common scene in a master coordinate system. Transformation is also useful in other areas of the image synthesis process (e.g. viewing transformation in Chap. 5).

There are two complementary points of view for describing object transformation. The first is that the object itself is transformed relative to a stationary coordinate system or background. The mathematical statement of this viewpoint is described by *geometric transformations* applied to each point of the object. The second point of view holds that the object is held stationary while the coordinate system is transformed relative to the object. This effect is attained through the application of *coordinate transformations*. An example that helps to distinguish these two viewpoints involves the movement of an automobile against a scenic background. We can simulate this by moving the automobile while keeping the backdrop fixed (a geometric transformation). Or we can keep the car fixed while moving the backdrop scenery (a coordinate transformation).

This chapter covers transformations in the plane, i.e., the two-dimensional (2D) space. We detail three basic transformations: translation, rotation, and scaling, along with other transformations that can be accomplished in terms of a sequence of basic transformations. We describe these operations in mathematical form suitable for computer processing and show how they are used to achieve the ends of object manipulation.

4.1 GEOMETRIC TRANSFORMATIONS

Let us impose a coordinate system on a plane. An object *Obj* in the plane can be considered as a set of points. Every object point *P* has coordinates (x, y), and so the object is the sum total of all its coordinate points (Fig. 4-1). If the object is moved to a new position, it can be regarded as a new object *Obj′*, all of whose coordinate points *P′* can be obtained from the original points *P* by the application of a geometric transformation.

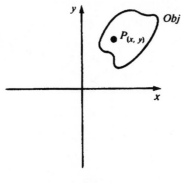

Fig. 4-1

Translation

In *translation*, an object is displaced a given distance and direction from its original position. If the displacement is given by the vector $\mathbf{v} = t_x\mathbf{I} + t_y\mathbf{J}$, the new object point $P'(x', y')$ can be found by applying the transformation $T_{\mathbf{v}}$ to $P(x, y)$ (see Fig. 4-2).

$$P' = T_{\mathbf{v}}(P)$$

where $x' = x + t_x$ and $y' = y + t_y$.

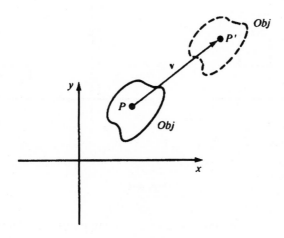

Fig. 4-2

Rotation about the Origin

In *rotation*, the object is rotated $\theta°$ about the origin. The convention is that the direction of rotation is counterclockwise if θ is a positive angle and clockwise if θ is a negative angle (see Fig. 4-3). The transformation of rotation R_θ is

$$P' = R_\theta(P)$$

where $x' = x\cos(\theta) - y\sin(\theta)$ and $y' = x\sin(\theta) + y\cos(\theta)$.

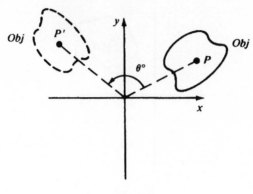

Fig. 4-3

Scaling with Respect to the Origin

Scaling is the process of expanding or compressing the dimensions of an object. Positive scaling constants s_x and s_y are used to describe changes in length with respect to the x direction and y direction, respectively. A scaling constant greater than one indicates an expansion of length, and less than one, compression of length. The scaling transformation S_{s_x,s_y} is given by $P' = S_{s_x,s_y}(P)$ where $x' = s_x x$ and $y' = s_y y$. Notice that, after a scaling transformation is performed, the new object is located at a different position relative to the origin. In fact, in a scaling transformation the only point that remains fixed is the origin. Figure 4-4 shows scaling transformation with scaling factors $s_x = 2$ and $s_y = \frac{1}{2}$.

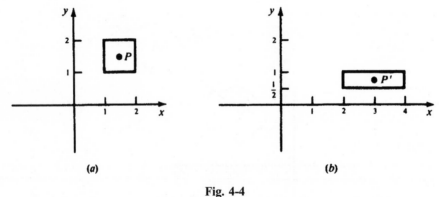

(a)   (b)

Fig. 4-4

If both scaling constants have the same value s, the scaling transformation is said to be *homogeneous* or *uniform*. Furthermore, if $s > 1$, it is a *magnification* and for $s < 1$, a *reduction*.

Mirror Reflection about an Axis

If either the x or y axis is treated as a mirror, the object has a mirror image or reflection. Since the reflection P' of an object point P is located the same distance from the mirror as P (Fig. 4-5), the mirror reflection transformation M_x about the x axis is given by

$$P' = M_x(P)$$

where $x' = x$ and $y' = -y$.

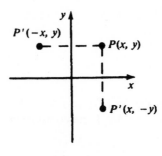

Fig. 4-5

Similarly, the mirror reflection about the y axis is

$$P' = M_y(P)$$

where $x' = -x$ and $y' = y$.

Note that $M_x = S_{1,-1}$ and $M_{xy} = S_{-1,1}$. The two reflection transformations are simply special cases of scaling.

Inverse Geometric Transformations

Each geometric transformation has an inverse (see App. 1) which is described by the opposite operation performed by the transformation:

Translation: $T_{\mathbf{v}}^{-1} = T_{-\mathbf{v}}$, or translation in the opposite direction

Rotation: $R_\theta^{-1} = R_{-\theta}$, or rotation in the opposite direction

Scaling: $S_{s_x,s_y}^{-1} = S_{1/s_x,1/s_y}$

Mirror reflection: $M_x^{-1} = M_x$ and $M_y^{-1} = M_y$.

4.2   COORDINATE TRANSFORMATIONS

Suppose that we have two coordinate systems in the plane. The first system is located at origin O and has coordinates axes xy. The second coordinate system is located at origin O' and has coordinate axes $x'y'$ (Fig. 4-6). Now each point in the plane has two coordinate descriptions: (x, y) or (x', y'), depending on which coordinate system is used. If we think of the second system $x'y'$ as arising from a transformation applied to the first system xy, we say that a *coordinate transformation* has been applied. We can describe

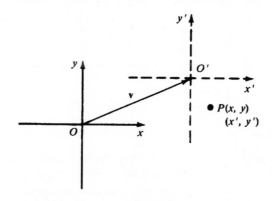

Fig. 4-6

this transformation by determining how the (x', y') coordinates of a point P are related to the (x, y) coordinates of the same point.

Translation

If the xy coordinate system is displaced to a new position, where the direction and distance of the displacement is given by the vector $\mathbf{v} = t_x\mathbf{I} + t_y\mathbf{J}$, the coordinates of a point in both systems are related by the translation transformation $\bar{T}_\mathbf{v}$:

$$(x', y') = \bar{T}_\mathbf{v}(x, y)$$

where $x' = x - t_x$ and $y' = y - t_y$.

Rotation about the Origin

The xy system is rotated $\theta°$ about the origin (see Fig. 4-7). Then the coordinates of a point in both systems are related by the rotation transformation $\bar{R}_\theta$:

$$(x', y') = \bar{R}_\theta(x, y)$$

where $x' = x\cos(\theta) + y\sin(\theta)$ and $y' = -x\sin(\theta) + y\cos(\theta)$.

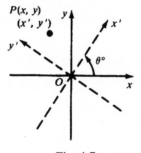

Fig. 4-7

Scaling with Respect to the Origin

Suppose that a new coordinate system is formed by leaving the origin and coordinate axes unchanged, but introducing different units of measurement along the x and y axes. If the new units are obtained from the old units by a scaling of s_x along the x axis and s_y along the y axis, the coordinates in the new system are related to coordinates in the old system through the scaling transformation $\bar{S}_{s_x, s_y}$:

$$(x', y') = \bar{S}_{s_x, s_y}(x, y)$$

where $x' = (1/s_x)x$ and $y' = (1/s_y)y$. Figure 4-8 shows coordinate scaling transformation using scaling factors $s_x = 2$ and $s_y = \frac{1}{2}$.

Mirror Reflection about an Axis

If the new coordinate system is obtained by reflecting the old system about either x or y axis, the relationship between coordinates is given by the coordinate transformations $\bar{M}_x$ and $\bar{M}_y$. For reflection about the x axis [Fig. 4-9(a)]

$$(x', y') = \bar{M}_x(x, y)$$

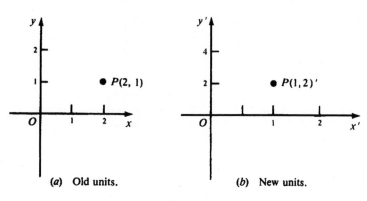

(a) Old units.   (b) New units.

Fig. 4-8

where $x' = x$ and $y' = -y$. For reflection about the y axis [Fig. 4-9(b)]

$$(x', y') = \bar{M}_y(x, y)$$

where $x' = -x$ and $y' = y$.

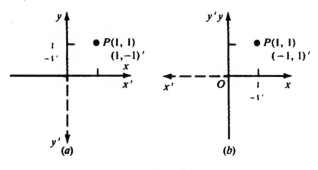

Fig. 4-9

Notice that the reflected coordinate system is left-handed; thus reflection changes the orientation of the coordinate system. Also note that $\bar{M}_x = \bar{S}_{1,-1}$ and $\bar{M}_y = \bar{S}_{-1,1}$.

Inverse Coordinate Transformations

Each coordinate transformation has an inverse (see App. 1) which can be found by applying the opposite transformation:

Translation: $\bar{T}_{\mathbf{v}}^{-1} = \bar{T}_{-\mathbf{v}}$, translation in the opposite direction

Rotation: $\bar{R}_\theta^{-1} = \bar{R}_{-\theta}$, rotation in the opposite direction

Scaling: $\bar{S}_{s_x, s_y}^{-1} = \bar{S}_{1/s_x, 1/s_y}$

Mirror reflection: $\bar{M}_x^{-1} = \bar{M}_x$ and $\bar{M}_y^{-1} = \bar{M}_y$.

4.3   COMPOSITE TRANSFORMATIONS

More complex geometric and coordinate transformations can be built from the basic transformations described above by using the process of *composition of functions* (see App. 1). For example, such operations as rotation about a point other than the origin or reflection about lines other than the axes can be constructed from the basic transformations.

EXAMPLE 1.   Magnification of an object while keeping its center fixed (see Fig. 4-10). Let the geometric center be located at $C(h, k)$ [Fig. 4-10(a)]. Choosing a magnification factor $s > 1$, we construct the transformation by

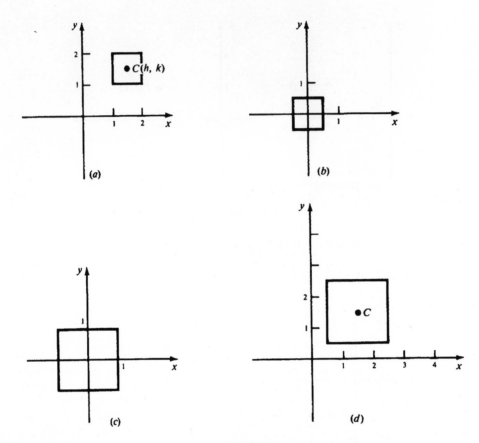

Fig. 4-10

performing the following sequence of basic transformations: (1) translate the object so that its center coincides with the origin [Fig. 4-10(b)], (2) scale the object with respect to the origin [Fig. 4-10(c)], and (3) translate the scaled object back to the original position [Fig. 4-10(d)].

The required transformation $S_{s,C}$ can be formed by compositions $S_{s,C} = T_{\mathbf{v}} \cdot S_{s,s} \cdot T_{\mathbf{v}}^{-1}$ where $\mathbf{v} = h\mathbf{I} + k\mathbf{J}$. By using composition, we can build more general scaling, rotation, and reflection transformations. For these transformations, we shall use the following notations: (1) $S_{s_x,s_y,P}$—scaling with respect to a fixed point P; (2) $R_{\theta,P}$—rotation about a point P; and (3) M_L—reflection about a line L.

The matrix description of these transformations can be found in Probs. 4.4, 4.7, and 4.10.

Matrix Description of the Basic Transformations

The transformations of rotation, scaling, and reflection can be represented as matrix functions:

Geometric transformations	**Coordinate transformations**

$$R_\theta = \begin{pmatrix} \cos(\theta) & -\sin(\theta) \\ \sin(\theta) & \cos(\theta) \end{pmatrix} \qquad \bar{R}_\theta = \begin{pmatrix} \cos(\theta) & \sin(\theta) \\ -\sin(\theta) & \cos(\theta) \end{pmatrix}$$

$$S_{s_x,s_y} = \begin{pmatrix} s_x & 0 \\ 0 & s_y \end{pmatrix} \qquad \bar{S}_{s_x,s_y} = \begin{pmatrix} \dfrac{1}{s_x} & 0 \\ 0 & \dfrac{1}{s_y} \end{pmatrix}$$

$$M_x = \begin{pmatrix} 1 & 0 \\ 0 & -1 \end{pmatrix} \qquad \bar{M}_x = \begin{pmatrix} 1 & 0 \\ 0 & -1 \end{pmatrix}$$

$$M_y = \begin{pmatrix} -1 & 0 \\ 0 & 1 \end{pmatrix} \qquad \bar{M}_y = \begin{pmatrix} -1 & 0 \\ 0 & 1 \end{pmatrix}$$

The translation transformation cannot be expressed as a 2×2 matrix function. However, a certain artifice allows us to introduce a 3×3 matrix function which performs the translation transformation.

We represent the coordinate pair (x, y) of a point P by the triple $(x, y, 1)$. This is simply the homogeneous representation of P (App. 2). Then translation in the direction $\mathbf{v} = t_x\mathbf{I} + t_y\mathbf{J}$ can be expressed by the matrix function

$$T_{\mathbf{v}} = \begin{pmatrix} 1 & 0 & t_x \\ 0 & 1 & t_y \\ 0 & 0 & 1 \end{pmatrix}$$

Then

$$\begin{pmatrix} 1 & 0 & t_x \\ 0 & 1 & t_y \\ 0 & 0 & 1 \end{pmatrix}\begin{pmatrix} x \\ y \\ 1 \end{pmatrix} = \begin{pmatrix} x+t_x \\ y+t_y \\ 1 \end{pmatrix}$$

From this we extract the coordinate pair $(x+t_x, y+t_y)$.

Concatenation of Matrices

The advantage of introducing a matrix form for translation is that we can now build complex transformations by multiplying the basic matrix transformations. This process is sometimes called *concatenation of matrices* and the resulting matrix is often referred to as the *composite transformation matrix* (CTM). Here, we are using the fact that the composition of matrix functions is equivalent to matrix multiplication (App. 1). We must be able to represent the basic transformations as 3×3 *homogeneous coordinate matrices* (App. 2) so as to be compatible (from the point of view of matrix multiplication) with the matrix of translation. This is accomplished by augmenting the 2×2 matrices with a third column $\begin{pmatrix} 0 \\ 0 \\ 1 \end{pmatrix}$ and a third row $(0\,0\,1)$. That is

$$\begin{pmatrix} a & b & 0 \\ c & d & 0 \\ 0 & 0 & 1 \end{pmatrix}$$

EXAMPLE 2. Express as a matrix (i.e., CTM) the transformation which magnifies an object about its center $C(h, k)$. From Example 1, the required transformation $S_{s,C}$ can be written as

$$S_{s,C} = T_{\mathbf{v}} \cdot S_{s,s} \cdot T_{\mathbf{v}}^{-1}$$
$$= \begin{pmatrix} 1 & 0 & h \\ 0 & 1 & k \\ 0 & 0 & 1 \end{pmatrix}\begin{pmatrix} s & 0 & 0 \\ 0 & s & 0 \\ 0 & 0 & 1 \end{pmatrix}\begin{pmatrix} 1 & 0 & -h \\ 0 & 1 & -k \\ 0 & 0 & 1 \end{pmatrix} = \begin{pmatrix} s & 0 & -sh+h \\ 0 & s & -sk+k \\ 0 & 0 & 1 \end{pmatrix}$$

Caution on Matrix Notations

The reader should be alerted to the fact that, within the field of computer graphics, there are two different matrix notations that are used. This book represents points by column vectors and applies transformations by left-multiplying by the transformation matrix. We have chosen this approach because it is the standard used in mathematics and computer science texts. The other notation represents points by row vectors and applies transformations by right-multiplying by the transformation matrix. It is used in much of the computer graphics literature.

To change from one notational style to another, it is necessary to take the transpose of the matrices that appear in any expression. For example, translation of point (x, y) in the direction $\mathbf{v} = t_x \mathbf{I} + t_y \mathbf{J}$ can also be expressed as

$$(x \quad y \quad 1) \begin{pmatrix} 1 & 0 & 0 \\ 0 & 1 & 0 \\ t_x & t_y & 1 \end{pmatrix} = (x + t_x \quad y + t_y \quad 1)$$

EXAMPLE 2 continued.   Using the row-vector notation, we have

$$S_{s,C} = \begin{pmatrix} 1 & 0 & 0 \\ 0 & 1 & 0 \\ -h & -k & 1 \end{pmatrix} \begin{pmatrix} s & 0 & 0 \\ 0 & s & 0 \\ 0 & 0 & 1 \end{pmatrix} \begin{pmatrix} 1 & 0 & 0 \\ 0 & 1 & 0 \\ h & k & 1 \end{pmatrix} = \begin{pmatrix} s & 0 & 0 \\ 0 & s & 0 \\ -sh + h & -sk + k & 1 \end{pmatrix}$$

4.4 INSTANCE TRANSFORMATIONS

Quite often a picture or design is composed of many objects used several times each. In turn, these objects may also be composed of other symbols and objects. We suppose that each object is defined, independently of the picture, in its own coordinate system. We wish to place these objects together to form the picture or at least part of the picture, called a *subpicture*. We can accomplish this by defining a transformation of coordinates, called an *instance transformation*, which converts object coordinates to picture coordinates so as to place or create an *instance* of the object in the picture coordinate system.

The *instance transformation* $N_{\text{picture,object}}$ is formed as a composition or concatenation of scaling, rotation, and translation operations, usually performed in this order (although any order can be used):

$$N_{\text{picture,object}} = T_{\mathbf{v}} \cdot R_{\theta,P} \cdot S_{a,b,P}$$

With the use of different instance transformations, the same object can be placed in different positions, sizes, and orientations within a subpicture. For instance, Fig. 4-11(*a*) is placed in the picture coordinate system of Fig. 4-11(*b*) by using the instance transformations $N_{\text{picture,object}}$.

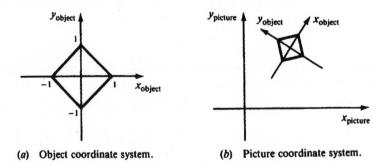

(*a*) Object coordinate system.   (*b*) Picture coordinate system.

Fig. 4-11

Nested Instances and Multilevel Structures

A subpicture or picture may exhibit a multilevel or nested structure by being composed of objects which are, in turn, composed of still other objects, and so on. Separate instance transformations must then be applied, in principle, at each level of the picture structure for each picture component.

EXAMPLE 3.   A picture of an apple tree contains branches, and an apple hangs on each branch. Suppose that each branch and apple is described in its own coordinate system [Figs. 4-12(*a*) and 4-12(*b*)]. Then a subpicture call to place

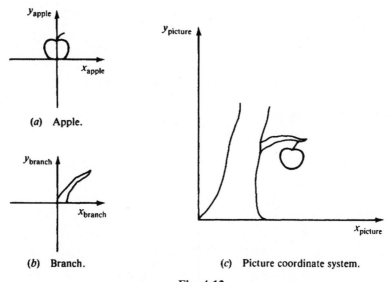

(a) Apple.

(b) Branch.

(c) Picture coordinate system.

Fig. 4-12

an instance of this branch in the picture of the tree requires an additional subpicture call to place an instance of the apple into the branch coordinate system.

We can perform each instance transformation separately, i.e., instance the apple in the branch coordinate system and then instance both branch and apple from the branch coordinate system to the picture coordinate system. However, it is much more efficient to transform the apple directly into picture coordinates [see Fig. 4-12(c)]. This is accomplished by defining the composite transformation matrix $C_{\text{picture,object}}$ to be the composition of the nested instance transformations from apple coordinates to branch coordinates and then from branch coordinates to picture coordinates:

$$C_{\text{picture,apple}} = N_{\text{picture,branch}} \cdot N_{\text{branch,apple}}$$

Since the branch subpicture is only one level below the picture

$$C_{\text{picture,branch}} = N_{\text{picture,branch}}$$

Solved Problems

4.1   Derive the transformation that rotates an object point $\theta°$ about the origin. Write the matrix representation for this rotation.

SOLUTION

Refer to Fig. 4-13. Definition of the trigonometric functions sin and cos yields

$$x' = r\cos(\theta + \phi) \qquad y' = r\sin(\theta + \phi)$$

and

$$x = r\cos\phi \qquad y = r\sin\phi$$

Using trigonometric identities, we obtain

$$r\cos(\theta + \phi) = r(\cos\theta\cos\phi - \sin\theta\sin\phi) = x\cos\theta - y\sin\theta$$

and

$$r\sin(\theta + \phi) = r(\sin\theta\cos\phi + \cos\theta\sin\phi) = x\sin\theta - y\cos\theta$$

or

$$x' = x\cos\theta - y\sin\theta \qquad y' = x\sin\theta + y\cos\theta$$

Writing $P' = \begin{pmatrix} x' \\ y' \end{pmatrix}$, $P = \begin{pmatrix} x \\ y \end{pmatrix}$, and

$$R_\theta = \begin{pmatrix} \cos\theta & -\sin\theta \\ \sin\theta & \cos\theta \end{pmatrix}$$

we can now write $P' = R_\theta \cdot P$.

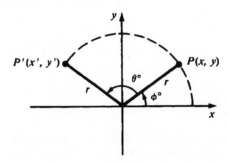

Fig. 4-13

4.2   (a) Find the matrix that represents rotation of an object by $30°$ about the origin.
         (b) What are the new coordinates of the point $P(2, -4)$ after the rotation?

SOLUTION

(a) From Prob. 4.1:

$$R_{30°} = \begin{pmatrix} \cos 30° & -\sin 30° \\ \sin 30° & \cos 30° \end{pmatrix} = \begin{pmatrix} \dfrac{\sqrt{3}}{2} & -\dfrac{1}{2} \\ \dfrac{1}{2} & \dfrac{\sqrt{3}}{2} \end{pmatrix}$$

(b) So the new coordinates can be found by multiplying:

$$\begin{pmatrix} \dfrac{\sqrt{3}}{2} & -\dfrac{1}{2} \\ \dfrac{1}{2} & \dfrac{\sqrt{3}}{2} \end{pmatrix} \begin{pmatrix} 2 \\ -4 \end{pmatrix} = \begin{pmatrix} \sqrt{3} + 2 \\ 1 - 2\sqrt{3} \end{pmatrix}$$

4.3   Describe the transformation that rotates an object point, $Q(x, y)$, $\theta°$ about a fixed center of rotation $P(h, k)$ (Fig. 4-14).

SOLUTION

We determine the transformation $R_{\theta,P}$ in three steps: (1) translate so that the center of rotation P is at the origin, (2) perform a rotation of θ degrees about the origin, and (3) translate P back to (h, k).

Using $\mathbf{v} = h\mathbf{I} + k\mathbf{J}$ as the translation vector, we build $R_{\theta,P}$ by composition of transformations:

$$R_{\theta,O'} = T_{\mathbf{v}} \cdot R_\theta \cdot T_{-\mathbf{v}}$$

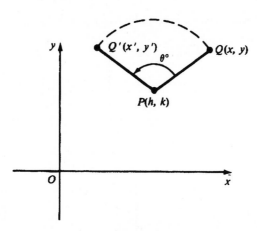

Fig. 4-14

4.4   Write the general form of the matrix for rotation about a point $P(h, k)$.

SOLUTION

Following Prob. 4.3, we write $R_{\theta,P} = T_{\mathbf{v}} \cdot R_{\theta} \cdot T_{-\mathbf{v}}$, where $\mathbf{v} = h\mathbf{I} + k\mathbf{J}$. Using the 3×3 homogeneous coordinate form for the rotation and translation matrices, we have

$$
R_{\theta,P} = \begin{pmatrix} 1 & 0 & h \\ 0 & 1 & k \\ 0 & 0 & 1 \end{pmatrix} \begin{pmatrix} \cos(\theta) & -\sin(\theta) & 0 \\ \sin(\theta) & \cos(\theta) & 0 \\ 0 & 0 & 1 \end{pmatrix} \begin{pmatrix} 1 & 0 & -h \\ 0 & 1 & -k \\ 0 & 0 & 1 \end{pmatrix}
$$

$$
= \begin{pmatrix} \cos(\theta) & -\sin(\theta) & [-h\cos(\theta) + k\sin(\theta) + h] \\ \sin(\theta) & \cos(\theta) & [-h\sin(\theta) - k\cos(\theta) + k] \\ 0 & 0 & 1 \end{pmatrix}
$$

4.5   Perform a $45°$ rotation of triangle $A(0,0)$, $B(1,1)$, $C(5,2)$ (a) about the origin and (b) about $P(-1, -1)$.

SOLUTION

We represent the triangle by a matrix formed from the homogeneous coordinates of the vertices:

$$
\begin{array}{ccc} A & B & C \end{array}
$$
$$
\begin{pmatrix} 0 & 1 & 5 \\ 0 & 1 & 2 \\ 1 & 1 & 1 \end{pmatrix}
$$

(a)   The matrix of rotation is

$$
R_{45°} = \begin{pmatrix} \cos 45° & -\sin 45° & 0 \\ \sin 45° & \cos 45° & 0 \\ 0 & 0 & 1 \end{pmatrix} = \begin{pmatrix} \dfrac{\sqrt{2}}{2} & -\dfrac{\sqrt{2}}{2} & 0 \\ \dfrac{\sqrt{2}}{2} & \dfrac{\sqrt{2}}{2} & 0 \\ 0 & 0 & 1 \end{pmatrix}
$$

So the coordinates $A'B'C'$ of the rotated triangle ABC can be found as

$$
[A'B'C'] = R_{45°} \cdot [ABC] = \begin{pmatrix} \dfrac{\sqrt{2}}{2} & -\dfrac{\sqrt{2}}{2} & 0 \\ \dfrac{\sqrt{2}}{2} & \dfrac{\sqrt{2}}{2} & 0 \\ 0 & 0 & 1 \end{pmatrix} \begin{pmatrix} 0 & 1 & 5 \\ 0 & 1 & 2 \\ 1 & 1 & 1 \end{pmatrix} = \begin{pmatrix} 0 & 0 & \dfrac{3\sqrt{2}}{2} \\ 0 & \sqrt{2} & \dfrac{7\sqrt{2}}{2} \\ 1 & 1 & 1 \end{pmatrix} \begin{array}{ccc} A' & B' & C' \end{array}
$$

Thus $A' = (0,0)$, $B' = (0, \sqrt{2})$, and $C' = (\frac{3}{2}\sqrt{2}, \frac{7}{2}\sqrt{2})$.

(b) From Prob. 4.4, the rotation matrix is given by $R_{45°,P} = T_\mathbf{v} \cdot R_{45°} \cdot T_{-\mathbf{v}}$, where $\mathbf{v} = -\mathbf{I} - \mathbf{J}$. So

$$R_{45°,P} = \begin{pmatrix} 1 & 0 & -1 \\ 0 & 1 & -1 \\ 0 & 0 & 1 \end{pmatrix} \begin{pmatrix} \frac{\sqrt{2}}{2} & -\frac{\sqrt{2}}{2} & 0 \\ \frac{\sqrt{2}}{2} & \frac{\sqrt{2}}{2} & 0 \\ 0 & 0 & 1 \end{pmatrix} \begin{pmatrix} 1 & 0 & 1 \\ 0 & 1 & 1 \\ 0 & 0 & 1 \end{pmatrix} = \begin{pmatrix} \frac{\sqrt{2}}{2} & -\frac{\sqrt{2}}{2} & -1 \\ \frac{\sqrt{2}}{2} & \frac{\sqrt{2}}{2} & (\sqrt{2} - 1) \\ 0 & 0 & 1 \end{pmatrix}$$

Now

$$[A'B'C'] = R_{45°,P} \cdot [ABC] = \begin{pmatrix} \frac{\sqrt{2}}{2} & -\frac{\sqrt{2}}{2} & -1 \\ \frac{\sqrt{2}}{2} & \frac{\sqrt{2}}{2} & (\sqrt{2} - 1) \\ 0 & 0 & 1 \end{pmatrix} \begin{pmatrix} 0 & 1 & 5 \\ 0 & 1 & 2 \\ 1 & 1 & 1 \end{pmatrix}$$

$$= \begin{pmatrix} -1 & -1 & (\frac{3}{2}\sqrt{2} - 1) \\ (\sqrt{2} - 1) & (2\sqrt{2} - 1) & (\frac{9}{2}\sqrt{2} - 1) \\ 1 & 1 & 1 \end{pmatrix}$$

So $A' = (-1, \sqrt{2} - 1)$, $B' = (-1, 2\sqrt{2} - 1)$, and $C' = (\frac{3}{2}\sqrt{2} - 1, \frac{9}{2}\sqrt{2} - 1)$.

4.6 Find the transformation that scales (with respect to the origin) by (a) a units in the X direction, (b) b units in the Y direction, and (c) simultaneously a units in the X direction and b units in the Y direction.

SOLUTION

(a) The scaling transformation applied to a point $P(x, y)$ produces the point (ax, y). We can write this in matrix form as $S_{a,1} \cdot P$, or

$$\begin{pmatrix} a & 0 \\ 0 & 1 \end{pmatrix}\begin{pmatrix} x \\ y \end{pmatrix} = \begin{pmatrix} ax \\ y \end{pmatrix}$$

(b) As in part (a), the required transformation can be written in matrix form as $S_{1,b} \cdot P$. So

$$\begin{pmatrix} 1 & 0 \\ 0 & b \end{pmatrix}\begin{pmatrix} x \\ y \end{pmatrix} = \begin{pmatrix} x \\ by \end{pmatrix}$$

(c) Scaling in both directions is described by the transformation $x' = ax$ and $y' = by$. Writing this in matrix form as $S_{a,b} \cdot P$, we have

$$\begin{pmatrix} a & 0 \\ 0 & b \end{pmatrix}\begin{pmatrix} x \\ y \end{pmatrix} = \begin{pmatrix} ax \\ by \end{pmatrix}$$

4.7 Write the general form of a scaling matrix with respect to a fixed point $P(h, k)$.

SOLUTION

Following the same general procedure as in Probs. 4.3 and 4.4, we write the required transformation with

$\mathbf{v} = h\mathbf{I} + k\mathbf{J}$ as

$$S_{a,b,P} = T_{\mathbf{v}} \cdot S_{a,b} \cdot T_{-\mathbf{v}}$$

$$= \begin{pmatrix} 1 & 0 & h \\ 0 & 1 & k \\ 0 & 0 & 1 \end{pmatrix} \begin{pmatrix} a & 0 & 0 \\ 0 & b & 0 \\ 0 & 0 & 1 \end{pmatrix} \begin{pmatrix} 1 & 0 & -h \\ 0 & 1 & -k \\ 0 & 0 & 1 \end{pmatrix}$$

$$= \begin{pmatrix} a & 0 & -ah+h \\ 0 & b & -bk+k \\ 0 & 0 & 1 \end{pmatrix}$$

4.8   Magnify the triangle with vertices $A(0,0)$, $B(1,1)$, and $C(5,2)$ to twice its size while keeping $C(5,2)$ fixed.

SOLUTION

From Prob. 4.7, we can write the required transformation with $\mathbf{v} = 5\mathbf{I} + 2\mathbf{J}$ as

$$S_{2,2,C} = T_{\mathbf{v}} \cdot S_{2,2} \cdot T_{-\mathbf{v}}$$

$$= \begin{pmatrix} 1 & 0 & 5 \\ 0 & 1 & 2 \\ 0 & 0 & 1 \end{pmatrix} \begin{pmatrix} 2 & 0 & 0 \\ 0 & 2 & 0 \\ 0 & 0 & 1 \end{pmatrix} \begin{pmatrix} 1 & 0 & -5 \\ 0 & 1 & -2 \\ 0 & 0 & 1 \end{pmatrix} = \begin{pmatrix} 2 & 0 & -5 \\ 0 & 2 & -2 \\ 0 & 0 & 1 \end{pmatrix}$$

Representing a point P with coordinates (x, y) by the column vector $\begin{pmatrix} x \\ y \\ 1 \end{pmatrix}$, we have

$$S_{2,2,C} \cdot A = \begin{pmatrix} 2 & 0 & -5 \\ 0 & 2 & -2 \\ 0 & 0 & 1 \end{pmatrix} \begin{pmatrix} 0 \\ 0 \\ 1 \end{pmatrix} = \begin{pmatrix} -5 \\ -2 \\ 1 \end{pmatrix}$$

$$S_{2,2,C} \cdot B = \begin{pmatrix} 2 & 0 & -5 \\ 0 & 2 & -2 \\ 0 & 0 & 1 \end{pmatrix} \begin{pmatrix} 1 \\ 1 \\ 1 \end{pmatrix} = \begin{pmatrix} -3 \\ 0 \\ 1 \end{pmatrix}$$

$$S_{2,2,C} \cdot C = \begin{pmatrix} 2 & 0 & -5 \\ 0 & 2 & -2 \\ 0 & 0 & 1 \end{pmatrix} \begin{pmatrix} 5 \\ 2 \\ 1 \end{pmatrix} = \begin{pmatrix} 5 \\ 2 \\ 1 \end{pmatrix}$$

So $A' = (-5, -2)$, $B' = (-3, 0)$, and $C' = (5, 2)$. Note that, since the triangle ABC is completely determined by its vertices, we could have saved much writing by representing the vertices using a 3×3 matrix

$$[ABC] = \begin{pmatrix} 0 & 1 & 5 \\ 0 & 1 & 2 \\ 1 & 1 & 1 \end{pmatrix}$$

and applying $S_{2,2,C}$ to this. So

$$S_{2,2,C} \cdot [ABC] = \begin{pmatrix} 2 & 0 & -5 \\ 0 & 2 & -2 \\ 0 & 0 & 1 \end{pmatrix} \begin{pmatrix} 0 & 1 & 5 \\ 0 & 1 & 2 \\ 1 & 1 & 1 \end{pmatrix} = \begin{pmatrix} -5 & -3 & 5 \\ -2 & 0 & 2 \\ 1 & 1 & 1 \end{pmatrix} = [A'B'C']$$

4.9   Describe the transformation M_L which reflects an object about a line L.

SOLUTION

Let line L in Fig. 4-15 have a y intercept $(0, b)$ and an angle of inclination $\theta°$ (with respect to the x axis). We reduce the description to known transformations:

1. Translate the intersection point B to the origin.
2. Rotate by $-\theta°$ so that line L aligns with the x axis.
3. Mirror-reflect about the x axis.
4. Rotate back by $\theta°$.
5. Translate B back to $(0, b)$.

In transformation notation, we have

$$M_L = T_\mathbf{v} \cdot R_\theta \cdot M_x \cdot R_{-\theta} \cdot T_{-\mathbf{v}}$$

where $\mathbf{v} = b\mathbf{J}$.

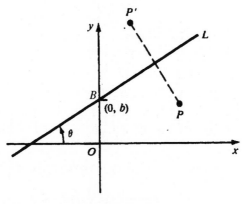

Fig. 4-15

4.10 Find the form of the matrix for reflection about a line L with slope m and y intercept $(0, b)$.

SOLUTION

Following Prob. 4.9 and applying the fact that the angle of inclination of a line is related to its slope m by the equation $\tan(\theta) = m$, we have with $\mathbf{v} = b\mathbf{J}$,

$$M_L = T_\mathbf{v} \cdot R_\theta \cdot M_x \cdot R_{-\theta} \cdot T_{-\mathbf{v}}$$
$$= \begin{pmatrix} 1 & 0 & 0 \\ 0 & 1 & b \\ 0 & 0 & 1 \end{pmatrix} \begin{pmatrix} \cos(\theta) & -\sin(\theta) & 0 \\ \sin(\theta) & \cos(\theta) & 0 \\ 0 & 0 & 1 \end{pmatrix} \begin{pmatrix} 1 & 0 & 0 \\ 0 & -1 & 0 \\ 0 & 0 & 1 \end{pmatrix} \begin{pmatrix} \cos(\theta) & \sin(\theta) & 0 \\ -\sin(\theta) & \cos(\theta) & 0 \\ 0 & 0 & 1 \end{pmatrix} \begin{pmatrix} 1 & 0 & 0 \\ 0 & 1 & -b \\ 0 & 0 & 1 \end{pmatrix}$$

Now if $\tan(\theta) = m$, standard trigonometry yields $\sin(\theta) = m/\sqrt{m^2 + 1}$ and $\cos(\theta) = 1/\sqrt{m^2 + 1}$. Substituting these values for $\sin(\theta)$ and $\cos(\theta)$ after matrix multiplication, we have

$$M_L = \begin{pmatrix} \dfrac{1 - m^2}{m^2 + 1} & \dfrac{2m}{m^2 + 1} & \dfrac{-2bm}{m^2 + 1} \\[3mm] \dfrac{2m}{m^2 + 1} & \dfrac{m^2 - 1}{m^2 + 1} & \dfrac{2b}{m^2 + 1} \\[3mm] 0 & 0 & 1 \end{pmatrix}$$

4.11 Reflect the diamond-shaped polygon whose vertices are $A(-1, 0)$, $B(0, -2)$, $C(1, 0)$, and $D(0, 2)$ about (a) the horizontal line $y = 2$, (b) the vertical line $x = 2$, and (c) the line $y = x + 2$.

SOLUTION

We represent the vertices of the polygon by the homogeneous coordinate matrix

$$V = \begin{pmatrix} -1 & 0 & 1 & 0 \\ 0 & -2 & 0 & 2 \\ 1 & 1 & 1 & 1 \end{pmatrix}$$

From Prob. 4.9, the reflection matrix can be written as

$$M_L = T_{\mathbf{v}} \cdot R_{\theta} \cdot M_x \cdot R_{-\theta} \cdot T_{-\mathbf{v}}$$

(a) The line $y = 2$ has y intercept $(0, 2)$ and makes an angle of $0°$ with the x axis. So with $\theta = 0$ and $\mathbf{v} = 2\mathbf{J}$, the transformation matrix is

$$M_L = \begin{pmatrix} 1 & 0 & 0 \\ 0 & 1 & 2 \\ 0 & 0 & 1 \end{pmatrix} \begin{pmatrix} 1 & 0 & 0 \\ 0 & 1 & 0 \\ 0 & 0 & 1 \end{pmatrix} \begin{pmatrix} 1 & 0 & 0 \\ 0 & -1 & 0 \\ 0 & 0 & 1 \end{pmatrix} \begin{pmatrix} 1 & 0 & 0 \\ 0 & 1 & 0 \\ 0 & 0 & 1 \end{pmatrix} \begin{pmatrix} 1 & 0 & 0 \\ 0 & 1 & -2 \\ 0 & 0 & 1 \end{pmatrix} = \begin{pmatrix} 1 & 0 & 0 \\ 0 & -1 & 4 \\ 0 & 0 & 1 \end{pmatrix}$$

This same matrix could have been obtained directly by using the results of Prob. 4.10 with slope $m = 0$ and y intercept $b = 2$. To reflect the polygon, we set

$$M_L \cdot V = \begin{pmatrix} 1 & 0 & 0 \\ 0 & -1 & 4 \\ 0 & 0 & 1 \end{pmatrix} \begin{pmatrix} -1 & 0 & 1 & 0 \\ 0 & -2 & 0 & 2 \\ 1 & 1 & 1 & 1 \end{pmatrix} = \overset{\displaystyle \begin{matrix} A' & B' & C' & D' \end{matrix}}{\begin{pmatrix} -1 & 0 & 1 & 0 \\ 4 & 6 & 4 & 2 \\ 1 & 1 & 1 & 1 \end{pmatrix}}$$

Converting from homogeneous coordinates, $A' = (-1, 4)$, $B' = (0, 6)$, $C' = (1, 4)$, and $D' = (0, 2)$.

(b) The vertical line $x = 2$ has no y intercept and an infinite slope! We can use M_y, reflection about the y axis, to write the desired reflection by (1) translating the given line two units over to the y axis, (2) reflect about the y axis, and (3) translate back two units. So with $\mathbf{v} = 2\mathbf{I}$,

$$M_L = T_{\mathbf{v}} \cdot M_y \cdot T_{-\mathbf{v}}$$

$$= \begin{pmatrix} 1 & 0 & 2 \\ 0 & 1 & 0 \\ 0 & 0 & 1 \end{pmatrix} \begin{pmatrix} -1 & 0 & 0 \\ 0 & 1 & 0 \\ 0 & 0 & 1 \end{pmatrix} \begin{pmatrix} 1 & 0 & -2 \\ 0 & 1 & 0 \\ 0 & 0 & 1 \end{pmatrix} = \begin{pmatrix} -1 & 0 & 4 \\ 0 & 1 & 0 \\ 0 & 0 & 1 \end{pmatrix}$$

Finally

$$M_L \cdot V = \begin{pmatrix} -1 & 0 & 4 \\ 0 & 1 & 0 \\ 0 & 0 & 1 \end{pmatrix} \begin{pmatrix} -1 & 0 & 1 & 0 \\ 0 & -2 & 0 & 2 \\ 1 & 1 & 1 & 1 \end{pmatrix} = \begin{pmatrix} 5 & 4 & 3 & 4 \\ 0 & -2 & 0 & 2 \\ 1 & 1 & 1 & 1 \end{pmatrix}$$

or $A' = (5, 0)$, $B' = (4, -2)$, $C' = (3, 0)$, and $D' = (4, 2)$.

(c) The line $y = x + 2$ has slope 1 and a y intercept $(0, 2)$. From Prob. 4.10, with $m = 1$ and $b = 2$, we find

$$M_L = \begin{pmatrix} 0 & 1 & -2 \\ 1 & 0 & 2 \\ 0 & 0 & 1 \end{pmatrix}$$

The required coordinates A', B', C', and D' can now be found.

$$M_L \cdot V = \begin{pmatrix} 0 & 1 & -2 \\ 1 & 0 & 2 \\ 0 & 0 & 1 \end{pmatrix} \begin{pmatrix} -1 & 0 & 1 & 0 \\ 0 & -2 & 0 & 2 \\ 1 & 1 & 1 & 1 \end{pmatrix} = \begin{pmatrix} -2 & -4 & -2 & 0 \\ 1 & 2 & 3 & 2 \\ 1 & 1 & 1 & 1 \end{pmatrix}$$

So $A' = (-2, 1)$, $B' = (-4, 2)$, $C' = (-2, 3)$, and $D' = (0, 2)$.

4.12 The matrix $\begin{pmatrix} 1 & a \\ b & 1 \end{pmatrix}$ defines a transformation called a *simultaneous shearing* or *shearing* for short.

The special case when $b = 0$ is called *shearing in the x direction*. When $a = 0$, we have *shearing in the y direction*. Illustrate the effect of these shearing transformations on the square $A(0, 0)$, $B(1, 0)$, $C(1, 1)$, and $D(0, 1)$ when $a = 2$ and $b = 3$.

SOLUTION

Figure 4-16(*a*) shows the original square, Fig. 4-16(*b*) shows shearing in the *x* direction, Fig. 4-16(*c*) shows shearing in the *y* direction, and Fig. 4-16(*d*) shows shearing in both directions.

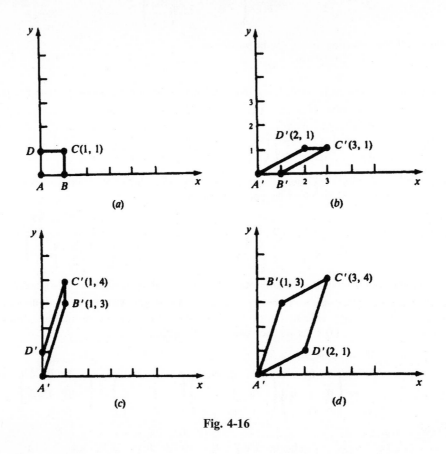

Fig. 4-16

4.13   An observer standing at the origin sees a point $P(1, 1)$. If the point is translated one unit in the direction $\mathbf{v} = \mathbf{I}$, its new coordinate position is $P'(2, 1)$. Suppose instead that the observer stepped back one unit along the *x* axis. What would be the apparent coordinates of *P* with respect to the observer?

SOLUTION

The problem can be set up as a transformation of coordinate systems. If we translate the origin *O* in the direction $\mathbf{v} = -\mathbf{I}$ (to a new position at O') the coordinates of *P* in this system can be found by the translation $\bar{T}_\mathbf{v}$:

$$\bar{T}_\mathbf{v} \cdot P = \begin{pmatrix} 1 & 0 & 1 \\ 0 & 1 & 0 \\ 0 & 0 & 1 \end{pmatrix} \begin{pmatrix} 1 \\ 1 \\ 1 \end{pmatrix} = \begin{pmatrix} 2 \\ 1 \\ 1 \end{pmatrix}$$

So the new coordinates are $(2, 1)'$. This has the following interpretation: a displacement of one unit in a given direction can be achieved by either moving the object forward or stepping back from it.

4.14   An object is defined with respect to a coordinate system whose units are measured in feet. If an observer's coordinate system uses inches as the basic unit, what is the coordinate transformation used to describe object coordinates in the observer's coordinate system?

SOLUTION

Since there are 12 inches to a foot, the required transformation can be described by a coordinate scaling transformation with $s = \frac{1}{12}$ or

$$\bar{S}_{1/12} = \begin{pmatrix} \frac{1}{1/12} & 0 \\ 0 & \frac{1}{1/12} \end{pmatrix} = \begin{pmatrix} 12 & 0 \\ 0 & 12 \end{pmatrix}$$

and so

$$\bar{S}_{1/12} \cdot \begin{pmatrix} x \\ y \end{pmatrix} = \begin{pmatrix} 12 & 0 \\ 0 & 12 \end{pmatrix} \begin{pmatrix} x \\ y \end{pmatrix} = \begin{pmatrix} 12x \\ 12y \end{pmatrix}$$

4.15 Find the equation of the circle $(x')^2 + (y')^2 = 1$ in terms of xy coordinates, assuming that the $x'y'$ coordinate system results from a scaling of a units in the x direction and b units in the y direction.

SOLUTION

From the equations for a coordinate scaling transformation, we find

$$x' = \frac{1}{a}x \qquad y' = \frac{1}{b}y$$

Substituting, we have

$$\left(\frac{x}{a}\right)^2 + \left(\frac{y}{b}\right)^2 = 1$$

Notice that as a result of scaling, the equation of the circle is transformed to the equation of an ellipse in the xy coordinate system.

4.16 Find the equation of the line $y' = mx' + b$ in xy coordinates if the $x'y'$ coordinate system results from a 90° rotation of the xy coordinate system.

SOLUTION

The rotation coordinate transformation equations can be written as

$$x' = x\cos(90°) + y\sin(90°) = y \qquad y' = -x\sin(90°) + y\cos(90°) = -x$$

Substituting, we find $-x = my + b$. Solving for y, we have $y = (-1/m)x - b/m$.

4.17 Find the instance transformation which places a half-size copy of the square $A(0,0)$, $B(1,0)$, $C(1,1)$, $D(0,1)$ [Fig. 4-17(a)] into a master picture coordinate system so that the center of the square is at $(-1,-1)$ [Fig. 4-17(b)].

SOLUTION

The center of the square $ABCD$ is at $P(\frac{1}{2}, \frac{1}{2})$. We shall first apply a scaling transformation while keeping P fixed (see Prob. 4.7). Then we shall apply a translation that moves the center P to $P'(-1, -1)$. Taking $t_x = (-1) - (\frac{1}{2}) = -\frac{3}{2}$ and similarly $t_y = -\frac{3}{2}$ (so $\mathbf{v} = -\frac{3}{2}\mathbf{I} - \frac{3}{2}\mathbf{J}$), we obtain

$$N_{\text{picture,square}} = T_{\mathbf{v}} \cdot S_{1/2,1/2,P} = \begin{pmatrix} 1 & 0 & -\frac{3}{2} \\ 0 & 1 & -\frac{3}{2} \\ 0 & 0 & 1 \end{pmatrix} \begin{pmatrix} \frac{1}{2} & 0 & \frac{1}{4} \\ 0 & \frac{1}{2} & \frac{1}{4} \\ 0 & 0 & 1 \end{pmatrix} = \begin{pmatrix} \frac{1}{2} & 0 & -\frac{5}{4} \\ 0 & \frac{1}{2} & -\frac{5}{4} \\ 0 & 0 & 1 \end{pmatrix}$$

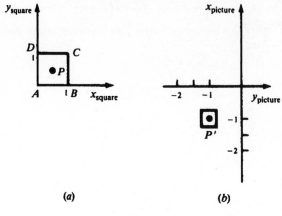

(a)   (b)

Fig. 4-17

4.18 Write the composite transformation that creates the design in Fig. 4-19 from the symbols in Fig. 4-18.

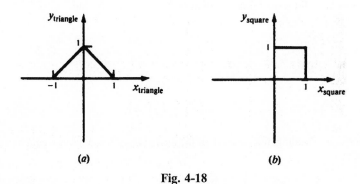

(a)   (b)

Fig. 4-18

SOLUTION

First we create an instance of the triangle [Fig. 4-18(a)] in the square [Fig. 4-18(b)]. Since the base of the triangle must be halved while keeping the height fixed at one unit, the appropriate instance transformation is $N_{\text{square,triangle}} = T_{1/2,\mathbf{I}} \cdot S_{1/2,1}$.

The instance transformation needed to place the square at the desired position in the picture coordinate system (Fig. 4-19) is a translation in the direction $\mathbf{v} = \mathbf{I} + \mathbf{J}$:

$$N_{\text{picture,square}} = T_{\mathbf{v}}$$

Then the composite transformation for placing the triangle into the picture is

$$C_{\text{picture,triangle}} = N_{\text{picture,square}} \cdot N_{\text{square,triangle}}$$

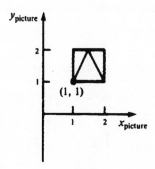

Fig. 4-19

and the composite transformation to place the square into the picture is

$$C_{\text{picture,square}} = N_{\text{picture,square}}$$

Supplementary Problems

4.19   What is the relationship between the rotations R_θ, $R_{-\theta}$, and R_θ^{-1}?

4.20   Describe the transformations used in magnification and reduction with respect to the origin. Find the new coordinates of the triangle $A(0,0)$, $B(1,1)$, $C(5,2)$ after it has been (a) magnified to twice its size and (b) reduced to half its size.

4.21   Show that reflection about the line $y = x$ is attained by reversing coordinates. That is,

$$M_L(x, y) = (y, x)$$

4.22   Show that the order in which transformations are performed is important by the transformation of triangle $A(1,0)$, $B(0,1)$, $C(1,1)$, by (a) rotating $45°$ about the origin and then translating in the direction of vector $\mathbf{I}$, and (b) translating and then rotating.

4.23   An object point $P(x, y)$ is translated in the direction $\mathbf{v} = a\mathbf{I} + b\mathbf{J}$ and simultaneously an observer moves in the direction $\mathbf{v}$. Show that there is no apparent motion (from the point of view of the observer) of the object point.

4.24   Assuming that we have a mathematical equation defining a curve in $x'y'$ coordinates, and the $x'y'$ coordinate system is the result of a coordinate transformation from the xy coordinate system, write the equation in terms of xy coordinates.

4.25   Show that

$$T_{\mathbf{V}_1} \cdot T_{\mathbf{V}_2} = T_{\mathbf{V}_2} \cdot T_{\mathbf{V}_1} = T_{\mathbf{V}_1 + \mathbf{V}_2}$$

4.26   Show that $S_{a,b} \cdot S_{c,d} = S_{c,d} \cdot S_{a,b} = S_{ac,bd}$.

4.27   Show that $R_\alpha \cdot R_\beta = R_\beta \cdot R_\alpha = R_{\alpha+\beta}$.

4.28   Find the condition under which we have

$$S_{s_x,s_y} \cdot R_\theta = R_\theta \cdot S_{s_x,s_y}$$

4.29   Is a simultaneous shearing the same as a shearing in one direction followed by a shearing in another direction? Why?

4.30   Find the condition under which we can switch the order of a rotation and a simultaneous shearing and still get the same result.

4.31   Express a simultaneous shearing in terms of rotation and scaling transformations.

4.32   Express R_θ in terms of shearing and scaling transformations.

4.33   Express R_θ in terms of shearing transformations.

4.34   Prove that the 2D composite transformation matrix is always in the following form:

$$\begin{pmatrix} a & b & c \\ d & e & f \\ 0 & 0 & 1 \end{pmatrix}$$

4.35   Consider a line from P_1 to P_2 and an arbitrary point P on the line. Prove that for any given composite transformation the transformed P is on the line between the transformations of P_1 and P_2.

CHAPTER 5

Two-Dimensional Viewing and Clipping

Much like what we see in real life through a small window on the wall or the viewfinder of a camera, a computer-generated image often depicts a partial view of a large scene. Objects are placed into the scene by modeling transformations to a master coordinate system, commonly referred to as the *world coordinate system* (WCS). A rectangular *window* with its edges parallel to the axes of the WCS is used to select the portion of the scene for which an image is to be generated (see Fig. 5-1). Sometimes an additional coordinate system called the *viewing coordinate system* is introduced to simulate the effect of moving and/or tilting the camera.

On the other hand, an image representing a view often becomes part of a larger image, like a photo on an album page, which models a computer monitor's display area. Since album pages vary and monitor sizes differ from one system to another, we want to introduce a device-independent tool to describe the display area. This tool is called the *normalized device coordinate system* (NDCS) in which a unit (1×1) square whose lower left corner is at the origin of the coordinate system defines the display area of a virtual display device. A rectangular *viewport* with its edges parallel to the axes of the NDCS is used to specify a sub-region of the display area that embodies the image.

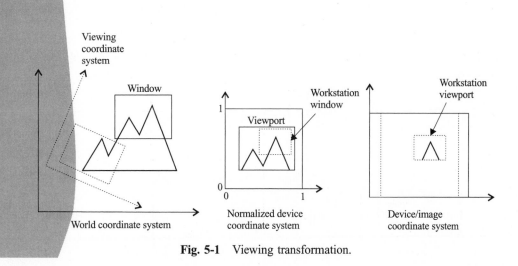

Fig. 5-1 Viewing transformation.

The process that converts object coordinates in WCS to normalized device coordinates is called *window-to-viewport mapping* or *normalization transformation*, which is the subject of Sect. 5.1. The process that maps normalized device coordinates to discrete device/image coordinates is called *workstation transformation*, which is essentially a second window-to-viewport mapping, with a workstation window in the normalized device coordinate system and a workstation viewport in the device coordinate system. Collectively, these two coordinate-mapping operations are referred to as *viewing transformation*.

Workstation transformation is dependent on the resolution of the display device/frame buffer. When the whole display area of the virtual device is mapped to a physical device that does not have a 1/1 aspect ratio, it may be mapped to a square sub-region (see Fig. 5-1) so as to avoid introducing unwanted geometric distortion.

Along with the convenience and flexibility of using a window to specify a localized view comes the need for *clipping*, since objects in the scene may be completely inside the window, completely outside the window, or partially visible through the window (e.g. the mountain-like polygon in Fig. 5-1). The clipping operation eliminates objects or portions of objects that are not visible through the window to ensure the proper construction of the corresponding image.

Note that clipping may occur in the world coordinate or viewing coordinate space, where the window is used to clip the objects; it may also occur in the normalized device coordinate space, where the viewport/workstation window is used to clip. In either case we refer to the window or the viewport/workstation window as the *clipping window*. We discuss point clipping, line clipping, and polygon clipping in Secs. 5.2, 5.3, and 5.4, respectively.

5.1 WINDOW-TO-VIEWPORT MAPPING

A window is specified by four world coordinates: wx_{min}, wx_{max}, wy_{min}, and wy_{max} (see Fig. 5-2). Similarly, a viewport is described by four normalized device coordinates: vx_{min}, vx_{max}, vy_{min}, and vy_{max}. The objective of window-to-viewport mapping is to convert the world coordinates (wx, wy) of an arbitrary point to its corresponding normalized device coordinates (vx, vy). In order to maintain the same relative placement of the point in the viewport as in the window, we require:

$$\frac{wx - wx_{min}}{wx_{max} - wx_{min}} = \frac{vx - vx_{min}}{vx_{max} - vx_{min}} \quad \text{and} \quad \frac{wy - wy_{min}}{wy_{max} - wy_{min}} = \frac{vy - vy_{min}}{vy_{max} - vy_{min}}$$

Thus

$$\begin{cases} vx = \dfrac{vx_{max} - vx_{min}}{wx_{max} - wx_{min}}(wx - wx_{min}) + vx_{min} \\[2ex] vy = \dfrac{vy_{max} - vy_{min}}{wy_{max} - wy_{min}}(wy - wy_{min}) + vy_{min} \end{cases}$$

Since the eight coordinate values that define the window and the viewport are just constants, we can express these two formulas for computing (vx, vy) from (wx, wy) in terms of a translate–scale–translate transformation N

$$\begin{pmatrix} vx \\ vy \\ 1 \end{pmatrix} = N \cdot \begin{pmatrix} wx \\ wy \\ 1 \end{pmatrix}$$

where

$$N = \begin{pmatrix} 1 & 0 & vx_{min} \\ 0 & 1 & vy_{min} \\ 0 & 0 & 1 \end{pmatrix} \cdot \begin{pmatrix} \dfrac{vx_{max} - vx_{min}}{wx_{max} - wx_{min}} & 0 & 0 \\ 0 & \dfrac{vy_{max} - vy_{min}}{wy_{max} - wy_{min}} & 0 \\ 0 & 0 & 1 \end{pmatrix} \cdot \begin{pmatrix} 1 & 0 & -wx_{min} \\ 0 & 1 & -wy_{min} \\ 0 & 0 & 1 \end{pmatrix}$$

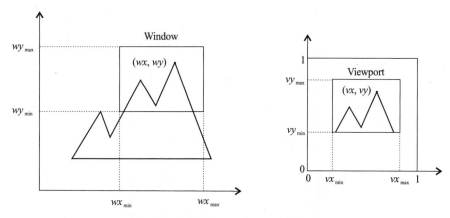

Fig. 5-2   Window-to-viewport mapping.

Note that geometric distortions occur (e.g. squares in the window become rectangles in the viewport) whenever the two scaling constants differ.

5.2   POINT CLIPPING

Point clipping is essentially the evaluation of the following inequalities:

$$x_{\min} \leq x \leq x_{\max} \qquad \text{and} \qquad y_{\min} \leq y \leq y_{\max}$$

where $x_{\min}$, $x_{\max}$, $y_{\min}$ and $y_{\max}$ define the clipping window. A point (x, y) is considered inside the window when the inequalities all evaluate to true.

5.3   LINE CLIPPING

Lines that do not intersect the clipping window are either completely inside the window or completely outside the window. On the other hand, a line that intersects the clipping window is divided by the intersection point(s) into segments that are either inside or outside the window. The following algorithms provide efficient ways to decide the spatial relationship between an arbitrary line and the clipping window and to find intersection point(s).

The Cohen–Sutherland Algorithm

In this algorithm we divide the line clipping process into two phases: (1) identify those lines which intersect the clipping window and so need to be clipped and (2) perform the clipping.

All lines fall into one of the following *clipping categories*:

1. *Visible*—both endpoints of the line lie within the window.

2. *Not visible*—the line definitely lies outside the window. This will occur if the line from (x_1, y_1) to (x_2, y_2) satisfies any one of the following four inequalities:

$$x_1, x_2 > x_{\max} \qquad y_1, y_2 > y_{\max}$$
$$x_1, x_2 < x_{\min} \qquad y_1, y_2 < y_{\min}$$

3. *Clipping candidate*—the line is in neither category 1 nor 2.

In Fig. 5-3, line *AB* is in category 1 (visible); lines *CD* and *EF* are in category 2 (not visible); and lines *GH*, *IJ*, and *KL* are in category 3 (clipping candidate).

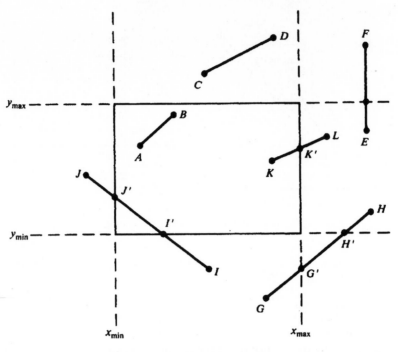

Fig. 5-3

The algorithm employs an efficient procedure for finding the category of a line. It proceeds in two steps:

1. Assign a 4-bit region code to each endpoint of the line. The code is determined according to which of the following nine regions of the plane the endpoint lies in

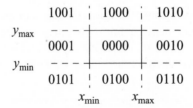

Starting from the leftmost bit, each bit of the code is set to true (1) or false (0) according to the scheme

$$\text{Bit } 1 \equiv \text{endpoint is above the window} = \text{sign } (y - y_{max})$$
$$\text{Bit } 2 \equiv \text{endpoint is below the window} = \text{sign } (y_{min} - y)$$
$$\text{Bit } 3 \equiv \text{endpoint is to the right of the window} = \text{sign } (x - x_{max})$$
$$\text{Bit } 4 \equiv \text{endpoint is to the left of the window} = \text{sign } (x_{min} - x)$$

We use the convention that $\text{sign}(a) = 1$ if a is positive, 0 otherwise. Of course, a point with code 0000 is inside the window.

2. The line is visible if both region codes are 0000, and not visible if the bitwise logical AND of the codes is not 0000, and a candidate for clipping if the bitwise logical AND of the region codes is 0000 (see Prob. 5.8).

For a line in category 3 we proceed to find the intersection point of the line with one of the boundaries of the clipping window, or to be exact, with the infinite extension of one of the boundaries (see Fig. 5-4). We choose an endpoint of the line, say (x_1, y_1), that is outside the window, i.e., whose region code is not

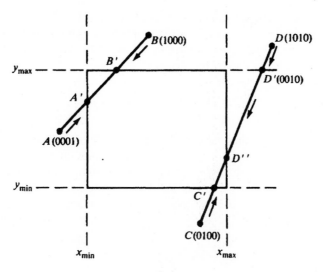

Fig. 5-4

0000. We then select an extended boundary line by observing that those boundary lines that are candidates for intersection are the ones for which the chosen endpoint must be "pushed across" so as to change a "1" in its code to a "0" (see Fig. 5-4). This means:

If bit 1 is 1, intersect with line $y = y_{max}$.

If bit 2 is 1, intersect with line $y = y_{min}$.

If bit 3 is 1, intersect with line $x = x_{max}$.

If bit 4 is 1, intersect with line $x = x_{min}$.

Consider line CD in Fig. 5-4. If endpoint C is chosen, then the bottom boundary line $y = y_{min}$ is selected for computing intersection. On the other hand, if endpoint D is chosen, then either the top boundary line $y = y_{max}$ or the right boundary line $x = x_{max}$ is used. The coordinates of the intersection point are

$$\begin{cases} x_i = x_{min} \text{ or } x_{max} & \text{if the boundary line is vertical} \\ y_i = y_1 + m(x_i - x_1) \end{cases}$$

or

$$\begin{cases} x_i = x_1 + (y_i - y_1)/m & \text{if the boundary line is horizontal} \\ y_i = y_{min} \text{ or } y_{max} \end{cases}$$

where $m = (y_2 - y_1)/(x_2 - x_1)$ is the slope of the line.

Now we replace endpoint (x_1, y_1) with the intersection point (x_i, y_i), effectively eliminating the portion of the original line that is on the outside of the selected window boundary. The new endpoint is then assigned an updated region code and the clipped line re-categorized and handled in the same way. This iterative process terminates when we finally reach a clipped line that belongs to either category 1 (visible) or category 2 (not visible).

Midpoint Subdivision

An alternative way to process a line in category 3 is based on binary search. The line is divided at its midpoint into two shorter line segments. The clipping categories of the two new line segments are then determined by their region codes. Each segment in category 3 is divided again into shorter segments and categorized. This bisection and categorization process continues until each line segment that spans across a window boundary (hence encompasses an intersection point) reaches a threshold for line size and all other segments are either in category 1 (visible) or in category 2 (invisible). The midpoint coordinates (x_m, y_m) of a line joining (x_1, y_1) and (x_2, y_2) are given by

$$x_m = \frac{x_1 + x_2}{2} \qquad y_m = \frac{y_1 + y_2}{2}$$

The example in Fig. 5-5 illustrates how midpoint subdivision is used to zoom in onto the two intersection points I_1 and I_2 with 10 bisections. The process continues until we reach two line segments that are, say, pixel-sized, i.e., mapped to one single pixel each in the image space. If the maximum number of pixels in a line is M, this method will yield a pixel-sized line segment in N subdivisions, where $2^N = M$ or $N = \log_2 M$. For instance, when $M = 1024$ we need at most $N = \log_2 1024 = 10$ subdivisions.

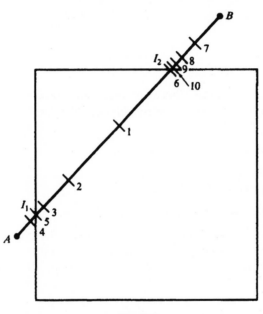

Fig. 5-5

The Liang–Barsky Algorithm

The following parametric equations represent a line from (x_1, y_1) to (x_2, y_2) along with its infinite extension:

$$\begin{cases} x = x_1 + \Delta x \cdot u \\ y = y_1 + \Delta y \cdot u \end{cases}$$

where $\Delta x = x_2 - x_1$ and $\Delta y = y_2 - y_1$. The line itself corresponds to $0 \leq u \leq 1$ (see Fig. 5-6). Notice that when we traverse along the extended line with u increasing from $-\infty$ to $+\infty$, we first move from the outside to the inside of the clipping window's two boundary lines (bottom and left), and then move from the inside to the outside of the other two boundary lines (top and right). If we use u_1 and u_2, where $u_1 \leq u_2$, to represent the beginning and end of the visible portion of the line, we have $u_1 = \text{maximum}(0, u_l, u_b)$ and $u_2 = \text{minimum}(1, u_t, u_r)$, where u_l, u_b, u_t, and u_r correspond to the intersection point of the extended line with the window's left, bottom, top, and right boundary, respectively.

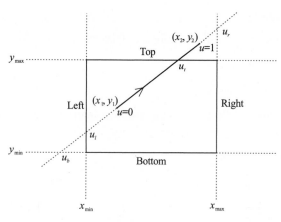

Fig. 5-6

Now consider the tools we need to turn this basic idea into an efficient algorithm. For point (x, y) inside the clipping window, we have

$$x_{\min} \leq x_1 + \Delta x \cdot u \leq x_{\max}$$
$$y_{\min} \leq y_1 + \Delta y \cdot u \leq y_{\max}$$

Rewrite the four inequalities as

$$p_k u \leq q_k, \qquad k = 1, 2, 3, 4$$

where

$$
\begin{array}{lll}
p_1 = -\Delta x & q_1 = x_1 - x_{\min} & \text{(left)} \\
p_2 = \Delta x & q_2 = x_{\max} - x_1 & \text{(right)} \\
p_3 = -\Delta y & q_3 = y_1 - y_{\min} & \text{(bottom)} \\
p_4 = \Delta y & q_4 = y_{\max} - y_1 & \text{(top)}
\end{array}
$$

Observe the following facts:

- if $p_k = 0$, the line is parallel to the corresponding boundary and

$$
\begin{cases}
\text{if } q_k < 0, & \text{the line is completely outside the boundary and can be eliminated} \\
\text{if } q_k \geq 0, & \text{the line is inside the boundary and needs further consideration,}
\end{cases}
$$

- if $p_k < 0$, the extended line proceeds from the outside to the inside of the corresponding boundary line,
- if $p_k > 0$, the extended line proceeds from the inside to the outside of the corresponding boundary line,
- when $p_k \neq 0$, the value of u that corresponds to the intersection point is q_k/p_k.

The Liang–Barsky algorithm for finding the visible portion of the line, if any, can be stated as a four-step process:

1. If $p_k = 0$ and $q_k < 0$ for any k, eliminate the line and stop. Otherwise proceed to the next step.
2. For all k such that $p_k < 0$, calculate $r_k = q_k/p_k$. Let u_1 be the maximum of the set containing 0 and the calculated r values.
3. For all k such that $p_k > 0$, calculate $r_k = q_k/p_k$. Let u_2 be the minimum of the set containing 1 and the calculated r values.
4. If $u_1 > u_2$, eliminate the line since it is completely outside the clipping window. Otherwise, use u_1 and u_2 to calculate the endpoints of the clipped line.

5.4 POLYGON CLIPPING

In this section we consider the case of using a polygonal clipping window to clip a polygon.

Convex Polygonal Clipping Windows

A polygon is called *convex* if the line joining any two interior points of the polygon lies completely inside the polygon (see Fig. 5-7). A non-convex polygon is said to be *concave*.

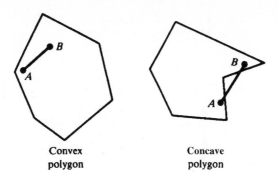

Convex
polygon

Concave
polygon

Fig. 5-7

By convention, a polygon with vertices $P_1, \ldots, P_N$ (and edges $P_{i-1}P_i$ and $P_N P_1$) is said to be *positively oriented* if a tour of the vertices in the given order produces a counterclockwise circuit.

Equivalently, the left hand of a person standing along any directed edge $\overline{P_{i-1}P_i}$ or $\overline{P_N P_1}$ would be pointing inside the polygon [see orientations in Figs. 5-8(*a*) and 5-8(*b*)].

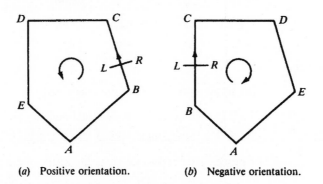

(*a*) Positive orientation.   (*b*) Negative orientation.

Fig. 5-8

Let $A(x_1, y_1)$ and $B(x_2, y_2)$ be the endpoints of a directed line segment. A point $P(x, y)$ will be to the *left* of the line segment if the expression $C = (x_2 - x_1)(y - y_1) - (y_2 - y_1)(x - x_1)$ is positive (see Prob. 5.13). We say that the point is to the *right* of the line segment if this quantity is negative. If a point P is to the right of any one edge of a positively oriented, convex polygon, it is outside the polygon. If it is to the left of *every* edge of the polygon, it is inside the polygon.

This observation forms the basis for clipping any polygon, convex or concave, against a convex polygonal clipping window.

The Sutherland–Hodgman Algorithm

Let $P_1, \ldots, P_N$ be the vertex list of the polygon to be clipped. Let edge E, determined by endpoints A and B, be any edge of the positively oriented, convex clipping polygon. We clip each edge of the polygon in turn against the edge E of the clipping polygon, forming a new polygon whose vertices are determined as follows.

Consider the edge $\overline{P_{i-1}P_i}$:

1. If both P_{i-1} and P_i are to the left of the edge, vertex P_i is placed on the *vertex output list* of the clipped polygon [Fig. 5-9(a)].
2. If both P_{i-1} and P_i are to the right of the edge, nothing is placed on the vertex output list [Fig. 5-9(b)].
3. If P_{i-1} is to the left and P_i is to the right of the edge E, the intersection point I of line segment $\overline{P_{i-1}P_i}$ with the extended edge E is calculated and placed on the vertex output list [Fig. 5-9(c)].
4. If P_{i-1} is to the right and P_i is to the left of edge E, the intersection point I of the line segment $\overline{P_{i-1}P_i}$ with the extended edge E is calculated. Both I and P_i are placed on the vertex output list [Fig. 5-9(d)].

The algorithm proceeds in stages by passing each clipped polygon to the next edge of the window and clipping. See Probs. 5.14 and 5.15.

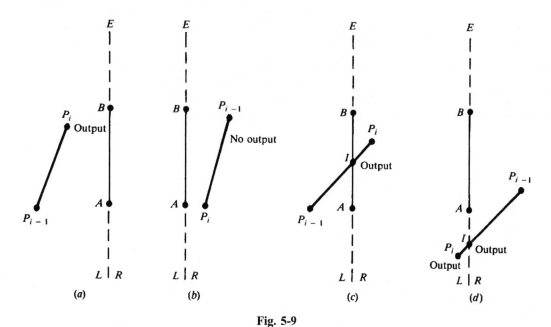

Fig. 5-9

Special attention is necessary in using the Sutherland–Hodgman algorithm in order to avoid unwanted effects. Consider the example in Fig. 5-10(a). The correct result should consist of two disconnected parts, a square in the lower left corner of the clipping window and a triangle at the top [see Fig. 5-10(b)]. However, the algorithm produces a list of vertices (see Prob. 5.16) that forms a figure with the two parts connected by extra edges [see Fig. 5-10(c)]. The fact that these edges are drawn twice in opposite direction can be used to devise a post-processing step to eliminate them.

The Weiler–Atherton Algorithm

Let the clipping window be initially called the clip polygon, and the polygon to be clipped the subject polygon [see Fig. 5-11(a)]. We start with an arbitrary vertex of the subject polygon and trace around its border in the clockwise direction until an intersection with the clip polygon is encountered:

- If the edge enters the clip polygon, record the intersection point and continue to trace the subject polygon.

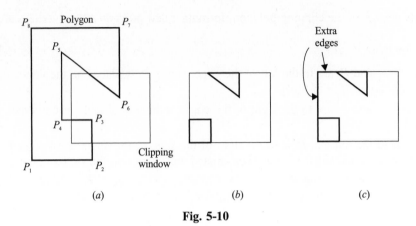

Fig. 5-10

- If the edge leaves the clip polygon, record the intersection point and make a right turn to follow the clip polygon in the same manner (i.e., treat the clip polygon as subject polygon and the subject polygon as clip polygon and proceed as before).

Whenever our path of traversal forms a sub-polygon we output the sub-polygon as part of the overall result. We then continue to trace the rest of the original subject polygon from a recorded intersection point that marks the beginning of a not-yet-traced edge or portion of an edge. The algorithm terminates when the entire border of the original subject polygon has been traced exactly once.

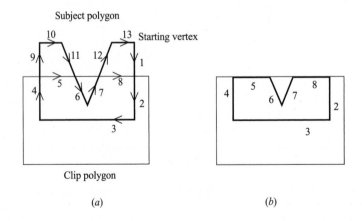

Fig. 5-11

For example, the numbers in Fig. 5-11(a) indicate the order in which the edges and portions of edges are traced. We begin at the starting vertex and continue along the same edge (from 1 to 2) of the subject polygon as it enters the clip polygon. As we move along the edge that is leaving the clip polygon we make a right turn (from 4 to 5) onto the clip polygon, which is now considered the subject polygon. Following the same logic leads to the next right turn (from 5 to 6) onto the current clip polygon, which is really the original subject polygon. With the next step done (from 7 to 8) in the same way we have a sub-polygon for output [see Fig. 5-11(b)]. We then resume our traversal of the original subject polygon from the recorded intersection point where we first changed our course. Going from 9 to 10 to 11 produces no output. After skipping the already-traversed 6 and 7, we continue with 12 and 13 and come to an end. The figure in Fig. 5-11(b) is the final result.

Applying the Weiler–Atherton algorithm to clip the polygon in Fig. 5-10(a) produces correct result [see Fig. 5-12(a) and (b)].

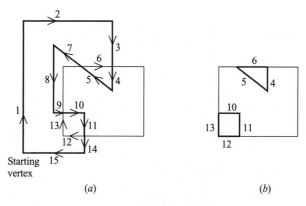

(a)   (b)

Fig. 5-12

5.5   EXAMPLE: A 2D GRAPHICS PIPELINE

Shared by many graphics systems is the overall system architecture called the graphics pipeline. The operational organization of a 2D graphics pipeline is shown in Fig. 5-13. Although 2D graphics is typically treated as a special case ($z = 0$) of three-dimensional graphics, it demonstrates the common working principle and basic application of these pipelined systems.

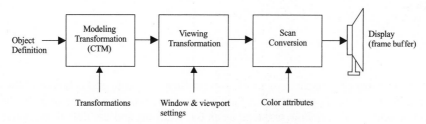

Fig. 5-13   A 2D graphics pipeline.

At the beginning of the pipeline we have object data (e.g., vertex coordinates for lines and polygons that make up individual objects) stored in application-specific data structures. A graphics application uses system subroutines to initialize and to change, among other things, the transformations that are to be applied to the original data, window and viewport settings, and the color attributes of the objects. Whenever a drawing subroutine is called to render a pre-defined object, the graphics system first applies the specified modeling transformation to the original data, then carries out viewing transformation using the current window and viewport settings, and finally performs scan conversion to set the proper pixels in the frame buffer with the specified color attributes.

Suppose that we have an object centered in its own coordinate system [see Fig. 5-14(a)], and we are to construct a sequence of images that animates the object rotating around its center and moving along a circular path in a square display area [see Fig. 5-14(b)]. We generate each image as follows: first rotate the object around its center by angle α, then translate the rotated object by offset $\cdot$ **I** to position its center on the positive x axis of the WCS, and rotate it with respect to the origin of the WCS by angle β. We control the amount of the first rotation from one image to the next by $\Delta\alpha$, and that of the second rotation by $\Delta\beta$.

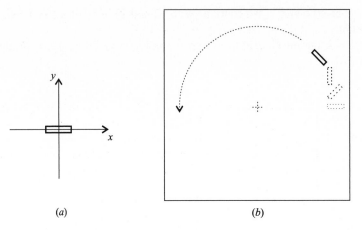

(a)   (b)

Fig. 5-14

```
window(-winsize/2, winsize/2, -winsize/2, winsize/2);
α = 0;
while (1) {
    setColor(background);
    clear();
    setColor(color);
    pushCTM();
    translate(offset, 0);
    rotate(α);
    drawObject();
    popCTM();
    α = α + Δα;
    rotate(Δβ);
}
```

We first set the window of winsize by winsize to be sufficiently large and centered at the origin of the WCS to cover the entire scene. The system's default viewport coincides with the unit display area in the NDCS. The default workstation window is the same as the viewport and the default workstation viewport corresponds to the whole square display area.

The graphics system maintains a stack of composite transformation matrices. The CTM on top of the stack, called the current CTM, is initially an identity matrix and is automatically used in modeling transformation. Each call to translate, scale, and rotate causes the system to generate a corresponding transformation matrix and to reset the current CTM to take into account the generated matrix. The order of transformation is maintained in such a way that the most recently specified transformation is applied first. When pushCTM() is called, the system makes a copy of the current CTM and pushes it onto the stack (now we have two copies of the current CTM on the stack). When popCTM() is called, the system simply removes the CTM on top of the stack (now we have restored the CTM that was second to the removed CTM to be the current CTM).

Panning and Zooming

Two simple camera effects can be achieved by changing the position or size of the window. When the position of the window is, for example, moved to the left, an object in the scene that is visible through the window would appear moved to the right, much like what we see in the viewfinder when we move or pan a camera. On the other hand, if we fix the window on an object but reduce or increase its size, the object would appear bigger (zoom in) or smaller (zoom out), respectively.

Double Buffering

Producing an animation sequence by clearing the display screen and constructing the next frame of image often leads to flicker, since an image is erased almost as soon as it is completed. An effective solution to this problem is to have two frame buffers: one holds the image on display while the system draws a new image into the other. Once the new image is drawn, a call that looks like swapBuffer() would cause the two buffers to switch their roles.

Lookup Table Animation

We can sometimes animate a displayed image in the lookup table representation by changing or cycling the color values in the lookup table. For example, we may draw the monochromatic object in Fig. 5-14(a) into the frame buffer in several pre-determined locations, using consecutive lookup table entries for the color attribute in each location (see Fig. 5-15). We initialize lookup table entry 0 with the color of the object, and all other entries with the background color. This means that in the beginning the object is visible only in its first position (labeled 0). Now if we simply reset entry 0 with the background color and entry 1 with the object color, we would have the object "moved" to its second position (labeled 1) without redrawing the image. The object's circular motion could hence be produced by cycling the object color through all relevant lookup table entries.

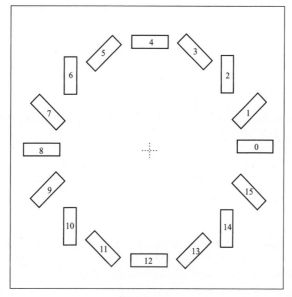

Fig. 5-15

Solved Problems

5.1   Let

$$s_x = \frac{vx_{\max} - vx_{\min}}{wx_{\max} - wx_{\min}} \quad \text{and} \quad s_y = \frac{vy_{\max} - vy_{\min}}{wy_{\max} - wy_{\min}}$$

Express window-to-viewport mapping in the form of a composite transformation matrix.

SOLUTION

$$N = \begin{pmatrix} 1 & 0 & vx_{\min} \\ 0 & 1 & vy_{\min} \\ 0 & 0 & 1 \end{pmatrix} \cdot \begin{pmatrix} s_x & 0 & 0 \\ 0 & s_y & 0 \\ 0 & 0 & 1 \end{pmatrix} \cdot \begin{pmatrix} 1 & 0 & -wx_{\min} \\ 0 & 1 & -wy_{\min} \\ 0 & 0 & 1 \end{pmatrix}$$

$$= \begin{pmatrix} s_x & 0 & -s_x wx_{\min} + vx_{\min} \\ 0 & s_y & -s_y wy_{\min} + vy_{\min} \\ 0 & 0 & 1 \end{pmatrix}$$

5.2   Find the normalization transformation that maps a window whose lower left corner is at $(1, 1)$ and upper right corner is at $(3, 5)$ onto (*a*) a viewport that is the entire normalized device screen and (*b*) a viewport that has lower left corner at $(0, 0)$ and upper right corner $(\frac{1}{2}, \frac{1}{2})$.

SOLUTION

From Prob. 5.1, we need only identify the appropriate parameters.

(*a*)   The window parameters are $wx_{\min} = 1$, $wx_{\max} = 3$, $wy_{\min} = 1$, and $wy_{\max} = 5$. The viewport parameters are $vx_{\min} = 0$, $vx_{\max} = 1$, $vy_{\min} = 0$, and $vy_{\max} = 1$. Then $s_x = \frac{1}{2}$, $s_y = \frac{1}{4}$, and

$$N = \begin{pmatrix} \frac{1}{2} & 0 & -\frac{1}{2} \\ 0 & \frac{1}{4} & -\frac{1}{4} \\ 0 & 0 & 1 \end{pmatrix}$$

(*b*)   The window parameters are the same as in (*a*). The viewport parameters are now $vx_{\min} = 0$, $vx_{\max} = \frac{1}{2}$, $vy_{\min} = 0$, $vy_{\max} = \frac{1}{2}$. Then $s_x = \frac{1}{4}$, $s_y = \frac{1}{8}$, and

$$N = \begin{pmatrix} \frac{1}{4} & 0 & -\frac{1}{4} \\ 0 & \frac{1}{8} & -\frac{1}{8} \\ 0 & 0 & 1 \end{pmatrix}$$

5.3   Find the complete viewing transformation that maps a window in world coordinates with x extent 1 to 10 and y extent 1 to 10 onto a viewport with x extent $\frac{1}{4}$ to $\frac{3}{4}$ and y extent 0 to $\frac{1}{2}$ in normalized device space, and then maps a workstation window with x extent $\frac{1}{4}$ to $\frac{1}{2}$ and y extent $\frac{1}{4}$ to $\frac{1}{2}$ in the normalized device space into a workstation viewport with x extent 1 to 10 and y extent 1 to 10 on the physical display device.

SOLUTION

From Prob. 5.1, the parameters for the normalization transformation are $wx_{\min} = 1$, $wx_{\max} = 10$, $wy_{\min} = 1$, $wy_{\max} = 10$, and $vx_{\min} = \frac{1}{4}$, $vx_{\max} = \frac{3}{4}$, $vy_{\min} = 0$, and $vy_{\max} = \frac{1}{2}$. Then

$$s_x = \frac{1/2}{9} = \frac{1}{18} \qquad s_y = \frac{1/2}{9} = \frac{1}{18}$$

and

$$N = \begin{pmatrix} \frac{1}{18} & 0 & \frac{7}{36} \\ 0 & \frac{1}{18} & -\frac{1}{18} \\ 0 & 0 & 1 \end{pmatrix}$$

The parameters for the workstation transformation are $wx_{\min} = \frac{1}{4}$, $wx_{\max} = \frac{1}{2}$, $wy_{\min} = \frac{1}{4}$, $wy_{\max} = \frac{1}{2}$, and $vx_{\min} = 1$, $vx_{\max} = 10$, $vy_{\min} = 1$, and $vy_{\max} = 10$. Then

$$s_x = \frac{9}{1/4} = 36 \qquad s_y = \frac{9}{1/4} = 36$$

and

$$W = \begin{pmatrix} 36 & 0 & -8 \\ 0 & 36 & -8 \\ 0 & 0 & 1 \end{pmatrix}$$

The complete viewing transformation V is

$$V = W \cdot N = \begin{pmatrix} 36 & 0 & -8 \\ 0 & 36 & -8 \\ 0 & 0 & 1 \end{pmatrix} \begin{pmatrix} \frac{1}{18} & 0 & \frac{7}{36} \\ 0 & \frac{1}{18} & -\frac{1}{18} \\ 0 & 0 & 1 \end{pmatrix} = \begin{pmatrix} 2 & 0 & -1 \\ 0 & 2 & -10 \\ 0 & 0 & 1 \end{pmatrix}$$

5.4 Find a normalization transformation from the window whose lower left corner is at $(0, 0)$ and upper right corner is at $(4, 3)$ onto the normalized device screen so that aspect ratios are preserved.

SOLUTION

The window aspect ratio is $a_w = \frac{4}{3}$. Unless otherwise indicated, we shall choose a viewport that is as large as possible with respect to the normalized device screen. To this end, we choose the x extent from 0 to 1 and the y extent from 0 to $\frac{3}{4}$. So

$$a_v = \frac{1}{3/4} = \frac{4}{3}$$

As in Prob. 5.2, with parameters $wx_{\min} = 0$, $wx_{\max} = 4$, $wy_{\min} = 0$, $wy_{\max} = 3$ and $vx_{\min} = 0$, $vx_{\max} = 1$, $vy_{\min} = 0$, $vy_{\max} = \frac{3}{4}$,

$$N = \begin{pmatrix} \frac{1}{4} & 0 & 0 \\ 0 & \frac{1}{4} & 0 \\ 0 & 0 & 1 \end{pmatrix}$$

5.5 Find the normalization transformation N which uses the rectangle $A(1, 1)$, $B(5, 3)$, $C(4, 5)$, $D(0, 3)$ as a window [Fig. 5-16(a)] and the normalized device screen as a viewport [Fig. 5-16(b)].

SOLUTION

We will first rotate the rectangle about A so that it is aligned with the coordinate axes. Next, as in Prob. 5.1, we calculate s_x and s_y and finally we compose the rotation and the transformation N (from Prob. 5.1) to find the required normalization transformation N_R.

The slope of the line segment $\overline{AB}$ is

$$m = \frac{3 - 1}{5 - 1} = \frac{1}{2}$$

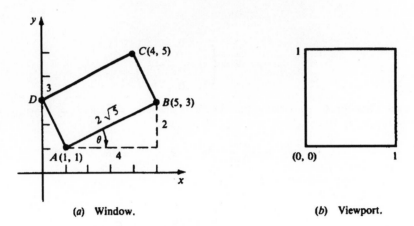

(a) Window.   (b) Viewport.

Fig. 5-16

Looking at Fig. 5-11, we see that $-\theta$ will be the direction of the rotation. The angle θ is determined from the slope of a line (App. 1) by the equation $\tan \theta = \frac{1}{2}$. Then

$$\sin \theta = \frac{1}{\sqrt{5}}, \qquad \text{and so} \qquad \sin(-\theta) = -\frac{1}{\sqrt{5}}, \qquad \cos \theta = \frac{2}{\sqrt{5}}, \qquad \cos(-\theta) = \frac{2}{\sqrt{5}}$$

The rotation matrix about $A(1, 1)$ is then (Chap. 4, Prob. 4.4):

$$R_{-\theta, A} = \begin{pmatrix} \dfrac{2}{\sqrt{5}} & \dfrac{1}{\sqrt{5}} & \left(1 - \dfrac{3}{\sqrt{5}}\right) \\ -\dfrac{1}{\sqrt{5}} & \dfrac{2}{\sqrt{5}} & \left(1 - \dfrac{1}{\sqrt{5}}\right) \\ 0 & 0 & 1 \end{pmatrix}$$

The x extent of the rotated window is the length of $\overline{AB}$. Similarly, the y extent is the length of $\overline{AD}$. Using the distance formula (App. 1) to calculate these lengths yields

$$d(A, B) = \sqrt{2^2 + 4^2} = \sqrt{20} = 2\sqrt{5} \qquad d(A, D) = \sqrt{1^2 + 2^2} = \sqrt{5}$$

Also, the x extent of the normalized device screen is 1, as is the y extent. Calculating s_x and s_y,

$$s_x = \frac{\text{viewport } x \text{ extent}}{\text{window } x \text{ extent}} = \frac{1}{2\sqrt{5}} \qquad s_y = \frac{\text{viewport } y \text{ extent}}{\text{window } y \text{ extent}} = \frac{1}{\sqrt{5}}$$

So

$$N = \begin{pmatrix} \dfrac{1}{2\sqrt{5}} & 0 & -\dfrac{1}{2\sqrt{5}} \\ 0 & \dfrac{1}{\sqrt{5}} & -\dfrac{1}{\sqrt{5}} \\ 0 & 0 & 1 \end{pmatrix}$$

The normalization transformation is then

$$N_R = N \cdot R_{-\theta, A} = \begin{pmatrix} \frac{1}{5} & \frac{1}{10} & -\frac{3}{10} \\ -\frac{1}{5} & \frac{2}{5} & -\frac{1}{5} \\ 0 & 0 & 1 \end{pmatrix}$$

5.6   Let R be the rectangular window whose lower left-hand corner is at $L(-3, 1)$ and upper right-hand corner is at $R(2, 6)$. Find the region codes for the endpoints in Fig. 5-17.

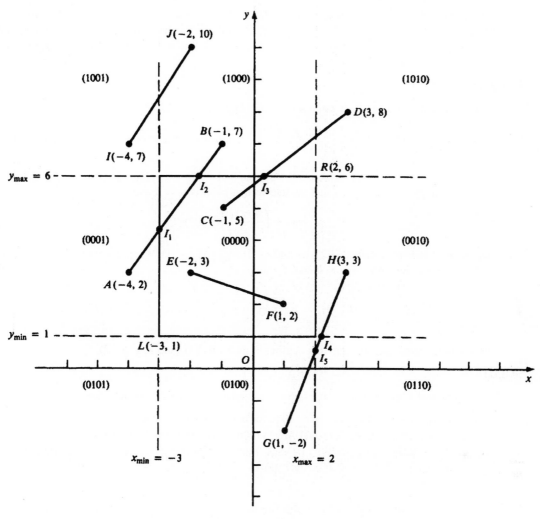

Fig. 5-17

SOLUTION

The region code for point (x, y) is set according to the scheme

$$\text{Bit 1} = \text{sign}(y - y_{\max}) = \text{sign}(y - 6) \qquad \text{Bit 3} = \text{sign}(x - x_{\max}) = \text{sign}(x - 2)$$
$$\text{Bit 2} = \text{sign}(y_{\min} - y) = \text{sign}(1 - y) \qquad \text{Bit 4} = \text{sign}(x_{\min} - x) = \text{sign}(-3 - x)$$

Here

$$\text{Sign}(a) = \begin{cases} 1 & \text{if } a \text{ is positive} \\ 0 & \text{otherwise} \end{cases}$$

So

$$\begin{array}{ll} A(-4, 2) \to 0001 & F(1, 2) \to 0000 \\ B(-1, 7) \to 1000 & G(1, -2) \to 0100 \\ C(-1, 5) \to 0000 & H(3, 3) \to 0010 \\ D(3, 8) \to 1010 & I(-4, 7) \to 1001 \\ E(-2, 3) \to 0000 & J(-2, 10) \to 1000 \end{array}$$

5.7   Clipping against rectangular windows whose sides are aligned with the x and y axes involves computing intersections with vertical and horizontal lines. Find the intersection of a line segment $\overline{P_1P_2}$ [joining $P_1(x_1, y_1)$ to $P_2(x_2, y_2)$] with (a) the vertical line $x = a$ and (b) the horizontal line $y = b$.

SOLUTION

We write the equation of $\overline{P_1P_2}$ in parametric form (App. 1, Prob. A1.23):

$$\begin{cases} x = x_1 + t(x_2 - x_1) \\ y = y_1 + t(y_2 - y_1), \end{cases} \quad 0 \le t \le 1 \qquad \begin{matrix} (5.1) \\ (5.2) \end{matrix}$$

(a)   Since $x = a$, we substitute this into equation (5.1) and find $t = (a - x_1)/(x_2 - x_1)$. Then, substituting this value into equation (5.2), we find that the intersection point is $x_I = a$ and

$$y_I = y_1 + \left(\frac{a - x_1}{x_2 - x_1}\right)(y_2 - y_1)$$

(b)   Substituting $y = b$ into equation (5.2), we find $t = (b - y_1)/(y_2 - y_1)$. When this is placed into equation (5.1), the intersection point is $y_I = b$ and

$$x_I = x_1 + \left(\frac{b - y_1}{y_2 - y_1}\right)(x_2 - x_1)$$

5.8   Find the clipping categories for the line segments in Prob. 5.6 (see Fig. 5-17).

SOLUTION

We place the line segments in their appropriate categories by testing the region codes found in Prob. 5.6.

Category 1 (visible): $\overline{EF}$ since the region code for both endpoints is 0000.
Category 2 (not visible): $\overline{IJ}$ since (1001) AND (1000) = 1000 (which is not 0000).
Category 3 (candidates for clipping): $\overline{AB}$ since (0001) AND (1000) = 0000, $\overline{CD}$ since (0000) AND (1010) = 0000, and $\overline{GH}$ since (0100) AND (0010) = 0000.

5.9   Use the Cohen–Sutherland algorithm to clip the line segments in Prob. 5.6 (see Fig. 5-17).

SOLUTION

From Prob. 5.8, the candidates for clipping are $\overline{AB}$, $\overline{CD}$, and $\overline{GH}$.

In *clipping $\overline{AB}$*, the code for A is 0001. To push the 1 to 0, we clip against the boundary line $x_{\min} = -3$. The resulting intersection point is $I_1(-3, 3\frac{2}{3})$. We clip (do not display) $\overline{AI_1}$ and work on $\overline{I_1B}$. The code for I_1 is 0000. The clipping category for $\overline{I_1B}$ is 3 since (0000) AND (1000) is (0000). Now B is outside the window (i.e., its code is 1000), so we push the 1 to a 0 by clipping against the line $y_{\max} = 6$. The resulting intersection is $I_2(-1\frac{3}{5}, 6)$. Thus $\overline{I_2B}$ is clipped. The code for I_2 is 0000. The remaining segment $\overline{I_1I_2}$ is displayed since both endpoints lie in the window (i.e., their codes are 0000).

For *clipping $\overline{CD}$*, we start with D since it is outside the window. Its code is 1010. We push the first 1 to a 0 by clipping against the line $y_{\max} = 6$. The resulting intersection I_3 is $(\frac{1}{3}, 6)$ and its code is 0000. Thus $\overline{I_3D}$ is clipped and the remaining segment $\overline{CI_3}$ has both endpoints coded 0000 and so it is displayed.

For *clipping $\overline{GH}$*, we can start with either G or H since both are outside the window. The code for G is 0100, and we push the 1 to a 0 by clipping against the line $y_{\min} = 1$. The resulting intersection point is $I_4(2\frac{1}{5}, 1)$, and its code is 0010. We clip $\overline{GI_4}$ and work on $\overline{I_4H}$. Segment $\overline{I_4H}$ is not displayed since (0010) AND (0010) = 0010.

5.10   Clip line segment $\overline{CD}$ of Prob. 5.6 by using the midpoint subdivision process.

SOLUTION

The midpoint subdivision process is based on repeated bisections. To avoid continuing indefinitely, we agree to say that a point (x_1, y_1) lies on any of the boundary lines of the rectangle, say, boundary line $x = x_{max}$, for example, if $-\text{TOL} \leq x_1 - x_{max} \leq \text{TOL}$. Here TOL is a prescribed tolerance, some small number, that is set before the process begins.

To clip $\overline{CD}$, we determine that it is in category 3. For this problem we arbitrarily choose $\text{TOL} = 0.1$. We find the midpoint of $\overline{CD}$ to be $M_1(1, 6.5)$. Its code is 1000.

So $\overline{M_1 D}$ is not displayed since (1000) AND (1010) = 1000. We further subdivide $\overline{CM_1}$ since (0000) AND (1000) = 0000. The midpoint of $\overline{CM_1}$ is $M_2(0, 5.75)$; the code for M_2 is 0000. Thus $\overline{CM_2}$ is displayed since both endpoints are 0000 and $\overline{M_2 M_1}$ is a candidate for clipping. The midpoint of $\overline{M_2 M_1}$ is $M_3(0.5, 6.125)$, and its code is 1000. Thus $\overline{M_3 M_1}$ is chipped and $\overline{M_2 M_3}$ is subdivided. The midpoint of $\overline{M_2 M_3}$ is $M_4(0.25, 5.9375)$, whose code is 0000. However, since $y_1 = 5.9375$ lies within the tolerance 0.1 of the boundary line $y_{max} = 6$—that is, $6 - 5.9375 = 0.0625 < 0.1$, we agree that M_4 lies on the boundary line $y_{max} = 6$. Thus $\overline{M_2 M_4}$ is displayed and $\overline{M_4 M_3}$ is not displayed. So the original line segment $\overline{CD}$ is clipped at M_4 and the process stops.

5.11   Suppose that in an implementation of the Cohen–Sutherland algorithm we choose boundary lines in the top–bottom–right–left order to clip a line in category 3, draw a picture to show a worst-case scenario, i.e., one that involves the highest number of iterations.

SOLUTION

   See Fig. 5-18.

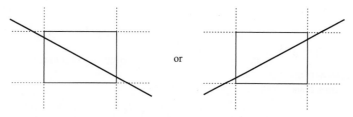

Fig. 5-18

5.12   Use the Liang–Barsky algorithm to clip the lines in Fig. 5-19.

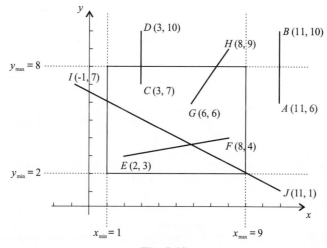

Fig. 5-19

SOLUTION

For line AB, we have

$$
\begin{aligned}
p_1 &= 0 & q_1 &= 10 \\
p_2 &= 0 & q_2 &= -2 \\
p_3 &= -4 & q_3 &= 4 \\
p_4 &= 4 & q_4 &= 2
\end{aligned}
$$

Since $p_2 = 0$ and $q_2 < -2$, AB is completely outside the right boundary.

For line CD, we have

$$
\begin{aligned}
p_1 &= 0 & q_1 &= 2 \\
p_2 &= 0 & q_2 &= 6 \\
p_3 &= -3 & q_3 &= 5 & r_3 &= -\tfrac{5}{3} \\
p_4 &= 3 & q_4 &= 1 & r_4 &= \tfrac{1}{3}
\end{aligned}
$$

Thus $u_1 = \max(0, -\tfrac{5}{3}) = 0$ and $u_2 = \min(1, \tfrac{1}{3}) = \tfrac{1}{3}$. Since $u_1 < u_2$, the two endpoints of the clipped line are $(3, 7)$ and $(3, 7 + 3(\tfrac{1}{3})) = (3, 8)$.

For line EF, we have

$$
\begin{aligned}
p_1 &= -6 & q_1 &= 1 & r_1 &= -\tfrac{1}{6} \\
p_2 &= 6 & q_2 &= 7 & r_2 &= \tfrac{7}{6} \\
p_3 &= -1 & q_3 &= 1 & r_3 &= -\tfrac{1}{1} \\
p_4 &= 1 & q_4 &= 5 & r_4 &= \tfrac{5}{1}
\end{aligned}
$$

Thus $u_1 = \max(0, -\tfrac{1}{6}, -1) = 0$ and $u_2 = \min(1, \tfrac{7}{6}, 5) = 1$. Since $u_1 = 0$ and $u_2 = 1$, line EF is completely inside the clipping window.

For line GH, we have

$$
\begin{aligned}
p_1 &= -2 & q_1 &= 5 & r_1 &= -\tfrac{5}{2} \\
p_2 &= 2 & q_2 &= 3 & r_2 &= \tfrac{3}{2} \\
p_3 &= -3 & q_3 &= 4 & r_3 &= -\tfrac{4}{3} \\
p_4 &= 3 & q_4 &= 2 & r_4 &= \tfrac{2}{3}
\end{aligned}
$$

Thus $u_1 = \max(0, -\tfrac{5}{2}, -\tfrac{4}{3}) = 0$ and $u_2 = \min(1, \tfrac{3}{2}, \tfrac{2}{3}) = \tfrac{2}{3}$. Since $u_1 < u_2$, the two endpoints of the clipped line are $(6, 6)$ and $(6 + 2(\tfrac{2}{3}), 6 + 3(\tfrac{2}{3})) = (7\tfrac{1}{3}, 8)$.

For line IJ, we have

$$
\begin{aligned}
p_1 &= -12 & q_1 &= -2 & r_1 &= \tfrac{1}{6} \\
p_2 &= 12 & q_2 &= 10 & r_2 &= \tfrac{5}{6} \\
p_3 &= 6 & q_3 &= 5 & r_3 &= \tfrac{5}{6} \\
p_4 &= -6 & q_4 &= 1 & r_4 &= -\tfrac{1}{6}
\end{aligned}
$$

Thus $u_1 = \max(0, \tfrac{1}{6}, -\tfrac{1}{6}) = \tfrac{1}{6}$ and $u_2 = \min(1, \tfrac{5}{6}, \tfrac{5}{6}) = \tfrac{5}{6}$. Since $u_1 < u_2$, the two endpoints of the clipped line are $(-1 + 12(\tfrac{1}{6}), 7 + (-6)(\tfrac{1}{6})) = (1, 6)$ and $(-1 + 12(\tfrac{5}{6}), 7 + (-6)(\tfrac{5}{6})) = (9, 2)$.

5.13   How can we determine whether a point $P(x, y)$ lies to the left or to the right of a line segment joining the points $A(x_1, y_1)$ and $B(x_2, y_2)$?

SOLUTION

Refer to Fig. 5-20. Form the vectors **AB** and **AP**. If the point P is to the left of **AB**, then by the definition of the cross product of two vectors (App. 2) the vector $\mathbf{AB} \times \mathbf{AP}$ points in the direction of the vector **K** perpendicular to the xy plane (see Fig. 5-20). If it lies to the right, the cross product points in the direction

$-\mathbf{K}$. Now

$$\mathbf{AB} = (x_2 - x_1)\mathbf{I} + (y_2 - y_1)\mathbf{J} \qquad \mathbf{AP} = (x - x_1)\mathbf{I} + (y - y_1)\mathbf{J}$$

So

$$\mathbf{AB} \times \mathbf{AP} = [(x_2 - x_1)(y - y_1) - (y_2 - y_1)(x - x_1)]\mathbf{K}$$

Then the direction of this cross product is determined by the number

$$\bar{C} = (x_2 - x_1)(y - y_1) - (y_2 - y_1)(x - x_1)$$

If $\bar{C}$ is positive, P lies to the left of $\mathbf{AB}$. If $\bar{C}$ is negative, then P lies to the right of $\mathbf{AB}$.

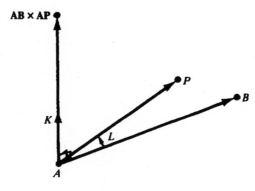

Fig. 5-20

5.14   Draw a flowchart illustrating the logic of the Sutherland–Hodgman algorithm.

SOLUTION

The algorithm inputs the vertices of a polygon one at a time. For each input vertex, either zero, one, or two output vertices will be generated depending on the relationship of the input vertices to the clipping edge E.

We denote by P the input vertex, S the previous input vertex, and F the first arriving input vertex. The vertex or vertices to be output are determined according to the logic illustrated in the flowchart in Fig. 5-21. Recall that a polygon with n vertices $P_1, P_2, \ldots, P_n$ has n edges $\overline{P_1 P_2}, \ldots, \overline{P_{n-1} P_n}$ and the edge $\overline{P_n P_1}$ closing the polygon. In order to avoid the need to duplicate the input of P_1 as the final input vertex (and a corresponding mechanism to duplicate the final output vertex to close the polygon), the closing logic shown in the flowchart in Fig. 5-22 is called after processing the final input vertex P_n.

5.15   Clip the polygon $P_1, \ldots, P_9$ in Fig. 5-23 against the window $ABCD$ using the Sutherland–Hodgman algorithm.

SOLUTION

At each stage the new output polygon, whose vertices are determined by applying the Sutherland–Hodgman algorithm (Prob. 5.14), is passed on to the next clipping edge of the window $ABCD$. The results are illustrated in Figs. 5-24 through 5-27.

5.16   Clip the polygon $P_1, \ldots, P_8$ in Fig. 5-10 against the rectangular clipping window using the Sutherland–Hodgman algorithm.

SOLUTION

We first clip against the top boundary line, then the left, and finally the bottom. The right boundary is omitted since it does not affect any vertex list. The intermediate and final results are in Fig. 5-28.

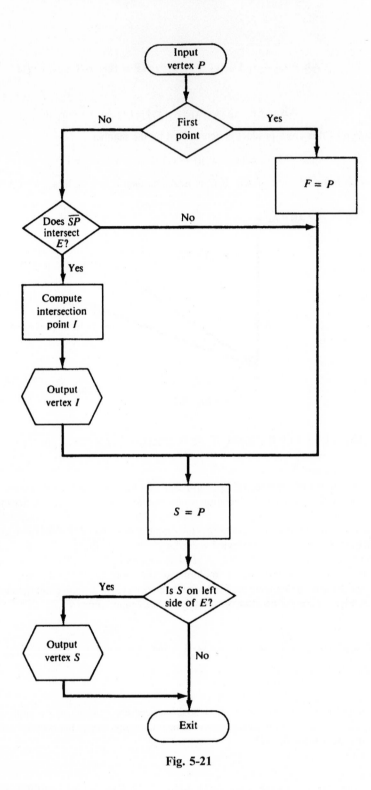

Fig. 5-21

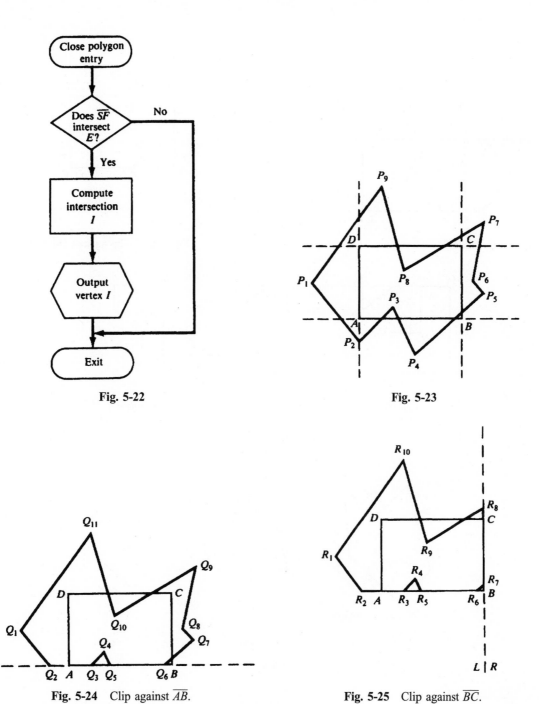

Fig. 5-22

Fig. 5-23

Fig. 5-24   Clip against $\overline{AB}$.

Fig. 5-25   Clip against $\overline{BC}$.

5.17   Use the Weiler–Atherton algorithm to clip the polygon in Fig. 5-29(*a*).

SOLUTION

   See Fig. 5-29(*b*) and (*c*).

5.18   Consider the example in Sect. 5.5, where the object would appear turning slowly around its center even if we set $\Delta\alpha = 0$. How to keep the orientation of the object constant while making it rotate around the center of the display area?

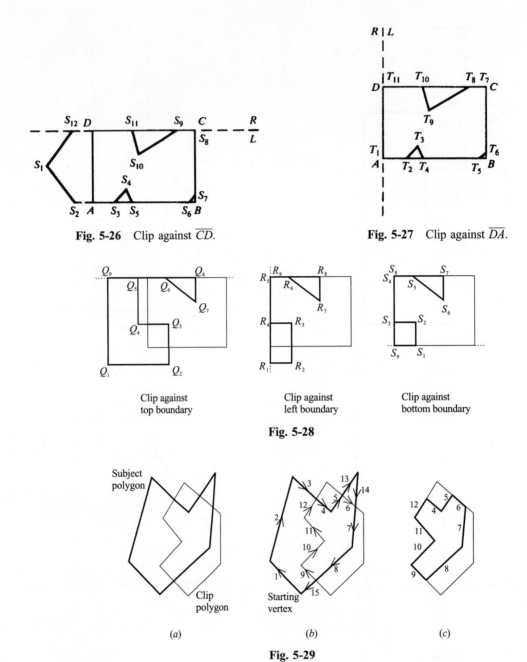

Fig. 5-26 Clip against $\overline{CD}$.

Fig. 5-27 Clip against $\overline{DA}$.

Clip against top boundary

Clip against left boundary

Clip against bottom boundary

Fig. 5-28

(a)

(b)

(c)

Fig. 5-29

SOLUTION

$\Delta\alpha = -\Delta\beta$, i.e., $\alpha = -\beta$.

5.19 How to animate the flag in Fig. 5-30(a) that may be in two different positions using lookup table animation?

SOLUTION

See Fig. 5-30(b). The area where position 1 overlaps position 2 is assigned entry 0 that has the color of the flag. The rest of position 1 is assigned entry 1 and that of position 2 entry 2. Now we only need to alternate entries 1 and 2 between the flag color and the background color.

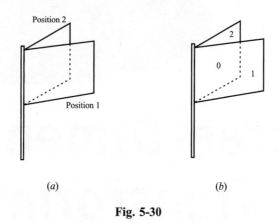

(a)   (b)

Fig. 5-30

Supplementary Problems

5.20 Find the workstation transformation that maps the normalized device screen onto a physical device whose x extent is 0 to 199 and y extent is 0 to 639 where the origin is located at the (a) lower left corner and (b) upper left corner of the device.

5.21 Show that for a viewing transformation, $s_x = s_y$ if and only if $a_w = a_v$, where a_w is the aspect ratio of the window and a_v the aspect ratio of the viewport.

5.22 Find the normalization transformation which uses a circle of radius five units and center $(1, 1)$ as a window and a circle of radius $\frac{1}{2}$ and center $(\frac{1}{2}, \frac{1}{2})$ as a viewport.

5.23 Describe how clipping a line against a circular window (or viewport) might proceed. Refer to Fig. 5-31.

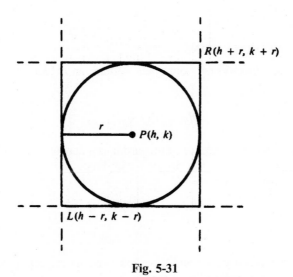

Fig. 5-31

5.24 Use the Sutherland–Hodgman algorithm to clip the line segment joining $P_1(-1, 2)$ to $P_2(6, 4)$ against the rotated window in Prob. 5.5.

CHAPTER 6

Three-Dimensional Transformations

Manipulation, viewing, and construction of three-dimensional graphic images requires the use of three-dimensional geometric and coordinate transformations. These transformations are formed by composing the basic transformations of translation, scaling, and rotation. Each of these transformations can be represented as a matrix transformation. This permits more complex transformations to be built up by use of matrix multiplication or concatenation.

As with two-dimensional transformations, two complementary points of view are adopted: either the object is manipulated directly through the use of geometric transformations, or the object remains stationary and the viewer's coordinate system is changed by using coordinate transformations. In addition, the construction of complex objects and scenes is facilitated by the use of instance transformations. The concepts and transformations introduced here are direct generalizations of those introduced in Chap. 4 for two-dimensional transformations.

6.1 GEOMETRIC TRANSFORMATIONS

With respect to some three-dimensional coordinate system, an object *Obj* is considered as a set of points:

$$Obj = \{P(x, y, z)\}$$

If the object is moved to a new position, we can regard it as a new object *Obj'*, all of whose coordinate points $P'(x', y', z')$ can be obtained from the original coordinate points $P(x, y, z)$ of *Obj* through the application of a geometric transformation.

Translation

An object is displaced a given distance and direction from its original position. The direction and displacement of the translation is prescribed by a vector

$$\mathbf{V} = a\mathbf{I} + b\mathbf{J} + c\mathbf{K}$$

The new coordinates of a translated point can be calculated by using the transformation

$$T_v: \begin{cases} x' = x + a \\ y' = y + b \\ z' = z + c \end{cases}$$

(see Fig. 6-1). In order to represent this transformation as a matrix transformation, we need to use homogeneous coordinates (App. 2). The required homogeneous matrix transformation can then be expressed as

$$\begin{pmatrix} x' \\ y' \\ z' \\ 1 \end{pmatrix} = \begin{pmatrix} 1 & 0 & 0 & a \\ 0 & 1 & 0 & b \\ 0 & 0 & 1 & c \\ 0 & 0 & 0 & 1 \end{pmatrix} \begin{pmatrix} x \\ y \\ z \\ 1 \end{pmatrix}$$

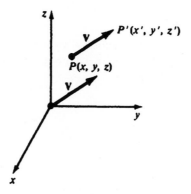

Fig. 6-1

Scaling

The process of scaling changes the dimensions of an object. The scale factor s determines whether the scaling is a magnification, $s > 1$, or a reduction, $s < 1$.

Scaling with respect to the origin, where the origin remains fixed, is effected by the transformation

$$S_{s_x,s_y,s_z}: \begin{cases} x' = s_x \cdot x \\ y' = s_y \cdot y \\ z' = s_z \cdot z \end{cases}$$

In matrix form this is

$$S_{s_x,s_y,s_z} = \begin{pmatrix} s_x & 0 & 0 \\ 0 & s_y & 0 \\ 0 & 0 & s_z \end{pmatrix}$$

Rotation

Rotation in three dimensions is considerably more complex than rotation in two dimensions. In two dimensions, a rotation is prescribed by an angle of rotation θ and a center of rotation P. Three-dimensional rotations require the prescriptioin of an angle of rotation and an axis of rotation. The *canonical* rotations are defined when one of the positive x, y, or z coordinate axes is chosen as the axis of rotation. Then the construction of the rotation transformation proceeds just like that of a rotation in two dimensions about the origin (see Fig. 6-2).

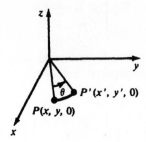

Fig. 6-2

Rotation about the z Axis

From Chap. 4 we know that

$$R_{\theta,\mathbf{K}}: \begin{cases} x' = x\cos\theta - y\sin\theta \\ y' = x\sin\theta + y\cos\theta \\ z' = z \end{cases}$$

Rotation about the y Axis

An analogous derivation leads to

$$R_{\theta,\mathbf{J}}: \begin{cases} x' = x\cos\theta + z\sin\theta \\ y' = y \\ z' = -x\sin\theta + z\cos\theta \end{cases}$$

Rotation about the x Axis

Similarly:

$$R_{\theta,\mathbf{I}}: \begin{cases} x' = x \\ y' = y\cos\theta - z\sin\theta \\ z' = y\sin\theta + z\cos\theta \end{cases}$$

Note that the direction of a positive angle of rotation is chosen in accordance to the right-hand rule with respect to the axis of rotation (App. 2).

The corresponding matrix transformations are

$$R_{\theta,\mathbf{K}} = \begin{pmatrix} \cos\theta & -\sin\theta & 0 \\ \sin\theta & \cos\theta & 0 \\ 0 & 0 & 1 \end{pmatrix}$$

$$R_{\theta,\mathbf{J}} = \begin{pmatrix} \cos\theta & 0 & \sin\theta \\ 0 & 1 & 0 \\ -\sin\theta & 0 & \cos\theta \end{pmatrix}$$

$$R_{\theta,\mathbf{I}} = \begin{pmatrix} 1 & 0 & 0 \\ 0 & \cos\theta & -\sin\theta \\ 0 & \sin\theta & \cos\theta \end{pmatrix}$$

The general use of rotation about an axis L can be built up from these canonical rotations using matrix multiplication (Prob. 6.3).

6.2   COORDINATE TRANSFORMATIONS

We can also achieve the effects of translation, scaling, and rotation by moving the observer who views the object and by keeping the object stationary. This type of transformation is called a *coordinate*

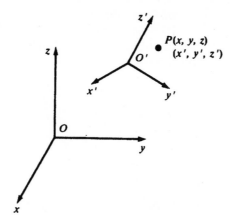

Fig. 6-3

transformation. We first attach a coordinate system to the observer and then move the observer and the attached coordinate system. Next, we recalculate the coordinates of the observed object with respect to this new observer coordinate system. The new coordinate values will be exactly the same as if the observer had remained stationary and the object had moved, corresponding to a geometric transformation (see Fig. 6-3).

If the displacement of the observer coordinate system to a new position is prescribed by a vector $\mathbf{V} = a\mathbf{I} + b\mathbf{J} + c\mathbf{K}$, a point $P(x, y, z)$ in the original coordinate system has coordinates $P(x', y', z')$ in the new coordinate system, and

$$\bar{T}_\mathbf{v}: \begin{cases} x' = x - a \\ y' = y - b \\ z' = z - c \end{cases}$$

The derivation of this transformation is completely analogous to that of the two-dimensional transformation (see Chap. 4).

Similar derivations hold for coordinate scaling and coordinate rotation transformations.

As in the two-dimensional case, we summarize the relationships between the matrix forms of the coordinate transformations and the geometeric transformations:

	Coordinate Transformations	**Geometric Transformations**
Translation	$\bar{T}_\mathrm{V}$	$T_{-\mathrm{V}}$
Rotation	$\bar{R}_\theta$	$R_{-\theta}$
Scaling	$\bar{S}_{s_x, s_y, s_z}$	$S_{1/s_x, 1/s_y, 1/s_z}$

Inverse geometric and coordinate transformations are constructed by performing the reverse operation. Thus, for coordinate transformations (and similarly for geometric transformations):

$$\bar{T}_\mathbf{v}^{-1} = \bar{T}_{-\mathbf{v}} \qquad \bar{R}_\theta^{-1} = \bar{R}_{-\theta} \qquad \bar{S}_{s_x, s_y, s_z}^{-1} = \bar{S}_{1/x_x, 1/s_y, 1/s_z}$$

6.3   COMPOSITE TRANSFORMATIONS

More complex geometric and coordinate transformations are formed through the process of *composition of functions*. For matrix functions, however, the process of composition is equivalent to matrix multiplication or concatenation. In Probs. 6.2, 6.3, 6.5, and 6.13, the following transformations are constructed:

1. $A_{V,N}$ = aligning a vector V with a vector N.
2. $R_{\theta,L}$ = rotation about an axis L. This axis is prescribed by giving a direction vector V and a point P through which the axis passes.
3. $S_{s_x,s_y,s_z,P}$ = scaling with respect to an arbitrary point P.

In order to build these more complex transformations through matrix concatenation, we must be able to multiply translation matrices with rotation and scaling matrices. This necessitates the use of homogeneous coordinates and 4×4 matrices (App. 2). The standard 3×3 matrices of rotation and scaling can be represented as 4×4 homogeneous matrices by adjoining an extra row and column as follows:

$$\begin{pmatrix} a & b & c & 0 \\ d & e & f & 0 \\ g & h & i & 0 \\ 0 & 0 & 0 & 1 \end{pmatrix}$$

These transformations are then applied to points $P(x, y, z)$ having the homogeneous form:

$$\begin{pmatrix} x \\ y \\ z \\ 1 \end{pmatrix}$$

EXAMPLE 1.   The matrix of rotation about the y axis has the homogeneous 4×4 form:

$$R_{\theta,J} = \begin{pmatrix} \cos \theta & 0 & \sin \theta & 0 \\ 0 & 1 & 0 & 0 \\ -\sin \theta & 0 & \cos \theta & 0 \\ 0 & 0 & 0 & 1 \end{pmatrix}$$

6.4   INSTANCE TRANSFORMATIONS

If an object is created and described in coordinates with respect to its own object coordinate space, we can place an instance or copy of it within a larger scene that is described in an independent coordinate space by the use of three-dimensional coordinate transformations. In this case, the transformations are referred to as *instance transformations*. The concepts and construction of three-dimensional instance transformations and the composite transformation matrix are completely analogous to the two-dimensional cases described in Chap. 4.

Solved Problems

6.1   Define *tilting* as a rotation about the x axis followed by a rotation about the y axis: (*a*) find the tilting matrix; (*b*) does the order of performing the rotation matter?

SOLUTION

(a)   We can find the required transformation T by composing (concatenating) two rotation matrices:

$$T = R_{\theta_y, \mathbf{J}} \cdot R_{\theta_x, \mathbf{I}}$$

$$= \begin{pmatrix} \cos\theta_y & 0 & \sin\theta_y & 0 \\ 0 & 1 & 0 & 0 \\ -\sin\theta_y & 0 & \cos\theta_y & 0 \\ 0 & 0 & 0 & 1 \end{pmatrix} \begin{pmatrix} 1 & 0 & 0 & 0 \\ 0 & \cos\theta_x & -\sin\theta_x & 0 \\ 0 & \sin\theta_x & \cos\theta_x & 0 \\ 0 & 0 & 0 & 1 \end{pmatrix}$$

$$= \begin{pmatrix} \cos\theta_y & \sin\theta_y\sin\theta_x & \sin\theta_y\cos\theta_x & 0 \\ 0 & \cos\theta_x & -\sin\theta_x & 0 \\ -\sin\theta_y & \cos\theta_y\sin\theta_x & \cos\theta_y\cos\theta_x & 0 \\ 0 & 0 & 0 & 1 \end{pmatrix}$$

(b)   We multiply $R_{\theta_x, \mathbf{I}} \cdot R_{\theta_y, \mathbf{J}}$ to obtain the matrix

$$\begin{pmatrix} \cos\theta_y & 0 & \sin\theta_y & 0 \\ \sin\theta_x\sin\theta_y & \cos\theta_x & -\sin\theta_x\cos\theta_y & 0 \\ -\cos\theta_x\sin\theta_y & \sin\theta_x & \cos\theta_x\cos\theta_y & 0 \\ 0 & 0 & 0 & 1 \end{pmatrix}$$

This is not the same matrix as in part a; thus the order of rotation matters.

6.2   Find a transformation $A_\mathbf{V}$ which aligns a given vector $\mathbf{V}$ with the vector $\mathbf{K}$ along the positive z axis.

SOLUTION

See Fig. 6-4(a). Let $\mathbf{V} = a\mathbf{I} + b\mathbf{J} + c\mathbf{K}$. We perform the alignment through the following sequence of transformations [Figs. 6-4(b) and 6-4(c)]:

1.   Rotate about the x axis by an angle θ_1 so that V rotates into the upper half of the xz plane (as the vector $\mathbf{V}_1$).
2.   Rotate the vector $\mathbf{V}_1$ about the y axis by an angle $-\theta_2$ so that $\mathbf{V}_1$ rotates to the positive z axis (as the vector $\mathbf{V}_2$).

Implementing step 1 from Fig. 6-4(b), we observe that the required angle of rotation θ_1 can be found by looking at the projection of $\mathbf{V}$ onto the yz plane. (We assume that b and c are not both zero.) From triangle $OP'B$:

$$\sin\theta_1 = \frac{b}{\sqrt{b^2 + c^2}} \qquad \cos\theta_1 = \frac{c}{\sqrt{b^2 + c^2}}$$

The required rotation is

$$R_{\theta_1, \mathbf{I}} = \begin{pmatrix} 1 & 0 & 0 & 0 \\ 0 & \dfrac{c}{\sqrt{b^2 + c^2}} & -\dfrac{b}{\sqrt{b^2 + c^2}} & 0 \\ 0 & \dfrac{b}{\sqrt{b^2 + c^2}} & \dfrac{c}{\sqrt{b^2 + c^2}} & 0 \\ 0 & 0 & 0 & 1 \end{pmatrix}$$

Applying this rotation to the vector $\mathbf{V}$ produces the vector $\mathbf{V}_1$ with the components $(a, 0, \sqrt{b^2 + c^2})$.

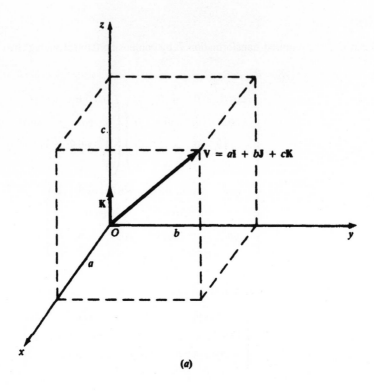

(a)

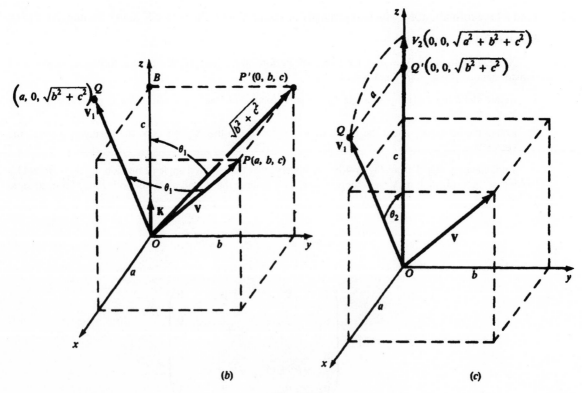

(b)   (c)

Fig. 6-4

Implementing step 2 from Fig. 6-4(c), we see that a rotation of $-\theta_2$ degrees is required, and so from triangle OQQ':

$$\sin(-\theta_2) = -\sin\theta_2 = -\frac{a}{\sqrt{a^2+b^2+c^2}} \qquad \text{and} \qquad \cos(-\theta_2) = \cos\theta_2 = \frac{\sqrt{b^2+c^2}}{\sqrt{a^2+b^2+c^2}}$$

Then

$$R_{-\theta_2,\mathbf{J}} = \begin{pmatrix} \dfrac{\sqrt{b^2+c^2}}{\sqrt{a^2+b^2+c^2}} & 0 & \dfrac{-a}{\sqrt{a^2+b^2+c^2}} & 0 \\ 0 & 1 & 0 & 0 \\ \dfrac{a}{\sqrt{a^2+b^2+c^2}} & 0 & \dfrac{\sqrt{b^2+c^2}}{\sqrt{a^2+b^2+c^2}} & 0 \\ 0 & 0 & 0 & 1 \end{pmatrix}$$

Since $|\mathbf{V}| = \sqrt{a^2+b^2+c^2}$, and introducing the notation $\lambda = \sqrt{b^2+c^2}$, we find

$$A_\mathbf{V} = R_{-\theta_2,\mathbf{J}} \cdot R_{\theta_1,\mathbf{I}}$$

$$= \begin{pmatrix} \dfrac{\lambda}{|\mathbf{V}|} & \dfrac{-ab}{\lambda|\mathbf{V}|} & \dfrac{-ac}{\lambda|\mathbf{V}|} & 0 \\ 0 & \dfrac{c}{\lambda} & \dfrac{-b}{\lambda} & 0 \\ \dfrac{a}{|\mathbf{V}|} & \dfrac{b}{|\mathbf{V}|} & \dfrac{c}{|\mathbf{V}|} & 0 \\ 0 & 0 & 0 & 1 \end{pmatrix}$$

If both b and c are zero, then $\mathbf{V} = a\mathbf{I}$, and so $\lambda = 0$. In this case, only a $\pm 90°$ rotation about the y axis is required. So if $\lambda = 0$, it follows that

$$A_\mathbf{v} = R_{-\theta_2,\mathbf{J}} = \begin{pmatrix} 0 & 0 & \dfrac{-a}{|a|} & 0 \\ 0 & 1 & 0 & 0 \\ \dfrac{a}{|a|} & 0 & 0 & 0 \\ 0 & 0 & 0 & 1 \end{pmatrix}$$

In the same manner we calculate the inverse transformation that aligns the vector $\mathbf{K}$ with the vector $\mathbf{V}$:

$$A_\mathbf{v}^{-1} = (R_{-\theta_2,\mathbf{J}} \cdot R_{\theta_1,\mathbf{I}})^{-1} = R_{\theta_1,\mathbf{I}}^{-1} \cdot R_{-\theta_2,\mathbf{J}}^{-1} = R_{-\theta_1,\mathbf{I}} \cdot R_{\theta_2,\mathbf{J}}$$

$$= \begin{pmatrix} \dfrac{\lambda}{|\mathbf{V}|} & 0 & \dfrac{a}{|\mathbf{V}|} & 0 \\ \dfrac{-ab}{\lambda|\mathbf{V}|} & \dfrac{c}{\lambda} & \dfrac{b}{|\mathbf{V}|} & 0 \\ \dfrac{-ac}{\lambda|\mathbf{V}|} & -\dfrac{b}{\lambda} & \dfrac{c}{|\mathbf{V}|} & 0 \\ 0 & 0 & 0 & 1 \end{pmatrix}$$

6.3   Let an axis of rotation L be specified by a direction vector $\mathbf{V}$ and a location point P. Find the transformation for a rotation of $\theta°$ about L. Refer to Fig. 6-5.

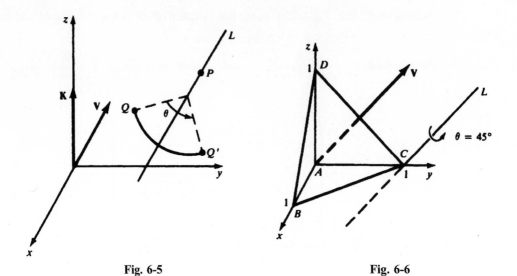

Fig. 6-5   Fig. 6-6

SOLUTION

We can find the required transformation by the following steps:

1. Translate P to the origin.
2. Align $\mathbf{V}$ with the vector $\mathbf{K}$.
3. Rotate by $\theta°$ about $\mathbf{K}$.
4. Reverse steps 2 and 1.

So

$$R_{\theta,L} = T_{-P}^{-1} \cdot A_{\mathbf{V}}^{-1} \cdot R_{\theta,\mathbf{K}} \cdot A_{\mathbf{V}} \cdot T_{-P}$$

Here, $A_{\mathbf{v}}$ is the transformation described in Prob. 6.2.

6.4 The pyramid defined by the coordinates $A(0, 0, 0)$, $B(1, 0, 0)$, $C(0, 1, 0)$, and $D(0, 0, 1)$ is rotated $45°$ about the line L that has the direction $\mathbf{V} = \mathbf{J} + \mathbf{K}$ and passing through point $C(0, 1, 0)$ (Fig. 6-6). Find the coordinates of the rotated figure.

SOLUTION

From Prob. 6.3, the rotation matrix $R_{\theta,L}$ can be found by concatenating the matrices

$$R_{\theta,L} = T_{-P}^{-1} \cdot A_{\mathbf{V}}^{-1} \cdot R_{\theta,\mathbf{K}} \cdot A_{\mathbf{V}} \cdot T_{-P}$$

With $P = (0, 1, 0)$, then

$$T_{-P} = \begin{pmatrix} 1 & 0 & 0 & 0 \\ 0 & 1 & 0 & -1 \\ 0 & 0 & 1 & 0 \\ 0 & 0 & 0 & 1 \end{pmatrix}$$

Now $\mathbf{V} = \mathbf{J} + \mathbf{K}$. So from Prob. 6.2, with $a = 0$, $b = 1$, $c = 1$, we find $\lambda = \sqrt{2}$, $|\mathbf{V}| = \sqrt{2}$, and

$$A_{\mathbf{V}} = \begin{pmatrix} 1 & 0 & 0 & 0 \\ 0 & \dfrac{1}{\sqrt{2}} & \dfrac{-1}{\sqrt{2}} & 0 \\ 0 & \dfrac{1}{\sqrt{2}} & \dfrac{1}{\sqrt{2}} & 0 \\ 0 & 0 & 0 & 1 \end{pmatrix} \qquad A_{\mathbf{V}}^{-1} = \begin{pmatrix} 1 & 0 & 0 & 0 \\ 0 & \dfrac{1}{\sqrt{2}} & \dfrac{1}{\sqrt{2}} & 0 \\ 0 & \dfrac{-1}{\sqrt{2}} & \dfrac{1}{\sqrt{2}} & 0 \\ 0 & 0 & 0 & 1 \end{pmatrix}$$

Also

$$R_{45°, \mathbf{K}} = \begin{pmatrix} \dfrac{1}{\sqrt{2}} & \dfrac{-1}{\sqrt{2}} & 0 & 0 \\ \dfrac{1}{\sqrt{2}} & \dfrac{1}{\sqrt{2}} & 0 & 0 \\ 0 & 0 & 1 & 0 \\ 0 & 0 & 0 & 1 \end{pmatrix} \qquad T_{-P}^{-1} = \begin{pmatrix} 1 & 0 & 0 & 0 \\ 0 & 1 & 0 & 1 \\ 0 & 0 & 1 & 0 \\ 0 & 0 & 0 & 1 \end{pmatrix}$$

Then

$$R_{\theta, L} = \begin{pmatrix} \dfrac{\sqrt{2}}{2} & -\dfrac{1}{2} & \dfrac{1}{2} & \dfrac{1}{2} \\ \dfrac{1}{2} & \dfrac{2+\sqrt{2}}{4} & \dfrac{2-\sqrt{2}}{4} & \dfrac{2-\sqrt{2}}{4} \\ -\dfrac{1}{2} & \dfrac{2-\sqrt{2}}{4} & \dfrac{2+\sqrt{2}}{4} & \dfrac{\sqrt{2}-2}{4} \\ 0 & 0 & 0 & 1 \end{pmatrix}$$

To find the coordinates of the rotated figure, we apply the rotation matrix $R_{\theta, L}$ to the matrix of homogeneous coordinates of the vertices A, B, C, and D:

$$C = (ABCD) = \begin{pmatrix} 0 & 1 & 0 & 0 \\ 0 & 0 & 1 & 0 \\ 0 & 0 & 0 & 1 \\ 1 & 1 & 1 & 1 \end{pmatrix}$$

So

$$R_{\theta, L} \cdot C = \begin{pmatrix} \dfrac{1}{2} & \dfrac{1+\sqrt{2}}{2} & 0 & 1 \\ \dfrac{2-\sqrt{2}}{4} & \dfrac{4-\sqrt{2}}{4} & 1 & \dfrac{2-\sqrt{2}}{2} \\ \dfrac{\sqrt{2}-2}{4} & \dfrac{\sqrt{2}-4}{4} & 0 & \dfrac{\sqrt{2}}{2} \\ 1 & 1 & 1 & 1 \end{pmatrix}$$

The rotated coordinates are (Fig. 6-7)

$$A' = \left(\frac{1}{2}, \frac{2-\sqrt{2}}{4}, \frac{\sqrt{2}-2}{4} \right) \qquad C' = (0, 1, 0)$$

$$B' = \left(\frac{1+\sqrt{2}}{2}, \frac{4-\sqrt{2}}{4}, \frac{\sqrt{2}-4}{4} \right) \qquad D' = \left(1, \frac{2-\sqrt{2}}{2}, \frac{\sqrt{2}}{2} \right)$$

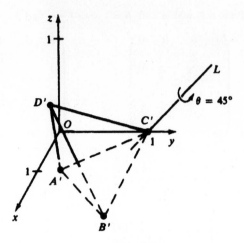

Fig. 6-7

6.5   Find a transformation $A_{V,N}$ which aligns a vector $\mathbf{V}$ with a vector $\mathbf{N}$.

SOLUTION

   We form the transformation in two steps. First, align $\mathbf{V}$ with vector $\mathbf{K}$, and second, align vector $\mathbf{K}$ with vector $\mathbf{N}$. So from Prob. 6.2,

$$\mathbf{A_{V,N}} = \mathbf{A_N^{-1}} \cdot \mathbf{A_V}$$

Referring to Prob. 6.12, we could also get $\mathbf{A_{V,N}}$ by rotating $\mathbf{V}$ towards $\mathbf{N}$ about the axis $\mathbf{V} \times \mathbf{N}$.

6.6   Find the transformation for mirror reflection with respect to the xy plane.

SOLUTION

   From Fig. 6-8, it is easy to see that the reflection of $P(x, y, z)$ is $P'(x, y, -z)$. The transformation that performs this reflection is

$$M = \begin{pmatrix} 1 & 0 & 0 \\ 0 & 1 & 0 \\ 0 & 0 & -1 \end{pmatrix}$$

6.7   Find the transformation for mirror reflection with respect to a given plane. Refer to Fig. 6-9.

SOLUTION

   Let the plane of reflection be specified by a normal vector $\mathbf{N}$ and a reference point $P_0(x_0, y_0, z_0)$. To reduce the reflection to a mirror reflection with respect to the xy plane:

1.   Translate P_0 to the origin:
2.   Align the normal vector $\mathbf{N}$ with the vector $\mathbf{K}$ normal to the xy plane.
3.   Perform the mirror reflection in the xy plane (Prob. 6.6).
4.   Reverse steps 1 and 2.

So, with translation vector $\mathbf{V} = -x_0\mathbf{I} - y_0\mathbf{J} - z_0\mathbf{K}$

$$M_{N,P_0} = T_V^{-1} \cdot A_N^{-1} \cdot M \cdot A_N \cdot T_V$$

Here, A_N is the alignment matrix defined in Prob. 6.2. So if the vector $\mathbf{N} = n_1\mathbf{I} + n_2\mathbf{J} + n_3\mathbf{K}$, then from Prob.

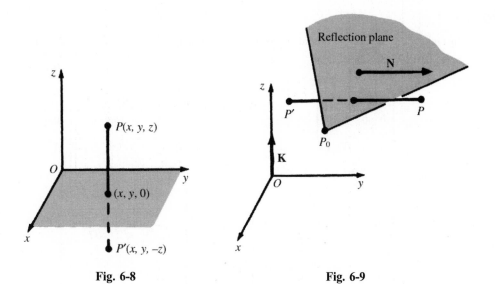

Fig. 6-8   **Fig. 6-9**

6.2, with $|\mathbf{N}| = \sqrt{n_1^2 + n_2^2 + n_3^2}$ and $\lambda = \sqrt{n_2^2 + n_3^2}$, we find

$$
A_{\mathbf{N}} =
\begin{pmatrix}
\dfrac{\lambda}{|\mathbf{N}|} & \dfrac{-n_1 n_2}{\lambda |\mathbf{N}|} & \dfrac{-n_1 n_3}{\lambda |\mathbf{N}|} & 0 \\[2mm]
0 & \dfrac{n_3}{\lambda} & \dfrac{-n_2}{\lambda} & 0 \\[2mm]
\dfrac{n_1}{|\mathbf{N}|} & \dfrac{n_2}{|\mathbf{N}|} & \dfrac{n_3}{|\mathbf{N}|} & 0 \\[2mm]
0 & 0 & 0 & 1
\end{pmatrix}
\quad \text{and} \quad
A_{\mathbf{N}}^{-1} =
\begin{pmatrix}
\dfrac{\lambda}{|\mathbf{N}|} & 0 & \dfrac{n_1}{|\mathbf{N}|} & 0 \\[2mm]
\dfrac{-n_1 n_2}{\lambda |\mathbf{N}|} & \dfrac{n_3}{\lambda} & \dfrac{n_2}{|\mathbf{N}|} & 0 \\[2mm]
\dfrac{-n_1 n_3}{\lambda |\mathbf{N}|} & \dfrac{-n_2}{\lambda} & \dfrac{n_3}{|\mathbf{N}|} & 0 \\[2mm]
0 & 0 & 0 & 1
\end{pmatrix}
$$

In addition

$$
T_{\mathbf{V}} =
\begin{pmatrix}
1 & 0 & 0 & -x_0 \\
0 & 1 & 0 & -y_0 \\
0 & 0 & 1 & -z_0 \\
0 & 0 & 0 & 1
\end{pmatrix}
\quad \text{and} \quad
T_{\mathbf{V}}^{-1} =
\begin{pmatrix}
1 & 0 & 0 & x_0 \\
0 & 1 & 0 & y_0 \\
0 & 0 & 1 & z_0 \\
0 & 0 & 0 & 1
\end{pmatrix}
$$

Finally, from Prob. 6.6, the homogeneous form of M is

$$
M =
\begin{pmatrix}
1 & 0 & 0 & 0 \\
0 & 1 & 0 & 0 \\
0 & 0 & -1 & 0 \\
0 & 0 & 0 & 1
\end{pmatrix}
$$

6.8 Find the matrix for mirror reflection with respect to the plane passing through the origin and having a normal vector whose direction is $\mathbf{N} = \mathbf{I} + \mathbf{J} + \mathbf{K}$.

SOLUTION

From Prob. 6.7, with $P_0(0, 0, 0)$ and $\mathbf{N} = \mathbf{I} + \mathbf{J} + \mathbf{K}$, we find $|\mathbf{N}| = \sqrt{3}$ and $\lambda = \sqrt{2}$. Then

$$T_{\mathbf{V}} = \begin{pmatrix} 1 & 0 & 0 & 0 \\ 0 & 1 & 0 & 0 \\ 0 & 0 & 1 & 0 \\ 0 & 0 & 0 & 1 \end{pmatrix} \quad (\mathbf{V} = 0\mathbf{I} + 0\mathbf{J} + 0\mathbf{K}) \quad T_{\mathbf{V}}^{-1} = \begin{pmatrix} 1 & 0 & 0 & 0 \\ 0 & 1 & 0 & 0 \\ 0 & 0 & 1 & 0 \\ 0 & 0 & 0 & 1 \end{pmatrix}$$

$$A_{\mathbf{N}} = \begin{pmatrix} \dfrac{\sqrt{2}}{\sqrt{3}} & \dfrac{-1}{\sqrt{2}\sqrt{3}} & \dfrac{-1}{\sqrt{2}\sqrt{3}} & 0 \\ 0 & \dfrac{1}{\sqrt{2}} & \dfrac{-1}{\sqrt{2}} & 0 \\ \dfrac{1}{\sqrt{3}} & \dfrac{1}{\sqrt{3}} & \dfrac{1}{\sqrt{3}} & 0 \\ 0 & 0 & 0 & 1 \end{pmatrix} \quad A_{\mathbf{N}}^{-1} = \begin{pmatrix} \dfrac{\sqrt{2}}{\sqrt{3}} & 0 & \dfrac{1}{\sqrt{3}} & 0 \\ \dfrac{-1}{\sqrt{2}\sqrt{3}} & \dfrac{1}{\sqrt{2}} & \dfrac{1}{\sqrt{3}} & 0 \\ \dfrac{-1}{\sqrt{2}\sqrt{3}} & \dfrac{-1}{\sqrt{2}} & \dfrac{-1}{\sqrt{3}} & 0 \\ 0 & 0 & 0 & 1 \end{pmatrix}$$

and

$$M = \begin{pmatrix} 1 & 0 & 0 & 0 \\ 0 & 1 & 0 & 0 \\ 0 & 0 & -1 & 0 \\ 0 & 0 & 0 & 1 \end{pmatrix}$$

The reflection matrix is

$$M_{\mathbf{N},O} = T_{\mathbf{V}}^{-1} \cdot A_{\mathbf{N}}^{-1} \cdot M \cdot A_{\mathbf{N}} \cdot T_{\mathbf{V}}$$

$$= \begin{pmatrix} \frac{1}{3} & -\frac{2}{3} & -\frac{2}{3} & 0 \\ -\frac{2}{3} & \frac{1}{3} & -\frac{2}{3} & 0 \\ -\frac{2}{3} & -\frac{2}{3} & \frac{1}{3} & 0 \\ 0 & 0 & 0 & 1 \end{pmatrix}$$

Supplementary Problems

6.9 Align the vector $\mathbf{V} = \mathbf{I} + \mathbf{J} + \mathbf{K}$ with the vector $\mathbf{K}$.

6.10 Find a transformation which aligns the vector $\mathbf{V} = \mathbf{I} + \mathbf{J} + \mathbf{K}$ with the vector $\mathbf{N} = 2\mathbf{I} - \mathbf{J} - \mathbf{K}$.

6.11 Show that the alignment transformation satisfies the relation $A_{\mathbf{V}}^{-1} = A_{\mathbf{V}}^T$.

6.12 Show that the alignment transformation $A_{\mathbf{V},\mathbf{N}}$ is equivalent to a rotation of $\theta°$ about an axis having the direction of the vector $\mathbf{V} \times \mathbf{N}$ and passing through the origin (see Fig. 6-10). Here θ is the angle between vectors $\mathbf{V}$ and $\mathbf{N}$.

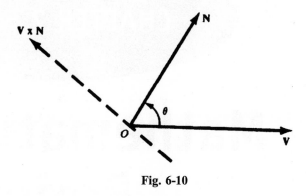

Fig. 6-10

6.13   How can scaling with respect to a point $P_0(x_0, y_0, z_0)$ be defined in terms of scaling with respect to the origin?

CHAPTER 7

Mathematics of Projection

Needless to say, there are fundamental differences between the true three-dimensional world and its pictorial description. For centuries, artists, engineers, designers, drafters, and architects have tried to come to terms with the difficulties and constraints imposed by the problem of representing a three-dimensional object or scene in a two-dimensional medium—the problem of *projection*. The implementers of a computer graphics system face the same challenge.

Projection can be defined as a mapping of point $P(x, y, z)$ onto its image $P'(x', y', z')$ in the *projection plane* or *view plane*, which constitutes the display surface (see Fig. 7-1). The mapping is determined by a projection line called the *projector* that passes through P and intersects the view plane. The intersection point is P'.

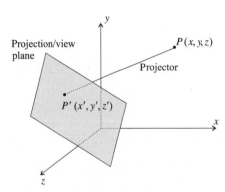

Fig. 7-1   The problem of projection.

The result of projecting an object is dependent on the spatial relationship among the projectors that project the points on the object, and the spatial relationship between the projectors and the view plane (see Sec. 7.1). An important observation is that projection preserves lines. That is, the line joining the projected images of the endpoints of the original line is the same as the projection of that line.

The two basic methods of projection—*perspective* and *parallel*—are designed to solve the basic but mutually exclusive problems of pictorial representation: showing an object as it appears and preserving its

128

true size and shape. We characterize each method and introduce the mathematical description of the projection process in Sec. 7.2 and 7.3, respectively.

7.1 TAXONOMY OF PROJECTION

We can construct different projections according to the view that is desired.

Figure 7-2 provides a taxonomy of the families of perspective and parallel projections. Some projections have names—cavalier, cabinet, isometric, and so on. Other projections qualify the main type of projection—one principal vanishing-point perspective, and so forth.

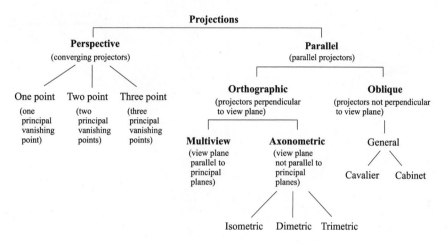

Fig. 7-2   Taxonomy of projection.

7.2 PERSPECTIVE PROJECTION

Basic Principles

The techniques of perspective projection are generalizations of the principles used by artists in preparing perspective drawings of three-dimensional objects and scenes. The eye of the artist is placed at the *center of projection*, and the canvas, or more precisely the plane containing the canvas, becomes the view plane. An image point is determined by a projector that goes from an object point to the center of projection (see Fig. 7-3).

Perspective drawings are characterized by perspective foreshortening and vanishing points. *Perspective foreshortening* is the illusion that objects and lengths appear smaller as their distance from the center of projection increases. The illusion that certain sets of parallel lines appear to meet at a point is another feature of perspective drawings. These points are called *vanishing points*. *Principal vanishing points* are formed by the apparent intersection of lines parallel to one of the three principal x, y, or z axes. The number of principal vanishing points is determined by the number of principal axes intersected by the view plane (Prop. 7.7).

Mathematical Description of a Perspective Projection

A perspective transformation is determined by prescribing a center of projection and a view plane. The view plane is determined by its *view reference point* R_0 and *view plane normal N*. The *object point P* is located in world coordinates at (x, y, z). The problem is to determine the *image point* coordinates $P'(x', y', z')$ (see Fig. 7-3).

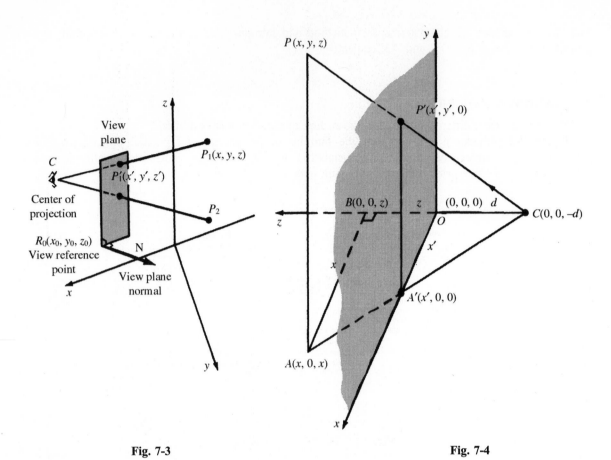

Fig. 7-3   Fig. 7-4

EXAMPLE 1.   The standard perspective projection is shown in Fig. 7-4. Here, the view plane is the xy plane, and the center of projection is taken as the point $C(0, 0, -d)$ on the negative z axis.

Using similar triangles ABC and $A'OC$, we find

$$x' = \frac{d \cdot x}{z + d} \qquad y' = \frac{d \cdot y}{z + d} \qquad z' = 0$$

The perspective transformation between object and image point is nonlinear and so cannot be represented as a 3×3 matrix transformation. However, if we use homogeneous coordinates, the perspective transformation can be represented as a 4×4 matrix:

$$\begin{pmatrix} x' \\ y' \\ z' \\ 1 \end{pmatrix} = \begin{pmatrix} d \cdot x \\ d \cdot y \\ 0 \\ z + d \end{pmatrix} = \begin{pmatrix} d & 0 & 0 & 0 \\ 0 & d & 0 & 0 \\ 0 & 0 & 0 & 0 \\ 0 & 0 & 1 & d \end{pmatrix} \begin{pmatrix} x \\ y \\ z \\ 1 \end{pmatrix}$$

The general form of a perspective transformation is developed in Prob. 7.5.

Perspective Anomalies

The process of constructing a perspective view introduces certain anomalies which enhance realism in terms of depth cues but also distort actual sizes and shapes.

1. *Perspective foreshortening.* The farther an object is from the center of projection, the smaller it appears (i.e. its projected size becomes smaller). Refer to Fig. 7-5.

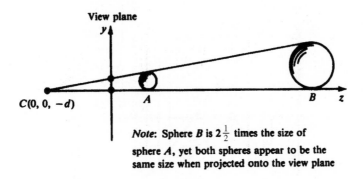

Note: Sphere B is $2\frac{1}{2}$ times the size of sphere A, yet both spheres appear to be the same size when projected onto the view plane

Fig. 7-5

2. *Vanishing points.* Projections of lines that are not parallel to the view plane (i.e. lines that are not perpendicular to the view plane normal) appear to meet at some point on the view plane. A common manifestation of this anomaly is the illusion that railroad tracks meet at a point on the horizon.

EXAMPLE 2.   For the standard perspective projection, the projections L_1' and L_2' of parallel lines L_1 and L_2 having the direction of the vector **K** appear to meet at the origin (Prob. 7.8). Refer to Fig. 7-6.

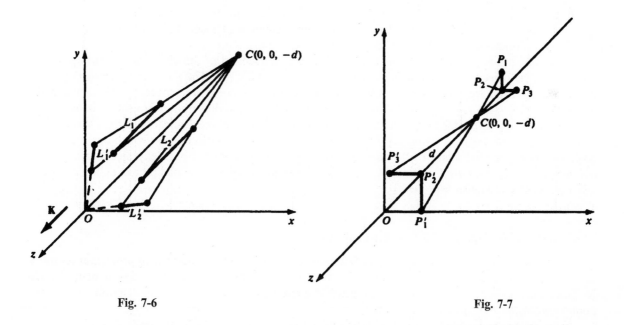

Fig. 7-6   Fig. 7-7

3. *View confusion.* Objects behind the center of projection are projected upside down and backward onto the view plane. Refer to Fig. 7-7.

4. *Topological distortion.* Consider the plane that passes through the center of projection and is parallel to the view plane. The points of this plane are projected to infinity by the perspective transformation. In particular, a finite line segment joining a point which lies in front of the viewer to a point in back of the viewer is actually projected to a broken line of infinite extent (Prob. 7.2) (see Fig. 7-8).

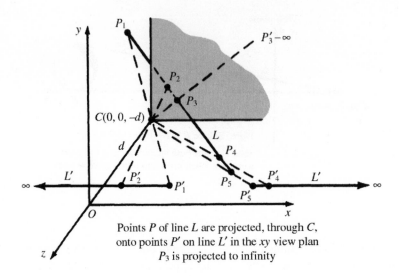

Points P of line L are projected, through C,
onto points P' on line L' in the xy view plan
P_3 is projected to infinity

Fig. 7-8

7.3   PARALLEL PROJECTION

Basic Principles

Parallel projection methods are used by drafters and engineers to create working drawings of an object which preserves its scale and shape. The complete representation of these details often requires two or more views (projections) of the object onto different view planes.

In parallel projection, image points are found as the intersection of the view plane with a projector drawn from the object point and having a fixed direction (see Fig. 7-9). The *direction of projection* is the prescribed direction for all projectors. *Orthographic projections* are characterized by the fact that the direction of projection is perpendicular to the view plane. When the direction of projection is parallel to any of the principal axes, this produces the front, top, and side views of mechanical drawings (also referred to as *multiview drawings*). *Axonometric projections* are orthographic projections in which the direction of projection is not parallel to any of the three principal axes. Nonorthograhic parallel projections are called *oblique parallel projections*. Further subcategories of these main types of parallel projection are described in the problems. (See also Fig. 7-10.)

Mathematical Description of a Parallel Projection

A *parallel projective transformation* is determined by prescribing a *direction of projection vector* $\mathbf{V}$ and a view plane. The view plane is specified by its view plane reference point R_0, and view plane normal $\mathbf{N}$. The object point P is located at (x, y, z) in world coordinates. The problem is to determine the image point coordinates $P'(x', y', z')$. See Fig. 7-9.

If the projection vector $\mathbf{V}$ has the direction of the view plane normal $\mathbf{N}$, the projection is said to be *orthographic*. Otherwise it is called *oblique* (see Fig. 7-10).

Some common subcategories of orthographic projections are:

1. *Isometric*—the direction of projection makes equal angles with all of the three principal axes (Prob. 7.14).

2. *Dimetric*—the direction of projection makes equal angles with exactly two of the principal axes (Prob. 7.15).

3. *Trimetric*—the direction of projection makes unequal angles with the three principal axes.

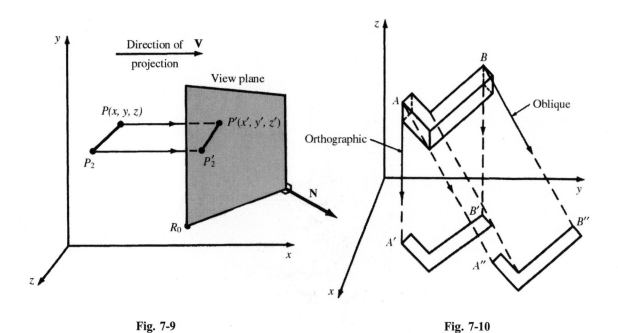

Fig. 7-9   Fig. 7-10

Some common subcategories of oblique projections are:

1. *Cavalier*—the direction of projection is chosen so that there is no foreshortening of lines perpendicular to the xy plane (Prob. 7.13).

2. *Cabinet*—the direction of projection is chosen so that lines perpendicular to the xy planes are foreshortened by half their lengths (Prob. 7.13).

EXAMPLE 3.   For orthographic projection onto the xy plane, from Fig. 7-11 it is easy to see that

$$Par_{\mathbf{K}}: \begin{cases} x' = x \\ y' = y \\ z' = 0 \end{cases}$$

The matrix form of $Par_{\mathbf{K}}$ is

$$Par_{\mathbf{K}} = \begin{pmatrix} 1 & 0 & 0 & 0 \\ 0 & 1 & 0 & 0 \\ 0 & 0 & 0 & 0 \\ 0 & 0 & 0 & 1 \end{pmatrix}$$

The general parallel projective transformation is derived in Prob. 7.11.

Solved Problems

7.1   The unit cube (Fig. 7-12) is projected onto the xy plane. Note the position of the x, y, and z axes. Draw the projected image using the standard perspective transformation with (a) $d = 1$ and (b) $d = 10$, where d is distance from the view plane.

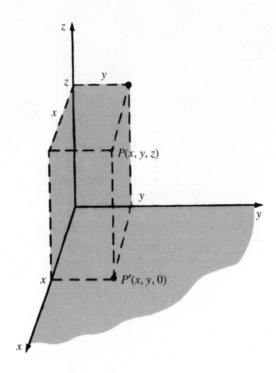

Fig. 7-11

SOLUTION

We represent the unit cube in terms of the homogeneous coordinates of its vertices:

$$\mathbf{V} = (ABCDEFGH) = \begin{pmatrix} 0 & 1 & 1 & 0 & 0 & 0 & 1 & 1 \\ 0 & 0 & 1 & 1 & 1 & 0 & 0 & 1 \\ 0 & 0 & 0 & 0 & 1 & 1 & 1 & 1 \\ 1 & 1 & 1 & 1 & 1 & 1 & 1 & 1 \end{pmatrix}$$

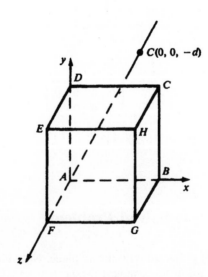

Fig. 7-12

From Example 1 the standard perspective matrix is

$$Per_{\mathbf{K}} = \begin{pmatrix} d & 0 & 0 & 0 \\ 0 & d & 0 & 0 \\ 0 & 0 & 0 & 0 \\ 0 & 0 & 1 & d \end{pmatrix}$$

(a) With $d = 1$, the projected coordinates are found by applying the matrix $Per_{\mathbf{K}}$ to the matrix of coordinates **V**. Then

$$Per_{\mathbf{K}} \cdot \mathbf{V} = \begin{pmatrix} 0 & 1 & 1 & 0 & 0 & 0 & 1 & 1 \\ 0 & 0 & 1 & 1 & 1 & 0 & 0 & 1 \\ 0 & 0 & 0 & 0 & 0 & 0 & 0 & 0 \\ 1 & 1 & 1 & 1 & 2 & 2 & 2 & 2 \end{pmatrix}$$

If these homogeneous coordinates are changed to three-dimensional coordinates, the projected image has coordinates:

$$A' = (0, 0, 0) \qquad E' = (0, \tfrac{1}{2}, 0)$$
$$B' = (1, 0, 0) \qquad F' = (0, 0, 0)$$
$$C' = (1, 1, 0) \qquad G' = (\tfrac{1}{2}, 0, 0)$$
$$D' = (0, 1, 0) \qquad H' = (\tfrac{1}{2}, \tfrac{1}{2}, 0)$$

We draw the projected image by preserving the edge connections of the original object (see Fig. 7-13). [Note the vanishing point at $(0, 0, 0)$.]

(b) With $d = 10$, the perspective matrix is

$$Per_{\mathbf{K}} = \begin{pmatrix} 10 & 0 & 0 & 0 \\ 0 & 10 & 0 & 0 \\ 0 & 0 & 0 & 0 \\ 0 & 0 & 1 & 10 \end{pmatrix}$$

Then

$$Per_{\mathbf{K}} \cdot \mathbf{V} = \begin{pmatrix} 0 & 10 & 10 & 0 & 0 & 0 & 10 & 10 \\ 0 & 0 & 10 & 10 & 10 & 0 & 0 & 10 \\ 0 & 0 & 0 & 0 & 0 & 0 & 0 & 0 \\ 10 & 10 & 10 & 10 & 11 & 11 & 11 & 11 \end{pmatrix}$$

is the matrix image coordinates in homogeneous form. The projected image coordinates are then

$$A' = (0, 0, 0) \qquad E' = (0, \tfrac{10}{11}, 0)$$
$$B' = (1, 0, 0) \qquad F' = (0, 0, 0)$$
$$C' = (1, 1, 0) \qquad G' = (\tfrac{10}{11}, 0, 0)$$
$$D' = (0, 1, 0) \qquad H' = (\tfrac{10}{11}, \tfrac{10}{11}, 0)$$

Note the different perspectives of the face $E'F'G'H'$ in Figs. 7-13 and 7-14. [To a viewer standing at the center of projection $(0, 0, -d)$, this face is the back face of the unit cube.]

7.2   Under the standard perspective transformation $Per_{\mathbf{K}}$, what is the projected image of (a) a point in the plane $z = -d$ and (b) the line segment joining $P_1(-1, 1, -2d)$ to $P_2(2, -2, 0)$? (See Fig. 7-15.)

SOLUTION

(a) The plane $z = -d$ is the plane parallel to the xy view plane and located at the center of projection $C(0, 0, -d)$. If $P(x, y, -d)$ is any point in this plane, the line of projection $\overline{CP}$ does not intersect the xy view plane. We then say that P is projected out to infinity (∞).

(b) The line $\overline{P_1 P_2}$ passes through the plane $z = -d$. Writing the equation of the line (App. 2), we have

$$x = -1 + 3t \qquad y = 1 - 3t \qquad z = -2d + 2dt$$

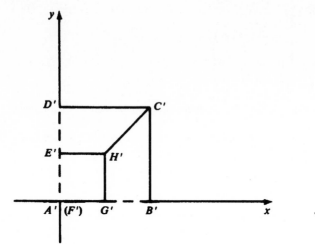

Fig. 7-13   Fig. 7-14

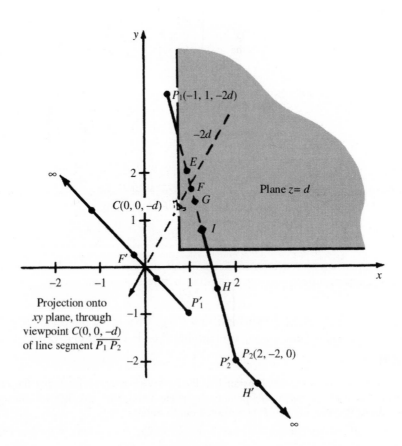

Fig. 7-15

We see that at $t = \frac{1}{2}$: $x = \frac{1}{2}$, $y = -\frac{1}{2}$, and $z = -d$. These are the coordinates of the intersection point I.
We now describe the perspective projection of this line segment.
Applying the standard projection to the equation of the line, we find

$$\begin{pmatrix} d & 0 & 0 & 0 \\ 0 & d & 0 & 0 \\ 0 & 0 & 0 & 0 \\ 0 & 0 & 1 & d \end{pmatrix} \begin{pmatrix} -1 + 3t \\ 1 - 3t \\ -2d + 2dt \\ 1 \end{pmatrix} = \begin{pmatrix} -d + 3dt \\ d - 3dt \\ 0 \\ -d + 2dt \end{pmatrix}$$

Changing from homogeneous to three-dimensional coordinates, the equations of the projected line segment are

$$x = \frac{-d + 3dt}{-d + 2dt} = \frac{-1 + 3t}{-1 + 2t} \qquad y = \frac{d - 3dt}{-d + 2dt} = \frac{1 - 3t}{-1 + 2t} \qquad z = 0$$

(In App. 1, Prob. A1.12, it is shown that this is the equation of a line.) When $t = 0$, then $x = 1$ and $y = -1$. These are the coordinates of the projection P_1' of point P_1. When $t = 1$, it follows that $x = 2$ and $y = -2$ (the coordinates of the projection P_2' of point P_2). However, when $t = \frac{1}{2}$, the denominator is 0. Thus this line segment "passes" through the point at infinity in joining $P_1'(1, -1)$ to $P_2'(2, -2)$. In other words, when a line segment joining endpoints P_1 and P_2 passes through the plane containing the center of projection and which is parallel to the view plane, the projection of this line segment is *not* the simple line segment joining the projected endpoints P_1' and P_2'. (See also Prob. A1.13 in App. 1.)

7.3 Using the origin as the center of projection, derive the perspective transformation onto the plane passing through the point $R_0(x_0, y_0, z_0)$ and having the normal vector $\mathbf{N} = n_1 I + n_2 J + n_3 K$.

SOLUTION

Let $P(x, y, z)$ be projected onto $P'(x', y', z')$. From Fig. 7-16, the vectors $\overline{PO}$ and $\overline{P'O}$ have the same direction. Thus there is a number α so that $\overline{P'O} = \alpha \overline{PO}$. Comparing components, we have

$$x' = \alpha x \qquad y' = \alpha y \qquad z' = \alpha z$$

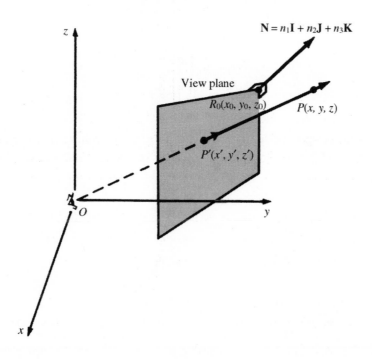

Fig. 7-16

We now find the value of α. Since any point $P'(x', y', z')$ lying on the plane satisfies the equation (App. 2)

$$n_1 x' + n_2 y' + n_3 z' = d_0$$

(where $d_0 = n_1 x_0 + n_2 y_0 + n_3 z_0$), substitution of $x' = \alpha x$, $y' = \alpha y$, and $z' = \alpha z$ into this equation gives

$$\alpha = \frac{d_0}{n_1 x + n_2 y + n_3 z}$$

This projection transformation cannot be represented as a 3×3 matrix transformation. However, by using the homogeneous coordinate representation for three-dimensional points, we can write the projection transformation as a 4×4 matrix:

$$Per_{\mathbf{N}, R_0} = \begin{pmatrix} d_0 & 0 & 0 & 0 \\ 0 & d_0 & 0 & 0 \\ 0 & 0 & d_0 & 0 \\ n_1 & n_2 & n_3 & 0 \end{pmatrix}$$

Application of this matrix to the homogeneous representation $P(x, y, z, 1)$ of points P gives $P'(d_0 x, d_0 y, d_0 z, n_1 x + n_2 y + n_3 z)$, which is the homogeneous representation of $P'(x', y', z')$ found above.

7.4   Find the perspective projection onto the view plane $z = d$ where the center of projection is the origin $(0, 0, 0)$.

SOLUTION

The plane $z = d$ is parallel to the xy plane (and d units away from it). Thus the view plane normal vector $\mathbf{N}$ is the same as the normal vector $\mathbf{K}$ to the xy plane, that is, $\mathbf{N} = \mathbf{K}$. Choosing the view reference point as $R_0(0, 0, d)$, then from Prob. 7.3, we identify the parameters

$$\mathbf{N}(n_1, n_2, n_3) = (0, 0, 1) \qquad R_0(x_0, y_0, z_0) = (0, 0, d)$$

So

$$d_0 = n_1 x_0 + n_2 y_0 + n_3 z_0 = d$$

and then the projection matrix is

$$Per_{\mathbf{K}, R_0} = \begin{pmatrix} d & 0 & 0 & 0 \\ 0 & d & 0 & 0 \\ 0 & 0 & d & 0 \\ 0 & 0 & 1 & 0 \end{pmatrix}$$

7.5   Derive the general perspective transformation onto a plane with reference point $R_0(x_0, y_0, z_0)$, normal vector $\mathbf{N} = n_1 \mathbf{I} + n_2 \mathbf{J} + n_3 \mathbf{K}$, and using $C(a, b, c)$ as the center of projection. Refer to Fig. 7-17.

SOLUTION

As in Prob. 7.3, we can conclude that the vectors $\overline{PC}$ and $\overline{P'C}$ satisfy (see Fig. 7-17) $\overline{P'C} = \alpha \overline{PC}$. Then

$$x' = \alpha(x - a) + a \qquad y' = \alpha(y - b) + b \qquad z' = \alpha(z - c) + c$$

Also, we find (by using the equation of the view plane) that

$$\alpha = \frac{d}{n_1(x - a) + n_2(y - b) + n_3(z - c)}$$

[i.e. $P'(x', y', z')$ is on the view plane and thus satisfies the view plane equation $n_1(x' - x_0) + n_2(y' - y_0) + n_3(z' - z_0) = 0$]. Here, $d = (n_1 x_0 + n_2 y_0 + n_3 z_0) - (n_1 a + n_2 b + n_3 c)$.

From App. 2, Prob. A2.13, d is proportional to the distance D from the view plane to the center of projection, that is, $d = \pm |\mathbf{N}| D$.

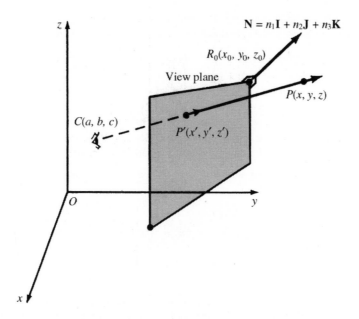

Fig. 7-17

To find the homogeneous coordinate matrix representation, it is easiest to proceed as follows:

1. Translate so that the center of projection C lies at the origin. Now $R'_0 = (x_0 - a, y_0 - b, z_0 - c)$ becomes the reference point of the translated plane (the normal vector is unchanged by translation).

2. Project onto the translated plane using the origin as the center of projection by constructing the transformation Per_{N,R'_0} (Prob. 7.3).

3. Translate back.

Introducing the intermediate quantities

$$d_0 = n_1 x_0 + n_2 y_0 + n_3 z_0 \qquad \text{and} \qquad d_1 = n_1 a + n_2 b + n_3 c$$

we obtain $d = d_0 - d_1$, and so $Per_{N,R_0,C} = T_C \cdot Per_{N,R'_0} \cdot T_{-C}$. Then with R'_0 used as the reference point in constructing the projection P_{N,R'_0},

$$
Per_{N,R_0,C} = \begin{pmatrix} 1 & 0 & 0 & a \\ 0 & 1 & 0 & b \\ 0 & 0 & 1 & c \\ 0 & 0 & 0 & 1 \end{pmatrix} \begin{pmatrix} d & 0 & 0 & 0 \\ 0 & d & 0 & 0 \\ 0 & 0 & d & 0 \\ n_1 & n_2 & n_3 & 0 \end{pmatrix} \begin{pmatrix} 1 & 0 & 0 & -a \\ 0 & 1 & 0 & -b \\ 0 & 0 & 1 & -c \\ 0 & 0 & 0 & 1 \end{pmatrix}
$$

$$
= \begin{pmatrix} d + an_1 & an_2 & an_3 & -ad_0 \\ bn_1 & d + bn_2 & bn_3 & -bd_0 \\ cn_1 & cn_2 & d + cn_3 & -cd_0 \\ n_1 & n_2 & n_3 & -d_1 \end{pmatrix}
$$

7.6   Find the (*a*) vanishing points for a given perspective transformation in the direction given by a vector **U** and (*b*) principal vanishing points.

SOLUTION

(*a*) The family of (parallel) lines having the direction of $\mathbf{U} = u_1 \mathbf{I} + u_2 \mathbf{J} + u_3 \mathbf{K}$ can be written in parametric form as

$$x = u_1 t + p \qquad y = u_2 t + q \qquad z = u_3 t + r$$

where $P(p, q, r)$ is any point (see App. 2). Application of the perspective transformation (Prob. 7.5) to the homogeneous point $(x, y, z, 1)$ produces the result (x', y', z', h), where

$$x' = (d + an_1)(u_1t + p) + an_2(u_2t + q) + an_3(u_3t + r) - ad_0$$
$$y' = bn_1(u_1t + p) + (d + bn_2)(u_2t + q) + bn_3(u_3t + r) - bd_0$$
$$z' = cn_1(u_1t + p) + cn_2(u_2t + q) + (d + cn_3)(u_3t + r) - cd_0$$
$$h = n_1(u_1t + p) + n_2(u_2t + q) + n_3(u_3t + r) - d_1$$

The vanishing point corresponds to the infinite point obtained when $t = \infty$. So after dividing x', y', and z' by h, we let $t \to \infty$ to find the coordinates of the vanishing point:

$$x_u = \frac{(d + an_1)u_1 + an_2u_2 + an_3u_3}{k} = a + \frac{du_1}{k}$$

(Here, $k = \mathbf{N} \cdot \mathbf{U} = n_1u_1 + n_2u_2 + n_3u_3$.)

$$y_u = \frac{bn_1u_1 + (d + bn_2)u_2 + bn_3u_3}{k} = b + \frac{du_2}{k}$$
$$z_u = \frac{cn_1u_1 + cn_2u_2 + (d + cn_3)u_3}{k} = c + \frac{du_3}{k}$$

This point lies on the line passing through the center of projection and parallel to the vector $\mathbf{U}$ (see Fig. 7-18). Note that $k = 0$ only when $\mathbf{U}$ is parallel to the projection plane, in which case there is no vanishing point.

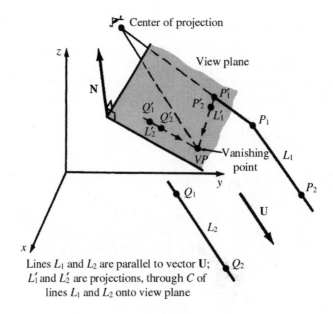

Lines L_1 and L_2 are parallel to vector $\mathbf{U}$;
L_1' and L_2' are projections, through C of
lines L_1 and L_2 onto view plane

Fig. 7-18

(b) The principal vanishing points P_1, P_2, and P_3 correspond to the vector directions $\mathbf{I}$, $\mathbf{J}$, and $\mathbf{K}$. In these cases

$$P_1: \begin{cases} x_1 = a + \dfrac{d}{n_1} \\ y_1 = b \\ z_1 = c \end{cases} \qquad P_2: \begin{cases} x_2 = a \\ y_2 = b + \dfrac{d}{n_2} \\ z_2 = c \end{cases} \qquad P_3: \begin{cases} x_3 = a \\ y_3 = b \\ z_3 = c + \dfrac{d}{n_3} \end{cases}$$

(Recall from Prob. 7.5 that a, b, c are the coordinates of the center of projection. Also, n_1, n_2, n_3 are the components of the view plane normal vector and d is proportional to the distance D from the view plane to the center of projection.) (*Note*: If any of the components of the normal vector are zero, say, $n_1 = 0$, then $k = \mathbf{N} \cdot \mathbf{I} = 0$, and there is no principal vanishing point in the $\mathbf{I}$ direction.)

7.7   Describe the (*a*) one-principal-vanishing-point perspective, (*b*) two-principal-vanishing-point perspective, and (*c*) three-principal-vanishing-point perspective.

SOLUTION

(*a*)   The one-principal-vanishing-point perspective occurs when the projection plane is perpendicular to one of the principal axes (x, y, or z). Assume that it is the z axis. In this case the view plane normal vector $\mathbf{N}$ is the vector $\mathbf{K}$, and from prob. 7.6, the principal vanishing point is

$$P_3: \begin{cases} x_3 = a \\ y_3 = b \\ z_3 = c + \dfrac{d}{n_3} \end{cases}$$

(*b*)   The two-principal-vanishing-point projection occurs when the projection plane intersects exactly two of the principal axes. Refer to Fig. 7-19, which is a perspective drawing with two principal vanishing points. In the case where the projection plane intersects the x and y axes, for example, the normal vector satisfies the relatioinship $\mathbf{N} \cdot \mathbf{K} = 0$ or $n_3 = 0$, and so the principal vanishing points are

$$P_1: \begin{cases} x_1 = a + \dfrac{d}{n_1} \\ y_1 = b \\ z_1 = c \end{cases} \qquad P_2: \begin{cases} x_2 = a \\ y_2 = b + \dfrac{d}{n_2} \\ z_2 = c \end{cases}$$

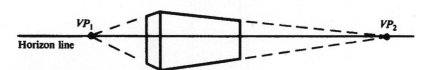

Fig. 7-19

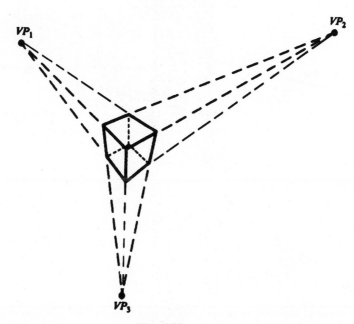

Fig. 7-20

(c)   The three-vanishing-point perspective projection occurs when the projection plane intersects all three of the principal axes—x, y, and z axes. Refer to Fig. 7-20, which is a perspective drawing with three principal vanishing points. In this case, the principal vanishing points are points P_1, P_2, and P_3 from Prob. 7.6(b).

7.8   What are the principal vanishing points for the standard perspective transforamtion?

SOLUTION

In this case, the view plane normal $\mathbf{N}$ is the vector $\mathbf{K}$. From Prob. 7.6(b), since $\mathbf{N} \cdot \mathbf{I} = 0$ and $\mathbf{N} \cdot \mathbf{J} = 0$, there are no vanishing points in the directions $\mathbf{I}$ and $\mathbf{J}$. On the other hand, $\mathbf{N} \cdot \mathbf{K} = \mathbf{K} \cdot \mathbf{K} = 1$. Thus there is only one principal vanishing point, and it is in the $\mathbf{K}$ direction. From Prob. 7.7(a), the coordinates of the principal vanishing point VP in the $\mathbf{K}$ direction are

$$x = a = 0 \qquad y = b = 0 \qquad z = -d + \frac{d}{1} = 0$$

So $VP = (0, 0, 0)$ is the principal vanishing point.

7.9   An artist constructs a two-vanishing-point perspective by locating the vanishing points VP_1 and VP_2 on a given horizon line in the view plane. The horizon line is located by its height h above the ground (Fig. 7-21). Construct the corresponding perspective projection transformation for the cube shown in Fig. 7-21.

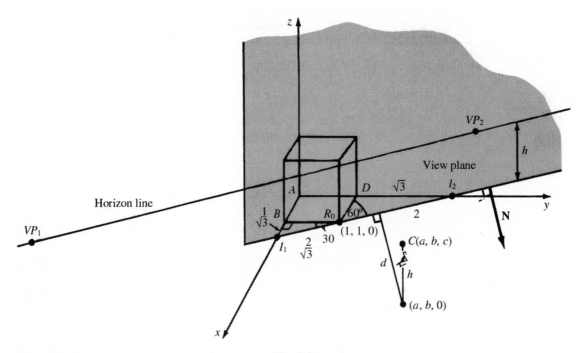

Fig. 7-21

SOLUTION

A two-principal-vanishing-point perspective must intersect two axes, say, x and y. We locate the view plane at the point $R_0(1, 1, 0)$ so that it makes angles of $30°$ and $60°$ with the corresponding faces of the cube (see Fig. 7-21). In this plane we locate the horizon line a given height h above the "ground" (the xy plane).

The vanishing points VP_1 and VP_2 are located on this horizon line. To construct the perspective transformation, we need to find the normal vector $\mathbf{N} = n_1\mathbf{I} + n_2\mathbf{J} + n_3\mathbf{K}$ of the view plane, the coordinates $C(a, b, c)$ of the center of projection, and the view parameters d_0, d_1, and d (Prob. 7.5). To calculate the coordinates of the vanishing points, we first find the equation of the horizon line. Let I_1 and I_2 be the points of intersection of the view plane and the x and y axes. The horizon line is parallel to the line $\overline{I_1 I_2}$ and lies h units above it.

From triangles $I_1 B R_0$ and $I_2 D R_0$, we find

$$I_1 = \left(1 + \frac{1}{\sqrt{3}}, 0, 0\right) = \left(\frac{1+\sqrt{3}}{\sqrt{3}}, 0, 0\right) \quad \text{and} \quad I_2 = (0, 1 + \sqrt{3}, 0)$$

The equation of the line through I_1 and I_2 (App. 2) is

$$x = \left(\frac{1+\sqrt{3}}{\sqrt{3}}\right) - \left(\frac{1+\sqrt{3}}{\sqrt{3}}\right)t \qquad y = (1+\sqrt{3})t \qquad z = 0$$

This line lies in the view plane. So if the equation of the horizon line is then taken to be a line parallel to this line and h units above it, the horizon line is guaranteed to be in the view plane. The equation of the horizon line is then

$$x = \left(\frac{1+\sqrt{3}}{\sqrt{3}}\right)(1-t) \qquad y = (1+\sqrt{3})t \qquad z = h$$

The vanishing points VP_1 and VP_2 are chosen to lie on the horizon line. So VP_1 has coordinates of the form

$$VP_1 = \left[\left(\frac{1+\sqrt{3}}{\sqrt{3}}\right)(1-t_1), (1+\sqrt{3})t_1, h\right] \quad \text{and} \quad VP_2 = \left[\left(\frac{1+\sqrt{3}}{\sqrt{3}}\right)(1-t_2), (1+\sqrt{3})t_2, h\right]$$

(Here, t_1 and t_2 are chosen so as to place the vanishing points at the desired locations.)

To find the normal vector $\mathbf{N}$ and the center of projection C, we use the equations in Prob. 7.6, part (b) for locating the vanishing points of a given perspective transformation. So

$$a + \frac{d}{n_1} = \left(\frac{1+\sqrt{3}}{\sqrt{3}}\right)(1-t_1) \qquad \text{and} \qquad a = \left(\frac{1+\sqrt{3}}{\sqrt{3}}\right)(1-t_2)$$

and

$$b = (1+\sqrt{3})t_1 \qquad \text{and} \qquad b + \frac{d}{n_2} = (1+\sqrt{3})t_2 \qquad \text{and} \qquad c = h$$

Using the values

$$a = \left(\frac{1+\sqrt{3}}{\sqrt{3}}\right)(1-t_2) \qquad b = (1+\sqrt{3})t_1 \qquad c = h$$

and then substituting, we find

$$\frac{d}{n_1} = \left(\frac{1+\sqrt{3}}{\sqrt{3}}\right)(t_2 - t_1) \tag{7.1}$$

and

$$\frac{d}{n_2} = (1+\sqrt{3})(t_2 - t_1) \tag{7.2}$$

Since the plane does not intersect the z axis, then $\mathbf{N} \cdot \mathbf{K} = 0$, or using components: $n_3 = 0$. Finally, we choose the normal vector $\mathbf{N}$ to be of unit length:

$$|\mathbf{N}| = \sqrt{n_1^2 + n_2^2 + n_3^2} = \sqrt{n_1^2 + n_2^2} = 1$$

From equations (7.1) and (7.2)

$$n_1 = \frac{d\sqrt{3}}{(1+\sqrt{3})(t_2 - t_1)} \qquad n_2 = \frac{d}{(1+\sqrt{3})(t_2 - t_1)}$$

So

$$|\mathbf{N}| = \sqrt{\frac{(d\sqrt{3})^2}{(1+\sqrt{3})^2(t_2-t_1)^2} + \frac{d^2}{(1+\sqrt{3})^2(t_2-t_1)^2}} = 1$$

or

$$\frac{2d}{(1+\sqrt{3})(t_2-t_1)} = 1 \qquad \text{and so} \qquad d = \frac{1+\sqrt{3}}{2}(t_2-t_1)$$

Also

$$n_1 = \frac{\sqrt{3}[(1+\sqrt{3})/2]}{1+\sqrt{3}} = \frac{\sqrt{3}}{2} \qquad \text{and} \qquad n_2 = \frac{(1+\sqrt{3})/2}{1+\sqrt{3}} = \frac{1}{2}$$

Finally, we have

$$d_1 = n_1 a + n_2 b + n_3 c = \left(\frac{\sqrt{3}}{2}\frac{1+\sqrt{3}}{\sqrt{3}}\right)(1-t_2) + \frac{1}{2}(1+\sqrt{3})t_1 = \frac{1+\sqrt{3}}{2}[1-(t_2-t_1)]$$

and

$$d_0 = d + d_1 = \frac{1+\sqrt{3}}{2}$$

From Prob. 7.5, the perspective transformation matrix is then

$$Per_{N,R_0,C} = \frac{1+\sqrt{3}}{2}\begin{pmatrix} 1-t_1 & \frac{1}{\sqrt{3}}(1-t_2) & 0 & -\left(\frac{1+\sqrt{3}}{\sqrt{3}}\right)(1-t_2) \\ \sqrt{3}t_1 & t_2 & 0 & -(1+\sqrt{3})t_1 \\ \frac{\sqrt{3}h}{1+\sqrt{3}} & \frac{h}{1+\sqrt{3}} & t_2-t_1 & -h \\ \frac{\sqrt{3}}{1+\sqrt{3}} & \frac{1}{1+\sqrt{3}} & 0 & -[1-(t_2-t_1)] \end{pmatrix}$$

In Chap. 8, Prob. 8.2, it is shown how to convert the transformed image of the cube into x, y coordinates for viewing.

7.10 Derive the equations of parallel projection onto the xy plane in the direction of projection $\mathbf{V} = a\mathbf{I} + b\mathbf{J} + c\mathbf{K}$.

SOLUTION

From Fig. 7-22 we see that the vectors $\mathbf{V}$ and $\overline{PP'}$ have the same direction. This means that $\overline{PP'} = k\mathbf{V}$. Comparing components, we see that

$$x' - x = ka \qquad y' - y = kb \qquad z' - z = kc$$

So

$$k = -\frac{z}{c} \qquad x' = x - \frac{a}{c}z \qquad \text{and} \qquad y' = y - \frac{b}{c}z$$

In 3×3 matrix form, this is

$$Par_{\mathbf{V}} = \begin{pmatrix} 1 & 0 & -\dfrac{a}{c} \\ 0 & 1 & -\dfrac{b}{c} \\ 0 & 0 & 0 \end{pmatrix}$$

and so $P' = Par_{\mathbf{V}} \cdot P$.

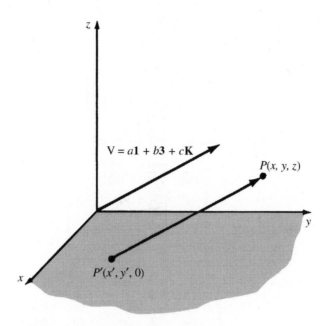

Fig. 7-22

7.11 Derive the general equation of parallel projection onto a given view plane in the direction of a given projector **V** (see Fig. 7-23).

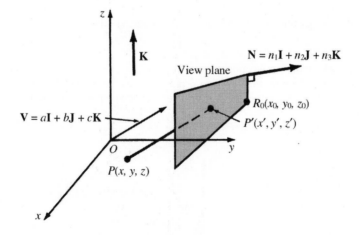

Fig. 7-23

SOLUTION

We reduce the problem to parallel projection onto the xy plane in the direction of the projector $\mathbf{V} = a\mathbf{I} + b\mathbf{J} + c\mathbf{K}$ by means of these steps:

1. Translate the view reference point R_0 of the view plane to the origin using the translation matrix T_{-R_0}.

2. Perform an alignment transformation $A_\mathbf{N}$ so that the view normal vector **N** of the view plane points in the direction **K** of the normal to the xy plane. The direction of projection vector **V** is transformed to a new vector $\mathbf{V}' = A_\mathbf{N}\mathbf{V}$.

3. Project onto the xy plane using $Par_{\mathbf{V}'}$.

4. Perform the inverse of steps 2 and 1. So finally $Par_{\mathbf{V},\mathbf{N},R_0} = T_{-R_0}^{-1} \cdot A_{\mathbf{N}}^{-1} \cdot Par_{\mathbf{V}'} \cdot A_{\mathbf{N}} \cdot T_{-R_0}$. From what we learned in Chap. 6, we know that

$$T_{-R_0} = \begin{pmatrix} 1 & 0 & 0 & -x_0 \\ 0 & 1 & 0 & -y_0 \\ 0 & 0 & 1 & -z_0 \\ 0 & 0 & 0 & 1 \end{pmatrix}$$

and further from Chap. 6, Prob. 6.2, where $\lambda = \sqrt{n_2^2 + n_3^2}$ and $\lambda \neq 0$, that

$$A_{\mathbf{N}} = \begin{pmatrix} \dfrac{\lambda}{|\mathbf{N}|} & \dfrac{-n_1 n_2}{\lambda|\mathbf{N}|} & \dfrac{-n_1 n_3}{\lambda|\mathbf{N}|} & 0 \\ 0 & \dfrac{n_3}{\lambda} & \dfrac{-n_2}{\lambda} & 0 \\ \dfrac{n_1}{|\mathbf{N}|} & \dfrac{n_2}{|\mathbf{N}|} & \dfrac{n_3}{|\mathbf{N}|} & 0 \\ 0 & 0 & 0 & 1 \end{pmatrix}$$

Then, after multiplying, we find

$$Par_{\mathbf{V},\mathbf{N},R_0} = \begin{pmatrix} d_1 - an_1 & -an_2 & -an_3 & ad_0 \\ -bn_1 & d_1 - bn_2 & -bn_3 & bd_0 \\ -cn_1 & -cn_2 & d_1 - cn_3 & cd_0 \\ 0 & 0 & 0 & d_1 \end{pmatrix}$$

Here $d_0 = n_1 x_0 + n_2 y_0 + n_3 z_0$ and $d_1 = n_1 a + n_2 b + n_3 c$. An alternative and much easier method to derive this matrix is by finding the intersection of the projector through P with the equation of the view plane (see Prob. A2.14).

7.12 Find the general form of an oblique projection onto the xy plane.

SOLUTION

Refer to Fig. 7-24. Oblique projections (to the xy plane) can be specified by a number f and an angle θ. The number f prescribes the ratio that any line L perpendicular to the xy plane will be foreshortened after projection. The angle θ is the angle that the projection of any line perpendicular to the xy plane makes with the (positive) x axis.

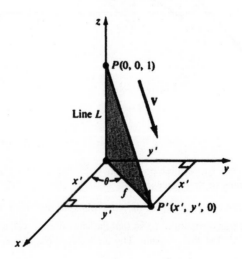

Fig. 7-24

To determine the projection transformation, we need to find the direction vector $\mathbf{V}$. From Fig. 7-24, with line L of length 1, we see that the vector $\overline{P'P}$ has the same direction as $\mathbf{V}$. We choose $\mathbf{V}$ to be this vector:

$$\mathbf{V} = \overline{P'P} = x'\mathbf{I} + y'\mathbf{J} - \mathbf{K} \qquad (=a\mathbf{I} + b\mathbf{J} + c\mathbf{K})$$

From Fig. 7-24 we find $a = x' = f\cos\theta$, $b = y' = f\sin\theta$, and $c = -1$.
    From Prob. 7.10, the required transformation is

$$Par_{\mathbf{V}} = \begin{pmatrix} 1 & 0 & f\cos\theta & 0 \\ 0 & 1 & f\sin\theta & 0 \\ 0 & 0 & 0 & 0 \\ 0 & 0 & 0 & 1 \end{pmatrix}$$

7.13 Find the transformation for (a) cavalier with $\theta = 45°$ and (b) cabinet projections with $\theta = 30°$. (c) Draw the projection of the unit cube for each transformation.

SOLUTION

(a)   A cavalier projection is an oblique projection where there is no foreshortening of lines perpendicular to the xy plane. From Prob. 7.12 we then see that $f = 1$. With $\theta = 45°$, we have

$$Par_{\mathbf{V}_1} = \begin{pmatrix} 1 & 0 & \dfrac{\sqrt{2}}{2} & 0 \\ 0 & 1 & \dfrac{\sqrt{2}}{2} & 0 \\ 0 & 0 & 0 & 0 \\ 0 & 0 & 0 & 1 \end{pmatrix}$$

(b)   A cabinet projection is an oblique projection with $f = \frac{1}{2}$. With $\theta = 30°$, we have

$$Par_{\mathbf{V}_2} = \begin{pmatrix} 1 & 0 & \dfrac{\sqrt{3}}{4} & 0 \\ 0 & 1 & \dfrac{1}{4} & 0 \\ 0 & 0 & 0 & 0 \\ 0 & 0 & 0 & 1 \end{pmatrix}$$

To construct the projections, we represent the vertices of the unit cube by a matrix whose columns are homogeneous coordinates of the vertices (see Prob. 7.1):

$$V = (ABCDEFGH) = \begin{pmatrix} 0 & 1 & 1 & 0 & 0 & 0 & 1 & 1 \\ 0 & 0 & 1 & 1 & 1 & 0 & 0 & 1 \\ 0 & 0 & 0 & 0 & 1 & 1 & 1 & 1 \\ 1 & 1 & 1 & 1 & 1 & 1 & 1 & 1 \end{pmatrix}$$

(c)   To draw the cavalier projection, we find the image coordinates by applying the transformation matrix $Par_{\mathbf{V}_1}$ to the coordinate matrix $\mathbf{V}$:

$$Par_{\mathbf{V}_1} \cdot V = \begin{pmatrix} 0 & 1 & 1 & 0 & \dfrac{\sqrt{2}}{2} & \dfrac{\sqrt{2}}{2} & 1+\dfrac{\sqrt{2}}{2} & 1+\dfrac{\sqrt{2}}{2} \\ 0 & 0 & 1 & 1 & 1+\dfrac{\sqrt{2}}{2} & \dfrac{\sqrt{2}}{2} & \dfrac{\sqrt{2}}{2} & 1+\dfrac{\sqrt{2}}{2} \\ 0 & 0 & 0 & 0 & 0 & 0 & 0 & 0 \\ 1 & 1 & 1 & 1 & 1 & 1 & 1 & 1 \end{pmatrix}$$

The image coordinates are then

$$A' = (0,0,0) \qquad E' = \left(\frac{\sqrt{2}}{2}, 1+\frac{\sqrt{2}}{2}, 0\right)$$

$$B' = (1,0,0) \qquad F' = \left(\frac{\sqrt{2}}{2}, \frac{\sqrt{2}}{2}, 0\right)$$

$$C' = (1,1,0) \qquad G' = \left(1+\frac{\sqrt{2}}{2}, \frac{\sqrt{2}}{2}, 0\right)$$

$$D' = (0,1,0) \qquad H' = \left(1+\frac{\sqrt{2}}{2}, 1+\frac{\sqrt{2}}{2}, 0\right)$$

Refer to Fig. 7-25.
To draw the cabinet projection:

$$Par_{V_2} \cdot V = \begin{pmatrix} 0 & 1 & 1 & 0 & \dfrac{\sqrt{3}}{4} & \dfrac{\sqrt{3}}{4} & 1+\dfrac{\sqrt{3}}{4} & 1+\dfrac{\sqrt{3}}{4} \\[2mm] 0 & 0 & 1 & 1 & 1\dfrac{1}{4} & \dfrac{1}{4} & \dfrac{1}{4} & 1\dfrac{1}{4} \\[2mm] 0 & 0 & 0 & 0 & 0 & 0 & 0 & 0 \\[1mm] 1 & 1 & 1 & 1 & 1 & 1 & 1 & 1 \end{pmatrix}$$

The image coordinates are then (see Fig. 7-26)

$$A' = (0,0,0) \qquad E' = \left(\frac{\sqrt{3}}{4}, 1\frac{1}{4}, 0\right)$$

$$B' = (1,0,0) \qquad F' = \left(\frac{\sqrt{3}}{4}, \frac{1}{4}, 0\right)$$

$$C' = (1,1,0) \qquad G' = \left(1+\frac{\sqrt{3}}{4}, \frac{1}{4}, 0\right)$$

$$D' = (0,1,0) \qquad H'\left(1+\frac{\sqrt{3}}{4}, 1\frac{1}{4}, 0\right)$$

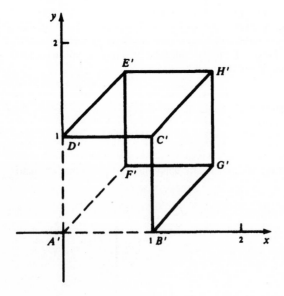

Fig. 7-25

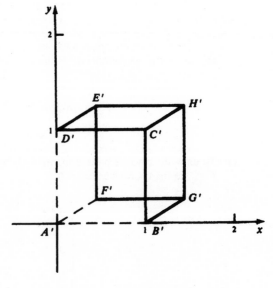

Fig. 7-26

7.14   Construct an isometric projection onto the xy plane. Refer to Fig. 7-27.

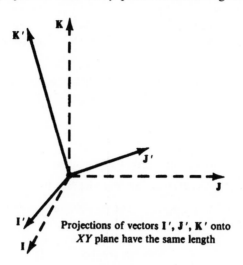

Projections of vectors **I′**, **J′**, **K′** onto
XY plane have the same length

Fig. 7-27

SOLUTION

We shall find a "tilting" of the x, y, z axes that transforms the **IJK** vector tried to a new set **I′J′K′** whose orthographic projections onto the xy plane produce vectors of equal lengths.

Denoting the tilting transformation by T and the orthographic projection onto the xy plane by Par_K, the final projection can be written as $Par = Par_K \cdot T$, where Par_K is as defined in Example 3 and T is as defined in Prob. 6.1 in Chap. 6. Multiplying, we find

$$Par = \begin{pmatrix} \cos\theta_y & \sin\theta_y\sin\theta_x & \sin\theta_y\cos\theta_x & 0 \\ 0 & \cos\theta_x & -\sin\theta_x & 0 \\ 0 & 0 & 0 & 0 \\ 0 & 0 & 0 & 1 \end{pmatrix}$$

Now

$$Par \cdot \mathbf{I} = (\cos\theta_y, 0, 0) \qquad Par \cdot \mathbf{J} = (\sin\theta_y\sin\theta_x, \cos\theta_x, 0) \qquad Par \cdot \mathbf{K} = (\sin\theta_y\cos\theta_x, -\sin\theta_x, 0)$$

(the projections of the vectors **I**, **J**, and **K**). To complete the specification of the transformation M, we need to find the angles θ_x and θ_y. To do this, we use the requirement that the images $Par \cdot \mathbf{I}$, $Par \cdot \mathbf{J}$, and $Par \cdot \mathbf{K}$ are to all have equal lengths. Now

$$|Par \cdot \mathbf{I}| = \sqrt{\cos^2\theta_y} \qquad |Par \cdot \mathbf{J}| = \sqrt{\sin^2\theta_y\sin^2\theta_x + \cos^2\theta_x}$$

and

$$|Par \cdot \mathbf{K}| = \sqrt{\sin^2\theta_y\cos^2\theta_x + \sin^2\theta_x}$$

Setting $|Par \cdot \mathbf{J}| = |Par \cdot \mathbf{K}|$ leads to the conclusion that $\sin^2\theta_x - \cos^2\theta_x = 0$ and to a solution $\theta_x = 45°$ (and so $\sin\theta_x = \cos\theta_x = \sqrt{2}/2$). Setting $|Par \cdot \mathbf{I}| = |Par \cdot \mathbf{J}|$ leads to $\cos^2\theta_y = \frac{1}{2}(\sin^2\theta_y + 1)$. Multiplying both sides by 2 and adding $\cos^2\theta_y$ to both sides gives $3\cos^2\theta_y = 2$ and a solution is $\theta_y = 35.26°$ (and so $\sin\theta_y = \sqrt{1/3}$, $\cos\theta_y = \sqrt{2/3}$). Finally

$$Par = \begin{pmatrix} \sqrt{\dfrac{2}{3}} & \dfrac{1}{2}\sqrt{\dfrac{2}{3}} & \dfrac{1}{2}\sqrt{\dfrac{2}{3}} & 0 \\ 0 & \dfrac{\sqrt{2}}{2} & -\dfrac{\sqrt{2}}{2} & 0 \\ 0 & 0 & 0 & 0 \\ 0 & 0 & 0 & 1 \end{pmatrix}$$

7.15 Construct a dimetric projection onto the xy plane.

SOLUTION

Following the procedures in Prob. 7.14, we shall tilt the x, y, z axes and then project on the xy plane. We then have, as before,

$$|Par \cdot \mathbf{I}| = \sqrt{\cos^2 \theta_y} \qquad |Par \cdot \mathbf{J}| = \sqrt{\sin^2 \theta_y \sin^2 \theta_x + \cos^2 \theta_x}$$

and

$$|Par \cdot \mathbf{K}| = \sqrt{\sin^2 \theta_y \cos^2 \theta_x + \sin^2 \theta_x}$$

To define a dimetric projection, we will specify the proportions

$$|Par \cdot \mathbf{I}| : |Par \cdot \mathbf{J}| : |Par \cdot \mathbf{K}| = l : 1 : 1 \qquad (l \neq 1)$$

Setting $|Par \cdot \mathbf{J}| = |Par \cdot \mathbf{K}|$, we find $\sin^2 \theta_x - \cos^2 \theta_x = 0$ and $\theta_x = 45°$, so $\sin \theta_x = \cos \theta_x = \sqrt{2}/2$. Setting $|Par \cdot \mathbf{I}| = l|Par \cdot \mathbf{J}|$ gives

$$\cos^2 \theta_y = \frac{l^2}{2}[\sin^2 \theta_y + 1] \tag{7.3}$$

Multiplying both sides by 2 and adding $l^2 \cos^2 \theta_y$ to both sides gives

$$(2 + l^2)\cos^2 \theta_y = 2l^2$$

So

$$\cos \theta_y = l\sqrt{\frac{2}{2 + l^2}}$$

From equation (7.3) we can also find

$$\sin^2 \theta_y = \frac{2 - l^2}{2 + l^2} \qquad \text{and} \qquad \sin \theta_y = \sqrt{\frac{2 - l^2}{2 + l^2}}$$

(Note the restriction $l \leq \sqrt{2}$.) Thus

$$Par = \begin{pmatrix} l\sqrt{\dfrac{2}{2 + l^2}} & \dfrac{\sqrt{2}}{2}\sqrt{\dfrac{2 - l^2}{2 + l^2}} & \dfrac{\sqrt{2}}{2}\sqrt{\dfrac{2 - l^2}{2 + l^2}} & 0 \\ 0 & \dfrac{\sqrt{2}}{2} & \dfrac{-\sqrt{2}}{2} & 0 \\ 0 & 0 & 0 & 0 \\ 0 & 0 & 0 & 1 \end{pmatrix}$$

and $0 \leq l \leq \sqrt{2}$.

Note that any other projection ratio, say, $1 : 1 : l$, can be achieved by performing an appropriate rotation before applying Par. In this example, a rotaiton of $90°$ about the y axis aligns the z axis with the x axis so that Par can be applied.

Supplementary Problems

7.16 Construct a perspective transformation given three principal vanishing points and the distance D from the center of projection to the projection plane.

7.17 Draw the (*a*) isometric and (*b*) dimetric projections of the unit cube onto the xy plane.

7.18 How many view planes (at the origin) produce isometric projections of an object?

CHAPTER 8

Three-Dimensional Viewing and Clipping

An important step in photography is to position and aim the camera at the scene in order to compose a picture. This parallels the specification of 3D viewing parameters in computer graphics that prescribe the projector (the center of projection for perspective projection or the direction of projection for parallel projection) along with the position and orientation of the projection/view plane.

In addition, a *view volume* defines the spatial extent that is visible through a rectangular window in the view plane. The bounding surfaces of this view volume is used to tailor/clip the objects that have been placed in the scene via modeling transformations (Chaps. 4 and 6) prior to viewing. The clipped objects are then projected into the window area, resulting in a specific view of the 3D scene that can be further mapped to the viewport in the NDCS (Chap. 5).

In this chapter we are concerned with the specification of 3D viewing parameters, including a viewing coordinate system for defining the view plane window, and the formation of the corresponding view volume (Sec. 8.1). We also discuss 3D clipping strategies and algorithms (Sec. 8.2). We then summarize the three-dimensional viewing process (Sec. 8.3). Finally, we examine the operational organization of a typical 3D graphics pipeline (Sec. 8.4).

8.1 THREE-DIMENSIONAL VIEWING

Three-dimensional viewing of objects requires the specification of a projection plane (called the *view plane*), a *center of projection* (*viewpoint*) or the direction of projection, and a *view volume* in world coordinates.

Specifying the View Plane

We specify the view plane by prescribing (1) a reference point $R_0(x_0, y_0, z_0)$ in world coordinates and (2) a *unit* normal vector $\mathbf{N} = n_1\mathbf{I} + n_2\mathbf{J} + n_3\mathbf{K}$, $|\mathbf{N}| = 1$, to the view plane (see Fig. 8-1). From this information, we can construct the projections used in presenting the required view with respect to the given viewpoint or direction of projection (Chap. 7).

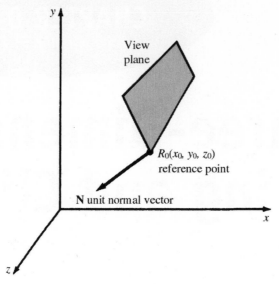

Fig. 8-1

View Plane Coordinates

The *view plane coordinate system* or *viewing coordinate system* can be specified as follows: (1) let the reference point $R_0(x_0, y_0, z_0)$ be the origin of the coordiante system and (2) determine the coordinate axes. To do this, we first choose a reference vector $\mathbf{U}$ called the *up vector*. A *unit* vector $\mathbf{J_q}$ can then be determined by the projection of the vector $\mathbf{U}$ onto the view plane. We let the vector $\mathbf{J_q}$ define the direction of the positive q axis for the view plane coordinate system. To calculate $\mathbf{J_q}$, we proceed as follows: with $\mathbf{N}$ being the view plane unit normal vector, let $\mathbf{U_q} = \mathbf{U} - (\mathbf{N} \cdot \mathbf{U})\mathbf{N}$ (App. 2, Prob. A2.14). Then

$$\mathbf{J_q} = \frac{\mathbf{U_q}}{|\mathbf{U_q}|}$$

is the unit vector that defines the direction of the positive q axis (see Fig. 8-2).

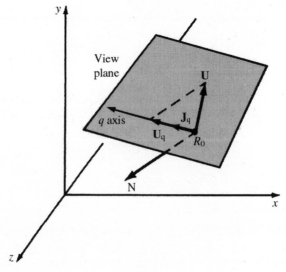

Fig. 8-2

Finally, the direction vector $\mathbf{I_p}$ of the positive p axis is chosen so that it is perpendicular to $\mathbf{J_q}$, and, by convention, so that the triad $\mathbf{I_p}$, $\mathbf{J_q}$, and $\mathbf{N}$ form a *left-handed* coordinate system. That is:

$$\mathbf{I_p} = \frac{\mathbf{N} \times \mathbf{J_q}}{|\mathbf{N} \times \mathbf{J_q}|}$$

This coordinate system is called the *view plane coordinate system* or *viewing coordinate system*. A left-handed system is traditionally chosen so that, if one thinks of the view plane as the face of a display device, then with the p and q coordinate axes superimposed on the display device, the normal vector $\mathbf{N}$ will point away from an observer facing the display. Thus the direction of increasing distance away from the observer is measured along $\mathbf{N}$ [see Fig. 8-3(a)].

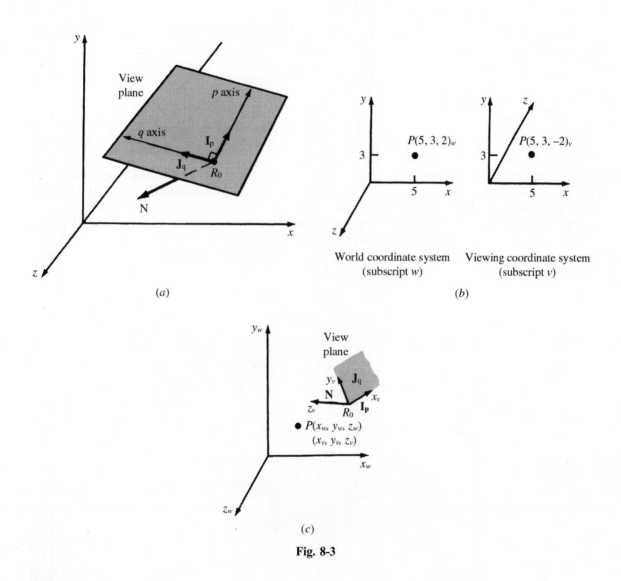

(a)

World coordinate system
(subscript w)

Viewing coordinate system
(subscript v)

(b)

(c)

Fig. 8-3

EXAMPLE 1. If the view plane is the xy plane, then $\mathbf{I_p} = \mathbf{I}$, $\mathbf{J_q} = \mathbf{J}$, and the unit normal $\mathbf{N} = -\mathbf{K}$ form a left-handed system. The z coordinate of a point measures the depth or distance of the point from the view plane. The sign indicates whether the point is in front or in back of the view plane with respect to the center or direction of projection. In this example, we change from right-handed world coordinates (x, y, z) to left-handed view plane coordinates

(x', y', z') [see Fig. 8-3(b)] be performing the transformation:

$$T_{RL}: \begin{cases} x' = x \\ y' = y \\ z' = -z \end{cases}$$

In matrix form, for homogeneous coordinates:

$$T_{RL} = \begin{pmatrix} 1 & 0 & 0 & 0 \\ 0 & 1 & 0 & 0 \\ 0 & 0 & -1 & 0 \\ 0 & 0 & 0 & 1 \end{pmatrix}$$

The general transformation for changing from world coordinates to view plane coordinates [see Fig. 8-3(c)] is developed in Prob. 8.3.

Specifying the View Volume

The view volume bounds a region in world coordinate space that will be clipped and projected onto the view plane. To define a view volume that projects onto a specified rectangular window defined in the view plane, we use view plane coordinates $(p, q)_v$ to locate points on the view plane. Then a rectangular view plane window is defined by prescribing the coordinates of the lower left-hand corner $L(p_{min}, q_{min})_v$ and upper right-hand corner $R(p_{max}, q_{max})_v$ (see Fig. 8-4). We can use the vectors $\mathbf{I_p}$ and $\mathbf{J_q}$ to find the equivalent world coordinates of L and R (see Prob. 8.1).

For a perspective view, the view volume, corresponding to the given window, is a semi-infinite pyramid, with apex at the viewpoint (Fig. 8-5). For views created using parallel projections (Fig. 8-6), the view volume is an infinite parallelepiped with sides parallel to the direction of projection.

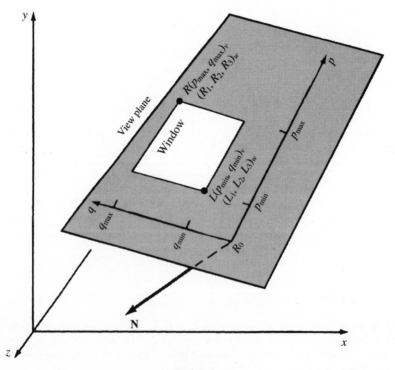

Fig. 8-4

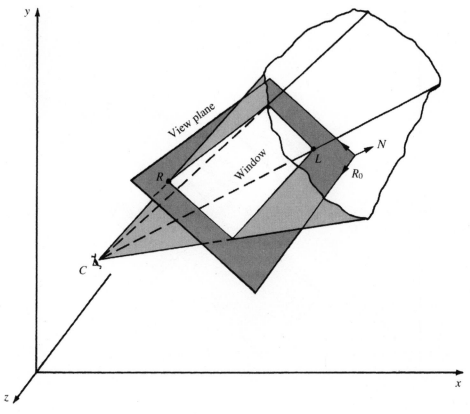

Fig. 8-5

8.2 CLIPPING

Clipping against a Finite View Volume

The view volumes created above are infinite in extent. In practice, we prefer to use a finite volume to limit the number of points to be projected. In addition, for perspective views, very distant objects from the view plane, when projected, appear as indistinguishable spots, while objects very close to the center of projection appear to have disjointed structure. This is another reason for using a finite view volume.

A finite volume is deliminated by using *front (near)* and *back (far) clipping planes* parallel to the view plane. These planes are specified by giving the front distance f and back distance b relative to the view plane reference point R_0 and measured along the normal vector **N**. The signed distance b and f can be positive or negative (Figs. 8-7 and 8-8).

Clipping Strategies

Two differing strategies have been devised to deal with the extraordinary computational effort required for three-dimensional clipping:

1. *Direct clipping*. In this method, as the name suggests, clipping is done directly against the view volume.

2. *Canonical clipping*. In this method, normalizing transformations are applied which transform the original view volume into a so-called canonical view volume. Clipping is then performed against the canonical view volume.

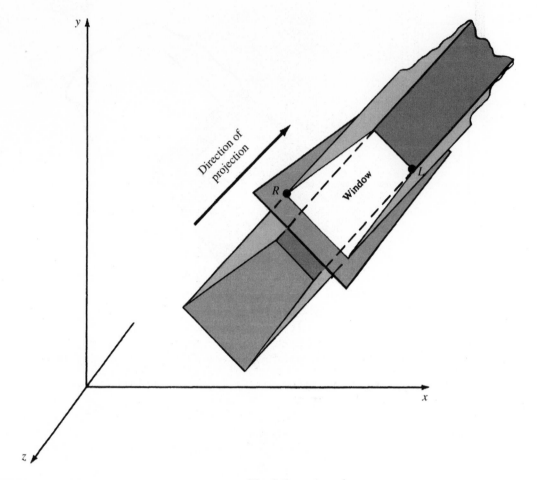

Fig. 8-6

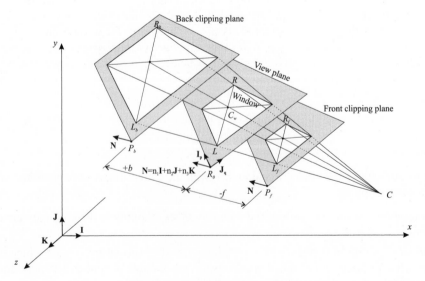

Fig. 8-7 Pespective view volume.

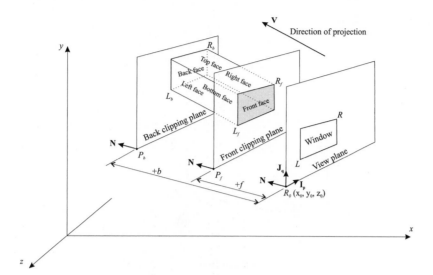

Fig. 8-8   Parallel view volume.

The canonical view volume for parallel projection is the unit cube whose faces are defined by the planes $x = 0$, $x = 1$, $y = 0$, $y = 1$, $z = 0$, and $z = 1$. The corresponding normalization transformation N_{par} is constructed in Prob. 8.5 (Fig. 8-9).

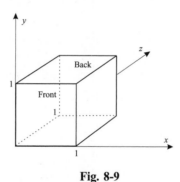

Fig. 8-9

The canonical view volume for perspective projections is the truncated pyramid whose faces are defined by the planes $x = z$, $x = -z$, $y = z$, $y = -z$, $z = z_f$, and $z = 1$ (where z_f is to be calculated) (Fig. 8-10). The corresponding normalization transformation N_{per} is constructed in Prob. 8.6.

The basis of the canonical clipping strategy is the fact that the computations involved such operations as finding the intersections of a line segment with the planes forming the faces of the canonical view volume are minimal (Prob. 8.9). This is balanced by the overhead involved in transforming points, many of which will be subsequently clipped.

For perspective views, additional clipping may be required to avoid the perspective anomalies produced by projecting objects that are behind the viewpoint (see Chap. 7).

Clipping Algorithms

Three-dimensional clipping algorithms are often direct adaptations of their two-dimensional counterparts (Chap. 5). The modifications necessary arise from the fact that we are now clipping against the six

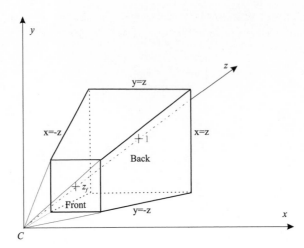

Figure 8-10

faces of the view volume, which are planes, as opposed to the four edges of the two-dimensional window, which are lines.

The technical differences involve:

1. Finding the intersection of a line and a plane (Prob. 8.12).

2. Assigning region codes to the endpoints of line segments for the Cohen–Sutherland algorithm (Prob. 8.8).

3. Deciding when a point is to the right (also said to be *outside*) or to the left (*inside*) of a plane for the Sutherland–Hodgman algorithm (Prob. 8.7).

4. Determining the inequalities for points inside the view volume (Prob. 8.10).

8.3   VIEWING TRANSFORMATION

Normalized Viewing Coordinates

We can view the normalizing transformations N_{par} and N_{per} from Sec. 8.2, under "Clipping Strategies," as geometric transformations. That is, *Obj* is an object defined in the world coordinate system, the transformation

$$Obj' = N_{par} \cdot Obj \qquad \text{or} \qquad Obj' = N_{per} \cdot Obj$$

yields an object *Obj'* defined in the *normalized viewing coordinate system.*

Canonical clipping is now equivalent to clipping in normalized viewing coordinates. That is, the transformed object *Obj'* is clipped against the canonical view volume. In Chap. 10, where hidden-surface algorithms are discussed, it is assumed that the coordinate description of geometric objects refers to normalized viewing coordinates.

Screen Projection Plane

After clipping in viewing coordinates, we project the resulting structure onto the *screen projection plane.* This is the plane that results from applying the transformations N_{par} or N_{per} to the given view plane. In the case N_{par}, from Prob. 8.5, we find that the screen projection plane is the plane $z = -f/(b-f)$ and that the direction of projection is that of the vector **K**. Thus the parallel projection is orthographic (Chap. 7), and, since the plane $z = -f/(b-f)$ is parallel to the xy plane, we can choose this latter plane as the projection plane. So parallel projection *Par* in normalized viewing coordinates reduces to orthographic projection onto the *xy* plane. The projection matrix is (Chap. 7, Sec. 7.3)

$$Par = \begin{pmatrix} 1 & 0 & 0 & 0 \\ 0 & 1 & 0 & 0 \\ 0 & 0 & 0 & 0 \\ 0 & 0 & 0 & 1 \end{pmatrix}$$

In the case of perspective projections, the screen projection plane is the plane $z = c_z'(c_z' + b)$ (Prob. 8.6). The transformed center of projection is the origin. So perspective projection *Per* in normalized viewing coordinates is accomplished by applying the matrix (Chap. 7, Prob. 7.4)

$$Per = \begin{pmatrix} \dfrac{c_z'}{c_z' + b} & 0 & 0 & 0 \\ 0 & \dfrac{c_z'}{c_z' + b} & 0 & 0 \\ 0 & 0 & \dfrac{c_z'}{c_z' + b} & 0 \\ 0 & 0 & 1 & 0 \end{pmatrix}$$

Constructing a Three-dimensional View

The complete three-dimensional viewing process (without hidden surface removal) is described by the following steps:

1. Transform from world coordinates to normalized viewing coordinates by applying the transformations N_{par} or N_{per}.
2. Clip in normalized viewing coordinates against the canonical clipping volumes.
3. Project onto the screen projection plane using the projections *Par* or *Per*.
4. Apply the appropriate (two-dimensional) viewing transformations (Chap. 5).

In terms of transformations, we can describe the above process in terms of a *viewing transformation* V_T, where

$$V_T = V_2 \cdot Par \cdot CL \cdot N_{\text{par}} \qquad \text{or} \qquad V_T = V_2 \cdot Per \cdot CL \cdot N_{\text{per}}$$

Here *CL* and V_2 refer to the appropriate clipping operations and two-dimensional viewing transformations.

8.4   EXAMPLE: A 3D GRAPHICS PIPELINE

The two-dimensional graphics pipeline introduced in Chap. 5 can non be extended to three dimensions (Fig. 8-11), where modeling transformation first places individually defined objectes into a common scene (i.e. the 3D WCS). Viewing transformation and projection are then carried out according to the viewing parameters set by the application. The result of projection in the view plane window is further mapped to

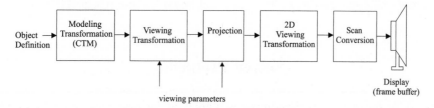

Fig. 8-11   A 3D graphics pipeline

the appropriate workstation viewpoint via 2D viewing transformation and scan-converted to a discrete image in the frame buffer for display.

An application typically specifies the method of projection and the corresponding view volume with system calls such as

$$\text{perspective } (\alpha, a_w, z_f, z_b)$$

where the viewpoint of perspective projection C is assumed to be at the origin of the WCS and the perspective view volume centers on the negative z axis (away from the viewer); α denotes the angle between the top and bottom clipping planes, a_w the aspect ratio of the view plane window, z_f the distance from C to the front clipping plane (which is essentially also the view plane), and z_b the distance from C to the back clipping plane.

On the other hand, orthographic parallel projection can be specified by

$$\text{orthographic } (x_{\min}, x_{\max}, y_{\min}, y_{\max}, z_f, z_b)$$

where the direction of projection is along the negative z axis of the WCS; the first four parameters of the call define the left, right, bottom, and top clipping planes, respectively; and the role of z_f and z_b remains the same as in the perspective case above.

Other calls to the system library often provide additional functionality. For example, the center of perspective projection can be placed anywhere in the WCS by a call that looks like

$$\text{lookat } (x_C, y_C, z_C, x_P, y_P, z_P)$$

where x_c, y_c, z_c are the coordinates of C and x_p, y_p, z_p are the coordinates of a reference point P—the perspective of view volume now centers on the line from C to P. The y axis of the WCS, or more precisely, vector $\mathbf{J}$, serves as the up vector that determines $\mathbf{I_p}$ and $\mathbf{J_q}$. An additional parameter may be included to allow rotation of the viewing coordinate system (with $R_0 = C_w$, the center of the view plane window) about its z axis, i.e. line CP.

Using perspective( ) and lookat( ), we can conveniently produce a sequence of images that animate a "walk-by" or "fly-by" experience by placing P on an object and moving C along the path of the camera from one frame to the next (Fig. 8-12).

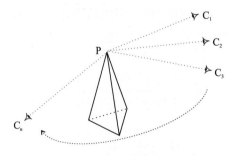

Fig. 8-12

Finally, we want to note a couple of crucial operations of the 3D graphics pipeline that have not yet been discussed. The first is to prevent objects and portions of objects that are hidden from the viewer's eyesight from being included in the projected view (Chap. 10). The second is to assign color attributes to pixels in a way that makes the objects in the image look more realistic (Chap. 11).

Solved Problems

8.1   Let $P(p, q)_v$ be the view plane coordinates of a point on the view plane. Find the world coordinates $P(x, y, z)_w$ of the point.

SOLUTION

Refer to Fig. 8-13. Let R_0 be the view plane reference point. Let $\mathbf{R}$ be the position vector of R_0 and $\mathbf{W}$ the position vector of P, both with respect to the world coordinate origin (see Fig. 8-13). Let $\mathbf{V}$ be the position vector of P with respect to the view plane origin R_0. Now

$$\mathbf{V} = p\mathbf{I_p} + q\mathbf{J_q} \qquad \text{and} \qquad \mathbf{W} = \mathbf{R} + \mathbf{V}$$

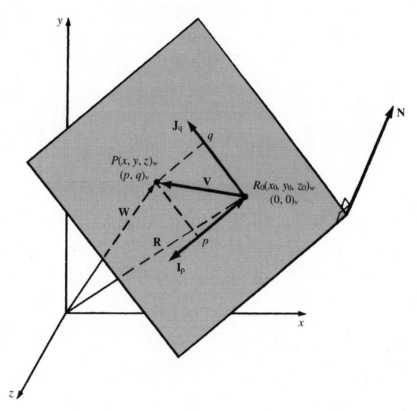

Fig. 8-13

So

$$\mathbf{W} = \mathbf{R} + p\mathbf{I_p} + q\mathbf{J_q}$$

Let the components of $\mathbf{I_p}$ and $\mathbf{J_q}$ be

$$\mathbf{I_p} = a_p\mathbf{I} + b_p\mathbf{J} + c_p\mathbf{K} \qquad \mathbf{J_q} = a_q\mathbf{I} + b_q\mathbf{J} + c_q\mathbf{K}$$

Also

$$\mathbf{R} = x_0\mathbf{I} + y_0\mathbf{J} + z_0\mathbf{K}$$

and so from $\mathbf{W} = \mathbf{R} + p\mathbf{I_p} + q\mathbf{J_q}$ we find

$$\mathbf{W} = (x_0 + pa_p + qa_q)\mathbf{I} + (y_0 + pb_p + qb_q)\mathbf{J} + (z_0 + pc_p + qc_q)\mathbf{K}$$

The required world coordinates of P can be read off from W:

$$P(x_0 + pa_p + qa_q, y_0 + pb_p + qb_q, z_0 + pc_p + qc_q)_w$$

8.2 Find the projection of the unit cube onto the view plane in Prob. 7.9 in Chap. 7. Find the corresponding view plane coordinates of the projected cube.

SOLUTION

Following Prob. 7.9, we must specify several parameters in order to calculate the corresponding perspective projection matrix $Per_{\mathbf{N},R_0,C}$. Choosing $h = \frac{1}{2}$, $t_1 = 1$, and $t_2 = (1 - \sqrt{3})/(1 + \sqrt{3})$, we obtain

$$Per_{\mathbf{N},R_0,C} = \frac{1+\sqrt{3}}{2} \begin{pmatrix} 0 & \dfrac{2}{1+\sqrt{3}} & 0 & -2 \\[2mm] \sqrt{3} & \dfrac{1-\sqrt{3}}{1+\sqrt{3}} & 0 & -(1+\sqrt{3}) \\[2mm] \dfrac{\sqrt{3}}{2(1+\sqrt{3})} & \dfrac{1}{2(1+\sqrt{3})} & \dfrac{-2\sqrt{3}}{1+\sqrt{3}} & -\dfrac{1}{2} \\[2mm] \dfrac{\sqrt{3}}{1+\sqrt{3}} & \dfrac{1}{1+\sqrt{3}} & 0 & -\left(\dfrac{1+3\sqrt{3}}{1+\sqrt{3}}\right) \end{pmatrix}$$

Applying $Per_{\mathbf{N},R_0,C}$ to the matrix V of homogeneous coordinates of the unit cube, we have $Per_{\mathbf{N},R_0,C} \cdot V = V'$, where V' is the matrix $(A'B'C'D'E'F'G'H')$. After matrix multiplication, we have

$$\mathbf{V'} = \frac{1+\sqrt{3}}{2} \times$$

$$\begin{pmatrix} -2 & -2 & \dfrac{-2\sqrt{3}}{1+\sqrt{3}} & \dfrac{-2\sqrt{3}}{1+\sqrt{3}} & \dfrac{-2\sqrt{3}}{1+\sqrt{3}} & -2 & -2 & \dfrac{-2\sqrt{3}}{1+\sqrt{3}} \\[2mm] -(1+\sqrt{3}) & -1 & \dfrac{-2\sqrt{3}}{1+\sqrt{3}} & -3 & -3 & -(1+\sqrt{3}) & -1 & \dfrac{-2\sqrt{3}}{1+\sqrt{3}} \\[2mm] -\dfrac{1}{2} & \dfrac{-1}{2(1+\sqrt{3})} & 0 & \dfrac{-\sqrt{3}}{2(1+\sqrt{3})} & \dfrac{-5\sqrt{3}}{2(1+\sqrt{3})} & -\left(\dfrac{1+5\sqrt{3}}{2(1+\sqrt{3})}\right) & -\left(\dfrac{1+4\sqrt{3}}{2(1+\sqrt{3})}\right) & \dfrac{-2\sqrt{3}}{1+\sqrt{3}} \\[2mm] -\left(\dfrac{1+3\sqrt{3}}{1+\sqrt{3}}\right) & -\left(\dfrac{1+2\sqrt{3}}{1+\sqrt{3}}\right) & \dfrac{-2\sqrt{3}}{1+\sqrt{3}} & \dfrac{-3\sqrt{3}}{(1+\sqrt{3})} & \dfrac{-3\sqrt{3}}{(1+\sqrt{3})} & -\left(\dfrac{1+3\sqrt{3}}{1+\sqrt{3}}\right) & -\left(\dfrac{1+2\sqrt{3}}{1+\sqrt{3}}\right) & \dfrac{-2\sqrt{3}}{1+\sqrt{3}} \end{pmatrix}$$

Changing from homogeneous coordinates to world coordinates (App. 2), we find the coordinates of the projected cube to be

$$A'\left[2\left(\frac{1+\sqrt{3}}{1+3\sqrt{3}}\right), 2\left(\frac{2+\sqrt{3}}{1+3\sqrt{3}}\right), \frac{1+\sqrt{3}}{2(1+3\sqrt{3})}\right] \qquad E'\left(\frac{2}{3}, \frac{1+\sqrt{3}}{\sqrt{3}}, \frac{5}{6}\right)$$

$$B'\left[2\left(\frac{1+\sqrt{3}}{1+2\sqrt{3}}\right), \frac{1+\sqrt{3}}{1+2\sqrt{3}}, \frac{1}{2(1+2\sqrt{3})}\right] \qquad F'\left[2\left(\frac{1+\sqrt{3}}{1+3\sqrt{3}}\right), \frac{2(2+\sqrt{3})}{1+3\sqrt{3}}, \frac{1+5\sqrt{3}}{2(1+3\sqrt{3})}\right]$$

$$C'(1,1,0) \qquad G'\left[2\left(\frac{1+\sqrt{3}}{1+2\sqrt{3}}\right), \frac{1+\sqrt{3}}{1+2\sqrt{3}}, \frac{1+4\sqrt{3}}{2(1+2\sqrt{3})}\right]$$

$$D'\left(\frac{2}{3}, \frac{1+\sqrt{3}}{\sqrt{3}}, \frac{1}{6}\right) \qquad H'(1,1,1)$$

To change from world coordinates to view plane coordinates, we first choose an up vector. Choosing the vector $\mathbf{K}$, the direction of the positive z axis, as the up vector, we next find the view plane coordinate vectors $\mathbf{I_p}$ and $\mathbf{J_q}$.

With our choices t_1 and t_2, we find that the unit normal vector $\mathbf{N}$ (Prob. 7.9) is

$$\mathbf{N} = \frac{\sqrt{3}}{2}\mathbf{I} + \frac{1}{2}\mathbf{J}$$

Choosing $\mathbf{U} = \mathbf{K}$, and using Prob. A2.14 (App. 2), we find that

$$\mathbf{U_q} = \mathbf{U} - (\mathbf{N} \cdot \mathbf{U})\mathbf{N} = \mathbf{U} \quad (\text{since } \mathbf{N} \cdot \mathbf{U} = 0) \quad = \mathbf{K} \qquad \text{and} \qquad \mathbf{J_q} = \frac{\mathbf{U_q}}{|\mathbf{U_q}|} = \mathbf{K}$$

(Note to student using equation (*A2-3*) of Prob. A2.14: we have used the fact that $|\mathbf{N}| = 1$ and replaced $\mathbf{V_p}$ with $\mathbf{U_q}$ and $\mathbf{V}$ and $\mathbf{U}$.)

Now

$$\mathbf{I_p} = \frac{\mathbf{N} \times \mathbf{J_q}}{|\mathbf{N} \times \mathbf{J_q}|}$$

Calculating (App. 2), we obtain

$$\mathbf{N} \times \mathbf{J_q} = \frac{1}{2}\mathbf{I} - \frac{\sqrt{3}}{2}\mathbf{J} \qquad \text{and} \qquad |\mathbf{N} \times \mathbf{J_q}| = 1$$

So

$$\mathbf{I_p} = \frac{1}{2}\mathbf{I} - \frac{\sqrt{3}}{2}\mathbf{J}$$

To convert a point P with world coordinates $(x, y, z)_w$ to view plane coordinates $(p, q)_v$, we use the equations from Prob. 8.1:

$$x = x_0 + pa_p + qa_q \qquad y = y_0 + pb_p + qb_q \qquad z = z_0 + pc_p + qc_q$$

where (x_0, y_0, z_0) are the coordinates of the view plane reference point R_0. Now

$$\mathbf{I_p} = a_p\mathbf{I} + b_p\mathbf{J} + c_p\mathbf{K} = \frac{1}{2}\mathbf{I} - \frac{\sqrt{3}}{2}\mathbf{J} + 0\mathbf{K} \qquad \mathbf{J_q} = a_q\mathbf{I} + b_q\mathbf{J} + c_q\mathbf{K} = 0\mathbf{I} + 0\mathbf{J} + 1\mathbf{K}$$

Choosing $R_0(1, 1, 0)$ as the view plane reference point, we find

$$x = \frac{1}{2}p + 1 \qquad y = \frac{-\sqrt{3}}{2}p + 1 \qquad z = q$$

Solving for p and q, we have

$$p = 2(x - 1) \qquad \text{and} \qquad q = z$$

Using these equations, we convert the transformed coordinates to view plane coordinates:

$$A'\left[2\left(\frac{1 - \sqrt{3}}{1 + 3\sqrt{3}}\right), \frac{1 + \sqrt{3}}{2(1 + 3\sqrt{3})}\right] \qquad E'\left(-\frac{2}{3}, \frac{5}{6}\right)$$

$$B'\left[\frac{2}{1 + 2\sqrt{3}}, \frac{1}{2(1 + 2\sqrt{3})}\right] \qquad F'\left[2\left(\frac{1 - \sqrt{3}}{1 + 3\sqrt{3}}\right), \frac{1 + 5\sqrt{3}}{2(1 + 3\sqrt{3})}\right]$$

$$C'(0, 0) \qquad G'\left[\frac{2}{1 + 2\sqrt{3}}, \frac{1 + 4\sqrt{3}}{2(1 + 2\sqrt{3})}\right]$$

$$D'\left(-\frac{2}{3}, \frac{1}{6}\right) \qquad H'(0, 1)$$

Refer to Fig. 8-14. Note also that the coordinates of the view point or center of projection C and the vanishing

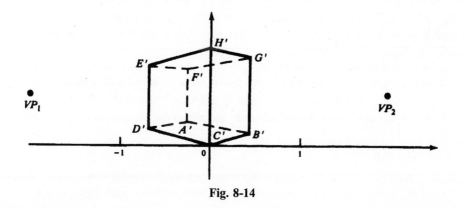

Fig. 8-14

points VP_1 and VP_2 can be found by using the equations from Prob. 7.9:

$$C(a, b, c) = C\left(2, 1 + \sqrt{3}, \frac{1}{2}\right) \qquad VP_1\left(0, 1 + \sqrt{3}, \frac{1}{2}\right)_w \qquad VP_2\left(2, 1 - \sqrt{3}, \frac{1}{2}\right)_w$$

In view plane coordinates:

$$VP_1\left(-2, \frac{1}{2}\right)_v \qquad \text{and} \qquad VP_2\left(2, \frac{1}{2}\right)_v$$

8.3   Find the transformation T_{wv} that relates world coordinates to view plane coordinates.

SOLUTION

The world coordinate axes are determined by the right-handed triad of unit vectors $[\mathbf{I}, \mathbf{J}, \mathbf{K}]$.

The view plane coordinate axes are determined by the left-handed triad of vectors $[\mathbf{I_p}, \mathbf{J_q}, \mathbf{N}]$ and the view reference point $R_0(x_0, y_0, z_0)$.

Referrring to Fig. 8-3(a), we construct the transformation T_{wv} through the concatenation of the matrices determined by the following steps:

1.   Translate the view plane reference point $R_0(x_0, y_0, z_0)$ to the world coordinate origin via the translation matrix $T_{\mathbf{v}}$. Here $\mathbf{V}$ is the vector with components $-x_0\mathbf{I} - y_0\mathbf{J} - z_0\mathbf{K}$.

2.   Align the view plane normal $\mathbf{N}$ with the vector $-\mathbf{K}$ (the direction of the negative z axis) using the transformation $A_{\mathbf{N},-\mathbf{K}}$ (Chap. 6, Prob. 6.5). Let $\mathbf{I'_p}$ be the new position of the vector $\mathbf{I_p}$ after performing the alignment transformation, i.e.

$$\mathbf{I'_p} = A_{\mathbf{N},-\mathbf{K}} \cdot \mathbf{I_p}$$

3.   Rotate $\mathbf{I'_p}$ about the z axis so that it aligns with $\mathbf{I}$, the direction of the x axis. With θ being the angle between $\mathbf{I'_p}$ and $\mathbf{I}$, the rotation is $R_{\theta,\mathbf{K}}$ (Chap. 6).

4.   Change from the right-handed coordinates to left-handed coordinates by applying the transformation T_{RL} from Example 1. Then $T_{wv} = T_{RL} \cdot R_{\theta,\mathbf{K}} \cdot A_{\mathbf{N},-\mathbf{K}} \cdot T_{\mathbf{v}}$. If (x_w, y_w, z_w) are the world coordinates of point P, the view plane coordinates (x_v, y_v, z_v) of P can be found by applying the transformation T_{wv}.

8.4   Find the equations of the planes forming the view volume for the general parallel projection.

SOLUTION

The equation of a plane is determined by two vectors that are contained in the plane and a reference point (App. 2, Prob. A2.10). The cross product of the two vectors determines the direction of the normal vector to the plane.

In Fig. 8-8, the sides of the window in the view plane have the directions of the view plane coordinate vectors $\mathbf{I_p}$ and $\mathbf{J_q}$. With $\mathbf{V}$ as the vector determining the direction of projection, we find the following planes:

1.   *Top plane*—determined by the vectors $\mathbf{I_p}$ and $\mathbf{V}$ and reference point R_f, measured f units along the unit normal vector $\mathbf{N} = n_1\mathbf{I} + n_2\mathbf{J} + n_3\mathbf{K}$ from the upper right corner $R(r_1, r_2, r_3)$ of the window. Reference point R_f has world coordinates $(r_1 + fn_1, r_2 + fn_2, r_3 + fn_3)$.

2.   *Bottom plane*—determined by the vectors $\mathbf{I_p}$ and $\mathbf{V}$ and the reference point L_f, measured from the lower left corner $L(l_1, l_2, l_3)$ of the window. Point L_f has world coordinates $(l_1 + fn_1, l_2 + fn_2, l_3 + fn_3)$.

3.   *Right side plane*—determined by the vectors $\mathbf{J_q}$ and $\mathbf{V}$ and the reference point R_f.

4.   *Left side plane*—determined by the vectors $\mathbf{J_q}$ and $\mathbf{V}$ and the reference point L_f.

Front and back clipping planes are parallel to the view plane, and thus have the same normal vector $\mathbf{N} = n_1\mathbf{I} + n_2\mathbf{J} + n_3\mathbf{K}$.

5.   *Front (near) plane*—determined by the normal vector $\mathbf{N}$ and reference point $P_f(x_0 + fn_1, y_0 + fn_2, z_0 + fn_3)$, measured from the view reference point $R_0(x_0, y_0, z_0)$.

6. *Back (far) plane*—determined by the normal vector **N** and reference point $P_b(x_0 + bn_1, y_0 + bn_2, z_0 + bn_3)$, measured b units from the view plane reference point R_0.

8.5 Find the normalizing transformation that transforms the parallel view volume to the canonical view volume determined by the planes $x = 0$, $x = 1$, $y = 0$, $y = 1$, $z = 0$, and $z = 1$ (the unit cube).

SOLUTION

Referring to Fig. 8-8, we see that the required transformation N_{par} is built by performing the following series of transformations:

1. Translate so that R_0, the view plane reference point, is at the origin. The required transformation is the translation T_{-R_0}.

2. The vectors $\mathbf{I_p}$, $\mathbf{J_q}$, and **N** form the left-handed view plane coordinate system. We next align the view plane normal vector **N** with the vector $-\mathbf{K}$ (the direction of the negative z axis). The alignment transformation $A_{\mathbf{N},-\mathbf{K}}$ was developed in Chap. 6, Prob. 6.5. Let $\mathbf{I'_p}$ be the new position of the vector $\mathbf{I_p}$; that is, $\mathbf{I'_p} = A_{\mathbf{N},-\mathbf{K}} \cdot \mathbf{I_p}$.

3. Align the vector $\mathbf{I'_p}$ with the vector **I** (the direction of the positive x axis) by rotating $\mathbf{I'_p}$ about the z axis. The required transformation is $R_{\theta,\mathbf{K}}$. Here, θ is the angle between $\mathbf{I'_p}$ and **I** (Chap. 6). When $R_{\theta,\mathbf{K}}$ aligns $\mathbf{I'_p}$ with **I**, the vector $\mathbf{J'_q}$ (where $\mathbf{J'_q} = A_{\mathbf{N},-\mathbf{K}} \cdot \mathbf{J_q}$) is aligned with the vector **J** (the direction of the positive y axis).

4. We change from the right-handed world coordinate system to a left-handed coordinate system. The required orientation changing transformation is [see Fig. 8-3(b)] (see also Example 1)

$$T_{RL} = \begin{pmatrix} 1 & 0 & 0 & 0 \\ 0 & 1 & 0 & 0 \\ 0 & 0 & -1 & 0 \\ 0 & 0 & 0 & 1 \end{pmatrix}$$

5. Let $\mathbf{V'}$ be the new position of the direction of projection vector **V**; that is, $\mathbf{V'} = T_{RL} \cdot R_{\theta,\mathbf{K}} \cdot A_{\mathbf{N},-\mathbf{K}} \cdot \mathbf{V}$. The new position of the transformed view volume is illustrated in Fig. 8-15. Note how the view volume is skewed along the line having the direction of the vector $\mathbf{V'}$. Suppose that the components of $\mathbf{V'}$ are $\mathbf{V'} = v'_x\mathbf{I} + v'_y\mathbf{J} + v'_z\mathbf{K}$. We now perform a shearing transformation that transforms the newly skewed view volume to a rectangular view volume aligned along the z axis. The required shearing transformation is determined by preserving the new view volume base vectors **I** and **J** and shearing $\mathbf{V'}$ to the vector $v'_z\mathbf{K}$ (the **K** component of $\mathbf{V'}$); that is, **I** is transformed to **I**, **J** is transformed to **J**, and $\mathbf{V'}$ is transformed to $v'_z\mathbf{K}$. The required transformation is the matrix

$$Sh = \begin{pmatrix} 1 & 0 & -\dfrac{v'_x}{v'_z} \\ 0 & 1 & -\dfrac{v'_y}{v'_z} \\ 0 & 0 & 1 \end{pmatrix}$$

In order to concatenate the transformation so as to build N_{par}, we use the 4×4 homogeneous form of Sh

$$\left(\begin{array}{ccc|c} & & & 0 \\ & Sh & & 0 \\ & & & 0 \\ \hline 0 & 0 & 0 & 1 \end{array} \right)$$

6. We now translate the new view volume so that its lower left corner L'_f will be at the origin. To do this, we note that the first four transformations correspond to the view plane coordinate system transformation in Prob. 8.3. So after performing these transformations, we find that the lower left corner of the view plane window $L(p_{min}, q_{min})_v$ (view plane coordinates) transforms to a point L' on the xy plane whose coordinates are $(p_{min}, q_{min}, 0)$. Similarly, the upper right corner R is transformed to $R'(p_{max}, q_{max}, 0)$. After performing the shearing transformation Sh, we see that the view volume is aligned with the z axis and the back and

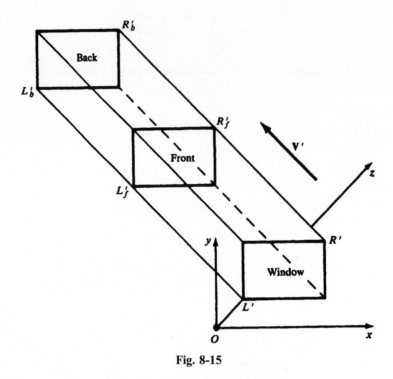

Fig. 8-15

front faces are, respectively, b and f units from the xy plane. Thus the lower left corner of the view volume is at $L'_f(p_{min}, q_{min}, f)$ and the bounds of the view volume are $p_{min} \leq x \leq p_{max}$, $q_{min} \leq y \leq q_{max}$, $f \leq z \leq b$. The required translation is $T_{-L'_f}$.

7. We now scale the rectangular view volume to the unit cube. The base of the present view volume has the dimensions of the base of the original volume, which corresponds to the view plane window; that is

$$w = p_{max} - p_{min} \text{ (width)} \qquad h = q_{max} - q_{min} \text{ (height)}$$

The depth of the new view volume is the distance from the front clipping plane to the back clipping plane: $d = b - f$. The required scaling is the matrix (in 4×4 homogeneous form)

$$S_{1/w, 1/h, 1/d} = \begin{pmatrix} \dfrac{1}{w} & 0 & 0 & 0 \\ 0 & \dfrac{1}{h} & 0 & 0 \\ 0 & 0 & \dfrac{1}{d} & 0 \\ 0 & 0 & 0 & 1 \end{pmatrix}$$

The required transformation is then

$$N_{par} = S_{1/w, 1/h, 1/d} \cdot T_{-L'_f} \cdot Sh \cdot T_{RL} \cdot R_{\theta, \mathbf{K}} \cdot A_{\mathbf{N}, -\mathbf{K}} \cdot T_{-R_0}$$

Note also that after performing the transformation N_{par}, the view plane transforms to the plane $z = -f/(b-f)$, parallel to the xy plane. Also, the direction of projection vector $\mathbf{V}$ transforms to a vector parallel to the vector $\mathbf{K}$ having the direction of the z axis.

8.6 Find the normalizing transformation that transforms the perspective view volume to the canonical view volume determined by the bounding planes $x = z$, $x = -z$, $y = z$, $y = -z$, $z = z_f$, and $z = 1$.

SOLUTION

Referring to Fig. 8-7, we build the normalizing transformation N_{per} through a series of transformations. As in Prob. 8.5:

1. Translate the center of projection C to the origin using the translation T_{-C}.
2. Align the view plane normal $\mathbf{N}$ with the vector $-\mathbf{K}$ using $A_{\mathbf{N},-\mathbf{K}}$.
3. Rotate $\mathbf{I'_p}$ to the vector $\mathbf{I}$ using the rotation $R_{\theta,\mathbf{K}}$. (Recall that $\mathbf{I'_p} = A_{\mathbf{N},-\mathbf{K}} \cdot \mathbf{I_p}$.)
4. We now change from right-handed world coordinates to left-handed coordinates by applying the transformation

$$T_{RL} = \begin{pmatrix} 1 & 0 & 0 & 0 \\ 0 & 1 & 0 & 0 \\ 0 & 0 & -1 & 0 \\ 0 & 0 & 0 & 1 \end{pmatrix}$$

5. The newly transformed view volume is skewed along the centerline joining the origin (the translated center of projection) with the center of the (transformed) view plane window (Fig. 8-16). Let C_w be the coordinates of the center of the original view plane window. Then C_w has view plane coordinates

$$\left(\frac{p_{min} + p_{max}}{2}, \frac{q_{min} + q_{max}}{2} \right)_v$$

These are changed to world coordinates as in Prob. 8.1. Let $\overline{CC}_w$ be the vector from the center of projection to the center of the window. Let $(\overline{CC}_w)'$ be the transformation of the vector $\overline{CC}_w$; that is, $(\overline{CC}_w)' = T_{RL} \cdot R_{\theta,\mathbf{K}} \cdot A_{\mathbf{N}-\mathbf{K}} \cdot \overline{CC}_w$. Then $(\overline{CC}_w)'$ is the vector that joins the origin to the center of the transformed view plane window (Fig. 8-16). Suppose that $(\overline{CC}_w)' = c'_x\mathbf{I} + c'_y\mathbf{J} + c'_z\mathbf{K}$. We shear the view volume so that it transforms to a view volume whose center line lies along the z axis. As in Prob. 8.5, the

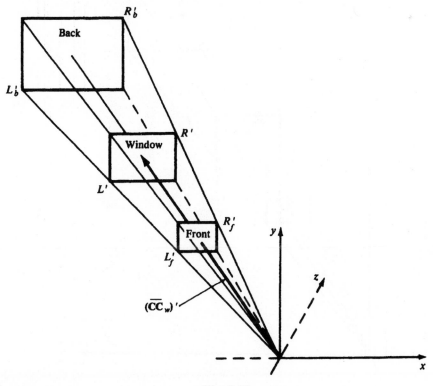

Fig. 8-16

required shearing transformation is

$$Sh = \begin{pmatrix} 1 & 0 & -\dfrac{c_x'}{c_z'} & 0 \\ 0 & 1 & -\dfrac{c_y'}{c_z'} & 0 \\ 0 & 0 & 1 & 0 \\ 0 & 0 & 0 & 1 \end{pmatrix}$$

The newly transformed window is, after applying the shearing transformation Sh, located on the z axis at $z_c = c_z'$.

6. Referring to Fig. 8-17, the transformed window is now centered on the z axis. The dimensions of the window are

$$w = p_{max} - p_{min} \text{ (width)} \quad \text{and} \quad h = q_{max} - q_{min} \text{ (height)}$$

The depth of the new view volume is the distance between the front and back clipping planes: $d = b - f$. The transformed window is centered on the z axis at $z_c = c_z'$ and is bounded by

$$-\frac{w}{2} \le x \le \frac{w}{2} \qquad -\frac{h}{2} \le y \le \frac{h}{2}$$

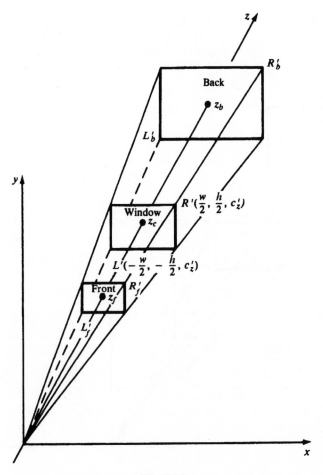

Fig. 8-17

The transformed view plane is located at $z_c = c'_z$. The transformed front clipping plane is located at $z_f = c'_z + f$. The back clipping plane is now located at $z_b = c'_z + b$.

To transform this view volume into the canonical view volume, we first scale in the z direction so that the back-clipping plane is transformed to $z = 1$. The required scale factor is

$$s_z = \frac{1}{c'_z + b}$$

The scaling matrix is

$$S_{1,1,s_z} = \begin{pmatrix} 1 & 0 & 0 & 0 \\ 0 & 1 & 0 & 0 \\ 0 & 0 & \dfrac{1}{c'_z + b} & 0 \\ 0 & 0 & 0 & 1 \end{pmatrix}$$

To find the new window boundaries R'' and L'', we apply this scaling transformation to the present window coordinates

$$R'\left(\frac{w}{2}, \frac{h}{2}, c'_z\right) \qquad L'\left(-\frac{w}{2}, -\frac{h}{2}, c'_z\right)$$

Then

$$R'' = \left(\frac{w}{2}, \frac{h}{2}, \frac{c'_z}{c'_z + b}\right) \qquad \text{and} \qquad L'' = \left(-\frac{w}{2}, -\frac{h}{2}, \frac{c'_z}{c'_z + b}\right)$$

Next we scale in the x and y directions so that the window boundaries will be

$$R'''\left(\frac{c'_z}{c'_z + b}, \frac{c'_z}{c'_z + b}, \frac{c'_z}{c'_z + b}\right) \qquad \text{and} \qquad L'''\left(-\frac{c'_z}{c'_z + b}, -\frac{c'_z}{c'_z + b}, \frac{c'_z}{c'_z + b}\right)$$

That is, the window boundaries will lie on the planes $x = z$, $x = -z$, $y = z$,and $y = -z$. The required scale factors are

$$s_x = \frac{2c'_z}{w(c'_z + b)} \qquad \text{and} \qquad s_y = \frac{2c'_z}{h(c'_z + b)}$$

The corresponding scaling transformation is

$$S_{s_x,s_y,1} = \begin{pmatrix} \dfrac{2c'_z}{w(c'_z + b)} & 0 & 0 & 0 \\ 0 & \dfrac{2c'_z}{h(c'_z + b)} & 0 & 0 \\ 0 & 0 & 1 & 0 \\ 0 & 0 & 0 & 1 \end{pmatrix}$$

Multiplication of these scaling transformations into one transformation yields

$$S_{s_x,s_y,s_z} = \begin{pmatrix} \dfrac{2c'_z}{w(c'_z + b)} & 0 & 0 & 0 \\ 0 & \dfrac{2c'_x}{h(c'_z + b)} & 0 & 0 \\ 0 & 0 & \dfrac{1}{c'_z + b} & 0 \\ 0 & 0 & 0 & 1 \end{pmatrix}$$

To find the location of the front clipping plane, z_f, we apply the transformation S_{s_x,s_y,s_z} to the present location of the center of the front clipping plane, which is $C_f(0, 0, c_z' + f)$. So

$$S_{s_x,s_y,s_z} \cdot C_f = \left(0, 0, \frac{c_z' + f}{c_z' + b}\right)$$

That is

$$z_f = \frac{c_z' + f}{c_z' + b}$$

The complete transformation can be written as

$$N_{\text{per}} = S_{s_x,s_y,s_z} \cdot Sh \cdot T_{RL} \cdot R_{\theta,\mathbf{K}} \cdot A_{\mathbf{N},-\mathbf{K}} \cdot T_{-C}$$

Note that after performing the transformation N_{per}, the view plane is transformed to the plane

$$z = \frac{c_z'}{c_z' + b}$$

parallel to the xy plane. Also, the center of projection C is transformed to the origin.

8.7   How do we determine whether a point P is inside or outside the view volume?

SOLUTION

A plane divides space into the two sides. The general equation of a plane is (App. 2)

$$n_1(x - x_0) + n_2(y - y_0) + n_3(z - z_0) = 0$$

We define a scalar function, $f(P)$, for any point $P(x, y, z)$ by

$$f(P) \equiv f(x, y, z) = n_1(x - x_0) + n_2(y - y_0) + n_3(z - z_0)$$

We say that a point P is on the same side (with respect to the plane) as point Q if sign $f(P) = \text{sign}\, f(Q)$. Referring to Figs. 8-7 or 8-8, let f_T, f_B, f_R, f_L, f_N, and f_F be the functions associated with the top, bottom, right, left, near (front), and far (back) planes, respectively (Probs. 8.4 and 8.10).

Also, L and R are the lower left and upper right corners of the window and P_b and P_f are the reference points of the back and front clipping planes, respectively.

Then a point P is inside the view volume if all the following hold:

P is on the same side as L with respect to f_T

P is on the same side as R with respect to f_B

P is on the same side as L with respect to f_R

P is on the same side as R with respect to f_L

P is on the same side as P_b with respect to f_N

P is on the same side as P_f with respect to f_F

Equivalently

$$\text{sign}\, f_T(P) = \text{sign}\, f_T(L) \qquad \text{sign}\, f_L(P) = \text{sign}\, f_L(R)$$
$$\text{sign}\, f_B(P) = \text{sign}\, f_B(R) \qquad \text{sign}\, f_N(P) = \text{sign}\, f_N(P_b)$$
$$\text{sign}\, f_R(P) = \text{sign}\, f_R(L) \qquad \text{sign}\, f_F(P) = \text{sign}\, f_F(P_f)$$

8.8   Show how region codes would be assigned to the endpoints of a line segment for the three-dimensional Cohen–Sutherland clipping algorithm for (*a*) the canonical parallel view volume and (*b*) the canonical perspective view volume.

SOLUTION

The procedure follows the logic of the two-dimensional algorithm in Chap. 5. For three dimensions, the planes describing the view volume divide three-dimensional space into six overlapping exterior regions (i.e., above, below, to right of, to left of, behind, and in front of view volume), plus the interior of the view volume; thus 6-bit codes are used. Let $P(x, y, z)$ be the coordinates of an endpoint.

(a) For the canonical parallel view volume, each bit is set to true (1) or false (0) according to the scheme

$$\text{Bit } 1 \equiv \text{endpoint is above view volume} = \text{sign} (y - 1)$$
$$\text{Bit } 2 \equiv \text{endpoint is below view volume} = \text{sign} (-y)$$
$$\text{Bit } 3 \equiv \text{endpoint is to the right of view volume} = \text{sign} (x - 1)$$
$$\text{Bit } 4 \equiv \text{endpoint is to the left of view volume} = \text{sign} (-x)$$
$$\text{Bit } 5 \equiv \text{endpoint is behind view volume} = \text{sign} (z - 1)$$
$$\text{Bit } 6 \equiv \text{endpoint is in front of view volume} = \text{sign} (-z)$$

Recall that sign $(a) = 1$ if a is positive, 0 otherwise.

(b) For the canonical perspective view volume:

$$\text{Bit } 1 \equiv \text{endpoint is above view volume} = \text{sign} (y - z)$$
$$\text{Bit } 2 \equiv \text{endpoint is below view volume} = \text{sign} (-z - y)$$
$$\text{Bit } 3 \equiv \text{endpoint is to the right of view volume} = \text{sign} (x - z)$$
$$\text{Bit } 4 \equiv \text{endpoint is to the left of view volume} = \text{sign} (-z - x)$$
$$\text{Bit } 5 \equiv \text{endpoint is behind view volume} = \text{sign} (z - 1)$$
$$\text{Bit } 6 \equiv \text{endpoint is in front of view volume} = \text{sign} (z_f - z)$$

The category of a line segment (Chap. 5) is (1) visible if both region codes are 000000, (2) not visible if the bitwise logical AND of the region codes is *not* 000000, and (3) clipping candidate if the bitwise logical AND of the region codes is 000000.

8.9 Find the intersecting points of a line segment with the bounding planes of the canonical view volumes for (a) parallel and (b) perspective projections.

SOLUTION

Let $P_1(x_1, y_1, z_1)$ and $P_2(x_2, y_2, z_2)$ be the endpoints of the line segment. The parametric equations of the line segment are

$$x = x_1 + (x_2 - x_1)t \qquad y = y_1 + (y_2 - y_1)t \qquad z = z_1 + (z_2 - z_1)t$$

From Prob. 8.11, the intersection parameter is

$$t_I = \frac{-\mathbf{N} \cdot \overline{\mathbf{R}_0\mathbf{P}_1}}{\mathbf{N} \cdot \overline{\mathbf{P}_1\mathbf{P}_2}}$$

where $\mathbf{N}$ is the normal vector and R_0 is a reference point on the plane.

(a) The bounding planes for the parallel canonical view volume are $x = 0$, $x = 1$, $y = 0$, $y = 1$, $z = 0$, and $z = 1$. For the plane $x = 1$, we have $\mathbf{N} = \mathbf{I}$ and $R_0 (1, 0, 0)$. Then

$$t_I = \frac{-(x_1 - 1)}{x_2 - x_1}$$

If $0 \le t_I \le 1$, the line segment intersects the plane. The point of intersection is then

$$x = x_1 + (x_2 - x_1)\left(-\frac{x_1 - 1}{x_2 - x_1}\right) = 1 \qquad y = y_1 + (y_2 - y_1)\left(-\frac{x_1 - 1}{x_2 - x_1}\right)$$
$$z = z_1 + (z_2 - z_1)\left(-\frac{x_1 - 1}{x_2 - x_1}\right)$$

The intersections with the other planes are found in the same way.

(b) The bounding planes for the perspective canonical view volume are $x = z$, $x = -z$, $y = z$, $y = -z$, $z = z_f$, and $z = 1$ (where z_f is calculated as in Prob. 8.6).

To find the intersection with the plane $x = z$, for example, we write the equation of the plane as $x - z = 0$. From this equation, we read off the normal vector as $\mathbf{N} = \mathbf{I} - \mathbf{K}$ (App. 2, Prob. A2.9), and the reference point is $R_0(0, 0, 0)$. Then

$$t_I = -\frac{x_1 - z_1}{(x_2 - x_1) - (z_2 - z_1)}$$

If $0 \leq t_I \leq 1$, we substitute t_I into the parametric equations of the line segment to calculate the intersection point.

The other intersections are found in the same way.

8.10   Determine the inequalities that are needed to extend the Liang–Barsky line-clipping algorithm to three dimensions for (a) the canonical parallel view volume and (b) the canonical perspective view volume.

SOLUTION

Let $P_1(x_1, y_1, z_1)$ and $P_2(x_2, y_2, z_2)$ be the endpoints of a line. The parametric representation of the line is

$$\begin{cases} x = x_1 + \Delta x \cdot u \\ y = y_1 + \Delta y \cdot u \\ z = z_1 + \Delta z \cdot u \end{cases}$$

where $0 \leq u \leq 1$, $\Delta x = x_2 - x_1$, $\Delta y = y_2 - y_1$, and $\Delta z = z_2 - z_1$. The infinite extension of the line corresponds to $u < 0$ and $1 < u$.

(a)   Points inside the canonical parallel view volume satisfy

$$x_{\min} \leq x_1 + \Delta x \cdot u \leq x_{\max}$$
$$y_{\min} \leq y_1 + \Delta y \cdot u \leq y_{\max}$$
$$z_{\min} \leq z_1 + \Delta z \cdot u \leq z_{\max}$$

where $x_{\min} = y_{\min} = z_{\min} = 0$ and $x_{\max} = y_{\max} = z_{\max} = 1$.
Rewrite the six inequalities as

$$p_k \cdot u \leq q_k, \qquad k = 1, 2, 3, 4, 5, 6$$

where

$$\begin{array}{llll} p_1 = -\Delta x, & q_1 = x_1 - x_{\min} = x_1 & \text{(left)} \\ p_2 = \Delta x, & q_2 = x_{\max} - x_1 = 1 - x_1 & \text{(right)} \\ p_3 = -\Delta y, & q_3 = y_1 - y_{\min} = y_1 & \text{(bottom)} \\ p_4 = \Delta y, & q_4 = y_{\max} - y_1 = 1 - y_1 & \text{(top)} \\ p_5 = -\Delta z, & q_5 = z_1 - z_{\min} = z_1 & \text{(front)} \\ p_6 = \Delta z, & q_6 = z_{\max} - z_1 = 1 - z_1 & \text{(back)} \end{array}$$

(b)   Points inside the canonical perspective view volume satisfy (see Fig. 8-10).

$$-z \leq x \leq z$$
$$-z \leq y \leq z$$
$$z_f \leq z \leq 1$$

i.e.

$$-z_1 - \Delta z \cdot u \leq x_1 + \Delta x \cdot u \leq z_1 + \Delta z \cdot u$$
$$-z_1 - \Delta z \cdot u \leq y_1 + \Delta y \cdot u \leq z_1 + \Delta z \cdot u$$
$$z_f \leq z_1 + \Delta z \cdot u \leq 1$$

Rewrite the six inequalities as

$$p_k \cdot u \leq q_k, \qquad k = 1, 2, 3, 4, 5, 6$$

where

$$
\begin{array}{lll}
p_1 = -\Delta x - \Delta z & q_1 = x_1 + z_1 & \text{(left)} \\
p_2 = \Delta x - \Delta z, & q_2 = z_1 - x_1 & \text{(right)} \\
p_3 = -\Delta y - \Delta z, & q_3 = y_1 + z_1 & \text{(bottom)} \\
p_4 = \Delta y - \Delta z, & q_4 = z_1 - y_1 & \text{(top)} \\
p_5 = -\Delta z, & q_5 = z_1 - z_f & \text{(front)} \\
p_6 = \Delta z, & q_6 = 1 - z_1 & \text{(back)}
\end{array}
$$

Supplementary Problems

8.11 Find the equations of the planes forming the view volume for the general perspective projection.

8.12 Find the intersection point of a plane and a line segment.

CHAPTER 9

Geometric Representation

One of the major concepts in computer graphics is *modeling* of objects. By this we mean numerical description of the objects in terms of their geometric property (size, shape) and how they interact with light (reflect, transmit). The focus of this chapter is on geometric representation of objects. We will discuss illumination and shading models in subsequent chapters.

A graphics system typically uses a set of primitives or geometric forms that are simple enough to be efficiently implemented on the computer but flexible enough to be easily manipulated (assembled, deformed) to represent or model a variety of objects. Geometric forms that are often used as primitives include, in order of complexity, points, lines, polylines, polygons, and polyhedra. More complex geometric forms include curves, curved surface patches, and quadric surfaces.

9.1 SIMPLE GEOMETRIC FORMS

Points and Lines

Points and lines are the basic building blocks of computer graphics. We specify a point by giving its coordinates in three- (or two-) dimensional space. A *line* or *line segment* is specified by giving its endpoints $P_1(x_1, y_1, z_1)$ and $P_2(x_2, y_2, z_2)$.

Polylines

A *polyline* is a chain of connected line segments. It is specified by giving the vertices (nodes) $P_0, \ldots, P_N$ defining the line segments. The first vertex is called the *initial* or *starting point* and the last vertex, the *final* or *terminal point* (see Fig. 9-1).

Polygons

A *polygon* is a closed polyline, that is, one in which the initial and terminal points coincide. A polygon is specified by its *vertex list* $P_0, \ldots, P_N, P_0$. The line segments $\overline{P_0 P_1}, \overline{P_1 P_2}, \ldots, \overline{P_N P_0}$ are called the *edges* of the polygon. (In general, we need not specify P_0 twice, especially when passing the polygon to the Sutherland–Hodgman clipping algorithm.)

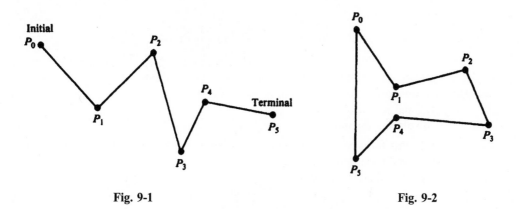

Fig. 9-1   Fig. 9-2

A *planar polygon* is a polygon in which all vertices (and thus the entire polygon) lie on the same plane (see Fig. 9-2).

9.2 WIREFRAME MODELS

A *wirefram model* consists of edges, vertices, and polygons. Here vertices are connected by edges, and polygons are sequences of vertices or edges. The edges may be curved or straight line segments. In the latter case, the wireframe model is called a *polygonal net* or *polygonal mesh* (Fig. 9-3).

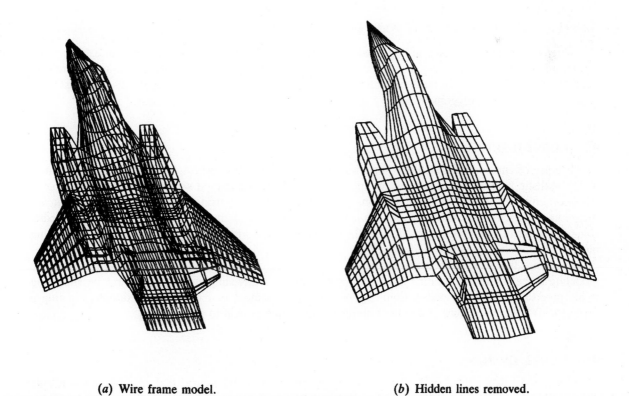

(*a*) Wire frame model.   (*b*) Hidden lines removed.

Fig. 9-3

Representing a Polygonal Net Model

There are several different ways of representing a polygonal net model.

1. *Explicit vertex list* $V = \{P_0, P_1, P_2, \ldots, P_N\}$. The points $P_i(x_i, y_i, z_i)$ are the vertices of the polygonal net, stored in the order in which they would be encountered by traveling around the model. Although this form of representation is useful for single polygons, it is quite inefficient for a complete polygonal net, in that shared vertices are repeated several times (see Prob. 9.1). In addition, when displaying the model by drawing the edges, shared edges are drawn several times.

2. *Polygon listing.* In this form of representation, each vertex is stored exactly once in a vertex list $V = (P_0, \ldots, P_N)$, and each polygon is defined by pointing or indexing into this vertex list (see Prob. 9.2). Again, shared edges are drawn several times in displaying the model.

3. *Explicit edge listing.* In this form of representation, we keep a vertex list in which each vertex is stored exactly once and an edge list in which each edge is stored exactly once. Each edge in the edge list points to the two vertices in the vertex list which define that edge. A polygon is now represented as a list of pointers or indices into the edge list. Additional information, such as those polygons sharing a given edge, can also be stored in the edge list (see Prob. 9.9). Explicit edge listing can be used to represent the more general wireframe model. The wireframe model is displayed by drawing all the edges, and each edge is drawn only once.

Polyhedron

A *polyhedron* is a closed polygonal net (i.e., one which encloses a definite volume) in which each polygon is planar. The polygons are called the *faces* of the polyhedron. In modeling, polyhedrons are quite often treated as solid (i.e., block) objects, as opposed to wireframes or two-dimensional surfaces.

Advantages and Disadvantages of Wireframe Models

Wireframe models are used in engineering applications. They are easy to construct and, if they are composed of straight lines, easy to clip and manipulate through the use of geometric and coordinate transformations. However, for building realistic models, especially of highly curved objects, we must use a very large number of polygons to achieve the illusions of roundness and smoothness.

9.3   CURVED SURFACES

The use of curved surfaces allows for a higher level of modeling, especially for the constructiodn of highly realistic models. There are several approaches to modeling curved surfaces. One is an analog of polyhedral models. Instead of using polygons, we model an object by using small, curved *surface patches* placed next to each other. Another approach is to use surfaces that define solid objects, such as polyhedra, spheres, cylinders, and cones. A model can then be constructed with these solid objects used as building blocks. This process is called *solid modeling*.

There are two ways to construct a model—*additive modeling* and *subtractive modeling*. Additive modeling is the process of building the model by assembling many simpler objects. Subtractive modeling is the process of removing pieces from a given object to create a new object, for example, creating a (cylindrical) hole in a sphere or a cube. Subtractive modeling is akin to sculpting.

9.4   CURVE DESIGN

Given $n + 1$ data points, $P_0(x_0, y_0), \ldots, P_n(x_n, y_n)$ we wish to find a curve that, in some sense, fits the shape outlined by these points. If we require the curve to pass through all the points, we are faced with the problem of *interpolation*. If we require only that the curve be near these points, we are faced with the problem of *approximation*. Interpolation arises, for example, in reconstructing the shape of a digitized curved objects. Approximation is used in computer graphics to design curves that "look good" or must meet some aesthetic goal. To solve these often quite distinct problems, it is necessary to find ways of building curves out of smaller pieces, or *curve segments*, in order to meet the design criteria. (Note that curves and curve segments can be modeled as polylines, i.e., drawn with extremely short line segments.) When modeling a curve $f(x)$ by using curve segments, we try to represent the curve as a sum of smaller segments $\Phi_i(x)$ (called *basis* or *blending functions*):

$$f(x) = \sum_{i=0}^{N} a_i \Phi_i(x)$$

We choose these blending functions with an eye toward computation and display. For this reason, polynomials are often the blending functions of choice.

A *polynomial of degree n* is a function that has the form

$$Q(x) = a_n x^n + a_{n-1} x^{n-1} + \cdots + a_1 x + a_0$$

This polynomial is determined by its $n + 1$ *coefficients* $[a_n, \ldots, a_0]$.

A *continuous piecewise polynomial* $Q(x)$ of degree n is a set of k polynomials $q_i(x)$, each of degree n and $k + 1$ *knots* (nodes) $t_0, \ldots, t_k$ so that

$$Q(x) = q_i(x) \qquad \text{for} \qquad t_i \leq x \leq t_{i+1} \qquad \text{and} \qquad i = 0, \ldots, k-1$$

Note that this definition requires the polynomials to match or piece together at the knots, that is, $q_{i-1}(t_i) = q_i(t_i)$, $i = 1, \ldots, k-1$. This requirement imposes no restrictions on how smoothly the polynomials $q_i(x)$ fit together. For example, there can be corners or sharp contours at the knots (see Fig. 9-4).

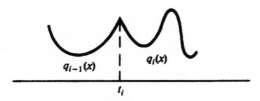

Fig. 9-4

Polynomials of high degree are not very useful for curve designing because of their oscillatory nature.

The most useful piecewise polynomials are those for which the polynomials $q_i(x)$ are cubic (degree 3). There are several reasons for this. One is that the piecewise cubic closely resembles the way a drafter uses a mechanical spline. In addition, 3 is the smallest degree which has the required smoothness properties for describing pleasing shapes. It is also the minimum number needed to represent three-dimensional curves.

9.5   POLYNOMIAL BASIS FUNCTIONS

Let $P_0(x_0, y_0), \ldots, P_n(x_n, y_n)$ represent $n + 1$ data points. In addition, let $t_0, t_1, t_2, \ldots,$ be any numbers (called *knots*). The following are common choices for basis or blending functions.

Lagrange Polynomials of Degree n

$$L_i(x) = \prod_{\substack{j=0 \\ j \neq i}}^{n} \frac{x - x_j}{x_i - x_j}, \qquad i = 0, 1, \ldots, n$$

Note that $L_i(x_i) = 1$ and $L_i(x_j) = 0$ for all $j \neq i$. (Here Π represents term-by-term multiplication.)

Hermite Cubic Polynomials

Refer to Fig. 9-5.

$$H_i(x) = \begin{cases} -\dfrac{2(x - t_{i-1})^3}{(t_i - t_{i-1})^3} + \dfrac{3(x - t_{i-1})^2}{(t_i - t_{i-1})^2} & t_{i-1} \leq x \leq t_i \\[4mm] -\dfrac{2(t_{i+1} - x)^3}{(t_{i+1} - t_i)^3} + \dfrac{3(t_{i+1} - x)^2}{(t_{i+1} - t_i)^2} & t_i \leq x \leq t_{i+1} \end{cases}$$

$$\bar{H}_i(x) = \begin{cases} \dfrac{(x - t_{i-1})^2(x - t_i)}{(t_i - t_{i-1})^2} & t_{i-1} \leq x \leq t_i \\[4mm] \dfrac{(x - t_i)(t_{i+1} - x)^2}{(t_{i+1} - t_i)^2} & t_i \leq x \leq t_{i+1} \end{cases}$$

B-Splines

Refer to Fig. 9-6. For the knot set $t_0, t_1, t_2, \ldots$, the nth-degree B-splines $B_{i,n}$ are defined recursively:

$$B_{i,0}(x) = \begin{cases} 1 & t_i \leq x \leq t_{i+1} \\ 0 & \text{otherwise} \end{cases} \qquad B_{i,n}(x) = \frac{x - t_i}{t_{i+n} - t_i} B_{i,n-1}(x) + \frac{t_{i+n+1} - x}{t_{i+n+1} - t_{i+1}} B_{i+1,n-1}(x)$$

for $t_i \leq x \leq t_{i+n+1}$. Note that $B_{i,n}(x)$ is nonzero only in the interval $[t_i, t_{i+n+1}]$. In particular, the cubic B-spline $B_{i,3}$ is nonzero over the interval $[t_i, t_{i+4}]$ (which spans the knots $t_i, t_{i+1}, t_{i+2}, t_{i+3}, t_{i+4}$). In addition, for nonrepeated knots, the B-spline is zero at the endknots t_i and t_{i+n+1} (from Prob. 9.3), that is,

$$\begin{aligned} B_{i,n}(t_i) &= 0 \\ B_{i,n}(t_{i+n+1}) &= 0 \end{aligned} \qquad (n \geq 1)$$

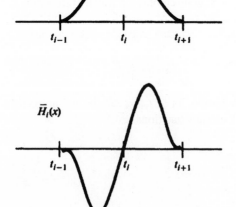

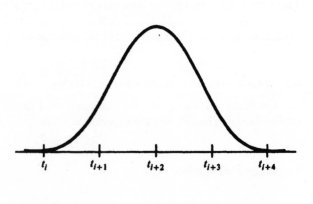

Fig. 9-5   Hermite cubic basis functions.   **Fig. 9-6**   Cubic B-spline $B_{i,3}(x)$.

In using B-splines, we allow for repeated knots, that is, $t_i = t_{i+1} = \cdots$. This means that $B_{i,n}$ can have the form $\frac{0}{0}$ in its definition. By letting $\frac{0}{0} = 0$, we extend the definition of $B_{i,n}$ to incorporate repeated knots.

Bernstein Polynomials

Refer to Fig. 9-7. The Bernstein polynomials of degree n over the interval [0, 1] are defined as

$$BE_{k,n}(x) = \frac{n!}{k!(n-k)!} x^k (1-x)^{n-k}, \qquad 0 \le x \le 1$$

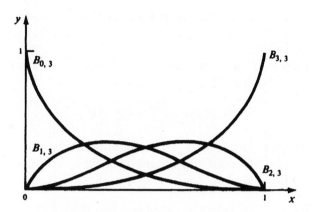

Fig. 9-7   Cubic Bernstein polynomials.

The cubic Bernstein polynomials are

$$B_{0,3}(x) = 1 - 3x + 3x^2 - x^3$$
$$B_{1,3}(x) = 3(x - 2x^2 + x^3)$$
$$B_{2,3}(x) = 3(x^2 - x^3)$$
$$B_{3,3}(x) = x^3$$

9.6   THE PROBLEM OF INTERPOLATION

Given data points $P_0(x_0, y_0), \ldots, P_n(x_n, y_n)$, we wish to find a curve which passes through these points.

Lagrange Polynomial Interpolation Solution

Here

$$L(x) = \sum_{i=0}^{n} y_i L_i(x)$$

where $L_i(x)$ are the Lagrange polynomials and $L(x)$ is the nth-degree polynomial interpolating the data points.

Hermitian Cubic Interpolation Solution

We wish to find a piecewise polynomial $H(x)$ of degree 3 which passes through the data points and is also continuously differentiable at these points. We also prescribe the values of the derivatives y' (or slope of the tangent line) at the given data points, that is, we prescribe the points $(x_0, y_0'), \ldots, (x_n, y_n')$:

$$H(x) = \sum_{i=0}^{n} [y_i H_i(x) + y_i' \bar{H}_i(x)]$$

where $H_i(x)$ and $\bar{H}_i(x)$ are the Hermitian cubic basis functions and $t_0 = x_0, t_1 = x_1, t_2 = x_2, \ldots, t_n = x_n$ are the choices for the knot set.

Spline Interpolation

If we require that the interpolating piecewise polynomial be joined as smoothly as possible at the data points, the resulting curve is called a *spline*. Therefore, a spline of degree m has continuous derivatives up to order $m - 1$ at the data points.

It can be shown that any mth-degree spline that passes through $n + 1$ data points can be represented in terms of the B-spline basis functions $B_{i,n}$ as

$$S_m(x) = \sum_{i=0}^{m+n-1} a_i B_{i,m}(x)$$

In order to define the B-spline functions $B_{i,m}(x)$ so as to solve the interpolation problem, the knots $t_0, t_1, \ldots, t_{m+n+1}$ must be chosen to satisfy the Shoenberg–Whitney condition:

$$t_i < x_i < t_{i+m+1}, \qquad i = 0, \ldots, n$$

The following choices for the knots satisfy this condition (see Prob. 9.4):

Step 1.   Choose

$$t_0 = \cdots = t_m < x_0 \qquad t_{n+1} = \cdots = t_{m+n+1} > x_n$$

Step 2.   Choose the remaining knots according to

$$t_{i+m+1} = \frac{x_{i+1} + \cdots + x_{i+m}}{m}, \qquad i = 0, \ldots, n - m - 1$$

For cubic splines ($m = 3$), an alternative to step 2, requiring less computation, is step 2'. Choose

$$t_{i+4} = x_{i+2}, \qquad i = 0, \ldots, n - 4$$

The splines $S_2(x)$ and $S_3(x)$ are called *quadratic* and *cubic splines*, respectively:

$$S_2(x) = \sum_{i=0}^{n+1} a_i B_{i,2}(x) \qquad \text{and} \qquad S_3(x) = \sum_{i=0}^{n+2} a_i B_{i,3}(x)$$

Confining our attention to the cubic spline, we see that there are $n + 3$ coefficients a_i to evaluate, requiring $n + 3$ equations.

The interpolation criterion $S_3(x_j) = y_j, j = 0, \ldots, n$ provides $n + 1$ equations:

$$y_j = S_3(x_j) = \sum_{i=0}^{n+2} a_i B_{i,3}(x_j)$$

The remaining two equations are usually specified as boundary conditions at the endpoints x_0 and x_n. Some choices for boundary conditions are

1.   *Natural spline condition*

$$S_3''(x_0) = 0 \qquad S_3''(x_n) = 0$$

2.   *Clamped spline condition*

$$S_3'(x_0) = y_0' \qquad S_3'(x_n) = y_n'$$

where y_0' and y_n' are prescribed derivative values.

3. *Cyclic spline condition*

$$S_3'(x_0) = S_3'(x_n) \qquad S_3''(x_0) = S_3''(x_n)$$

This is useful for producing closed curves.

4. *Anticyclic spline condition*

$$S_3'(x_0) = -S_3'(x_n) \qquad S_3''(x_0) = -S_3''(x_n)$$

This is useful in producing splines with parallel endings whose tangent vectors are equal in magnitude but opposite in direction.

For technical reasons, boundary condition 1, the so-called natural boundary condition, is the least preferred choice.

9.7   THE PROBLEM OF APPROXIMATION

The problem is to provide a smooth representation of a three-dimensional curve which approximates given data so as to yield a given shape. Usually the data is given interactively in the form of a guiding polyline determined by *control points* $P_0(x_0, y_0, z_0)$, $P_1(x_1, y_1, z_1), \ldots, P_n(x_n, y_n, z_n)$. We would like to find a curve which approximates the shape of this guiding polyline (see Fig. 9-8).

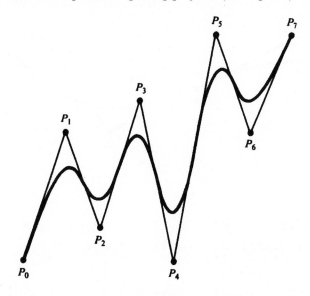

Fig. 9-8

Bézier–Bernstein Approximation

Using the Bernstein polynomials, we form the parametric curves:

$$P(t): \begin{cases} x(t) = \sum_{i=0}^{n} x_i BE_{i,n}(t) \\[2mm] y(t) = \sum_{i=0}^{n} y_i BE_{i,n}(t) \qquad 0 \le t \le 1 \\[2mm] z(t) = \sum_{i=0}^{n} z_i BE_{i,n}(t) \end{cases}$$

where $P(t)$ is called the *Bézier curve*.

Properties of the Bézier–Bernstein Approximation

There are four basic properties:

1. The Bézier curve has the same endpoints as the guiding polyline, that is:

$$P_0 = P(0) = [x(0), y(0), z(0)] \qquad P_n = P(1) = [x(1), y(1), z(1)]$$

2. The direction of the tangent vector at the endpoints P_0, P_n is the same as that of the vector determined by the first and last segments $\overline{P_0 P_1}$, $\overline{P_{n-1} P_n}$ of the guiding polyline. In particular $P'(0) = n \cdot (P_1 - P_0)$ [i.e., $x'(0) = n(x_1 - x_0)$, $y'(0) = n(y_1 - y_0)$, $z'(0) = n(z_1 - z_0)$] and $P'(1) = n \cdot (P_n - P_{n-1})$.

3. The Bézier curve lies entirely within the convex hull of the guiding polyline. In two dimensions, the *convex hull* is the polygon formed by placing a "rubber band" about the collection of points $P_0, \ldots, P_n$.

4. Bézier curves are suited to interactive design. In fact, Bézier curves can be pieced together so as to ensure continuous differentiability at their juncture by letting the edges of the two different guiding polylines that are adjacent to the common endpoint be collinear (see Fig. 9-9).

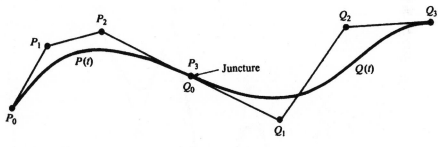

Fig. 9-9

Bézier–B-Spline Approximation

For this approximation, we use B-splines (see Fig. 9-10)

$$P(t): \begin{cases} x(t) = \displaystyle\sum_{i=0}^{n} x_i B_{i,m}(t) \\[2mm] y(t) = \displaystyle\sum_{i=0}^{n} y_i B_{i,m}(t) \qquad 0 \le t \le n - m + 1 \\[2mm] z(t) = \displaystyle\sum_{i=0}^{n} z_i B_{i,m}(t) \end{cases}$$

The mth-degree B-splines $B_{i,m}(t)$, $i = 0, \ldots, n$, are defined for t in the parameter range $[0, n - m + 1]$. The knot set $t_0, \ldots, t_{n+m+1}$ is chosen to be the set $\underbrace{0, \ldots, 0}_{m+1}, 1, 2, \ldots, n - m, \underbrace{n - m + 1, \ldots, n - m + 1}_{m+1}$.
This use of repeated knots ensures that the endpoints of the spline coincide with the endpoints of the guiding polyline (Prob. 9.6).

Since the knot spacing is uniform, we can also use an explicit form for calculating the B-splines (Prob. 9.10).

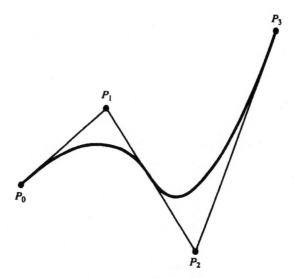

Fig. 9-10   Cubic Bézier B-spline.

Closed Curves

To construct a closed B-spline curve which approximates a given closed guiding polygon, we need only choose the knots $t_0, \ldots, t_{n+m+1}$ to be cyclic, i.e., $[0, 1, \ldots, n, 0, 1, \ldots]$. So

$$t_{m+1} = t_0 = 0 \qquad t_{m+2} = t_1 = 1 \qquad t_{m+1+i} = t_i$$

In practice, the quadratic and cubic B-splines $B_{i,2}$ and $B_{i,3}$ are the easiest to work with and provide enough flexibility for use in a wide range of curve design problems.

Properties of Bézier–B-Spline Approximation

There are five basic properties:

1. The Bézier–B-spline approximation has the same properties as the Bézier–Bernstein approximation; in fact, they are the same piecewise polynomial if $m = n$. This includes the properties of agreement with the guiding polygon and the tangent vectors at the endpoints and the convex hull property.

2. If the guiding polyline has $m + 1$ consecutive vertices (control points) which are collinear, the resulting span of the Bézier–B-spline will be linear. So this approximation allows for linear sections to be embedded within the curve.

3. The Bézier–B-spline approximation provides for the local control of curve shape. If a single control point is changed, portions of the curve that lie far away are not disturbed. In fact, only $m + 1$ of the spans are affected. This is due to the local nature of the B-spline basis functions.

4. Bézier–B-splines produce a closer fit to the guiding polygon than does the Bézier–Bernstein approximation.

5. The Bézier–B-spline approximation allows the use of control points P_i counted with *multiplicities* of 2 or more. That is, $P_i = P_{i+1} = \cdots = P_{i+k}$ for $k \geq 1$. This results in an approximation which is pulled closer toward this control point. In fact, if the point has multiplicity $m + 1$, the curve will pass through it.

9.8   CURVED-SURFACE DESIGN

The modeling and approximation of curved surfaces is difficult and involves many complex issues. We will look at two methods for representing a surface: *guiding nets* and *interpolating surface patches*.

Guiding Nets

This technique is a direct generalization of the Bézier–Bernstein and Bézier–B-spline approximation methods for curves. A *guiding net* is a polygonal net with vertices $P_{ij}(x_{ij}, y_{ij}, z_{ij})$, $i = 0, \ldots, m$, and $j = 0, \ldots, n$ (see Fig. 9-11).

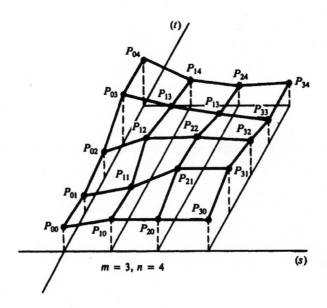

Fig. 9-11

1.   *Bézier–Bernstein surface.* This is the surface with parametric equations:

$$Q(s, t): \begin{cases} x(s, t) = \displaystyle\sum_{i=0}^{m} \sum_{j=0}^{n} x_{ij} BE_{i,m}(s) BE_{j,n}(t) \\[2ex] y(s, t) = \displaystyle\sum_{i=0}^{m} \sum_{j=0}^{n} y_{ij} BE_{i,m}(s) BE_{j,n}(t) \\[2ex] z(s, t) = \displaystyle\sum_{i=0}^{m} \sum_{j=0}^{n} z_{ij} BE_{i,m}(s) BE_{j,n}(t) \end{cases}$$

Here $0 \le s,\ t \le 1$ and BE are the Bernstein polynomials. This approximation has properties analogous to the one-dimensional case with respect to the corner points P_{00}, P_{m0}, P_{0n}, and P_{mn}. The convex hull property is also satisfied.

2. *Bézier–B-spline approximation*. In parametric form this is expressed as

$$Q(s, t): \begin{cases} x(s, t) = \sum_{i=0}^{m} \sum_{j=0}^{n} x_{ij} B_{i,\alpha}(s) B_{j,\beta}(t) \\[2mm] y(s, t) = \sum_{i=0}^{m} \sum_{j=0}^{n} y_{ij} B_{i,\alpha}(s) B_{j,\beta}(t) \\[2mm] z(s, t) = \sum_{i=0}^{m} \sum_{j=0}^{n} z_{ij} B_{i,\alpha}(s) B_{j,\beta}(t) \end{cases}$$

where $0 \le s \le m - \alpha + 1$ and $0 \le s \le n - \beta + 1$. The knot sets for s and t used to define the B-splines $B_{i,\alpha}(s)$ and $B_{j,\beta}(t)$ are determined as in the one-dimensional case.

Quadratic approximation occurs when $\alpha = \beta = 2$. Cubic approximation occurs when $\alpha = \beta = 3$. In general, quadratic or cubic B-splines are most often used. For both these methods, the construction of the guiding net (by locating the control points P_{ij}) is left to the user.

Interpolating Surface Patches

Instead of using a given set of points P_{ij} to construct a given surface, the process of interpolating surface patches is based upon prescribing boundary curves for a surface patch and "filling in" the interior of the patch by interpolating between the boundary curves.

1. *Coons surfaces*. For this technique, a patch is determined by specifying four bounding curves, denoted in parametric vector form as $P(s, 0)$, $P(s, 1)$, $P(0, t)$, and $P(1, t)$, $0 \le s, t \le 1$ (see Fig. 9-12).

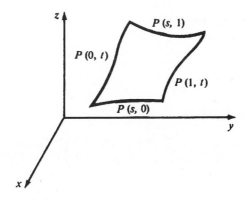

Fig. 9-12

The (linear) *Coons surface patch* interpolating the boundary curves can be written in vector form by using linear interpolation (or blending):

$$Q(s, t) = P(s, 0)(1 - t) + P(s, 1)t + P(0, t)(1 - s) + P(1, t)s - P(0, 0)(1 - s)(1 - t)$$
$$- P(0, 1)(1 - s)t - P(1, 0)s(1 - t) - P(1, 1)st$$

(The subtractions are required so that the interpolators between corner points are not counted twice.) This idea can be extended to define more general surface patches.

2. *Lofted surfaces*. *Lofting* is used where the surface to be constructed stretches in a given direction; an example is the hull of a ship.

Given two or more space curves, called *cross-section curves*, *lofting* is the process of blending the cross sections together using longitudinal blending curves. The simplest example is *linear blending* between cross-section curves $P_1(s)$ and $P_2(s)$. The lofted surface is $Q(s, t) = (1 - t)P_1(s) + tP_2(s)$ (see Fig. 9-13).

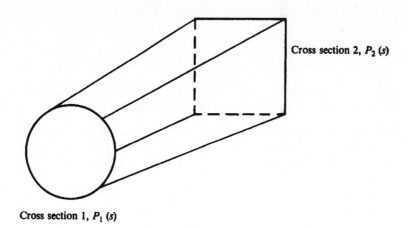

Cross section 2, $P_2(s)$

Cross section 1, $P_1(s)$

Fig. 9-13

9.9 TRANSFORMING CURVES AND SURFACES

All the curve and surface models that we have constructed have the general form

$$x = \Sigma x_i \Phi_i \qquad \text{and} \qquad y = \Sigma y_i \Phi_i$$

(Add a z component for three dimensions.)

If M is 2×2 transformation matrix

$$M = \begin{pmatrix} a & b \\ c & d \end{pmatrix}$$

we can apply M to the functions x and y:

$$\begin{pmatrix} a & b \\ c & d \end{pmatrix}\begin{pmatrix} \Sigma x_i \Phi_i \\ \Sigma y_i \Phi_i \end{pmatrix} = \begin{pmatrix} a(\Sigma x_i \Phi_i) + b(\Sigma y_i \Phi_i) \\ c(\Sigma x_i \Phi_i) + d(\Sigma y_i \Phi_i) \end{pmatrix} = \begin{pmatrix} \Sigma(a x_i + b y_i)\Phi_i \\ \Sigma(c x_i + d y_i)\Phi_i \end{pmatrix}$$

The transformed functions are then

$$\tilde{x} = \Sigma(a x_i + b y_i)\Phi_i \qquad \tilde{y} = \Sigma(c x_i + d y_i)\Phi_i$$

In other words, to transform these curves and surfaces, it is necessary only to transform the coefficients (x_i, y_i). In most cases these coefficients represent data or control points. So the transformation of the approximation of a curve or surface is found by first transforming the control points and then forming the approximation based on the transformed points.

9.10 QUADRIC SURFACES

Spheres, cylinders, and cones are part of the family of surfaces called *quadric surfaces*. A quadric surface is defined by an equation which is of the second degree (in x, y, or z).

The canonical quadric surfaces are as follows:

Sphere

From Fig. 9-14:

$$x^2 + y^2 + z^2 = R^2$$

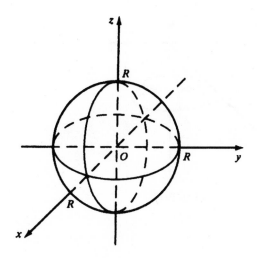

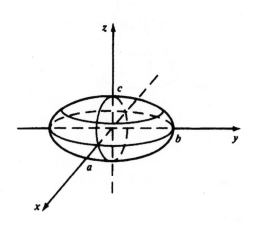

Fig. 9-14   **Fig. 9-15**

Ellipsoid

From Fig. 9-15:

$$\frac{x^2}{a^2} + \frac{y^2}{b^2} + \frac{z^2}{c^2} = 1$$

One-sheeted Hyperboloid

From Fig. 9-16:

$$\frac{x^2}{a^2} + \frac{y^2}{b^2} - \frac{z^2}{c^2} = 1$$

Two-sheeted Hyperboloid

From Fig. 9-17:

$$\frac{z^2}{c^2} - \frac{x^2}{a^2} - \frac{y^2}{b^2} = 1$$

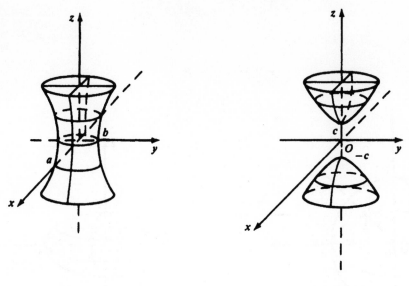

Fig. 9-16   Fig. 9-17

Elliptic Cylinder

From Fig. 9-18:

$$\frac{x^2}{a^2} + \frac{y^2}{b^2} = 1$$

When $a = b = R$, the cylinder is a circular cylinder of radius R.

Elliptic Paraboloid

From Fig. 9-19:

$$\frac{x^2}{a^2} + \frac{y^2}{b^2} = cz$$

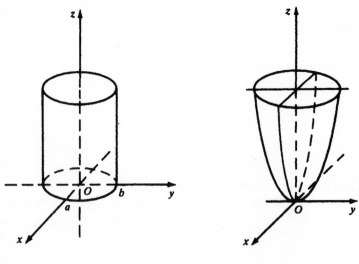

Fig. 9-18   Fig. 9-19

Hyperbolic Parboloid

From Fig. 9-20:

$$\frac{x^2}{a^2} - \frac{y^2}{b^2} = cz$$

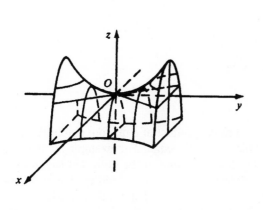

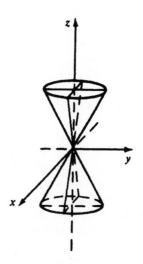

Fig. 9-20　　　　　　　　　　　　　　　　　Fig. 9-21

Elliptic Cone

From Fig. 9-21:

$$\frac{x^2}{a^2} + \frac{y^2}{b^2} = z^2$$

When $a = b = R$, we have a right circular cone. If we restrict z so that $z > 0$, we have the upper cone.

Note that, except for spheres and ellipsoids, the mathematical definition produces a figure of infinite extent. To use it for computer graphics, we must specify bounds for the surface in the form of bounding clipping planes having the form $z = h$.

9.11　EXAMPLE: TERRAIN GENERATION

We show two different ways to generate a *triangle mesh* (i.e., a polynomial net consisting of triangles) that models the random peaks and valleys of a mountainous landscape.

Midpoint Displacement

This is a recursive approach that begins with one or more triangles over the terrain area [see Fig. 9-22(a)]. We use the midpoints of the edges to subdivide each triangle into four smaller ones. The midpoints are randomly elevated to produce a rugged appearance [see Fig. 9-22(b)]. The coordinates (x_m, y_m, z_m) of the midpoint of the edge between $P_1(x_1, y_1, z_1)$ and $P_2(x_2, y_2, z_2)$ are calculated as follows:

$$\begin{cases} x_m = (x_2 - x_1)/2 \\ y_m = (y_2 - y_1)/2 + r \\ z_m = (z_2 - z_1)/2 \end{cases}$$

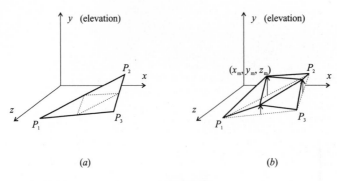

(a)   (b)

Fig. 9-22

where r is a random displacement that can be expressed as the product of a random number $0 \le \lambda \le 1$ and a function of the projected length (onto the x–z plane) of the edge. For example, if the function is $F(\rho) = \rho/2$, then the midpoint can be elevated by no more than half of the projected length of the edge. The subdivision process terminates when all edges project to a preset threshold or shorter length.

Since the original vertices are not moved and each midpoint is displaced only once, the resulting terrain tends to maintain the overall shape of the initial model. On the other hand, deep valleys that look unrealistic may appear along the original edges. We can alleviate this problem by adding a random displacement to the vertices as well as the midpoints at each recursion stage. The tradeoff here is less control over the shape of the final terrain structure.

Brownian Distribution of Disks

In this approach we superimpose a grid onto the terrain area and initialize a counter for each grid cell (see Fig. 9-23 for a rectangular area that can be represented by a two-dimensional counter array). We then randomly move a circular disk over the area. At each disk position we increment the counter for every grid cell that is covered by the disk. After a while the counter values form an elevation profile of a pile of randomly placed disks. Each elevation value describes the height of a point/vertex above the corresponding grid cell. A triangle-mesh model of the resulting terrain can thus be constructed by first connecting each vertex to its four neighbors [analogous to the four neighbouring pixels in Fig. 3-18(a)] to form a quadrilateral-mesh and then adding diagonal edges to divide each quadrilateral into two triangles.

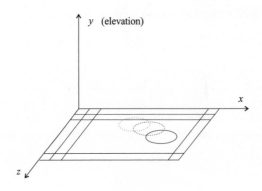

Fig. 9-23

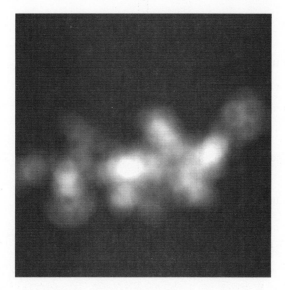

Fig. 9-24

For example, the gray-scale image in Fig. 9-24 represents the values in a 512×512 counter array. The values are obtained using a disk of radius 25 after 6000 random movements, each of which is a step of size 3 forward or backward and simultaneously a step of the same size to the left or to the right. Whenever the center of the disk moves beyond the image boundary it is reset to the middle of the image. The counter values are normalized so that the maximum count corresponds to white in the image. The resultant triangle-mesh is viewed in Fig. 9-25 using perspective projection, looking from a point near the lower-right corner of Fig. 9-24 towards the center (with hidden surfaces removed and visible surfaces lit by a light source).

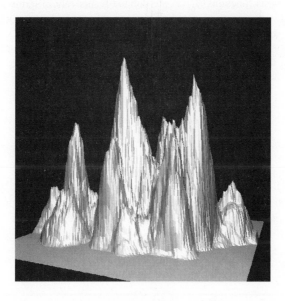

Fig. 9-25

Solved Problems

9.1   Represent a cube by using an explicit vertex list.

SOLUTION

Using the notation in Fig. 7-12, one possible representation is

$$V = \{ABCDAFEDCHEFGHGB\}$$

Note the vertex repetitions in the list V and the repetition of edge FE as EF.

9.2   Represent a cube by using polygon listing.

SOLUTION

Referring to Fig. 7-12, we form the vertex list

$$V = \{ABCDEFGH\}$$

The faces of the cube are polygons (which, in this case, are squares) $P_1, \ldots, P_6$, where

$$P_1 = \{ABCD\} \qquad P_4 = \{ABGF\}$$
$$P_2 = \{CDEH\} \qquad P_5 = \{BCHG\}$$
$$P_3 = \{ADEF\} \qquad P_6 = \{EFGH\}$$

Note the edge repetitions encountered in drawing the polygons. For example, polygons P_2 and P_3 share the edge DE.

9.3   Show that the nth-degree B-spline basis functions $B_{i,n}(x)$ satisfy

$$B_{i,n}(x) = 0 \quad \text{if} \quad x < t_i \quad \text{or} \quad x > t_{i+n+1}$$

SOLUTION

Since the B-spline basis functions $B_{i,n}(x)$ are defined recursively in terms of the lower-order B-splines $B_{i,n-1}(x)$ and $B_{i+1,n-1}(x)$ of degree $n-1$, we shall indicate only the first step of a general induction argument. Therefore, we illustrate what happens for the first-degree B-spline $B_{i,1}(x)$.

Now suppose that $x < t_i$. Then also $x < t_{i+1}$, so at x the zero-degree B-splines have the values $B_{i,0}(x) = 0$ and $B_{i+1,0}(x) = 0$. From these values we find, in turn, that $B_{i,1}(x) = 0$.

Now suppose that the knot set is nonrepeating. Let $x = t_i$. Then $B_{i,0}(t_i) = 1$, but $B_{i+1,0}(t_i) = 0$. So

$$B_{i,0}(t_i) = \frac{t_i - t_i}{t_{i+1} - t_i}(1) + \frac{t_{i+2} - t_i}{t_{i+2} - t_{i+1}}(0) = 0$$

Thus $B_{i,1}(x) = 0$ if $x \le t_i$. Similar arguments show that $B_{i,1}(x) = 0$ if $x \ge t_{i+1}$.

9.4   Let $P_0(0,0)$, $P_1(1,2)$, $P_2(2,1)$, $P_3(3,-1)$, $P_4(4,10)$, and $P_5(5,5)$ be given data points. If interpolation based on cubic B-splines is used to find a curve interpolating these data points, find a knot set $t_0, \ldots, t_9$ that can be used to define the cubic B-splines.

SOLUTION

The knot set can be chosen according to one of two schemes. With $m = 3$ and $n = 5$:

1.   Choose

$$t_0 = t_1 = t_2 = t_3 = -1 \ (< x_0) \qquad \text{and} \qquad t_6 = t_7 = t_8 = t_9 = 6 \ (> x_n)$$

The remaining knots are chosen according to

$$t_{i+m+1} = \frac{x_{i+1} + \cdots + x_{i+m}}{m}, \qquad i = 0, \ldots, n-m-1$$

So

$$t_4 = \frac{1+2+3}{3} = 2 \qquad t_5 = \frac{2+3+4}{3} = 3$$

2. An alternative scheme for cubic splines is

$$t_0 = t_1 = t_2 = t_3 = -1 \qquad t_6 = t_7 = t_8 = t_9 = 6$$

and the remaining knots are chosen according to

$$t_{i+4} = x_{i+2}, \qquad i = 0, \ldots, n-4$$

So

$$t_4 = 2 \qquad t_5 = 3$$

The agreement between knot sets chosen according to these two schemes is a result of the uniform spacing of the data points along the x axis.

9.5   Write the equations that can be used to find an interpolating cubic spline curve to fit the data in Prob. 9.4 using cubic B-spline basis functions.

SOLUTION

With $m = 3$ and $n = 5$, the interpolating spline can be written in terms of cubic B-splines as

$$S_3(x) = \sum_{i=0}^{7} a_i B_{i,3}(x)$$

The interpolation equations for the data points (x_j, y_j), $j = 0, \ldots, 5$ are

$$y_j = S_3(x_j), \qquad j = 0, \ldots, 5$$

With the knot set chosen in Prob. 9.4, the intervals $[t_j, t_{j+4}]$ defined by the knots t_j, $j = 0, \ldots, 9$ are

j	t_j	t_{j+4}
0	-1	2
1	-1	3
2	-1	6
3	-1	6
4	2	6
5	3	6

Because $B_{i,3}(x)$ is nonzero only for $t_i < x < t_{i+4}$, the interpolation equations become

$$y_j = S_3(x_j)$$

$$0 = a_0 B_{0,3}(0) + a_1 B_{1,3}(0) + a_2 B_{2,3}(0) + a_3 B_{3,3}(0)$$

$$2 = a_0 B_{0,3}(1) + a_1 B_{1,3}(1) + a_2 B_{2,3}(1) + a_3 B_{3,3}(1)$$

$$1 = a_1 B_{1,3}(2) + a_2 B_{2,3}(2) + a_3 B_{3,3}(2)$$

$$-1 = a_2 B_{2,3}(3) + a_3 B_{3,3}(3) + a_4 B_{4,3}(3)$$

$$10 = a_2 B_{2,3}(4) + a_3 B_{3,3}(4) + a_4 B_{4,3}(4) + a_5 B_{5,3}(4)$$

$$5 = a_2 B_{2,3}(5) + a_3 B_{3,3}(5) + a_4 B_{4,3}(5) + a_5 B_{5,3}(5)$$

The remaining two equations can be chosen to satisfy prescribed boundary conditions at $x_0 = 0$ and $x_5 = 5$.

9.6   Show that the knot set used in constructing the Bézier–B-spline approximation to a guiding polyline guarantees that the endpoints of the spline coincide with the endpoints of the guiding polyline.

SOLUTION

For an m-degree Bézier–B-spline approximation, the knot set used is

$$\underbrace{0,\ldots,0}_{m+1}, 1, 2, \ldots, n-m, \underbrace{n-m+1, n-m+1, \ldots, n-m+1}_{m+1}$$

Let $P_0(x_0, y_0, z_0)$ be the first control point of the guiding polyline and $P_n(x_n, y_n, z_n)$ the last. Now $x(t) = \sum_{i=0}^{n} x_i B_{i,m}(t)$ with similar expressions for $y(t)$ and $z(t)$. We wish to show that

$$x(0) = x_0, y(0) = y_0, z(0) = z_0 \quad \text{and} \quad x(n-1) = x_n, y(n-1) = y_n, z(n-1) = z_n$$

Let us restrict ourselves to $m = 2$ (quadratic) B-splines. Then the knot set is

$$0, 0, 0, 1, 2, 3, \ldots, n-2, n-1, n-1, n-1$$
$$t_0, t_1, t_2, t_3, t_4, t_5, \ldots, t_{n+1}, t_{n+2}, t_{n+3}, t_{n+4}$$

Since $B_{i,2}(x)$ is nonzero only over the interval $t_i \le x \le t_{i+3}$, it follows that $B_{i,2}(0)$ is nonzero only if $i = 0, 1$, and 2. So then

$$x(0) = \sum_{i=0}^{n} x_i B_{i,2}(0) = x_0 B_{0,2}(0) + x_1 B_{1,2}(0) + x_2 B_{2,2}(0)$$

To calculate $B_{0,2}$, using the definition and the convention that $\frac{0}{0} = 0$, we obtain

$$B_{0,2}(0) = B_{1,1}(0) \quad \text{and} \quad B_{1,1}(0) = B_{2,0}(0) \quad \text{and} \quad B_{2,0}(0) = 1$$

So $B_{0,2}(0) = 1$ (compare with Prob. 9.3).
To calculate $B_{1,2}(0)$, using the definition

$$B_{1,2}(0) = \frac{2}{2} B_{2,1}(0) \quad \text{and} \quad B_{2,1}(0) = \frac{2}{2-1} B_{3,0}(0) \quad \text{and} \quad B_{3,0}(0) = 0 \quad \text{since} \quad 0 \le t_3 = 1$$

So we have $B_{1,2}(0) = 0$. In a similar manner, we find $B_{2,2}(0) = 0$. Thus, $x(0) = x_0$ and the same for the y and z coordinates.
Similar calculations show that $x(n-1) = x_n$, $y(n-1) = y_n$, and $z(n-1) = z_n$.

9.7   Find the linear Coons surface patch that interpolates the curves of Fig. 9-26.

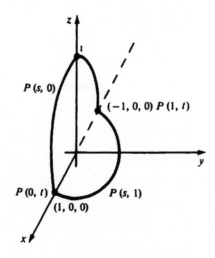

Fig. 9-26

SOLUTION

The four bounding curves can be described parametrically as follows (see Fig. 9-26):

1. $P(s, 0) = (\cos \pi s, 0, \sin \pi s)$ $0 \le s \le 1$
2. $P(1, t) = (-1, 0, 0)$ $0 \le t \le 1$
3    $P(s, 1) = (\cos \pi s, \sin \pi s, 0)$ $0 \le s \le 1$
4. $P(0, t) = (1, 0, 0)$ $0 \le t \le 1$

Note that curves 2 and 4 are constant curves, that is, points.
The linear Coons surface interpolating these curves can be written as

$$Q(s, t) = P(s, 0)(1 - t) + P(s, 1)t + P(0, t)(1 - s) + P(1, t)s - P(0, 0)(1 - s)(1 - t)$$
$$- P(0, 1)(1 - s)t - P(1, 0)s(1 - t) - p(1, 1)st$$

In terms of coordinates:

$$x(s, t) = (\cos \pi s)(1 - t) + (\cos \pi s)t + (1)(1 - s) + (-1)s$$
$$- (1)(1 - s)(1 - t) - (1)(1 - s)t - (-1)s(1 - t) - (-1)st$$

or

$$x(s, t) = \cos \pi s$$

Now

$$y(s, t) = (0)(1 - t) + (\sin \pi s)t + (0)(1 - s) + (0)s - (0)(1 - s)(1 - t) - (0)(1 - s)t - (0)s(1 - t) - (0)st$$

or

$$y(s, t) = t \sin \pi s$$

Finally

$$z(s, t) = (\sin \pi s)(1 - t) + (0)t + (0)(1 - s) + (0)s - (0)(1 - s)(1 - t) - (0)(1 - s)t - (0)s(1 - t) - (0)st$$

or

$$z(s, t) = (1 - t) \sin \pi s$$

The linear Coons surface is

$$Q(s, t) = [\cos \pi s, t \sin \pi s, (1 - t) \sin \pi s]   0 \le s, t \le 1$$

9.8   Find the lofting surface defined by linear blending between the cross-section curves in Fig. 9-27.

SOLUTION

The curves in Fig. 9-27 are circles whose equations can be defined parametrically as

$$P_1(s) = (\cos 2\pi s, \sin 2\pi s, 0)   0 \le s \le 1$$

and

$$P_2(s) = (2 \cos 2\pi s, 2 \sin 2\pi s, 4)   0 \le s \le 1$$

The lofting surface is then

$$Q(s, t) = (1 - t)P_1(s) + tP_2(s)$$

In terms of coordinates, we find that

$$x(s, t) = (1 - t)(\cos 2\pi s) + t(2 \cos 2\pi s) = (1 + t) \cos 2\pi s$$
$$y(s, t) = (1 - t)(\sin 2\pi s) + t(2 \sin 2\pi s) = (1 + t) \sin 2\pi s$$
$$z(s, t) = (1 - t)(0) + t(4) = 4t$$

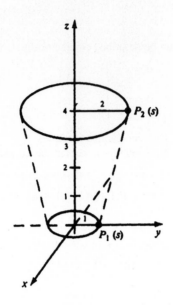

Fig. 9-27

Thus

$$Q(s, t) = [(1 + t) \cos 2\pi s, (1 + t) \sin 2\pi s, 4t] \qquad 0 \le s, t \le 1$$

Supplementary Problems

9.9   Represent a cube using an explicit edge listing.

9.10   Find an explicit representation for linear (degree 1) B-splines in the case of uniformly spaced knots, i.e., $t_{i+1} - t_i = L$.

9.11   For the knot set $t_1 = 1, t_2 = 2, \ldots, t_i = 1$, calculate $B_{i,3}$ (5.5).

CHAPTER 10

Hidden Surfaces

Opaque objects that are closer to the eye and in the line of sight of other objects will block those objects or portions of those objects from view. In fact, some surfaces of these opaque objects themselves are not visible because they are eclipsed by the objects' visible parts. The surfaces that are blocked or hidden from view must be "removed" in order to construct a realistic view of the 3D scene (see Fig. 1-3 where only three of the six faces of the cube are shown). The identification and removal of these surfaces is called the *hidden-surface problem*. The solution involves the determination of the closest visible surface along each projection line (Sec. 10.1).

There are many different hidden-surface algorithms. Each can be characterized as either an *image-space method*, in which the pixel grid is used to guide the computational activities that determine visibility at the pixel level (Secs. 10.2, 10.5, and 10.6), or an *object-space method*, in which surface visibility is determined using continuous models in the object space (or its transformation) without involving pixel-based operations (Secs. 10.3 and 10.4).

Notice that the hidden-surface problem has ties to the calculation of shadows. If we place a light source, such as a bulb, at the viewpoint, all surfaces that are visible from the viewpoint are lit directly by the light source and all surfaces that are hidden from the viewpoint are in the shadow of some opaque objects blocking the light.

10.1 DEPTH COMPARISONS

We assume that all coordinates (x, y, z) are described in the normalized viewing coordinate system (Chap. 8).

Any hidden-surface algorithm must determine which edges and surfaces are visible either from the center of projection for perspective projections or along the direction of projection for parallel projections.

The question of visibility reduces to this: given two points $P_1(x_1, y_1, z_1)$ and $P_2(x_2, y_2, z_2)$, does either point obscure the other? This is answered in two steps:

1. Are P_1 and P_2 on the same projection line?
2. If not, neither point obscures the other. If so, a depth comparison tells us which point is in front of the other.

For an orthographic parallel projection onto the xy plane, P_1 and P_2 are on the same projector if $x_1 = x_2$ and $y_1 = y_2$. In this case, depth comparison reduces to comparing z_1 and z_2. If $z_1 < z_2$, then P_1 obscures P_2 [see Fig. 10-1(a)].

For a perspective projection [see Fig. 10-1(b)], the calculations are more complex (Prob. 10.1). However, this complication can be avoided by transforming all three-dimensional objects so that parallel

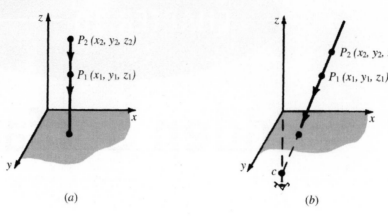

(a)   (b)

Fig. 10-1

projection of the transformed object is equivalent to a perspective projection of the original object (see Fig. 10-2). This is done with the use of the *perspective to parallel transform* T_p (Prob. 10.2).

If the original object lies in the normalized perspective view volume (Chap. 8), the *normalized perspective to parallel transform*

$$NT_p = \begin{pmatrix} \frac{1}{2} & 0 & \frac{1}{2} & 0 \\ 0 & \frac{1}{2} & \frac{1}{2} & 0 \\ 0 & 0 & \dfrac{1}{1-z_f} & \dfrac{-z_f}{1-z_f} \\ 0 & 0 & 1 & 0 \end{pmatrix}$$

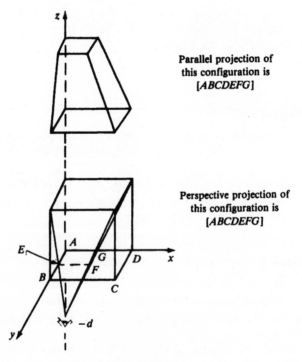

Parallel projection of this configuration is [ABCDEFG]

Perspective projection of this configuration is [ABCDEFG]

Fig. 10-2

(where z_f is the location of the front clipping plane of the normalized perspective view volume) transforms the normalized perspective view volume into the unit cube bounded by $0 \leq x \leq 1$, $0 \leq y \leq 1$, $0 \leq z \leq 1$ (Prob. 10.3). We call this cube the *normalized display space*. A critical fact is that the normalized perspective to parallel transform preserves lines, planes, and depth relationships.

If our display device has display coordinates $H \times V$, application of the scaling matrix

$$S_{H,V,1} = \begin{pmatrix} H & 0 & 0 & 0 \\ 0 & V & 0 & 0 \\ 0 & 0 & 1 & 0 \\ 0 & 0 & 0 & 1 \end{pmatrix}$$

transforms the normalized display space $0 \leq x \leq 1$, $0 \leq y \leq 1$, $0 \leq z \leq 1$ onto the region $0 \leq x \leq H$, $0 \leq y \leq V$, $0 \leq z \leq 1$. We cal this region the *display space*. The *display transform DT_p*:

$$DT_p = S_{H,V,1} \cdot NT_p$$

transforms the normalized perspective view volume onto the display space.

Clipping must be done against the normalized perspective view volume prior to applying the transform NT_p. An alternative to this is to combine NT_p with the normalizing transformation N_{per} (Chap. 8), forming the single transformation $NT_p' = NT_p \cdot N_{per}$. Then clipping is done in homogeneous coordinate space. This method for performing clipping is not covered in this book.

We now describe several algorithms for removing hidden surfaces from scenes containing objects defined with planar (i.e., flat), polygonal faces. We assume that the displays transform DT_p has been applied (if a perspective projection is being used), so that we always deal with parallel projections in display space.

10.2   Z-BUFFER ALGORITHM

We say that a point in display space is "seen" from pixel (x, y) if the projection of the point is scan-converted to this pixel (Chap. 3). The Z-buffer algorithm essentially keeps track of the smallest z coordinate (also called the *depth value*) of those points which are seen from pixel (x, y). These Z values are stored in what is called the Z buffer.

Let $Z_{buf}(x, y)$ denote the current depth value that is stored in the Z buffer at pixel (x, y). We work with the (already) projected polygons P of the scene to be rendered.

The Z-buffer algorithm consists of the following steps.

1. Initialize the screen to a background color. Initialize the Z buffer to the depth of the back clipping plane. That is, set

    $$Z_{buf}(x, y) = Z_{back}, \qquad \text{for every pixel } (x, y)$$

2. Scan-convert each (projected) polygon P in the scene (Chap. 3) and during this scan-conversion process, for each pixel (x, y) that lies inside the polygon:

    (a) Calculate $Z(x, y)$, the depth of the polygon at pixel (x, y).

    (b) If $Z(x, y) < Z_{buf}(x, y)$, set $Z_{buf}(x, y) = Z(x, y)$ and set the pixel value at (x, y) to the color of the polygon P at (x, y). In Fig. 10-3, points P_1 and P_2 are both scan-converted to pixel (x, y); however, since $z_1 < z_2$, P_1 will obscure P_2 and the P_1 z value, z_1, will be stored in the Z buffer.

Although the Z-buffer algorithm requires Z-buffer memory storage proportional to the number of pixels on the screen, it does not require additional memory for storing all the objects comprising the scene. In fact, since the algorithm processes polygons one at a time, the total number of objects in a scene can be arbitrarily large.

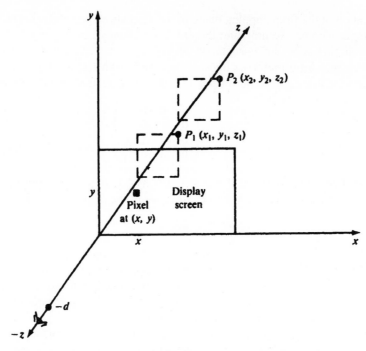

Fig. 10-3

10.3   BACK-FACE REMOVAL

Object surfaces that are orientated away from the viewer are called *back-faces*. The back-faces of an opaque polyhedron are completely blocked by the polyhedron itself and hidden from view. We can therefore identify and remove these back-faces based solely on their orientation without further processing (projection and scan-conversion) and without regard to other surfaces and objects in the scene.

Let $\mathbf{N} = (A, B, C)$ be the normal vector of a planar polygonal face, with $\mathbf{N}$ pointing in the direction the polygon is facing. Since the direction of viewing is the direction of the positive z axis (see Fig. 10-3), the polygon is facing away from the viewer when $C > 0$ (the angle between $\mathbf{N}$ and the z axis is less than 90°). The polygon is also classified as a back-face when $C = 0$, since in this case it is parallel to the line of sight and its projection is either hidden or overlapped by the edge(s) of some visible polygon(s).

Although this method identifies and removes back-faces quickly it does not handle polygons that face the viewer but are hidden (partially or completely) behind other surfaces. It can be used as a preprocessing step for other algorithms.

10.4   THE PAINTER'S ALGORITHM

Also called the *depth sort* or *priority algorithm*, the painter's algorithm processes polygons as if they were being painted onto the view plane in the order of their distance from the viewer. More distance polygons are painted first. Nearer polygons are painted on or over more distance polygons, partially or totally obscuring them from view. The key to implementing this concept is to find a priority ordering of the polygons in order to determine which polygons are to be painted (i.e., scan-converted) first.

Any attempt at a priority ordering based on depth sorting alone results in ambiguities that must be resolved in order to correctly assign priorities. For example, when two polygons overlap, how do we decide which one obscures the other? (See Fig. 10-4.)

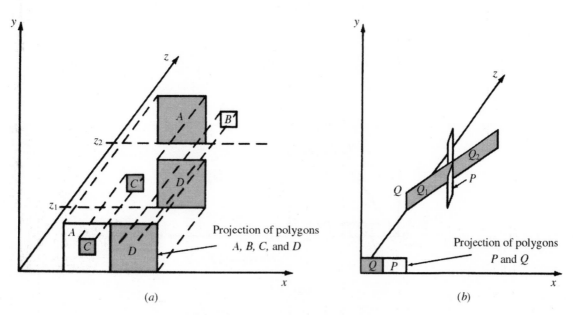

Fig. 10-4 Projection of opaque polygons.

Assigning Priorities

We assign priorities to polygons by determining if a given polygon P obscures other polygons. If the answer is no, then P should be painted first. Hence the key test is to determine whether polygon P does *not* obscure polygon Q.

The z extent of a polygon is the region between the planes $z = z_{min}$ and $z = z_{max}$ (Fig. 10-5). Here, z_{min} is the smallest of the z coordinates of all the polygon's vertices, and z_{max} is the largest.

Similar definitions hold for the x and y extents of a polygon. The intersection of the x, y, and z extents is called the *extent*, or bounding box, of the polygon.

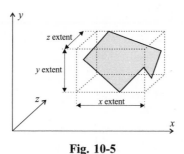

Fig. 10-5

Testing Whether P Obscures Q

Polygon P does not obscure polygon Q if any one of the following tests, applied in sequential order, is true.

Test 0: the z extents of P and Q do not overlap and $z_{Q_{max}}$ of Q is smaller than $z_{P_{min}}$ of P. Refer to Fig. 10-6.

Test 1: the y extents of P and Q do not overlap. Refer to Fig. 10-7.

Test 2: the x extents of P and Q do not overlap.

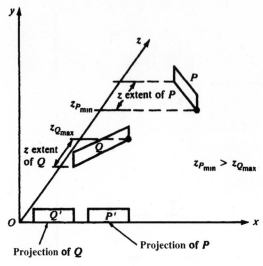

Fig. 10-6

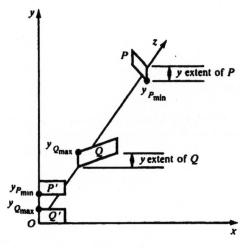

Fig. 10-7

Test 3: all the vertices of P lie on that side of the plane containing Q which is farthest from the viewpoint. Refer to Fig. 10-8.

Test 4: all the vertices of Q lie on that side of the plane containing P which is closest to the viewpoint. Refer to Fig. 10-9.

Test 5: the projections of the polygons P and Q onto the view plane do not overlap. This is checked by comparing each edge of one polygon against each edge of the other polygon to search for intersections.

The Algorithm

1. Sort all polygons into a polygon list according to $z_{\max}$ (the largest z coordinate of each polygon's vertices). Starting from the end of the list, assign priorities for each polygon P, in order, as described in steps 2 and 3 (below).

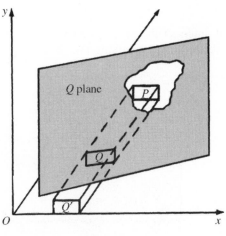

Fig. 10-8

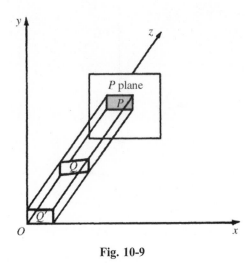

Fig. 10-9

2. Find all polygons Q (preceding P) in the polygon list whose z extents overlap that of P (test 0).

3. For each Q, perform tests 1 through 5 until true.

> (a)   If every Q passes, scan-convert polygon P.
>
> (b)   If false for some Q, swap P and Q on the list. Tag Q as swapped. If Q has already been tagged, use the plane containing polygon P to divide polygon Q into two polygons. Q_1 and Q_2 [see Fig. 10-4(b)]. The polygon-clipping techniques described in Chap. 5 can be used to perform the division. Remove Q from the list and place Q_1 and Q_2 on the list, in sorted order.

Sometimes the polygons are subdivided into triangles before processing, thus reducing the computational effort for polygon subdivision in step 3.

10.5   SCAN-LINE ALGORITHM

A scan-line algorithm consists essentially of two nested loops, an x-scan loop nested within a y-scan loop.

y Scan

For each y value, say, $y = \alpha$, intersect the polygons to be rendered with the scan plane $y = \alpha$. This scan plane is parallel to the xz plane, and the resulting intersections are line segments in this plane (see Fig. 10-10).

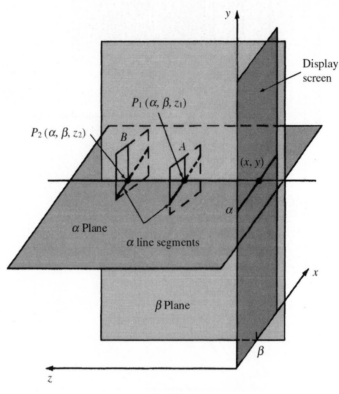

Fig. 10-10

x Scan

1. For each x value, say, $x = \beta$, intersect the line segments found above with the x-scan line $x = \beta$ lying on the y-scan plane. This intersection results in a set of points that lies on the x-scan line.

2. Sort these points with respect to their z coordinates. The point (x, y, z) with the smallest z value is visible, and the color of the polygon containing this point is the color set at the pixel corresponding to this point.

In order to reduce the amount of calculation in each scan-line loop, we try to take advantage of relationships and dependencies, called *coherences*, between different elements that comprise a scene.

Types of Coherence

1. *Scan-line coherence*. If a pixel on a scan line lies within a polygon, pixels near it will most likely lie within the polygon.

2. *Edge coherence*. If an edge of a polygon intersects a given scan line, it will mot likely intersect scan lines near the given one.

3.   *Area coherence*. A small area of an image will most likely lie within a single polygon.

4.   *Spatial coherence*. Certain properties of an object can be determined by examining the *extent* of the object, that is, a geometric figure which circumscribes the given object. Usually the extent is a rectangle or rectangle solid (also called a *bounding box*).

Scan-line coherence and edge coherence are both used to advantage in scan-converting polygons (Chap. 3).

Spatial coherence is often used as a preprocessing step. For example, when determining whether polygons intersect, we can eliminate those polygons that don't intersect by finding the rectangular extent of each polygon and checking whether the extents intersect—a much simpler problem (see Fig. 10-11). [*Note*: In Fig. 10-11 objects A and B do not intersect; however, objects A and C, and B and C, do intersect. In preprocessing, corner points would be compared to determine whether there is an intersection. For example, the edge of object A is at coordinate $P_3 = (6, 4)$ and the edge of object B is at coordinate $P_4 = (7, 3)$.] Of course, even if the extents intersect, this does not guarantee that the polygons intersect. See Fig. 10-12 and note that the extents of A' and B' overlap even though the polygons do not.

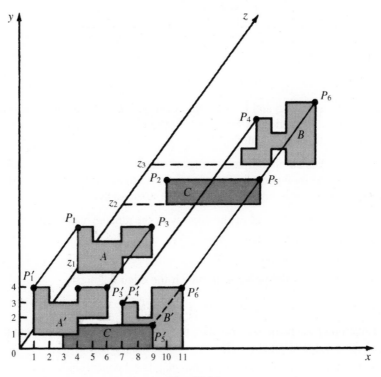

Fig. 10-11

Coherences can simplify calculations by making them incremental, as opposed to absolute. This is illustrated in Prob. 10.13.

A Scan-line Algorithm

In the following algorithm, scan line and edge coherence are used to enhance the processing done in the y-scan loop as follows. Since the y-scan loop constructs a list of potentially visible line segments, instead of reconstructing this list each time the y-scan line changes (absolute calculation), we keep the list and update it according to how it has changed (incremental calculation). This processing is facilitated by

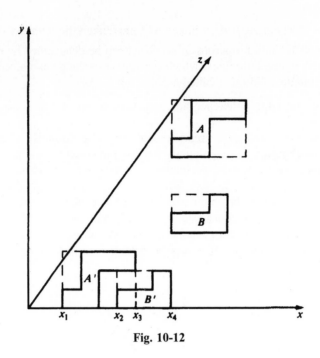

Fig. 10-12

the use of what is called the *edge list*, and its efficient construction and maintenance is at the heart of the algorithm (see Chap. 3, Sec. 3.7, under "A Scan-line Algorithm").

The following data structures are created:

1. *The edge list*—contains all nonhorizontal edges (horizontal edges are automatically displayed) of the projections of the polygons in the scene. The edges are sorted by the edge's smaller y coordinate ($y_{\min}$). Each edge entry in the edge list also contains:

   (a) The x coordinate of the end of the edge with the smaller y coordinate.

   (b) The y coordinate of the edge's other end ($y_{\max}$).

   (c) The increment $\Delta x = 1/m$.

   (d) A pointer indicating the polygon to which the edge belongs.

2. *The polygon list*—for each polygon, contains

   (a) The equation of the plane within which the polygon lies—used for depth determination, i.e., to find the z value at pixel (x, y).

   (b) An IN/OUT flag, initialized to OUT (this flag is set depending on whether a given scan line is in or out of the polygon).

   (c) Color information for the polygon.

The algorithm proceeds as follows.

I. *Initialization.*

   (a) Initialize each screen pixel to a background color.

   (b) Set y to the smallest $y_{\min}$ value in the edge list.

   Repeat steps II and III (below) until no further processing can be performed.

II. *y-scan loop.* Activate edges whose $y_{\min}$ is equal to y. Sort active edges in order of increasing x.

III. *x-scan loop.* Process, from left to right, each active edge as follows:

(a)   Invert the IN/OUT flag of the polygon in the polygon list which contains the edge. Count the number of active polygons whose IN/OUT flag is set to IN. If this number is 1, only one polygon is visible. All pixel values from this edge and up to the next edge are set to the color of the polygon. If this number is greater than 1, determine the visible polygon by the smallest z value of each polygon at the pixel under consideration. These z values are found from the equation of the plane containing the polygon. The pixels from this edge and up to the next edge are set to the color of this polygon, unless the polygon becomes obscured by another before the next edge is reached, in which case we set the remaining pixels to the color of the obscuring polygon. If this number is 0, pixels from this edge and up to the next one are left unchanged.

(b)   When the last active edge is processed, we then proceed as follows:

1.   Remove those edges for which the value of y_{max} equals the present scan-line value y. If no edges remain, the algorithm has finished.

2.   For each remaining active edge, in order, replace x by $x + 1/m$. This is the edge intersection with the next scan line $y + 1$ (see Prob. 10.13).

3.   Increment y to $y + 1$, the next scan line, and repeat step II.

10.6   SUBDIVISION ALGORITHM

The subdivision algorithm is a recursive procedure based on a two-step strategy that first decides which projected polygons overlap a given area A on the screen and are therefore potentially visible in that area. Second, in each area these polygons are further tested to determine which ones will be visible within this area and should therefore be displayed. If a visibility decision cannot be made, this screen area, usually a rectangular window, is further subdivided either until a visibility decision can be made, or until the screen area is a single pixel.

Starting with the full screen as the initial area, the algorithm divides an area at each stage into four smaller areas, thereby generating a quad tree (see Fig. 10-13).

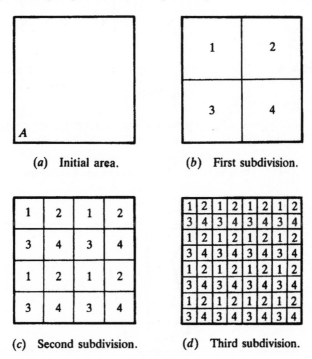

(a)   Initial area.   (b)   First subdivision.

(c)   Second subdivision.   (d)   Third subdivision.

Fig. 10-13

The processing exploits area coherence by classifying polygons P with respect to a given screen area A into the following categories: (1) *surrounding polygon*—polygon that completely contains the area [Fig. 10-14(a)], (2) *interesecting polygon*—polygon that intersects the area [Fig. 10-14(b)], (3) *contained polygon*—polygon that is completely contained within the area [Fig. 10-14(c)], and (4) *disjoint polygon*—polygon that is disjoint from the area [Fig. 10-14(d)].

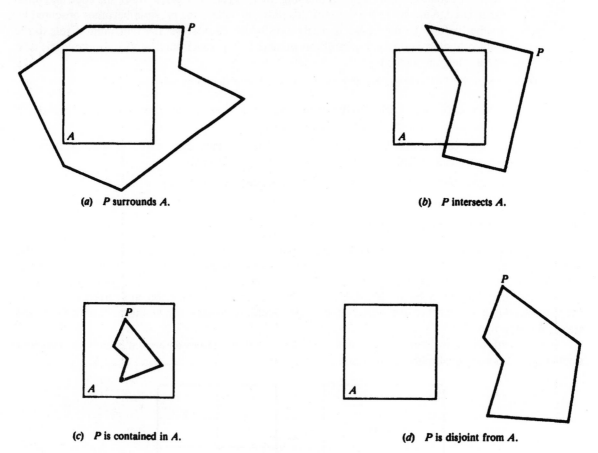

(a)   *P* surrounds *A*.   (b)   *P* intersects *A*.

(c)   *P* is contained in *A*.   (d)   *P* is disjoint from *A*.

Fig. 10-14

The classification of the polygons within a picture is the main computational expense of the algorithm and is analogous to the clipping algorithms discussed in Chap. 5. With the use of one of these clipping algorithms, a polygon in category 2 (intersecting polygon) can be clipped into a contained polygon and a disjoint polygon (see Fig. 10-15). Therefore, we could proceed as if category 2 were eliminated.

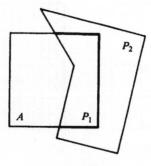

Fig. 10-15

For a given screen area, we keep a potentially visible polygons list (PVPL), those in categories 1, 2, and 3. (Disjoint polygons are clearly not visible.) Also, note that on subdivision of a screen area, surrounding and disjoint polygons remain surrounding and disjoint polygons of the newly formed areas. Therefore, only contained and intersecting polygons need to be reclassified.

Removing Polygons Hidden by a Surrounding Polygon

The key to efficient visibility computation lies in the fact that a polygon is not visible if it is in back of a surrounding polygon. Therefore, it can be removed from the PVPL. To facilitate processing, this list is sorted by z_{min}, the smallest z coordinate of the polygon within this area. In addition, for each surrounding polygon S, we also record its largest z coordinate, $z_{S_{max}}$.

If, for a polygon P on the list, $z_{P_{min}} > z_{S_{max}}$ (for a surrounding polygon S), then P is hidden by S and thus is not visible. In addition, all other polygons after P on the list will also be hidden by S, so we can remove these polygons from the PVPL.

Subdivision Algorithm

1. Initialize the area to be the whole screen.
2. Create a PVPL with respect to an area, sorted on z_{min} (the smallest z coordinate of the polygon within the area). Place the polygons in their appropriate categories. Remove polygons hidden by a surrounding polygon and remove disjoint polygons.
3. Perform the visibility decision tests:
    (*a*) If the list is empty, set all pixels to the background color.
    (*b*) If there is exactly one polygon in the list and it is a classified as intersecting (category 2) or contained (category 3), color (scan-convert) the polygon, and color the remaining area to the background color.
    (*c*) If there is exactly one polygon on the list and it is a surrounding one, color the area the color of the surrounding polygon.
    (*d*) If the area is the pixel (x, y), and neither *a*, *b*, nor *c* applies, compute the z coordinate $z(x, y)$ at pixel (x, y) of all polygons on the PVPL. The pixel is then set to the color of the polygon with the smallest z coordinate.
4. If none of the above cases has occurred, subdivide the screen area into fourths. For each area, go to step 2.

10.7   HIDDEN-LINE ELIMINATION

Although there are special-purpose hidden-line algorithms, each of the above algorithms can be modified to eliminate hidden lines or edges. This is especially useful for wireframe polygonal models where the polygons are unfilled. The idea is to use a color rule which fills all the polygons with the background color—say, black—and the edges and lines a different color—say, white. The use of a hidden-surface algorithm now becomes a hidden-line algorithm.

10.8   THE RENDERING OF MATHEMATICAL SURFACES

In plotting a mathematical surface described by an equation $z = F(x, y)$, where $x_{min} \leq x \leq x_{max}$ and $y_{min} \leq y \leq y_{max}$, we could use any of the hidden-surface algorithms so far described. However, these general algorithms are inefficient when compared to specialized algorithms that take advantage of the structure of this type of surface.

The mathematical surface is rendered as a wireframe model by drawing both the *x-constant curves* $z = F(\text{const}, y)$ and the *y-constant curves* $z = F(x, \text{const})$ (see Fig. 10-16). Each such curve is rendered as a polyline, where the illusion of smoothness is achieved by using a fine resolution (i.e., short line segments) in drawing the polyline (Chap. 3).

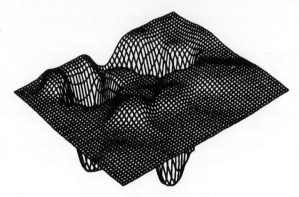

Fig. 10-16

Choose an $M \times N$ plotting resolution

$$x_{\min} \le x_1 < x_2 < \cdots < x_M \le x_{\max} \qquad \text{and} \qquad y_{\min} \le y_1 < y_2 < \cdots < y_N \le y_{\max}$$

The corresponding z values are $z_{ij} = F(x_i, y_j)$. An x-constant polyline, say $x = x_j$, has vertices

$$P_1(x_j, y_1), \ldots, P_N(x_j, y_N)$$

Similarly, the $y = y_k$ polyline has vertices

$$Q_1(x_1, y_k), \ldots, Q_M(x_M, y_k)$$

Choosing a view plane and a center of projection or viewpoint $C(a, b, c)$, we create a perspective view of the surface onto this view plane by using the transformations developed in Chap. 7. So a point $[x, y, F(x, y)]$ on the surface projects to a point (p, q) in view plane coordinates. By applying an appropriate 2D viewing transformation (Chap. 5), we can suppose that p and q line within the horizontal and vertical plotting dimensions of the plotting device, say, $H \times V$ pixels.

The Perimeter Method for Rendering the Surface

Each plotted x and y constant polyline outlines a polygonal region on the plotting screen (Fig. 10-17).

The algorithm is based on the following observations: (1) *ordering*—the x- and y-constant curves (i.e., polylines) are drawn in order starting with the one closest to the viewpoint and (2) *visibility*—we draw only that part of the polyline that is outside the perimeter of all previously drawn regions (Fig. 10-18). One implementation of the visibility condition uses a min–max array A, of length H (that of the plotting device), which contains, at each horizontal pixel position i, the maximum (and/or minimum) vertical pixel value

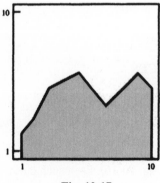

Fig. 10-17

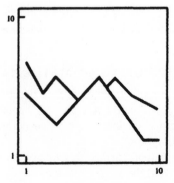

Fig. 10-18

drawn thus far at i; that is $A(i) = \frac{\max}{\min}$ (vertical pixel values drawn so far at i) (Fig. 10-19). Selection of the max results in a drawing of the top of the surface. The min is used to render the bottom of the surface, and the max and min yields both top and bottom.

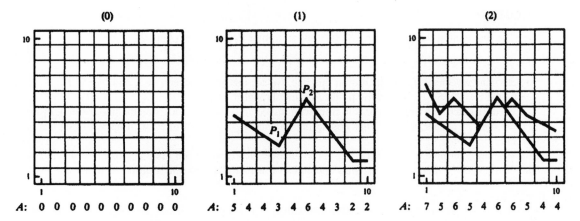

Fig. 10-19   Updating min–max array A (using maximum values only).

The Visibility Test

Suppose that (p', q') is the pixel that corresponds to the point (p, q). Then this pixel is *visible* if either

$$q' > A(p') \qquad \text{or} \qquad q' < A(p')$$

where A is the min–max array.

The visibility criteria for a line segment are: (1) the line segment is visible if both its endpoints are visible; (2) the line segment is invisible if both its endpoints are not visible; and (3) if only one endpoint is visible, the min–max array is tested to find the visible part of the line.

Drawing the x- or y-constant polylines thus consists of testing for the visibility of each line segment and updating the min–max array as necessary. Since a line segment will, in general, span several horizontal pixel positions (see segment $\overline{P_1 P_2}$ in Fig. 10-19), the computation of $A(i)$ for these intermediate pixels is found by using the slope of the line segment or by using Bresenham's method described in Chap. 3.

The Wright Algorithm for Rendering Mathematical Surfaces

The drawing of the surface $z = F(x, y)$ proceeds as follows.

1. To perform initialization, determine whether the viewpoint is closer to the x or the y axis. Suppose that it is closer to the x axis. We next locate the x-constant curve that is closest to the viewpoint at $x = 1$.

    (*a*)   Initialize the min–max array to some base value, say, zero.

    (*b*)   Start with the x-constant curve found above.

2. Repeat the following steps using the visibility test for drawing line segments and updating the min–max array each time a line segment is drawn:

    (*a*)   Draw the x-constant polyline.

    (*b*)   Draw those parts of each y-constant polyline that lie between the previously drawn x-constant polyline and the next one to be drawn.

    (*c*)   Proceed, in the direction of increasing x, to the next x-constant polyline.

Solved Problems

10.1 Given points $P_1(1, 2, 0)$, $P_2(3, 6, 20)$, and $P_3(2, 4, 6)$ and a viewpoint $C(0, 0, -10)$, determine which points obscure the others when viewed from C.

SOLUTION

The line joining the viewpoint $C(0, 0, -10)$ and point $P_1(1, 2, 0)$ is (App. 2)

$$x = t \qquad y = 2t \qquad z = -10 + 10t$$

To determine whether $P_2(3, 6, 20)$ lies on this line, we see that $x = 3$ when $t = 3$, and then at $t = 3$, $x = 3$, $y = 6$, and $z = 20$. So P_2 lies on the projection line through C and P_1.

Next we determine which point is in front with respect to C. Now C occurs on the line at $t = 0$, P_1 occurs at $t = 1$, and P_2 occurs at $t = 3$. Thus comapring t values, P_1 is in front of P_2 with respect to C; that is, P_1 obscures P_2.

We now determine whether $P_3(2, 4, 6)$ is on the line. Now $x = 2$ when $t = 2$ and then $y = 4$, and $z = 10$. Thus $P_3(2, 4, 6)$ is not on this projection line and so it nether obscures nor is obscured by P_1 and P_2.

10.2 Construct the perspective to parallel transform T_p which produces an object whose parallel projection onto the xy plane yields the same image as the perspective projection of the original object onto the normalized view plane $z = c_z'/(c_z' + b)$ (Chap. 8, Prob. 8.6) with respect to the origin as the center of projection.

SOLUTION

The perspective projection onto the plane $z = c_z'/(c_z' + b)$ with respect to the origin is (Chap. 7, Prob. 7.4):

$$Per = \begin{pmatrix} z_v & 0 & 0 & 0 \\ 0 & z_v & 0 & 0 \\ 0 & 0 & z_v & 0 \\ 0 & 0 & 1 & 0 \end{pmatrix}$$

where $z_v = c_z'/(c_z' + b)$. The perspective projection onto the view plane of a point $P(x, y, z)$ is the point

$$P'\left(\frac{z_v x}{z}, \frac{z_v y}{z}, z_v\right)$$

Define the perspective to parallel transform T_p to be

$$T_p = \begin{pmatrix} z_v & 0 & 0 & 0 \\ 0 & z_v & 0 & 0 \\ 0 & 0 & \dfrac{1}{1 - z_f} & \dfrac{-z_f}{1 - z_f} \\ 0 & 0 & 1 & 0 \end{pmatrix}$$

(where $z = z_f$ is the location of the normalized front clipping plane; see Chap. 8, Prob. 8.6).

Now, applying the perspective to parallel transform T_p to the point $P(x, y, z)$, we produce the point

$$Q'\left(\frac{z_v x}{z}, \frac{z_v y}{z}, \frac{z - z_f}{z(1 - z_f)}\right)$$

The parallel projection of Q' onto the xy plane produces the point

$$Q'\left(\frac{z_v x}{z}, \frac{z_v y}{z}, 0\right)$$

So Q' and P' produce the same projective image. Furthermore, T_p transforms the normalized perspective view volume bounded by $x = z$, $x = -z$, $y = z$, $y = -z$, $z = z_f$, and $z = 1$ to the rectangular volume bounded by $x = z_v$, $x = -z_v$, $y = z_v$, $y = -z_v$, $z = 0$, and $z = 1$.

10.3 Show that the normalized perspective to parallel transform NT_p preserves the relationships of the original perspective transformation while transforming the normalized perspective view volume into the unit cube.

SOLUTION

From Prob. 10.2, the perspective to parallel transform T_p transforms a point $P(x, y, z)$ to a point

$$Q\left(\frac{z_v x}{z}, \frac{z_v y}{z}, \frac{z - z_f}{z(1 - z_f)}\right)$$

The image under parallel projection of this point onto the xy plane is

$$Q'\left(\frac{z_v x}{z}, \frac{z_v y}{z}, 0\right)$$

The factor z_v can be set equal to 1 without changing the relation between points Q and Q'.

The matrix that transforms $P(x, y, z)$ to the point $Q\left(\dfrac{x}{z}, \dfrac{y}{z}, \dfrac{z - z_f}{z(1 - z_f)}\right)$ is then

$$\bar{T}_p = \begin{pmatrix} 1 & 0 & 0 & 0 \\ 0 & 1 & 0 & 0 \\ 0 & 0 & \dfrac{1}{1 - z_f} & \dfrac{-z_f}{1 - z_f} \\ 0 & 0 & 1 & 0 \end{pmatrix}$$

In addition, this matrix transforms the normalized perspective view volume to the rectangular view volume bounded by $x = 1$, $x = -1$, $y = 1$, $y = -1$, $z = 0$, and $z = 1$.

We next translate this view volume so that the corner point $(-1, -1, 0)$ translates to the origin. The translation matrix that does this is

$$T_{(1,1,0)} = \begin{pmatrix} 1 & 0 & 0 & 1 \\ 0 & 1 & 0 & 1 \\ 0 & 0 & 1 & 0 \\ 0 & 0 & 0 & 1 \end{pmatrix}$$

The new region is a volume bounded by $x = 0$, $x = 2$, $y = 0$, $y = 2$, $z = 0$, and $z = 1$.

Finally, we scale in the x and y direction by a factor $\frac{1}{2}$ so that the final view volume is the unit cube: $x = 0$, $x = 1$, $y = 0$, $y = 1$, $z = 0$, and $z = 1$. The scaling matrix is

$$S_{1/2,1/2,1} = \begin{pmatrix} \frac{1}{2} & 0 & 0 & 0 \\ 0 & \frac{1}{2} & 0 & 0 \\ 0 & 0 & 1 & 0 \\ 0 & 0 & 0 & 1 \end{pmatrix}$$

The final normalized perspective to parallel transform is

$$NT_p = S_{1/2,1/2,1} \cdot T_{(1,1,0)} \cdot \bar{T}_p = \begin{pmatrix} \frac{1}{2} & 0 & \frac{1}{2} & 0 \\ 0 & \frac{1}{2} & \frac{1}{2} & 0 \\ 0 & 0 & \dfrac{1}{1 - z_f} & \dfrac{-z_f}{1 - z_f} \\ 0 & 0 & 1 & 0 \end{pmatrix}$$

10.4 Why are hidden-surface algorithms needed?

SOLUTION

Hidden-surface algorithms are needed to determine which objects and surface will obscure those objects and surfaces that are in back of them, thus rendering a more realistic image.

10.5   What two steps are required to determine whether any given points $P_1(x_1, y_1, z_1)$ obscures another point $P_2(x_2, y_2, z_2)$? (See Fig. 10-1.)

SOLUTION

   It must be determined (1) whether the two points lie on the same projection line and (2) if they do, which point is in front of the other.

10.6   Why is it easier to locate hidden surfaces when parallel projection is used?

SOLUTION

   There are no vanishing points in parallel projection. As a result, any point $P(a, b, z)$ will line on the same projector as any other point having the same x and y coordinates (a, b). Thus only the z component must be compared to determine which point is closest to the viewer.

10.7   How does the Z-buffer algorithm determine which surfaces are hidden?

SOLUTION

   The Z-buffer algorithm sets up a two-dimensional array which is like the frame buffer; however the Z buffer stores the depth value at each pixel rather than the color, which is stored in the frame buffer. By setting the initial values of the Z buffer to some large number, usually the distance of back clipping plane, the problem of determining which surfaces are closer is reduced to simply comparing the present depth values stored in the Z buffer at pixel (x, y) with the newly calculated depth value at pixel (x, y). If this new value is less than the present Z-buffer value (i.e., closer along the line of sight), this value replaces the present value and the pixel color is changed to the color of the new surface.

10.8   Using a 2×2 pixel display, show how the Z-buffer algorithm would determine the color of each pixel for the given objects A and B in Fig. 10-20.

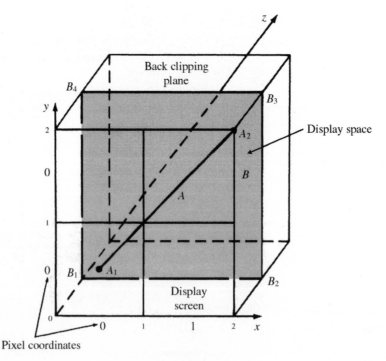

Fig. 10-20

SOLUTION

The display space for the 2×2 pixel display is the region $0 \leq x \leq 2$, $0 \leq y \leq 2$, and $0 \leq z \leq 1$. In Fig. 10-20, A is the line with display space coordinates $A_1(\frac{1}{2}, \frac{1}{2}, 0)$ and $A_2(2, 2, 0)$; line A is on the display screen in front of square B. B is the square with display space coordinates $B_1(0, 0, \frac{1}{2})$, $B_2(2, 0, \frac{1}{2})$, $B_3(2, 2, \frac{1}{2})$, and $B_4(0, 2, \frac{1}{2})$. The displayed image of A (after projection and scan conversion) would appear on a 2×2 pixel display as

	0	1
1	y	a
0	a	y

where a is the color of A and y is the background color. We have used the fact (Chap. 3, Sec. 3.1) that a point (x, y) scan-converts to the pixel [Floor(x), Floor(y)]. (We assume for consistency that $2 \equiv 1.99\ldots$.) The displayed image of B is

	0	1
1	b	b
0	b	b

where b is the color of B. We apply the Z-buffer algorithm to the picture composed of objects A and B as follows:

1. Perform initialization. The Z buffer is set equal to the depth of the back clipping plane $z = 1$, and the frame buffer is initialized to a background color y.

Frame buffer =

	0	1
1	y	y
0	y	y

Z buffer =

	0	1
1	1	1
0	1	1

2. Apply the algorithm to object A.

    (a) The present Z-buffer value at pixel $(0, 0)$ is that of the back clipping plane, i.e., $Z_{\text{buf}}(0, 0) = 1$. The depth vapue of A at pixel $(0, 0)$ is $z = 0$. Then $Z_{\text{buf}}(0, 0)$ is changed to 0 and pixel $(0, 0)$ has the color of A.

Frame buffer =

	0	1
1	y	y
0	a	y

Z buffer =

	0	1
1	1	1
0	0	1

    (b) Object A is not seen from pixel $(1, 0)$, so the Z-buffer value is unchanged.

Frame =

	0	1
1	y	y
0	a	y

Z_{buf} =

	0	1
1	1	1
0	0	1

    (c) Object A is not seen from pixel $(0, 1)$, so the Z-buffer value is unchanged.

Frame =

	0	1
1	y	y
0	a	y

Z_{buf} =

	0	1
1	1	1
0	0	1

(d) The depth value of A at pixel $(1, 1)$ is 0. Since this is less than the present Z-buffer value of 1, pixel $(1, 1)$ takes the color of A.

$$\text{Frame} = \begin{array}{c c} 1 & \begin{array}{|c|c|} \hline y & a \\ \hline a & y \\ \hline \end{array} \\ 0 & \\ & 0 \quad 1 \end{array} \qquad Z_{\text{buf}} = \begin{array}{c c} 1 & \begin{array}{|c|c|} \hline 1 & 0 \\ \hline 0 & 1 \\ \hline \end{array} \\ 0 & \\ & 0 \quad 1 \end{array}$$

3. Apply the algorithm to B.

(a) The depth value for B at pixel $(0, 0)$ is $\frac{1}{2}$, and $Z_{\text{buf}}(0, 0) = 0$. So the color of pixel $(0, 0)$ is unchanged.

$$\text{Frame} = \begin{array}{c c} 1 & \begin{array}{|c|c|} \hline y & a \\ \hline a & y \\ \hline \end{array} \\ 0 & \\ & 0 \quad 1 \end{array} \qquad Z_{\text{buf}} = \begin{array}{c c} 1 & \begin{array}{|c|c|} \hline 1 & 0 \\ \hline 0 & 1 \\ \hline \end{array} \\ 0 & \\ & 0 \quad 1 \end{array}$$

(b) The depth value of B at pixel $(1, 0)$ is $\frac{1}{2}$. The present Z-buffer value is 1. So the Z-buffer value is set to $\frac{1}{2}$ and pixel $(1, 0)$ takes the color of B.

$$\text{Frame} = \begin{array}{c c} 1 & \begin{array}{|c|c|} \hline y & a \\ \hline a & b \\ \hline \end{array} \\ 0 & \\ & 0 \quad 1 \end{array} \qquad Z_{\text{buf}} = \begin{array}{c c} 1 & \begin{array}{|c|c|} \hline 1 & 0 \\ \hline 0 & \frac{1}{2} \\ \hline \end{array} \\ 0 & \\ & 0 \quad 1 \end{array}$$

(c) The depth value of B at pixel $(0, 1)$ is $\frac{1}{2}$. The present Z-buffer value is 1, so the color at pixel $(0, 1)$ is set to that of B, and the Z buffer is updated.

$$\text{Frame} = \begin{array}{c c} 1 & \begin{array}{|c|c|} \hline b & a \\ \hline a & b \\ \hline \end{array} \\ 0 & \\ & 0 \quad 1 \end{array} \qquad Z_{\text{buf}} = \begin{array}{c c} 1 & \begin{array}{|c|c|} \hline \frac{1}{2} & 0 \\ \hline 0 & \frac{1}{2} \\ \hline \end{array} \\ 0 & \\ & 0 \quad 1 \end{array}$$

(d) The depth value of B at pixel $(1, 1)$ is $\frac{1}{2}$. The present Z-buffer value is 0. So the color at pixel $(1, 1)$ remains unchanged.

$$\text{Frame} = \begin{array}{c c} 1 & \begin{array}{|c|c|} \hline b & a \\ \hline a & b \\ \hline \end{array} \\ 0 & \\ & 0 \quad 1 \end{array} \qquad Z_{\text{buf}} = \begin{array}{c c} 1 & \begin{array}{|c|c|} \hline \frac{1}{2} & 0 \\ \hline 0 & \frac{1}{2} \\ \hline \end{array} \\ 0 & \\ & 0 \quad 1 \end{array}$$

The final form of the Z buffer indicates that line A lines in front of B.

10.9 What is the maximum number of objects that can be presented by using the Z-buffer algorithm?

SOLUTION

The total number of objects that can be handled by the Z-buffer algorithm is arbitrary because each object is processed one at a time.

10.10 How does the basic scan-line method determine which surfaces are hidden?

SOLUTION

The basic scan-line method looks one at a time at each of the horizontal lines of pixels in the display area. For example, at the horizontal pixel line $y = \alpha$, the graphics data structure (consisting of all scan-converted polygons) is searched to find all polygons with any horizontal (y) pixel values equal to α.

Next, the algorithm looks at each individual pixel in the α row. At pixel (α, β), the depth values (z values) of each polygon found above are compared to find the polygon having the smallest z value at this pixel. The color of pixel (α, β) is then set to the color of the corresponding polygon at this pixel.

10.11 Using the four pixel display and the graphics objects A and B from Prob. 10.8, show how the basic scan-line method would display these objects.

SOLUTION

First we initialize the display to the color y of the back clipping plane (located at $z = 1$).

$$\text{Frame buffer} = \begin{array}{c|c|c|} & & \\ 1 & y & y \\ \hline 0 & y & y \\ \hline & 0 & 1 \end{array}$$

1.   Set $y = 0$. The scan-converted representations of A and B contain pixels on the $y = 0$ scan line.

   (a)   Set $x = 0$. Comparing the z values of A and B at pixel $(0, 0)$, we find that the smaller z value is 0, which belongs to A. Thus A is seen from pixel $(0, 0)$; that is, pixel $(0, 0)$ is set to the color of A.

$$\begin{array}{c|c|c|} 1 & y & y \\ \hline 0 & a & y \\ \hline & 0 & 1 \end{array}$$

   (b)   Set $x = 1$. Since A is not seen from pixel $(1, 0)$ while B is seen, the color of pixel $(1, 0)$ is set to that of B.

$$\begin{array}{c|c|c|} 1 & y & y \\ \hline 0 & a & b \\ \hline & 0 & 1 \end{array}$$

2.   Set $y = 1$. The scan-converted representations of A and B contain pixels on the $y = 1$ scan line.

   (a)   Set $x = 0$. Because A is not seen at pixel $(0, 1)$ while B is seen, pixel $(0, 1)$ is set to the color of B.

$$\begin{array}{c|c|c|} 1 & b & y \\ \hline 0 & a & b \\ \hline & 0 & 1 \end{array}$$

   (b)   Set $x = 1$. Both A and B are "seen" from pixel $(1, 1)$. The depth of A at pixel $(1, 1)$ is 0, that of B is $\frac{1}{2}$. Thus A is visible at pixel $(1, 1)$.

$$\begin{array}{c|c|c|} 1 & b & a \\ \hline 0 & a & b \\ \hline & 0 & 1 \end{array}$$

This represents the final image displayed.

10.12 How does edge coherence help to reduce computational effort?

SOLUTION

It is based on the assumption that, if an edge or line intersects a given scan line, it will most likely intersect those scan lines next to it. Thus if the pixels that intersect the edge are to be found, instead of intersecting each scan line with the edge, it is necessary to locate only one intersection pixel and then find the others using the slope m of the edge (see Prob. 10.13).

10.13 Show how the calculation of the intersection of an edge with a scan line can be made incremental as opposed to absolute.

SOLUTION

The absolute calculation requires that we find the x intersection value of the edge (e.g., with equation $y = mx + b$) with the scan line $y = \alpha$ for each α.

The incremental solution to the problem is based on the following observations. Suppose that x_α is the x intersection of the edge with the scan line α. Then the intersection $x_{\alpha+1}$ of the edge with the next scan line $y = \alpha + 1$ can be found as illustrated in Fig. 10-21. From Fig. 10-21, where m is the slope of the edge,

$$\frac{\Delta y}{\Delta x} = \frac{(\alpha + 1) - \alpha}{x_{\alpha+1} - x_\alpha} = m$$

Solving for $x_{\alpha+1}$, we obtain

$$x_{\alpha+1} = x_\alpha + \frac{1}{m}$$

Thus the calculation of the next intersection point is incremental; that is, it is found from the previous intersection point by adding $1/m$ to it.

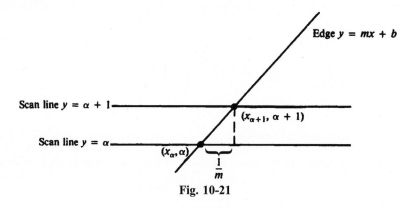

Fig. 10-21

10.14 How does area coherence reduce computational effort?

SOLUTION

Area coherence is based on the assumption that a small enough region of pixels will most likely lie within a single polygon. This reduces, as in the subdivision algorithm, computational effort in dealing with all those polygons that are potentially visible in a given screen area (region of pixels).

10.15 How is spatial coherence determined?

SOLUTION

Spatial coherence is determined by examining the extent of an object. The rectangular extent (bounding box) of an object is determined by finding the minimum and maximum x, y, and z coordinate values of the points that belong to the object. The extent is the rectangular region bounded by the planes $z = z_{min}$, $z = z_{max}$, $y = y_{min}$, $y = y_{max}$, $x = x_{min}$, and $x = x_{max}$.

10.16 Draw two polygons such that their extents intersect but the polygons themselves don't intersect.

SOLUTION

Figure 10-22 shows one possible solution.

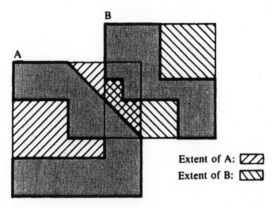

Extent of A: ▨
Extent of B: ▧

Fig. 10-22

10.17 Apply the scan-line algorithm from Sec. 10.5, under "A Scan-line algorithm," to the display of objects A and B in Prob. 10.8.

SOLUTION

As in Prob. 10.8, a point (x, y) scan converts to the pixel [Floor(x), Floor(y)]. Also note that a nonhorizontal line can be treated as a special polygon: a scanline enters into and exits from the polygon at the same pixel position.

We first construct the edge list (EL) and the polygon list (PL). From Fig. 10-20, the edge entries for the nonhorizontal edges $\overline{A_1A_2}$, $\overline{B_1B_4}$, and $\overline{B_2B_3}$ are

Edge	y_{min}	x	y_{max}	$\dfrac{1}{m}$	Polygon pointer
$\overline{A_1A_2}$	$\frac{1}{2}$	$\frac{1}{2}$	2	1	A
$\overline{B_1B_4}$	0	0	2	0	B
$\overline{B_2B_3}$	0	2	2	0	B

Here, y_{min} is the edge's smaller y coordinate and x the corresponding x coordinate; y_{max} is the larger y coordinate, and m is the slope of the edge. Form the PL:

$$PL = \begin{array}{|c|c|c|c|} \hline \text{Polygon} & \text{Equation} & \text{IN/OUT flag} & \text{Color} \\ \hline A & x = y & \text{OUT} & a \\ \text{(line)} & z = 0 & & \\ \hline B & z = \frac{1}{2} & \text{OUT} & b \\ \hline \end{array}$$

The algorithm proceeds as follows.

I.   *Initialization.*

(*a*)   We initialize the screen display to the color y of the back clipping plane (located at $z = 1$).

$$\text{Frame buffer} = \begin{array}{c} 1 \\ 0 \end{array} \begin{array}{|c|c|} \hline y & y \\ \hline y & y \\ \hline \end{array}$$
$$\qquad\qquad 0 \quad 1$$

(*b*)   Set the scan line to $y = 0$.

II.   *y-scan loop.* Activate edges that satisfy $\text{Floor}(y_{\min}) = 0$ and sort on x

Edges	x
$\overline{B_1 B_4}$	0
$\overline{A_1 A_2}$	$\frac{1}{2}$
$\overline{B_2 B_3}$	2

III.   *x-scan loop.*

(*a*)   Process edge $\overline{B_1 B_4}$. First invert the appropriate IN/OUT flags in the PL:

	Polygon	Equation	IN/OUT flag	Color
PL =	A	$x = y$ $z = 0$	OUT	a
	B	$z = \frac{1}{2}$	IN	b

The number of active polygons is one. Thus B is visible at pixel $(0, 0)$ and all pixels on scan line $y = 0$ between edges $\overline{B_1 B_4}$ and $\overline{A_1 A_2}$ are set to the color of B. In our case, this is just the pixel $(0, 0)$.

$$\begin{array}{c} 1 \\ 0 \end{array} \begin{array}{|c|c|} \hline y & y \\ \hline b & y \\ \hline \end{array}$$
$$\quad 0 \quad 1$$

(*a*)   Now we repeat step (*a*), processing edge $\overline{A_1 A_2}$. We update the PL:

	Polygon	Equation	IN/OUT flag	Color
PL =	A	$x = y$ $z = 0$	IN	a
	B	$z = \frac{1}{2}$	IN	b

The number of active polygons is 2. At pixel $(0, 0)$ the depth value (z value) of polygon A is 0 and of polygon B is $\frac{1}{2}$. Thus polygon A is visible at pixel $(0, 0)$, so the color is set to a.

1	y	y
0	a	y
	0	1

Since A is a line, set the IN/OUT flag of line A to OUT. The color of all pixels between edges $\overline{A_1A_2}$ and $\overline{B_2B_3}$ are determined by the remaining active polygon B.

	Polygon	. . .	IN/OUT flag	. . .
PL =	A	—	OUT	—
	B	—	IN	—

This means that we set the color of pixel $(1, 0)$ to b.

1	y	y
0	a	b
	0	1

(a)   Again, we repeat step (a), processing edge $\overline{B_2B_3}$. We update the PL:

	Polygon	. . .	IN/OUT flag	. . .
PL =	A	—	OUT	—
	B	—	OUT	—

The number of active polygons is 0.

(b)   Having processed $\overline{B_2B_3}$, the last active edge, we proceed:

(1)   All the $y_{\max}$ values are equal to 2. These values scan-convert (see Prob. 10.8) to 1. The present y scan line value is 0. So no edges are removed.

(2)   Incrementing x by $1/m$,

$\overline{B_1B_4}$	0
$\overline{A_1A_2}$	$\frac{3}{2}$
$\overline{B_2B_3}$	2

(3)   Set $y = 1$.

Now we repeat steps II and III.

II.   *y-scan loop.* With $y = 1$, no additional edge is activated. The result of sorting active edges remains as above.

III.   *x-scan loop.*

222 HIDDEN SURFACES [CHAP. 10

(a) Process edge $\overline{B_1B_4}$. We update the PL:

	Polygon	. . .	IN/OUT flag	. . .
PL =	A	—	OUT	—
	B	—	IN	—

The number of active polygons is 1. Thus B is visible at pixel $(0, 1)$ and all pixels between edge $\overline{B_1B_4}$ and $\overline{A_1A_2}$ on scan line $y = 1$ are set to the color of B.

1	b	b
0	a	b
	0	1

(a) Now we repeat step (a), processing edge $\overline{A_1A_2}$. We update the PL:

	Polygon	. . .	IN/OUT flag	. . .
PL =	A	—	IN	—
	B	—	IN	—

There are two active polygons. A depth comparison at pixel $(1, 1)$ shows that it is set to the color of line $\overline{A_1A_2}$.

1	b	a
0	a	b
	0	1

Since A is a line, we set the IN/OUT flag of A to OUT. And we proceed immediately to the next edge at the same pixel location.

(a) Again we repeat step (a), processing edge $\overline{B_2B_3}$. We update the PL:

	Polygon	Equation	IN/OUT flag	Color
PL =	A	$x = y$ $z = 0$	OUT	a
	B	$z = \frac{1}{2}$	OUT	b

The number of active polygons becomes 0.

(b) Having processed the last active edge $\overline{B_2B_3}$, we remove those edges for which y_{max} equals the y scan value of 1. Since this includes all the edges, i.e., $y_{max} = 2$, the algorithm stops.

10.18 What is the underlying concept of the painter's or the priority algorithm?

SOLUTION

The painter's algorithm sorts polygons by depth and then paints (scan-converts) each polygon onto the screen starting with the most distance polygon.

10.19 What difficulties are encountered in implementing the painter's algorithm?

SOLUTION

First, there is the question of what the "depth" of a polygon is, especially if the polygon is tilted out of the xy plane. Second, if two polygons have the same depth, which one should be painted first?

10.20 If polygon Q has the same depth value as polygon P, which polygon has priority, that is, which is painted first?

SOLUTION

We perform tests 0, 1, 2, 3, 4, 5 (from Sec. 10.4, under "Testing Whether P obscures Q") in order. If any one of the tests is true, we say that polygon P does not obscure polygon Q, and so polygon P is painted first.

If none of the tests is true, we have an ambiguity that must be resolved.

We resolve the ambiguity by switching the roles of P and Q and the reapply tests 0, 1, 2, 3, 4, and 5. If any one of these tests is true, Q does not obscure polygon P and so polygon Q is painted first.

If again none of the tests is true, polygon Q must be subdivided into two polygons Q_1 and Q_2, using the plane containing polygon P as the dividing plane [Fig. 10-4(b)].

10.21 Apply the painter's algorithm to display objects A and B in Prob. 10.8.

SOLUTION

We first find the depth values z_{max} for A and B. Since z_{max} is the largest z value from all the polygon's vertices, then for A, $z_{A_{max}} = 0$, and for B, $z_{B_{max}} = \frac{1}{2}$. Then sorting on z_{max}, we see that polygon B has a higher depth value than polygon A.

Next, we assign priorities by applying tests 0 through 5 in order (see Sec. 10.4). In test 0, the z extent of B is $z_{min} = \frac{1}{2}$, $z_{max} = \frac{1}{2}$. The z extent of A is $z_{min} = 0$, $z_{max} = 0$.

Thus the z extents of A and B do not overlap and $z_{A_{max}}$ is smaller than $z_{B_{min}}$. Thus test 0 is true, and so we scan-convert polygon B first:

$$\text{Frame buffer} = \begin{array}{c} 1 \\ 0 \end{array} \begin{array}{|c|c|} \hline b & b \\ \hline b & b \\ \hline \end{array}$$
$$ 0 \quad 1$$

Next, we scan-convert polygon A (i.e., we "paint" over polygon B):

$$\begin{array}{c} 1 \\ 0 \end{array} \begin{array}{|c|c|} \hline b & a \\ \hline a & b \\ \hline \end{array}$$
$$ 0 \quad 1$$

This is the final image displayed in the frame buffer.

10.22 What are the basic concepts underlying the subdivision algorithm?

SOLUTION

First, is that a polygon is seen from within a given area of the display screen if the projection of that polygon overlaps the given area. Second, of all polygons that overlap a given screen area, the one that is visible in this area is the one in front of all the others. Third, if we cannot decide which polygon is visible (in front of the others) from a given region, we subdivide the region into smaller regions until visbility decisions can be made (even if we must subdivide down to the pixel level).

10.23 Apply the subdivision algorithm to the display of objects A and B from Prob. 10.8.

SOLUTION

1. *Initialization.* We initialize the area to the whole screen.

2. *Forming the potentially visible polygon list.* We create the PVPL, sorted on z_{min}, the smallest of the z values of the polygon in the area.

PVPL =

Polygon	z_{min}	Category
A	0	Contained
B	$\frac{1}{2}$	Surrounding

3. *Visibility decision.* We apply criteria (a) through (d) in Sec. 10.6, step 3. Since all four tests fail, we pass to step 4 and subdivide the area into four subregions.

    After subdivision, the four newly formed regions are, in our example, the individual pixels. We apply the algorithm to each pixel in turn.

    Region 1: pixel (0, 0).

2. *Forming the PVPL.*

PVPL =

Polygon	z_{min}	Category
A	0	Intersecting
B	$\frac{1}{2}$	Surrounding

3. *Visibility decision.* Applying tests (a) thrpough (c), we now apply test (d) since the region is pixel size. The z coordinate of A at pixel (0, 0) is 0, and that of B is $\frac{1}{2}$. Thus A is visible at pixel (0, 0):

Frame buffer = (with values 1, 0 and a in lower left, axes 0, 1)

    Region 2: pixel (0, 1).

2. *Forming the PVPL.* Note that A is disjoint from this region:

PVPL =

Polygon	z_{min}	Category
B	$\frac{1}{2}$	Surrounding

3. *Visibility decision.* From test (c), there is only one polygon and it is surrounding, so we color pixel (0, 1)

that of B:

```
1  |   |   |
0  | a | b |
   0   1
```

Region 3: pixel $(0, 1)$.

2. *Forming the PVPL.* Since A is disjoint from this region, we have

$$\text{PVPL} = \begin{array}{|c|c|c|} \hline \text{Polygon} & z_{\min} & \text{Category} \\ \hline B & \frac{1}{2} & \text{Surrounding} \\ \hline \end{array}$$

3. *Visibility decision.* From test (c), there is only one polygon B and it is surrounding. So region 3 is colored b:

```
1  | b |   |
0  | a | b |
   0   1
```

Region 4: pixel $(1, 1)$.

2. *Forming the PVPL.*

$$\text{PVPL} = \begin{array}{|c|c|c|} \hline \text{Polygon} & z_{\min} & \text{Category} \\ \hline A & 0 & \text{Intersecting} \\ \hline B & \frac{1}{2} & \text{Surrounding} \\ \hline \end{array}$$

3. *Visibility decision.* Having applied tests (a) through (c), we now apply test (d). The z coordinate of A at pixel $(1, 1)$ is less than that of B. Thus pixel $(1, 1)$ is set to the color of A:

```
1  | b | a |
0  | a | b |
   0   1
```

This is the final image in the frame buffer.

10.24 How can we use the special structure of a convex polyhedron to identify its hidden faces for a general parallel or perspective projection?

SOLUTION

Suppose that on each face of the polyhedron there is an outward-pointing normal vector $\mathbf{N}$, attached at a point P of the face (Fig. 10-23). For each face of the polyhedron, let the *line-of-sight vector* $\mathbf{L}$ be the vector pointing from the face to the viewer. For a parallel projection, this is the direction of projection from the object to the projection plane. For a perspective projection, it is the vector $\overline{\mathbf{PC}}$ from the normal vector attached at point P to the viewpoint at point C (Fig. 10-23).

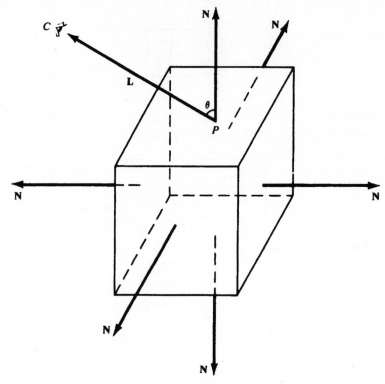

Fig. 10-23

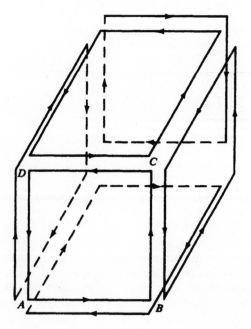

Fig. 10-24

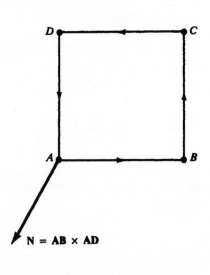

$$N = AB \times AD$$

Fig. 10-25

A face is *visible* if the angle θ made by the line-of-sight vector $\mathbf{L}$ and the normal vector $\mathbf{N}$ is less than 90°. It is *hidden* if this angle is larger than or equal to 90°. If $0° \leq \theta < 90°$, then $0 < \cos\theta \leq 1$; if $90° \leq \theta \leq 180°$, then $-1 \leq \cos\theta \leq 0$. Since (from App. 2)

$$\cos\theta = \frac{\mathbf{L}\cdot\mathbf{N}}{|\mathbf{L}||\mathbf{N}|}$$

the face is visible if

$$0 < \frac{\mathbf{L}\cdot\mathbf{N}}{|\mathbf{L}||\mathbf{N}|} \leq 1$$

and hidden otherwise. To use this visibility test, we need to find the outward-pointing normal vectors for the faces of the polyhedron. To do this, we label the faces of the polyhedron so that the polyhedron is *oriented*. That is, any edge shared by adjacent faces is traversed in opposite directions with respect to the faces (Fig. 10-24). This guarantees that the normal vectors will point outward. To construct the outward normal vectors, we label each polygon with a counterclockwise labeling (Fig. 10-25). Then a normal vector can be found by taking the cross product of vectors determined by two adjacent sides of the polygon and attaching it at one of the vertices (Fig. 10-25).

Supplementary Problems

10.25　How may the properties of parallel projection be used to simplify hidden-surface calculations for any form of projection?

10.26　What happens when two polygons have the same z value and the Z-buffer algorithm is used?

10.27　How would the Z-buffer algorithm be altered to allow figures to be superimposed on a surface (see Prob. 10.26)?

10.28　Assuming that one allows 2^{24} depth value levels to be used, how much memory would a 1024×768 pixel display require to store the Z buffer?

10.29　How can the amount of computation required by the scan-line method be reduced?

10.30　How does scan-line coherence help to reduce computation?

10.31　What is the extent of the polygon whose vertices are $A(0, 0, 1)$, $B(2, 0, 1)$, and $C(1, 2, 2)$ (see Fig. 10-26)?

10.32　Why are only nonhorizontal lines stored in the edge list of the scan-line algorithm?

10.33　How is the depth of a polygon determined by the painter's algorithm?

10.34　How does the subdivision algorithm exploit are coherence?

10.35　How can hidden-surface algorithms be used to eliminate hidden lines as applied to polygonal mesh models (Chap. 9)?

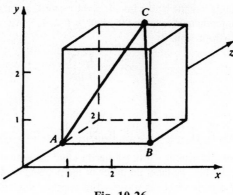

Fig. 10-26

CHAPTER 11

Color and Shading Models

Color is a fundamental attribute of our viewing experience. The perception of color arises from light energy entering our visual system and triggering a chain of not-yet-fully-understood neurological and psychological responses. This complex process is relevant to computer graphics because a realistic image is one that seems indistinguishable from a true record of the light energy coming from the real scene. It has been a constant challenge to find effective and efficient computational models for constructing such images.

In Sect. 11.1, we first outline the basic relationship between light (the physical stimulus) and the perception of color. This leads to an international standard for the specification and measurement of colors, and a better understanding of the widely used RGB color model. In Sect. 11.2, we use a well-known formula to mimic the effect of objects being lit by light sources (A more elaborate illumination model is discussed in Chap. 12). In Sects. 11.3 and 11.4, we describe several useful techniques for shading polygon-mesh objects and for depicting delicate surface details (surface texture).

11.1 LIGHT AND COLOR

Light, or visible light, is electromagnetic energy in the 400 to 700 nm, i.e., nanometer (10^{-9} meter), wavelength (λ) range of the spectrum (see Fig. 11-1). A typical light has its energy distributed across the visible band and the proportions are described by a spectral energy distribution function $P(\lambda)$ (see Fig. 11-2). To model a light or reproduce a given light with physical precision one would need to duplicate the exact energy distribution, which is commonly referred to as spectral reproduction.

On the other hand, it has been shown through carefully designed psychophysical experiments that discrepancy in spectral distribution does not necessarily lead to difference in perception. Less stringent approaches exist to reproduce light to the extent that the reproduction causes the same color sensation to an average human observer as the original. These results make it possible to specify or describe light in ways that are more perceptually oriented and are easier to handle.

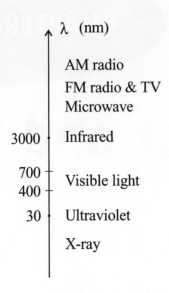

Fig. 11-1

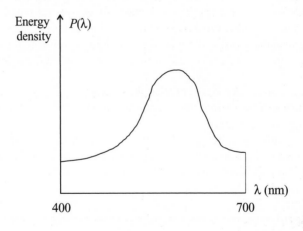

Fig. 11-2

Basic Characteristics of Light

Light can be characterized in three perceptual terms. The first one is *brightness*, which corresponds to its physical property called *luminance*. Luminance measures the total energy in the light. It is proportional to the area bounded by $P(\lambda)$ and the λ axis in the 400 to 700 nm range. The area can be calculated by

$$\int_\lambda P(\lambda)\mathrm{d}\lambda$$

The higher the luminance, the brighter the light to the observer.

The second perceptual term is *hue*, which distinguishes a white light from a red light or a green light. For a light with an idealized spectral distribution as shown in Fig. 11-3, hue corresponds to another physical property called the *dominant wavelength* of the distribution.

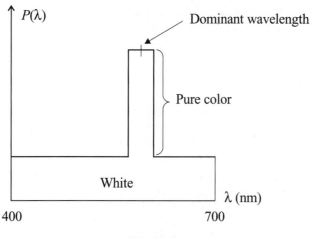

Fig. 11-3

The third perceptual term is *saturation*, which describes the degree of vividness. For example, two red lights may differ in luminance/brightness, and they may differ in degree of vividness (e.g., pure/saturated red vs. pale/unsaturated red). Saturation corresponds to the physical property called *excitation purity*, which is defined to be the percentage of luminance that is allocated to the dominant or pure color component (see Fig. 11-3). In other words, we have

$$\text{saturation} = \frac{\text{pure color}}{\text{pure color} + \text{white color}}$$

Although this simple scheme has its weaknesses (e.g., not all lights have an identifiable dominant wavelength), it bridges the physical aspects of light and the perceptual classification of color in a straightforward fashion.

The Trichromatic Generalization Theory

Let S be a given light or color stimulus. The effect of S (the color sensation of a human subject observing S) can be matched by combining light from three primary sources in appropriate proportions:

$$S = r \cdot \text{red} + g \cdot \text{green} + b \cdot \text{blue}$$

In other words, the given light and the proportional mix of the three primaries look the same to the observer.

Note that the theory stands with any triple of primaries. Three light sources form a triple of primaries as long as none of the three can be expressed as/matched by a linear combination of the other two. We use red, green, and blue in the formula mainly because they are the standard choice in color-matching experiments (with red = 700 nm, green = 546.1 nm, and blue = 435.8 nm). Moreover, these three colors roughly coincide with the wavelength values that cause peak response from the three types of color-sensitive receptor cells in the retina, a membrane that lines the back of the eye's wall. These receptor cells are called β, δ, and ρ cones, respectively. They are most sensitive to light in the wavelength range of $\beta : 440$–445 nm, $\delta : 535$–545 nm, and $\rho : 575$–580 nm. Another kind of receptor cells called rods are color-blind but are very sensitive to low intensity light.

A critical aspect of this tri-stimulus approach is that, in order to match all visible colors, the weight values sometimes have to be negative. For example, when red, green, and blue are used as primaries the value of b, the weight of the blue component, may be negative. A negative b value means that the effect of the given stimulus S cannot be matched normally through the additive process. But if S is mixed with some blue light, then the effect of the mix can be matched by a linear combination of red and green (Intuitively, we move the term $b \cdot$ blue to the other side of the equation).

CIE *XYZ* Color Model

Looking for a good compromise between the simple and effective tri-stimulus method and the fact that no naturally occurring primaries can be used to match all visible colors, the International Commission on Illumination (Commission Internationale de l'Eclairage, or CIE) defined three imaginary (non-realizable) primaries, vis., X, Y, and Z, in 1931. They were the result of an affine transformation applied to three real primaries to ensure that every single-wavelength light or spectral color can be expressed as a linear combination of the CIE primaries without any negative weight.

The relative amounts of X, Y, and Z that are needed to describe each spectral color are shown in Fig. 11-4 in the form of three color-matching functions $x(\lambda)$, $y(\lambda)$, and $z(\lambda)$. In order to match a color light of wavelength λ_0, the proper proportion is found by the line $\lambda = \lambda_0$ intersecting the curves representing the three functions. In addition, $y(\lambda)$ matches the *luminous efficiency* of the human eye and corresponds to the eye's response to light of constant luminance.

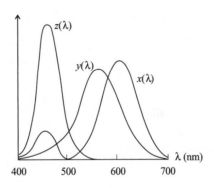

Fig. 11-4

To describe an arbitrary light S with spectral distribution $P(\lambda)$, we "add together" the respective amounts of the CIE primaries that are necessary to match all the spectral components of S. This is done with

$$X = k \int_\lambda P(\lambda)x(\lambda) \, d\lambda, \qquad Y = k \int_\lambda P(\lambda)y(\lambda) \, d\lambda, \qquad Z = k \int_\lambda P(\lambda)z(\lambda) d\lambda$$

where k is a light-source-dependent constant. The resultant X, Y (which carries luminance information due to the way $y(\lambda)$ is defined), and Z are used as weights to express S as follows:

$$S = X \cdot \boldsymbol{X} + Y \cdot \boldsymbol{Y} + Z \cdot \boldsymbol{Z}$$

CIE Chromaticity Diagram

Now we define x, y, and z by normalizing the above weights against $X + Y + Z$:

$$x = \frac{X}{X + Y + Z}, \qquad y = \frac{Y}{X + Y + Z}, \qquad z = \frac{Z}{X + Y + Z}$$

Clearly $x + y + z = 1$, and we have $z = 1 - x - y$. The two variables x and y represent colors by grouping them into sets, each of which has members that differ only in luminance.

Using x and y as the horizontal and vertical axes we can plot the well-known CIE Chromaticity Diagram (see Fig. 11-5). The curved triangular figure encompasses all perceivable colors by ignoring luminance. Only when two colors differ in chromaticity (hue and/or saturation) are they represented by two different points in the diagram (i.e., they have different chromaticity coordinates).

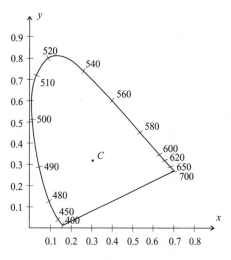

Fig. 11-5

To convert from chromaticity coordinates (x, y) back to a specific color in the XYZ color space we need an additional piece of information, typically Y:

$$X = \frac{x}{y}Y, \qquad Y = Y, \qquad Z = \frac{1 - x - y}{y}Y$$

We can find all spectral colors along the figure's upper border. Point C $(0.310, 0.316)$ is known as *Illuminant C*. It corresponds to a reference white that is obtained from a spectral distribution close to daylight.

The CIE chromaticity diagram serves as a universal reference for the specification and comparison of visible colors. The phosphors of a typical color monitor have the following chromaticity coordinates: R $(0.62, 0.34)$, G $(0.29, 0.59)$, and B $(0.15, 0.06)$. These coordinates define a triangular region within the diagram. The region is referred to as the *color gamut* of the monitor, which represents (the chromaticity range of) all the colors this monitor is able to display.

Color Gamut Mapping

Let (x_r, y_r), (x_g, y_g), and (x_b, y_b) be the chromaticity coordinates of the phosphors of an RGB color monitor. What are the XYZ coordinates of its colors? We first introduce auxiliary variables $C_r = X_r + Y_r + Z_r$, $C_g = X_g + Y_g + Z_g$, and $C_b = X_b + Y_b + Z_b$, where (X_r, Y_r, Z_r), (X_g, Y_g, Z_g), and (X_b, Y_b, Z_b) denote the respective XYZ coordinates of the red, green, and blue colors the monitor can display. We have

$$X_r = x_r C_r, \qquad Y_r = y_r C_r, \qquad Z_r = z_r C_r \qquad \text{where } z_r = 1 - x_r - y_r$$
$$X_g = x_g C_g, \qquad Y_g = y_g C_g, \qquad Z_g = z_g C_g \qquad \text{where } z_g = 1 - x_g - y_g$$
$$X_b = x_b C_b, \qquad Y_b = y_b C_b, \qquad Z_b = z_b C_b \qquad \text{where } z_b = 1 - x_b - y_b$$

Thus the *XYZ* coordinates of a composite *RGB* color can be expressed in terms of a transformation M:

$$\begin{pmatrix} X \\ Y \\ Z \end{pmatrix} = M \begin{pmatrix} R \\ G \\ B \end{pmatrix} = \begin{pmatrix} x_r C_r & x_g C_g & x_b C_b \\ y_r C_r & y_g C_g & y_b C_b \\ z_r C_r & z_g C_g & z_b C_b \end{pmatrix} \begin{pmatrix} R \\ G \\ B \end{pmatrix} = \begin{pmatrix} x_r & x_g & x_b \\ y_r & y_g & y_b \\ z_r & z_g & z_b \end{pmatrix} \begin{pmatrix} C_r & 0 & 0 \\ 0 & C_g & 0 \\ 0 & 0 & C_b \end{pmatrix} \begin{pmatrix} R \\ G \\ B \end{pmatrix}$$

There are two different ways to determine C_r, C_g, and C_b. One is to use a photometer to measure the luminance levels Y_r, Y_g, and Y_b of the red, green, and blue colors at their maximum intensity/brightness, respectively. Then

$$C_r = Y_r/y_r, \qquad C_g = Y_g/y_g, \qquad C_b = Y_b/y_b,$$

The other is to find/measure the *XYZ* coordinates (X_w, Y_w, Z_w) of the monitor's white color $(R = G = B = 1)$. Using these we have

$$\begin{pmatrix} X_w \\ Y_w \\ Z_w \end{pmatrix} = \begin{pmatrix} x_r & x_g & x_b \\ y_r & y_g & y_b \\ z_r & z_g & z_b \end{pmatrix} \begin{pmatrix} C_r \\ C_g \\ C_b \end{pmatrix}$$

We can now solve for C_r, C_g, and C_b.

If M_1 is the transformation for monitor 1 and M_2 is the transformation for monitor 2, then a color (R_1, G_1, B_1) on monitor 1 can be matched by a corresponding color (R_2, G_2, B_2) on monitor 2:

$$\begin{pmatrix} R_2 \\ G_2 \\ B_2 \end{pmatrix} = M_2^{-1} M_1 \begin{pmatrix} R_1 \\ G_1 \\ B_1 \end{pmatrix}$$

provided that (R_2, G_2, B_2) is within the color gamut of monitor 2.

The NTSC *YIQ* Color Model

The NTSC (National Television System Committee) *YIQ* color model is used for commercial television broadcasting in the US. It is defined to be a linear transformation of the *RGB* color model, with the Y component purposely made to be the same as the Y in the CIE *XYZ* color model. Since Y carries luminance information, black-and-white television sets can use it to display color images as gray-scale pictures. The mapping between *RGB* and *YIQ* is as follows:

$$\begin{pmatrix} Y \\ I \\ Q \end{pmatrix} = \begin{pmatrix} 0.299 & 0.587 & 0.114 \\ 0.596 & -0.275 & -0.321 \\ 0.212 & -0.523 & 0.311 \end{pmatrix} \begin{pmatrix} R \\ G \\ B \end{pmatrix}$$

The quantities in the transformation matrix are obtained using the standard NTSC *RGB* phosphors whose chromaticity coordinates are R $(0.67, 0.33)$, G $(0.21, 0.71)$, and B $(0.14, 0.08)$. It is also assumed that the white point is at $x_w = 0.31$, $y_w = 0.316$, and $Y_w = 1.0$.

11.2   THE PHONG MODEL

This is a widely used and highly effective way to mimic the reflection of light from object surfaces to the viewer's eye. It is considered an empirical approach because, although it is consistent with some basic principles of physics, it is largely based on our observation of the phenomenon. It is also referred to as a *local illumination model* because its main focus is on the direct impact of the light coming from the light source. On the other hand, a *global illumination model* attempts to include such secondary effects as light going through transparent/translucent material and light bouncing from one object surface to another.

Now consider a point light source [see Fig. 11-6(*a*)], which is an idealized light with all its energy coming out from a single point in space (a reasonable approximation to a bulb). Our eye is at the viewpoint

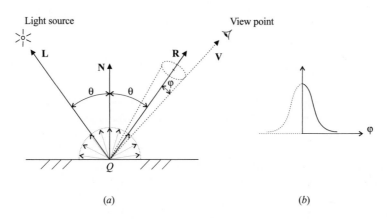

Fig. 11-6

looking at point Q on the surface of an object. What should be the color of Q? In other words, what should be the color of the light reflected into our eye from Q (in the direction of vector $\mathbf{V}$)?

There are two extreme cases of light reflection. The first is called *diffuse reflection*. In this case light energy from the light source (in the direction of $-\mathbf{L}$) gets reflected/bounced off equally in all directions (see the small arrows forming a half-circle/hemisphere). We also want the energy level of the reflection to be a function of the incident angle θ (between $\mathbf{L}$ and surface normal $\mathbf{N}$). The smaller the angle, the higher the reflection (kind of like bouncing a ball off a wall). The mathematical tool we use to achieve these is to have the reflection proportional to $\cos(\theta)$.

The second case is called *specular reflection*. It attempts to capture the characteristic of a shiny or mirror-like surface. Were the surface in Fig. 11-6(a) a perfect mirror, energy from the light source would be reflected in exactly one direction (the direction of vector $\mathbf{R}$). Since a perfect mirror is nonexistent we want to distribute reflected energy across a small cone-shaped space centered around $\mathbf{R}$, with the reflection being the strongest along the direction of $\mathbf{R}$ (i.e., $\varphi = 0$) and decreasing quickly as φ increases [see the bell-shaped curve in Fig. 11-6(b)]. The mathematical means for modeling this effect is $\cos^{k}(\varphi)$, where the parameter k provides for a convenient way to vary the degree of shininess ($k = 1$ for a dull surface and $k = 100$ for a mirror-like surface). For a given scene we can find out the amount of specular reflection in the direction of $\mathbf{V}$ using the actual angle φ between $\mathbf{R}$ and $\mathbf{V}$.

Furthermore, the complex inter-object reflection needs to be accounted for in some way because many surfaces we see are not lit directly by the light source. They are lit by light that is bouncing around the environment. For this we introduce a directionless ambient light, which illuminates all surfaces in the scene and gets reflected uniformly in all directions by each surface.

Thus in the Phong model, object surfaces are thought to produce a combination of ambient-light reflection and light-source-dependent diffuse/specular reflection. Mathematically we can state the total reflected energy intensity I as

$$I = I_{a}k_{a} + I_{p}(k_{d}\cos(\theta) + k_{s}\cos^{k}(\varphi))$$

where I_{a} is the intensity of the ambient light; I_{p} is the intensity of the point light; and $0 \le k_{a}, k_{d}, k_{s} \le 1.0$ are reflection coefficients that represent the surface's ability to reflect ambient light, to produce diffuse reflection, and to produce specular reflection, respectively (e.g., $k_{a} = 0.2$ means 20% reflection of I_{a}).

If $\mathbf{L}$, $\mathbf{N}$, $\mathbf{R}$, and $\mathbf{V}$ are all unit vectors, then $\mathbf{L} \cdot \mathbf{N} = \cos(\theta)$ and $\mathbf{R} \cdot \mathbf{V} = \cos(\varphi)$. We can write the formula as

$$I = I_{a}k_{a} + I_{p}(k_{d}\mathbf{L} \cdot \mathbf{N} + k_{s}(\mathbf{R} \cdot \mathbf{V})^{k})$$

Note that the term $\mathbf{L} \cdot \mathbf{N}$ is used in computing $\mathbf{R}$ (see Prob. 11.10). When there are two or more light sources in the scene, their effects are cumulative:

$$I = I_a k_a + \sum_{i=1}^{n} I_{p_i}(k_d \mathbf{L}_i \cdot \mathbf{N} + k_s(\mathbf{R}_i \cdot \mathbf{V})^k)$$

These formulas are typically used along with the *RGB* color model. Thus light intensity is in the form of an *RGB* color vector, e.g., $I = (I_r, I_g, I_b)$. Reflection coefficients are also three-dimensional vectors. For example, $k_d = (0.7, 0.7, 0.3)$ defines a surface that looks yellowish when illuminated with white light. The ambient reflection coefficient k_a can simply be the same as k_d. The three components of k_s are often made equal since the color of the reflection of a light source is typically the same as the color of the light source itself. When the light is white, the formula for a single point source becomes

$$\begin{cases} I_r = I_a k_{ar} + I_p(k_{dr} \mathbf{L} \cdot \mathbf{N} + k_s(\mathbf{R} \cdot \mathbf{V})^k) \\ I_g = I_a k_{ag} + I_p(k_{dg} \mathbf{L} \cdot \mathbf{N} + k_s(\mathbf{R} \cdot \mathbf{V})^k) \\ I_b = I_a k_{ab} + I_p(k_{db} \mathbf{L} \cdot \mathbf{N} + k_s(\mathbf{R} \cdot \mathbf{V})^k) \end{cases}$$

Figure 11-7 shows a gray scale image with 16 views of a sphere shaded using the Phong formula. The four rows from top to bottom are calculated using $k_d/k_s = 0.5/0.1$, $0.5/0.3$, $0.5/0.5$, and $0.5/0.7$, respectively. The four columns from left to right represent $k = 3$, 5, 20, and 100, respectively.

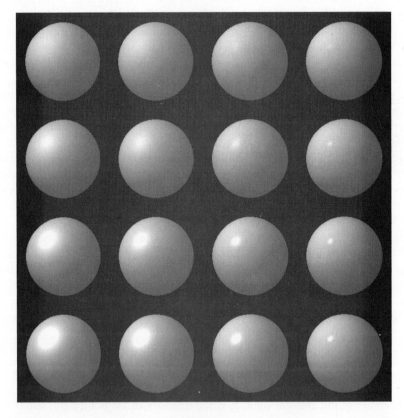

Fig. 11-7

11.3 INTERPOLATIVE SHADING METHODS

Computing surface color using an illumination model such as the Phong formula at every point of interest can be very expensive. It is even unnecessary when the image is used to preview the scene. To circumvent this problem, we apply the formula at full scale only at selected surface points. We then rely on such techniques as color interpolation and surface-normal interpolation to shade other surface points.

Constant Shading

The least time-consuming approach is not to perform calculation for additional surface points at all. The color values of those selected surface points are used to shade the entire surface.

For example, a cylindrical object may be modeled by a polygon mesh as shown in Fig. 11-8(a). We can evaluate the Phong formula using the geometric center of each polygon and set the resultant color to every pixel that belongs to the corresponding polygon [see Fig. 11-8(b)].

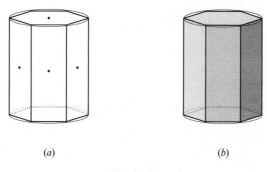

(a)   (b)

Fig. 11-8

Constant shading can produce good results for dull polyhedrons lit by light sources that are relatively far away (hence the diffuse component varies little within each polygonal face). The primary weakness of this method is that false contours appear between adjacent polygons that approximate a curved surface [see the cylindrical object in Fig. 11-8(b)]. In addition, the specular reflection of the light source (often referred to as the *specular highlight*) tends to get lost. On the other hand, if a selected surface point happens to be at the location of the strongest specular reflection of the light source, then the color of the corresponding polygon will be, for the most part, significantly distorted.

Gouraud Shading

In this approach we evaluate the illumination formula at the vertices of the polygon mesh. We then interpolate the resultant color values to get a gradual shading within each polygon.

For example, we use bilinear interpolation to find the color of point P inside a triangle whose vertices are P_1, P_2, and P_3 (see Fig. 11-9). The scan line containing P intersects the two edges at points P' and P''. We interpolate the color of P_1 and the color of P_2 to get the color of P'. We then interpolate the color of P_2 and the color of P_3 to get the color of P''. Finally, we interpolate the color of P' and the color of P'' to get the color of P (see Prob. 11.15).

When polygons are used to approximate a curved surface, there are two ways to determine the normal vectors at the vertices in order to get a smooth-looking transition between adjacent polygons. The first is to use the underlying curved surface to find the true surface normal at each vertex location. For example, the vertices of the polygon mesh in Fig. 11-8(a) are on the surface of an underlying cylinder. The normal vector at a point on the cylinder is perpendicular to the axis of the cylinder and points from the axis to the point [see Fig. 11-10(a)].

On the other hand, it may sometimes be difficult to find normal vectors from the underlying surface, or the polygon mesh may not come from any underlying surface. A second approach to deciding normal vectors at the vertices is to average the normal vectors of adjacent polygons. For example, to determine

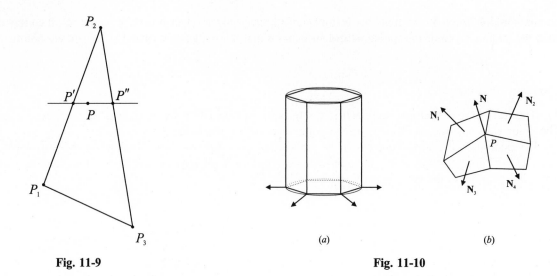

Fig. 11-9   Fig. 11-10

normal vector $\mathbf{N}$ at vertex $\mathbf{P}$ in Fig. 11-10(b), we use the average of the normal vectors of the polygons that meet at P:

$$\mathbf{N} = \mathbf{N}_1 + \mathbf{N}_2 + \mathbf{N}_3 + \mathbf{N}_4$$

where $\mathbf{N}$ is then normalized by dividing it by $|\mathbf{N}|$.

Common normal vectors at the vertices of a polygon mesh that approximates a curved surface result in color values that are shared by adjacent polygons, eliminating abrupt changes in shading characteristics across polygon edges. Even when the polygon mesh is relatively coarse, Gouraud shading is very effective in suppressing false contours. However, a much finer mesh is needed in order to show reasonably good specular reflection.

Phong Shading

Instead of color values, we may also interpolate normal vectors. For example, to find the normal vector $\mathbf{N}$ at point P in a triangle (see Fig. 11-11), we first interpolate $\mathbf{N}_1$ and $\mathbf{N}_2$ to get $\mathbf{N}'$, then interpolate $\mathbf{N}_2$ and $\mathbf{N}_3$ to get $\mathbf{N}''$, finally interpolate $\mathbf{N}'$ and $\mathbf{N}''$ to get $\mathbf{N}$.

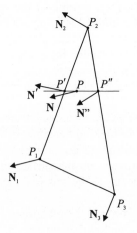

Fig. 11-11

This technique is relatively time-consuming since the illumination model is evaluated at every point of interest using the interpolated normal vectors. However, it is very effective in dealing with specular highlights.

11.4   TEXTURE

While gradual shading based on illumination is an important step towards achieving photo-realism, most real-life objects have regular or irregular surface features (e.g., wood grain). These surface details are collectively referred to as *surface texture*. In this section we present three approaches to adding surface texture: *projected texture, texture mapping,* and *solid texture*.

Projected Texture

Imagine putting a plain object between a slide projector and the projection screen. The surfaces of the object that face the projector will be covered by the projected image. If the image depicts wood grain then the affected surfaces will have the intricate wood texture superimposed onto its original shading.

In computer graphics, projecting texture onto an object is effectively the inverse of projecting an object onto the view plane (compare Fig. 7-1 and Fig. 11-12) . We now refer to the view plane as the reference plane, which contains a two-dimensional texture definition called the *texture map*. The projection line that associates point P with its image P' allows the shading of P to be determined or influenced by information in the texture map at location P'.

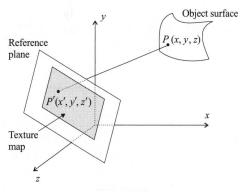

Fig. 11-12

The texture map is often a synthesized or scanned image, in which case it contains color attributes. There are several ways for the color attributes of P' to be used to shade point P. First, we may simply assign these attributes to P, replacing whatever color attributes P currently has. The net effect of this approach is to paint the color of the texture onto the object. Second, we may interpolate between the color C' of P' and the original color C of P using $(1 - k)C + kC'$ where $0 \leq k \leq 1.0$ to come up with a new color for P. The result of this calculation makes the texture appear blended into the original shading. Third, we may use a logical operation involving C and C' to compute a new color for P. For example, when the AND operation is used, a texture area with magenta shades will appear unaltered if the original color is white, but it will take on red shades if the original is yellow.

Projected texture is an effective tool when target surfaces are relatively flat and facing the reference plane. On the other hand, "hidden surfaces" are not affected, and features of the texture are distorted by the curvature of the surface.

Texture Mapping

Now imagine the texture map being a thin and flexible sheet made of elastic material. When we wrap it around the surface of an object we can stretch or shrink it so as to follow the shape of the object.

This approach is referred to as *texture mapping*. We describe the texture map in a two-dimensional space called the *texture space* with coordinates (u, w), and we represent the surface of an object in parametric form using (θ, φ). The mapping from the texture space to the object space is then defined by

$$\theta = f(u, w) \qquad \varphi = g(u, w)$$

and the inverse mapping by

$$u = r(\theta, \varphi) \qquad w = s(\theta, \varphi)$$

Although not necessary, these mapping functions are generally assumed to be linear (so the texture map stretches and shrinks proportionally). Thus we can write

$$\theta = Au + B \qquad \varphi = Cw + D$$

where the constants A, B, C, and D are obtained from the relationship between known points in the two spaces (e.g., corners of the texture map and the corresponding surface points).

As mentioned early, the texture map often contains color attributes that can be used in different ways to alter the original shading. In addition, its role may be extended to provide other kind of information that affects the outcome of the shading process. For example, a technique called *bump mapping* uses the quantities in the texture map to displace or perturb the normal vectors of the surface to produce an appearance of roughness (see Fig. 11-13 for a one-dimensional illustration of the effect).

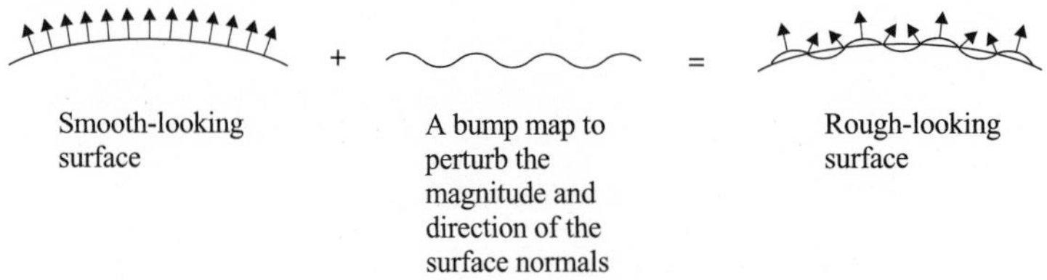

| Smooth-looking surface | A bump map to perturb the magnitude and direction of the surface normals | Rough-looking surface |

Fig. 11-13

In comparison with projected texture, the method of texture mapping can better adapt to a curved surface. However, complex shapes deter the derivation of mapping functions. Furthermore, both methods are particularly weak when features of the texture on one surface should "match" those on others. Consider a wood cube, for instance: the wood grain on one side should exhibit continuity and consistency with the wood grain on all adjacent sides. As we turn the wood cube into a sculpture, the complexity of this texture-matching problem simply multiplies.

Solid Texture

The weaknesses of projected texture and texture mapping largely stem from the inherent mismatch between a two-dimensional texture map and a three-dimensional surface. In this approach we define texture using a three-dimensional texture space. The texture definition, referred to as *solid texture*, is a three-dimensional representation of the internal structure of some nonhomogeneous material such as wood, marble, etc.

When rendering an object made of a specific material, we use transformations to place the object into the coordinate system where the texture for the material is defined. In other words, we map a surface point $P(x, y, z)$ to its coordinates (u, v, w) in the texture space. Information associated with this location is then used to control the shading of P. This makes the object look as if it were carved out of a solid piece of the chosen material.

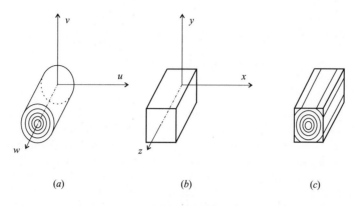

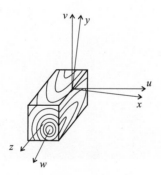

(a) (b) (c)

Fig. 11-14

Solid texture is often defined procedurally. The following is an example that shows the development of a model for wood grain. We begin by representing the most prominent feature of the material with a series of concentric cylinders in the texture space [see Fig. 11-14(a)]) . When an object such as the parallelepiped in Fig. 11-14(b) is placed into the texture field, the object intersects the cylinders, leaving intersection contours on its surfaces. The contours we get by aligning the object coordinate axes with the texture coordinate axes are shown in Fig. 11-14(c). We now rotate the front end of the parallelepiped slightly to the left about the v axis, and slightly up about the u axis. The result is our first approximation to wood grain (see Fig. 11-15).

Fig. 11-15

We can see that the contours on different sides are consistent with the underlying three-dimensional structure, but they are just too smooth and too perfect to look real. In order to incorporate some asymmetry and irregularity we need to bring two updates to the model. The first is to add ripples or sinusoidal perturbations to the cylinders so the intersection contours will have some minor and natural-looking oscillations. The second is to turn or twist the ripples slowly along the w axis to give the contours a skewed appearance. An implementation of the improved cylinder model is shown in the following pseudo-code procedure:

```
woodGrain(pt, kd)
{
    float radius, angle;
    radius = sqrt(pt[u]² + pt[v]²);
    angle = (pt[u] == 0) ? π/2 : arctan(pt[v]/pt[u]);
    radius = radius + m*sin( f*angle + r*pt[w]);
```

```
if ((int)radius % p < d)
    set the components of kd to produce a dark shade;
else
    set the components of kd to produce a light shade;
}
```

where array parameter *pt* represents the coordinates of surface point *P* in the texture space, and array parameter *kd* is used to return the proper reflection coefficients for shading point *P*.

The first instruction in woodGrain is to determine the radius of the cylinder that intersects *P*. The next instruction sets the base parameter value for the sine function that delivers the ripple effects. The magnitude of the perturbation is controlled by *m*, the frequency or number of ripples in a full circle is controlled by *f*, and the rate at which the ripples rotate along the *w* axis is controlled by *r*. Finally, we treat wood grain as alternating bands of dark and light cylinders of period *p*. Within a period the two bands are separated by threshold *d*. Although only two shades are shown in the procedure, the value of *kd* should be made to vary based on the relative position of *P* within each band to produce better results (see Fig. 11-16 for a ray-traced sphere).

Fig. 11-16

Solved Problems

11.1 Assuming that the medium of interest is air (or a vacuum) express the visible band of the spectrum in terms of a frequency range.

SOLUTION

Since frequency = speed of light/wavelength, and speed of light $\approx 3.0 \times 10^8$ m/s, we obtain the frequency range $(3.0 \times 10^8)/(700 \times 10^{-9})$ to $(3.0 \times 10^8)/(400 \times 10^{-9})$ Hz or 4.3×10^{14} to 7.5×10^{14} Hz.

11.2 Name the three perceptual terms for describing color and the corresponding physical properties of light.

SOLUTION

Brightness/luminance, hue/dominant wavelength, saturation/excitation purity.

11.3 Derive a simple formula to calculate the area bounded by the distribution function $P(\lambda)$ in Fig. 11-3.

SOLUTION

Let W and H be the width and height of the rectangular area that corresponds to white, and D and P be the width and height of the rectangular area that corresponds to pure color. The area bounded by $P(\lambda)$ is $W \times H + D \times P$.

11.4 Name the two kinds of receptor cells in the retina and describe their basic function.

SOLUTION

They are cones for seeing colors, and rods for perceiving low intensity light.

11.5 Why did we say that red, green, and blue only *roughly* coincide with the wavelength values that cause peak response from the three types of color-sensitive cones?

SOLUTION

The three colors have the following typical wavelength: red $= 700$ nm, green $= 546.1$ nm, and blue $= 435.8$ nm. Although blue and green closely match the sensitive range of two types of cones, $\beta : 440 - 445$ nm and $\delta : 535 - 545$ nm, the sensitive range of the third type, $\rho : 575 - 580$ nm, is actually yellow, not red.

11.6 Do we have to use Y in order to convert from chromaticity coordinates (x, y) back to a specific color in the XYZ color space?

SOLUTION

No. If we know X, we can use

$$X = X, \qquad Y = \frac{y}{x}X, \qquad Z = \frac{1-x-y}{x}X$$

11.7 Presume that a monitor produces what is called the standard white D_{65} with $x_w = 0.313$, $y_w = 0.329$, and $Y_w = 1.0$ when $R = G = B = 1$, and the chromaticity coordinates of its phosphors are as given in Sec. 11.1. Find the color transformation matrix M for the monitor.

SOLUTION

Since $Y_w = 1.0$, we have

$$X_w = x_w/y_w = 0.951 \qquad \text{and} \qquad Z_w = (1 - x_w - y_w)/y_w = 1.088$$

Use these and the chromaticity coordinates of the phosphors

$$\begin{pmatrix} 0.951 \\ 1.0 \\ 1.088 \end{pmatrix} = \begin{pmatrix} 0.62 & 0.29 & 0.15 \\ 0.34 & 0.59 & 0.06 \\ 0.04 & 0.12 & 0.79 \end{pmatrix} \begin{pmatrix} C_r \\ C_g \\ C_b \end{pmatrix}$$

Solve and get $C_r = 0.705$, $C_g = 1.170$, and $C_b = 1.164$. Now

$$M = \begin{pmatrix} x_r C_r & x_g C_g & x_b C_b \\ y_r C_r & y_g C_g & y_b C_b \\ z_r C_r & z_g C_g & z_b C_b \end{pmatrix} = \begin{pmatrix} 0.437 & 0.339 & 0.175 \\ 0.240 & 0.690 & 0.070 \\ 0.028 & 0.140 & 0.920 \end{pmatrix}$$

11.8   Verify the fact that the Y in the CIE XYZ color model is the same as the Y in the NTSC YIQ color model.

SOLUTION

Find the transformation to XYZ for the standard NTSC RGB display (see Sec. 11.1). Since $x_w = 0.31, y_w = 0.316$, and $Y_w = 1.0$, we have

$$X_w = x_w/y_w = 0.981 \qquad \text{and} \qquad Z_w = (1 - x_w - y_w)/y_w = 1.184$$

Use these and the chromaticity coordinates of the standard NTSC phosphors

$$\begin{pmatrix} 0.981 \\ 1.0 \\ 1.184 \end{pmatrix} = \begin{pmatrix} 0.67 & 0.21 & 0.14 \\ 0.33 & 0.71 & 0.08 \\ 0.0 & 0.08 & 0.78 \end{pmatrix} \begin{pmatrix} C_r \\ C_g \\ C_b \end{pmatrix}$$

Solve and get $C_r = 0.906, C_g = 0.826$, and $C_b = 1.432$. Now

$$M = \begin{pmatrix} x_r C_r & x_g C_g & x_b C_b \\ y_r C_r & y_g C_g & y_b C_b \\ z_r C_r & z_g C_g & z_b C_b \end{pmatrix} = \begin{pmatrix} 0.607 & 0.173 & 0.200 \\ 0.299 & 0.587 & 0.114 \\ 0.0 & 0.066 & 1.117 \end{pmatrix}$$

Since the middle row of M is the same as the top row of the matrix for mapping from RGB to YIQ, we can see that the Y in CIE XYZ is the same as the Y in NTSC YIQ.

11.9   What is the difference between a local illumination model and a global illumination model?

SOLUTION

A local illumination model focuses on the direct impact of the light coming from the light source. On the other hand, a global illumination model attempts to include such secondary effects as light going through transparent/translucent material and light bouncing from one object surface to another.

11.10   Refer to Fig. 11-6 in Sec. 11.2. Find a formula to compute **R**, the reflection of vector **L** with respect to normal vector **N**.

SOLUTION

Introducing auxiliary vectors **e** and **m** (see Fig. 11-17), we can write

$$\mathbf{R} = \mathbf{m} - \mathbf{e}$$

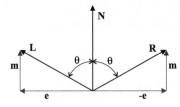

Fig. 11-17

Since $\mathbf{L} = \mathbf{e} + \mathbf{m}$, we have $\mathbf{e} = \mathbf{L} - \mathbf{m}$ and

$$\mathbf{R} = \mathbf{m} - (\mathbf{L} - \mathbf{m}) = 2\mathbf{m} - \mathbf{L}$$

Note that **m** is simply the perpendicular projection of **L** onto **N** (see Prob. A2.16) and **N** is a unit vector, hence

$$\mathbf{m} = (\mathbf{L} \cdot \mathbf{N})\mathbf{N}$$

Finally we have

$$\mathbf{R} = 2(\mathbf{L} \cdot \mathbf{N})\mathbf{N} - \mathbf{L}$$

11.11 The term $\mathbf{R} \cdot \mathbf{V}$ in the Phong formula is sometimes replaced by $\mathbf{N} \cdot \mathbf{H}$, where $\mathbf{H}$ is a unit vector that bisects the angle between $\mathbf{L}$ and $\mathbf{V}$. Show that $\mathbf{R} \cdot \mathbf{V} \neq \mathbf{N} \cdot \mathbf{H}$.

SOLUTION

Let $\mathbf{L}$, $\mathbf{N}$, and $\mathbf{V}$ be coplanar. Since $\mathbf{L}$, $\mathbf{N}$, and $\mathbf{R}$ must be coplanar from the laws of optics, and $\mathbf{L}$, $\mathbf{V}$, and $\mathbf{H}$, the bisector of the angle between $\mathbf{L}$ and $\mathbf{V}$, must also be coplanar, all the vectors are coplanar (see Fig. 11-18). From the angles shown on the left half of the drawing we have

$$\beta = \theta + \alpha$$

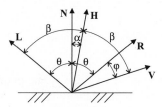

Fig. 11-18

From the angles shown on the right half of the drawing we have

$$\alpha + \beta = \theta + \varphi$$

Combining the two expressions we get

$$\varphi = 2\alpha$$

Unless $\varphi = \alpha = 0$, we have $\varphi \neq \alpha$ and $\cos(\varphi) \neq \cos(\alpha)$. Since $\mathbf{R} \cdot \mathbf{V} = \cos(\varphi)$ and $\mathbf{N} \cdot \mathbf{H} = \cos(\alpha)$, we have

$$\mathbf{R} \cdot \mathbf{V} \neq \mathbf{N} \cdot \mathbf{H}$$

11.12 The color of an object is largely determined by its diffuse reflection coefficient. If $k_d = (0.8, 0.4, 0)$ and the light is blue, what is the color of the object?

SOLUTION

Black, since the object does not reflect blue light and there is no red and green light for it to reflect.

11.13 Refer to Prob. 11.12. What if we use magenta light?

SOLUTION

Red, since the object only reflects the red component of the magenta light.

11.14 When a light source is relatively far away from a polyhedron, the diffuse reflection determined by the Phong formula varies little within each polygonal face. Why?

SOLUTION

All points on a polygonal face share the same normal vector $\mathbf{N}$. When the light is relatively far away, vector $\mathbf{L}$ (see Fig. 11-6) varies little from one surface point to another. (If the light is very distant, say, the sun, then **L** becomes a constant vector.) Hence $\mathbf{L} \cdot \mathbf{N}$, the term that determines the diffuse component in the Phong formula varies little within each polygonal face.

11.15 Refer to Fig. 11-9, and show exactly how to compute the color of P using bilinear interpolation.

SOLUTION

Let the coordinates of $P, P_1, P_2, P_3, P', $ and P'' be $(x, y), (x_1, y_1), (x_2, y_2), (x_3, y_3), (x', y'),$ and (x'', y''), respectively. Also let the color/intensity values at those points be $I, I_1, I_2, I_3, I',$ and I'', and respectively. We have

$$I' = I_1 \frac{y_2 - y'}{y_2 - y_1} + I_2 \frac{y' - y_1}{y_2 - y_1} \qquad I'' = I_2 \frac{y'' - y_3}{y_2 - y_3} + I_3 \frac{y_2 - y''}{y_2 - y_3}$$

and

$$I = I' \frac{x'' - x}{x'' - x'} + I'' \frac{x - x'}{x'' - x'}$$

For *RGB* colors, these formulas are applied to the values of each color component.

11.16 Suppose point P_1 with intensity I_1 is on scan line y_1 and point P_2 with intensity I_2 is on scan line y_2. Find an incremental formula to compute intensity values I' for all the scan lines between P_1 and P_2 using linear interpolation in the y direction.

SOLUTION

Let P_1 be the starting point, then the intensity change from one scan line to the next is

$$\Delta I = (I_2 - I_1)/(y_2 - y_1)$$

Hence

$$I_1' = I_1 \qquad \text{and} \quad I_i' = I_{i-1}' + \Delta I \qquad \text{where } i = 2, \ldots, y_2 - y_1$$

11.17 Refer to Prob. 11.16. If point P_1 on line 5 has an *RGB* color (1, 0.5, 0) and point P_2 on line 15 has an *RGB* color (0.2, 0.5, 0.6), what is the color for line 8?

SOLUTION

Since

$$\Delta R = (0.2 - 1)/(15 - 5) = -0.08$$
$$\Delta G = (0.5 - 0.5)/(15 - 5) = 0$$
$$\Delta B = (0.6 - 0)/(15 - 5) = 0.06$$

we have $(1 + 3 \times (-0.08), 0.5 + 3 \times 0, 0 + 3 \times 0.06) = (0.76, 0.5, 0.18)$ as the color for line 8.

11.18 Refer to Fig. 11-10(a). The vertices are shared by the rectangles that approximate the cylinder and the two polygons that represent the top and bottom of the object. Does each vertex have a unique normal vector?

SOLUTION

No. When a vertex is used to describe the top or bottom face, its normal vector is the normal of the corresponding face. When it is used to define the rectangle mesh, its normal vector is perpendicular to the cylinder as shown in the figure.

11.19 Refer to Fig. 11-11 and see Prob. 11.15. If the two normal vectors at P' and P'' are

$$\mathbf{N}' = -\frac{\sqrt{2}}{2}\mathbf{I} + \frac{\sqrt{2}}{2}\mathbf{J} \qquad \mathbf{N}'' = -\frac{\sqrt{2}}{2}\mathbf{I} + \frac{\sqrt{2}}{2}\mathbf{K}$$

and point P is half way between P' and P'', what is $\mathbf{N}$?

SOLUTION

Since P is in the middle of P' and P'', the last formula in Prob. 11.15 for linear interpolation in the x direction becomes

$$I = \frac{I'}{2} + \frac{I''}{2}$$

Use it to interpolate each component of $\mathbf{N}'$ and $\mathbf{N}''$:

$$\left(-\frac{\sqrt{2}}{4} - \frac{\sqrt{2}}{4}\right)\mathbf{I} + \frac{\sqrt{2}}{4}\mathbf{J} + \frac{\sqrt{2}}{4}\mathbf{K} = -\frac{\sqrt{2}}{2}\mathbf{I} + \frac{\sqrt{2}}{4}\mathbf{J} + \frac{\sqrt{2}}{4}\mathbf{K}$$

The magnitude of this vector is

$$\sqrt{\left(-\frac{\sqrt{2}}{2}\right)^2 + \left(\frac{\sqrt{2}}{4}\right)^2 + \left(\frac{\sqrt{2}}{4}\right)^2} = \sqrt{\frac{2}{4} + \frac{2}{16} + \frac{2}{16}} = \frac{\sqrt{3}}{2}$$

Use it to normalize the interpolated vector and get

$$\mathbf{N} = -\frac{\sqrt{6}}{3}\mathbf{I} + \frac{\sqrt{6}}{6}\mathbf{J} + \frac{\sqrt{6}}{6}\mathbf{K}$$

11.20 Show that when averaging or interpolating normal vectors we will get incorrect result if the vectors are not unit vectors (or vectors of equal magnitude).

SOLUTION

Consider $\mathbf{N}_1 = \mathbf{I}$ and $\mathbf{N}_2 = \mathbf{J}$: the average of the two is $\mathbf{I} + \mathbf{J}$, which bisects the 90° angle between $\mathbf{I}$ and $\mathbf{J}$. We can normalize it to get

$$\mathbf{N} = \frac{\sqrt{2}}{2}\mathbf{I} + \frac{\sqrt{2}}{2}\mathbf{J}$$

Now if we set $\mathbf{N}_2 = 2\mathbf{J}$, which has the same direction as $\mathbf{J}$, the average of $\mathbf{N}_1$ and $\mathbf{N}_2$ becomes $\mathbf{I} + 2\mathbf{J}$. Clearly, the direction of this vector differs from that of $\mathbf{N}$.

As for interpolation we can see from Prob. 11.19 that to compute a vector for the point halfway between two given points we apply

$$I = \frac{I'}{2} + \frac{I''}{2}$$

to each vector component. For $\mathbf{N}_1 = \mathbf{I}$ and $\mathbf{N}_2 = \mathbf{J}$, this produces

$$\tfrac{1}{2}\mathbf{I} + \tfrac{1}{2}\mathbf{J}$$

which is, after normalization, the same as $\mathbf{N}$ above. But, if we use $\mathbf{N}_2 = 2\mathbf{J}$, the result of interpolation becomes

$$\tfrac{1}{2}\mathbf{I} + \mathbf{J}$$

which has the direction of $\mathbf{I} + 2\mathbf{J}$, not the direction of $\mathbf{N}$.

11.21 Consider the texture-blending formula $(1 - k)C + kC'$ where $0 \leq k \leq 1.0$, C is the original color of the object, and C' is the color of the texture map. Describe in simple words the results that correspond to the two extreme cases: $k = 0$ and $k = 1$.

SOLUTION

The case $k = 0$ means no texture at all, whereas the case $k = 1$ means painting the texture over the original shading of the object.

11.22 When we use the logical-operation AND to combine the original color of the object and the color of the texture map, a texture area with magenta shades will appear unaltered if the original color is white, but it will take on red shades if the original is yellow. Why?

SOLUTION

Various shades of magenta can be described by RGB color vectors in the form of $(m, 0, m)$. The result of white $(1, 1, 1)$ AND $(m, 0, m)$ is $(m, 0, m)$, whereas the result of yellow $(1, 1, 0)$ AND $(m, 0, m)$ is $(m, 0, 0)$, which represents shades of red.

11.23 See Fig. 11-19, and find the linear functions that map the normalized image onto a square area of 50×50 in the middle of the front face of the cubic object.

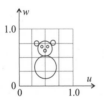 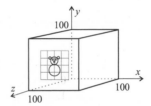

Fig. 11-19

SOLUTION

First find a parametric representation for the target area

$$\begin{cases} x = \theta & 25 \leq \theta \leq 75 \\ y = \varphi & 25 \leq \varphi \leq 75 \\ z = 100 \end{cases}$$

Note the relationship between the corner points

$$\begin{aligned} u = 0, \quad w = 0 &\rightarrow \theta = 25, \quad \varphi = 25 \\ u = 1, \quad w = 0 &\rightarrow \theta = 75, \quad \varphi = 25 \\ u = 0, \quad w = 1 &\rightarrow \theta = 25, \quad \varphi = 75 \\ u = 1, \quad w = 1 &\rightarrow \theta = 75, \quad \varphi = 75 \end{aligned}$$

Substitute these into $\theta = Au + B$ and $\varphi = Cw + D$, we get

$$A = 50, \quad B = 25, \quad C = 50, \quad \text{and} \quad D = 25$$

Hence the mapping functions are

$$\theta = 50u + 25 \quad \text{and} \quad \varphi = 50w + 25$$

The inverse mapping functions are

$$u = \frac{\theta - 25}{50} \quad \text{and} \quad w = \frac{\varphi - 25}{50}$$

11.24 See Fig. 11-20. Find the linear functions that map the normalized grid pattern onto the bottom portion ($\pi/4 \leq \varphi \leq \pi/2$) of the spherical surface in the first octant.

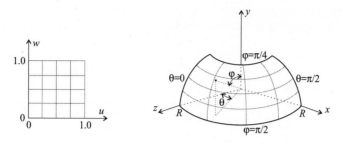

Fig. 11-20

SOLUTION

The parametric representation for the target area is

$$\begin{cases} x = R\sin(\theta)\sin(\varphi) & 0 \leq \theta \leq \pi/2 \\ y = R\cos(\varphi) & \pi/4 \leq \varphi \leq \pi/2 \\ z = R\cos(\theta)\sin\varphi \end{cases}$$

Note the relationship between the corner points

$$\begin{array}{llll} u = 0, & w = 0 \rightarrow \theta = 0, & \varphi = \pi/2 \\ u = 1, & w = 0 \rightarrow \theta = \pi/2, & \varphi = \pi/2 \\ u = 0, & w = 1 \rightarrow \theta = 0, & \varphi = \pi/4 \\ u = 1, & w = 1 \rightarrow \theta = \pi/2, & \varphi = \pi/4 \end{array}$$

Substitute these into $\theta = Au + B$ and $\varphi = Cw + D$, we get

$$A = \pi/2, \qquad B = 0, \qquad C = -\pi/4, \quad \text{and} \quad D = \pi/2$$

Hence the mapping functions are

$$\theta = \frac{\pi}{2}u \qquad \text{and} \qquad \varphi = \frac{\pi}{2} - \frac{\pi}{4}w$$

The inverse mapping functions are

$$u = \frac{\theta}{\pi/2} \qquad \text{and} \qquad w = \frac{\pi/2 - \varphi}{\pi/4}$$

Supplementary Problems

11.25 Given the distribution function $P(\lambda)$ in Fig. 11-3, derive a formula to calculate saturation.

11.26 Why everything looks gray or black in a dark room where we can barely see?

11.27 Can we use Z to convert from chromaticity coordinates (x, y) back to a specific color in the XYZ color space?

11.28 What's the difference between the Y in CMY and the Y in YIQ?

11.29 Consider a sphere of radius R, centered at (x_c, y_c, z_c). What is the normal vector $\mathbf{N}$ at point (x, y, z) on the sphere?

11.30 Find the linear functions that map a 1.0×2.0 texture map onto a cylindrical surface in the first octant (see Fig. 11-21) . The short sides of the texture map should align with the straight edges of the surface.

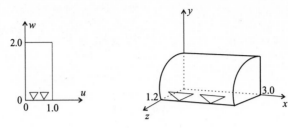

Fig. 11-21

CHAPTER 12

Ray Tracing

Ray tracing is a global illumination model that accounts for the transport of light energy beyond the direct/local contribution from the light sources. Its operation is largely based on the principles of geometric optics. By tracing the path of light rays it is able to integrate the tasks of shading, shadow generation, hidden surface removal, projection, and scan conversion into one single computational process.

In this chapter we first introduce the fundamental concepts that underlie this elegant approach (Sect. 12.1). We then discuss the basic ray-tracing algorithm (Sect. 12.2), the parametric vector representation of a ray (Sect. 12.3), and the mathematics of ray–surface intersection (Sect. 12.4). We also present techniques for improving execution efficiency (Sect. 12.5), anti-aliasing (Sect. 12.6), and achieving some desired visual effects (Sect. 12.7).

12.1 THE PINHOLE CAMERA

In theory one can take perfect pictures using a pinhole camera—a closed box with a tiny hole in the center of the front panel (see Fig. 12-1). The hole is so small that only one light ray passing through it can strike a particular point on the negative, which is mounted on the inside of the back panel. As light rays from across the scene expose the negative by hitting their respective target precisely, a sharp image depicting the scene emerges.

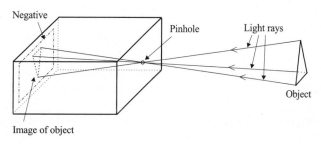

Fig. 12-1   A pinhole camera.

Now we place a screen between the pinhole and the object (see Fig. 12-2), causing the light rays to intersect the screen. If we can record each light ray as it intersects the screen, we will have a perfect picture of the object on the screen. Or, to put this in terms of image synthesis, if the screen resolution is arbitrarily high and we can set the pixel at each intersection point to match the color of the corresponding light ray, then the image will be indistinguishable from the real scene when viewed from the position of the pinhole.

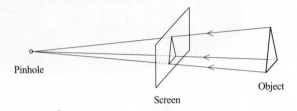

Fig. 12-2

12.2 A RECURSIVE RAY-TRACER

In order to construct an image based on the pinhole-camera model we need to determine the light rays that are responsible for the pixels. We do so by following their path in the opposite direction, i.e., from the viewpoint through the center of each pixel into the scene (see Fig. 12-3). These are called the *primary rays*. If a primary ray does not intersect any object in the scene, then the corresponding pixel is simply set to some background color.

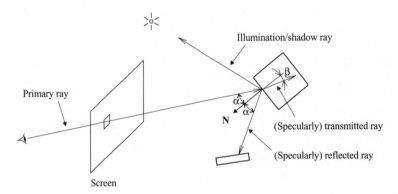

Fig. 12-3   Ray tracing.

On the other hand, if a primary ray intersects an object, then the color of the corresponding pixel is determined by the surface shading of the object at the intersection point. Several *secondary rays* are used to compute the three components of this surface shading. The first component is called the *local contribution*, which refers to the direct contribution from the light source(s). We send a *shadow ray* or *illumination ray* from the surface point to a light source. If the ray is blocked before reaching the light source, the surface point is in shadow (relative to this light source). The second component is called the *reflected contribution*, which refers to the reflection of light energy coming from another object surface (inter-object reflection). This is determined by a (*specularly*) *reflected ray*, a ray that represents the reflection of the primary ray with respect to normal vector $\mathbf{N}$. The third component is called the *transmitted contribution*, which refers to the transmission of light energy coming from behind the surface (transparent object). This is determined by a (*specularly*) *transmitted ray*, a ray that represents the refraction of the primary ray with respect to $\mathbf{N}$.

Note that, were the object surface a perfect mirror, the specularly reflected ray would represent the sole direction of light reflected towards the viewpoint. Also, if the object were made of perfectly homogeneous material, the specularly transmitted ray would represent the sole direction of light refracted towards the viewpoint.

Snell's law determines the relationship between angles α and β (see Fig. 12-3):

$$\frac{\sin(\alpha)}{\sin(\beta)} = \frac{\eta_2}{\eta_1}$$

where η_1 is the refraction index of the medium in which α is defined and η_2 is the refraction index of the medium in which β is defined. Although the refraction index of a medium is a function of temperature and wavelength, we can often use such values as 1.0 for air, 1.3 for water, and 1.5 for glass.

Employing the Phong formula to describe the local contribution, we express the intensity I of the light energy represented by the primary ray as

$$I = I_a k_a + \sum_{i=1}^{n} I_{p_i}(k_d \mathbf{L}_i \cdot \mathbf{N} + k_s(\mathbf{R}_i \cdot \mathbf{V})^k) + k_r I_r + k_t I_t$$

where the ambient term now represents the portion of inter-object reflection that is not accounted for by the term $k_r I_r$, which describes the reflected contribution as the product of the reflection coefficient k_r and the intensity I_r of the reflected ray; the last term $k_t I_t$ describes the transmitted contribution as the product of the transmission coefficient k_t and the intensity I_t of the transmitted ray. Both k_r and k_t are in the range of $[0, 1.0]$. I_r and I_t are obtained recursively by treating the reflected ray and the transmitted ray as a primary ray. In other words, we calculate I_r by evaluating the above equation at the closest surface the reflected ray intersects, in exactly the same way as the primary ray is handled. A pseudo-code description of the basic ray-tracing algorithm is as follows:

```
rayTrace{ray, depth, color}
{
   determine closest intersection of ray with an object;
   if (no intersection) color = background;
   else {
      color = local contribution;
      if (depth > 1) {
         calculate reflected ray;
         rayTrace(reflected ray, depth-1, ref_color);
         calculate transmitted ray;
         rayTrace(transmitted ray, depth-1, trans_color);
         color = color + k_r · ref_color + k_t · trans_color;
      }
   }
}
```

This procedure takes a ray and a depth value that is greater than or equal to 1 as input, and returns a color as output (typically an RGB vector, the above formula is used to compute the intensity of each individual color component). It treats the given ray as a primary ray and (when depth > 1) makes recursive calls to obtain the color (ref_color) of the reflected ray and the color (trans_color) of the transmitted ray.

Figures 12-4, 12-5, and 12-6 show the results of ray-tracing a scene consisting of three opaque spheres. The smaller one in the front is dull whereas the two larger ones in the back are shiny. The first image (depth = 1) is obtained using only the primary ray and shadow ray. The second image (depth = 2) depicts the effect of adding reflected contribution (one level beyond the primary ray). The third image (depth = 3) shows the cumulative effect of two levels of reflected contribution. In Fig. 12-7 (also depth = 3), the dull sphere is replaced by a shiny glass sphere (a check-board floor is also added) to illustrate the combined effect of all three shading components.

12.3 PARAMETRIC VECTOR REPRESENTATION OF A RAY

A ray is not a vector although it may look like one (see Fig. 12-3). The difference between the two is that, while a vector is defined by its direction and magnitude, a ray is determined by its direction and starting point.

Fig. 12-4

Fig. 12-5

We may represent a ray in terms of two vectors: **s** to specify its starting point, and **d** to describe its direction (see Fig. 12-8). These two vectors are used to provide a parametric vector representation for the ray:

$$\mathbf{r}(t) = \mathbf{s} + t\mathbf{d} \qquad (0 \leq t)$$

where $\mathbf{r}(t)$ denotes a family of vectors. When the tails of these vectors are placed at the origin, their heads make up the ray.

Fig. 12-6

Fig. 12-7

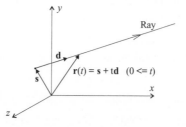

Fig. 12-8   Vector representation of a ray.

12.4   RAY–SURFACE INTERSECTION

A critical step in the implementation of ray tracing is to determine whether a ray intersects an object. This operation is performed for each primary ray (or a ray that is treated as a primary ray in a recursive call) and shadow ray. If a primary ray does intersect an object, we need to know exactly where the intersection point is.

Coordinate System Plane

Intersection of a ray with the xy plane can be determined by solving the following for t (see Fig. 12-9):

$$\mathbf{s} + t\mathbf{d} = x_i\mathbf{I} + y_i\mathbf{J}$$

With $\mathbf{s} = x_s\mathbf{I} + y_s\mathbf{J} + z_s\mathbf{K}$ and $\mathbf{d} = x_d\mathbf{I} + y_d\mathbf{J} + z_d\mathbf{K}$, we have

$$\begin{cases} x_s + tx_d = x_i \\ y_s + ty_d = y_i \\ z_s + tz_d = 0 \end{cases}$$

When $z_d = 0$, the ray is parallel to the plane (no intersection). When $z_s = 0$, the ray originates from the plane (no intersection). Otherwise, we calculate t using the third equation

$$t = -\frac{z_s}{z_d}$$

If $t < 0$, the negative extension of the ray intersects the plane. On the other hand, if $t > 0$, the ray itself intersects the plane and the coordinates x_i and y_i of the intersection point can be calculated from the first two equations.

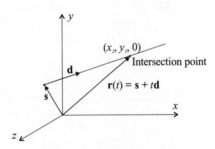

Fig. 12-9

Intersection with other coordinate system planes and planes that are parallel to a coordinate system plane can be handled similarly (see Probs. 12.9 and 12.30). We can also test to see if the intersection point is within a region (see Probs. 12.10, 12.11, and 12.12).

Arbitrary Plane

Let $\mathbf{n} = x_n\mathbf{I} + y_n\mathbf{J} + z_n\mathbf{K}$ be the normal vector to an arbitrary plane and $P_0\,(x_0, y_0, z_0)$ a point on the plane (see Fig. 12-10). The vector equation or point-normal equation of the plane is then (from App. 2, Sect. A2.3)

$$x_n(x - x_0) + y_n(y - y_0) + z_n(z - z_0) = 0$$

To determine if a ray $\mathbf{s} + t\mathbf{d}$ ($\mathbf{s} = x_s\mathbf{I} + y_s\mathbf{J} + z_s\mathbf{K}$ and $\mathbf{d} = x_d\mathbf{I} + y_d\mathbf{J} + z_d\mathbf{K}$) intersects the plane, we substitute $x_s + tx_d$, $y_s + ty_d$, and $z_s + tz_d$ for x, y, and z, respectively:

$$x_n(x_s + tx_d - x_0) + y_n(y_s + ty_d - y_0) + z_n(z_s + tz_d - z_0) = 0$$

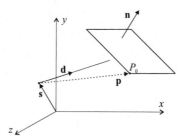

Fig. 12-10

Solving for t we get

$$t = -\frac{x_\mathbf{n}(x_\mathbf{s} - x_0) + y_\mathbf{n}(y_\mathbf{s} - y_0) + z_\mathbf{n}(z_\mathbf{s} - z_0)}{x_\mathbf{n}x_\mathbf{d} + y_\mathbf{n}y_\mathbf{d} + z_\mathbf{n}z_\mathbf{d}}$$

Introducing $\mathbf{p} = (x_0 - x_\mathbf{s})\mathbf{I} + (y_0 - y_\mathbf{s})\mathbf{J} + (z_0 - z_\mathbf{s})\mathbf{K}$, we can express t in vector form:

$$t = \frac{\mathbf{n} \cdot \mathbf{p}}{\mathbf{n} \cdot \mathbf{d}}$$

When $\mathbf{n} \cdot \mathbf{d} = 0$, the ray is parallel to the plane (no intersection). Otherwise, if $t < 0$, the negative extension of the ray intersects the plane; if $t = 0$, the ray originates from the plane. The ray intersects the plane only when $t > 0$.

Sometimes we want to further distinguish the two cases of intersection; intersecting the outside (front) of a plane versus intersecting its inside (back). The former occurs when $\mathbf{n} \cdot \mathbf{d} < 0$ whereas the latter occurs when $\mathbf{n} \cdot \mathbf{d} > 0$.

Sphere

Consider a sphere of radius R centered at $(x_\mathbf{c}, y_\mathbf{c}, z_\mathbf{c})$ and an arbitrary point (x, y, z) on the sphere (see Fig. 12-11). Define vectors $\mathbf{c} = x_\mathbf{c}\mathbf{I} + y_\mathbf{c}\mathbf{J} + z_\mathbf{c}\mathbf{K}$ and $\mathbf{p} = x\mathbf{I} + y\mathbf{J} + z\mathbf{K}$. The vector equation for the sphere is

$$|\mathbf{p} - \mathbf{c}| = R$$

To determine if a ray $\mathbf{r}(t) = \mathbf{s} + t\mathbf{d}$ intersects the sphere, we substitute $\mathbf{s} + t\mathbf{d}$ and $\mathbf{p}$ and square both sides:

$$|\mathbf{s} + t\mathbf{d} - \mathbf{c}|^2 = R^2$$

Since $\mathbf{v} \cdot \mathbf{v} = |\mathbf{v}|^2$ for any vector $\mathbf{v}$ (see Prob. A2.3), we have

$$\begin{aligned}
|\mathbf{s} - \mathbf{c} + t\mathbf{d}|^2 &= (\mathbf{s} - \mathbf{c} + t\mathbf{d}) \cdot (\mathbf{s} - \mathbf{c} + t\mathbf{d}) \\
&= (\mathbf{s} - \mathbf{c}) \cdot (\mathbf{s} - \mathbf{c} + t\mathbf{d}) + t\mathbf{d} \cdot (\mathbf{s} - \mathbf{c} + t\mathbf{d}) \quad \text{(Prob. A1.20)} \\
&= (\mathbf{s} - \mathbf{c}) \cdot (\mathbf{s} - \mathbf{c}) + 2(\mathbf{s} - \mathbf{c}) \cdot t\mathbf{d} + t\mathbf{d} \cdot t\mathbf{d} \quad \text{(Prob. A1.19)} \\
&= |\mathbf{s} - \mathbf{c}|^2 + 2t(\mathbf{s} - \mathbf{c}) \cdot \mathbf{d} + t^2|\mathbf{d}|^2 = R^2
\end{aligned}$$

This is in the form of a quadratic equation in t:

$$At^2 + 2Bt + C = 0$$

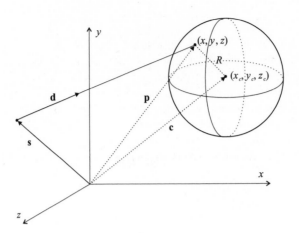

Fig. 12-11

where $A = |\mathbf{d}|^2$, $B = (\mathbf{s} - \mathbf{c}) \cdot \mathbf{d}$, $C = |\mathbf{s} - \mathbf{c}|^2 - R^2$, and the solution is

$$t = \frac{-B \pm \sqrt{B^2 - AC}}{A}$$

with

$$B^2 - AC \begin{cases} < 0 & \text{no intersection} \\ = 0 & \text{ray (or its negative extension) touching sphere} \\ > 0 & \text{two (possible) intersection points} \end{cases}$$

When $B^2 - AC > 0$ we get two t values: t_1 and t_2. If both are less than 0, the negative extension of the ray intersects the sphere (no intersection by the ray). If one of them is 0, the ray starts from a point on the sphere and intersects the sphere only if the other value is positive. If the two values differ in signs, the ray originates from inside the sphere and intersects the sphere once. If both are positive, the ray intersects the sphere twice (first enters and then exits), and the smaller t value corresponds to the intersection point that is closer to the starting point of the ray.

General Implicit Surface

Generally, to determine if a ray $\mathbf{s} + t\mathbf{d}$ ($\mathbf{s} = x_s\mathbf{I} + y_s\mathbf{J} + z_s\mathbf{K}$ and $\mathbf{d} = x_d\mathbf{I} + y_d\mathbf{J} + z_d\mathbf{K}$) intersects a surface that is represented by an implicit equation $F(x, y, z) = 0$, we solve

$$F(x_s + tx_d, y_s + ty_d, z_s + tz_d) = 0$$

for t (see Probs. 12.16, 12.17, and 12.31).

12.5 EXECUTION EFFICIENCY

Ray-tracing is time-consuming largely due to the recursive nature of the algorithm and the demanding task of computing ray–surface intersections. Several techniques are designed to improve execution efficiency by means of object/scene-dependent deployment of system resources.

Adaptive Depth Control

An opaque object ($k_t = 0$) does not transmit light. A dull object ($k_r = 0$) does not produce specular reflection. In these extreme cases there is clearly no need to trace the transmitted/reflected ray, since the transmitted/reflected contribution is zero regardless of the value of I_t/I_r.

Even in a more general situation, say, $k_r > 0$, the cumulative effect of the reflection coefficients of the surfaces along the path of reflection can render the contribution from additional recursive steps negligible. For example (see Fig. 12-12), if the reflection coefficients of the objects along the path of reflection are k_{r1}, k_{r2}, and k_{r3}, respectively, the eventual contribution of I_{r3} to the primary ray is $k_{r1}k_{r2}k_{r3}I_{r3}$. When $k_{r1} = k_{r2} = k_{r3} = 0.1$, this contribution is $0.001I_{r3}$ (negligible in most applications).

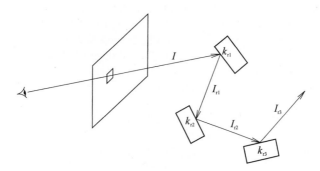

Fig. 12-12

Using adaptive depth control, the ray-tracer keeps track of the cumulative attenuation along the path of reflection (and transmission in a similar manner) and, before working on another reflected ray, compares the current value of cumulative attenuation to a present threshold. It continues its recursive execution to the required depth only if the cumulative attenuation does not fall below the threshold. For the example in Fig. 12-12, if $k_{r1} = k_{r2} = k_{r3} = 0.1$ and the threshold is 0.01, then the ray-tracer will not go beyond the second reflected ray because $k_{r1}k_{r2}k_{r3} < 0.01$.

Bounding Volume Extension

Since a ray travels along a narrow path in one specific direction, it normally misses most of the objects in the scene. This means that an object is more likely to get a "no" answer in a ray–surface intersection test than a "yes" answer. The purpose of this technique is to identify objects, especially complex objects, that are definitely not intersected by the ray as quickly as possible.

Each object or group of objects in close spatial proximity is surrounded by a capsule/bounding volume (e.g., a sphere, a box, etc.) that permits a simple intersection check. If the ray does not intersect the capsule, it does not intersect the object(s) inside the capsule, and no further testing involving the object(s) is necessary. On the other hand, if the ray does intersect the capsule, further testing involving the enclosed object(s) is necessary in order to reach a conclusion ("yes" or "no").

Hierarchy of Bounding Volumes

The bounding volume technique can be extended to a hierarchy of bounding volumes. For example, if a monitor and a printer are on top of a desk, we may introduce a large bounding volume encompassing all three objects, and three smaller bounding volumes inside the large one for the individual objects, respectively. Only if a ray intersects the large bounding volume it is necessary to go to the next level of the hierarchy to test against the three smaller bounding volumes.

Bounding volume techniques incur two types of overhead: maintaining bounding volumes and testing against bounding volumes. It is often worth the effort when the objects are complex and are not loosely distributed across the scene (see Prob. 12.20).

Spatial Coherence/Spatial Subdivision

This technique is based on the observation that only objects that are in the vicinity of the path of a ray may be intersected by the ray, objects that are away from the path do not have anything to do with the ray (and should be ignored in intersection testing).

We subdivide the scene space into regions (see Fig. 12-13 for a 2D illustration) and associate objects with the regions in which they appear. In other words, each region is linked to a list of objects that appear in that region. Since the regions are typically regularly spaced and aligned with the coordinate system axes/planes, only a minimum amount of computation is necessary to identify the regions that are intersected by a given ray (see Prob. 12.21). The actual test for ray–surface intersection is then performed only with the objects that appear in the identified regions.

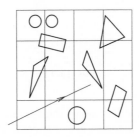

Fig. 12-13

Furthermore, we follow the ray from one region to the next and perform intersection tests as we enter each region (since an object may be associated with more than one region, care should be taken to avoid repeating intersection tests with the same object). Once an intersection point (closest to the starting point of the ray) is identified with the objects in the current region, there is no need to move forward into other regions.

The overhead for spatial subdivision is mainly the need to preprocess the scene in order to assign objects to regions. The technique is complementary to the bounding volume approach in that it is quite capable of dealing with objects that are scattered around the scene.

12.6   ANTI-ALIASING

Ray-tracing depicts a continuous scene by taking discrete samples from the scene. Hence the aliasing artifacts associated with scan-conversion (e.g., jagged edges, dropout of small parts/objects) are also present in ray-traced images. The following are some anti-aliasing techniques that can be incorporated into the ray-tracing process to alleviate the problem.

Supersampling

Each pixel is divided into subpixels (see Chap. 3, Fig. 3-27) and a separate primary ray is sent and traced through the center of each subpixel. The color/intensity values of the primary rays for the subpixels are then combined (averaged) to produce a value for the parent pixel.

Adaptive Supersampling

Supersampling often drastically increases the computational burden of ray tracing. In this approach we send one ray through the center of a pixel and four additional rays through its corners. If the five rays return similar colors the pixel will not be subdivided (it probably corresponds to a smoothly shaded area in the scene). Only if the returned colors are sufficiently different do we subdivide the pixel (it probably covers both sides of an edge) into 2×2 subpixels. Each subpixel is then handled in the same way, and the process terminates when a preset level of subdivision is reached.

Stochastic Supersampling

The effect of supersampling can often be enhanced with stochastic or distributed ray-tracing. In this approach we deviate from using the fixed (sub)pixel grid by scattering the rays evenly across the pixel area in a random fashion. A typical way to achieve this is to displace each ray from its normal position in the grid (see Prob. 12.24).

12.7   ADDITIONAL VISUAL EFFECTS

Various techniques have been developed to achieve certain desirable visual effects. Some methods below are applications of *distributed ray-tracing*, which means that we scatter rays around with respect to a certain parameter in the ray-tracing process (recall that in stochastic supersampling we displace rays from their normal position in the pixel grid).

Environment Mapping

A shiny (mirror-like) object reflects the surrounding environment. Instead of ray-tracing the three-dimensional scene to obtain the global reflection, we may map a picture of the environment onto the object (see Fig. 12-14). The object is typically placed in the middle of an enclosure such as a cube, cylinder, or sphere, with the environment map attached to the inside of the enclosing surface (facing the object). The color of a pixel is then a function (e.g., average by supersampling) of the area in the environment map that corresponds to the pixel.

Clearly this is only an approximation to ray-tracing the three-dimensional scene. The quality of the mapped reflection is dependent on the size (relative to the enclosure) and shape of the object. However,

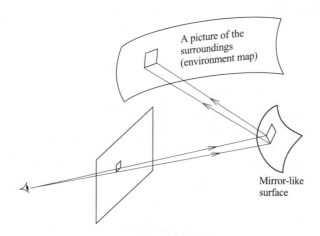

Fig. 12-14

environment mapping is often faster, and it is particularly useful in creating the illusion of a computer-generated shiny object amidst a real-world scene (which of course cannot be ray-traced).

Soft Shadow

Ray-traced images of scene involving fixed point-lights are characterized by the harsh edges of the shadow areas. However real lights are not mathematical points and they cast *soft shadows*, which consist of an *umbra* area surrounded by a *penumbra* area (see Fig. 12- 15).

Fig. 12-15

In order to produce soft shadows we model a light source by a region, called an *area light*. The area is subdivided into subareas or zones. Shadow rays are then distributed to these zones via random selection (with equal probability for each zone or weights that favor zones that correspond to higher intensity values).

Blurry Reflection

To get a blurry reflection of the surroundings on a glossy (not mirror-like) object, we distribute the reflected rays. This can be done by displacing a reflected ray from the position of its mirror reflection by a small angle. The distribution of the angle is subject to the same bell-shaped reflectance function that governs specular highlights (see Fig. 11-6).

Translucency

The difference between transparency (specular transmission) and translucency is somewhat analogous to the difference between specular reflection and blurry reflection. To achieve the effect of light going through translucent material, we distribute the transmitted rays by displacing each from the position of specular transmission by a small angle. The distribution of the angle is subject to a transmittance function similar to the aforementioned reflectance function. Furthermore, we may attenuate the transmitted intensity to account for the loss of energy.

Motion Blur

A fast-moving object tends to look blurry in a photograph (especially if the photo was taken with a low shutter speed). To mimic this phenomenon we distribute rays over time. In other words, we predetermine the path or a series of positions of a moving object based on the characteristics of the movement. We then displace the object along its path or between positions as each ray is traced.

Solved Problems

12.1   Describe how hidden surface removal and projection are integrated into the ray-tracing process.

SOLUTION

Each primary ray plays the role of a projector that maps a surface point P to its image P' in the view plane. If all primary rays emanate from a view point C we have the effect of perspective projection. If all primary rays are parallel to each other we have the effect of parallel projection. Furthermore, if a primary ray intersects several object surfaces, only the surface that is the closest to the view plane is chosen to determine the color of the corresponding pixel; all others are effectively treated as hidden surfaces and removed (not displayed).

12.2   Name the three components of surface shading and the secondary ray for computing each.

SOLUTION

Local contribution (shadow ray), reflected contribution (specularly reflected ray), and transmitted contribution (specularly transmitted ray).

12.3   The refraction index of a medium is the ratio of the speed of light in vacuum to the speed of light in that medium. Rewrite Snell's law in terms of the speed of light in the two participating media.

SOLUTION

Let c be the speed of light in vacuum, c_1 be the speed of light in the medium whose refraction index is η_1, and c_2 be the speed of light in the medium whose refraction index is η_2. We have $\eta_1 = c/c_1$ and $\eta_2 = c/c_2$. Hence Snell's law can be written as

$$\frac{\sin(\alpha)}{\sin(\beta)} = \frac{\eta_2}{\eta_1} = \frac{c/c_2}{c/c_1} = \frac{c_1}{c_2}$$

12.4   What is the difference between a vector and a ray?

SOLUTION

A vector is defined by its direction and magnitude, whereas a ray is determined by its direction and starting point.

12.5   A ray is represented by $\mathbf{r}(t) = \mathbf{s} + t\mathbf{d}$ where $\mathbf{s} = 2\mathbf{I} + \mathbf{J} - 3\mathbf{K}$ and $\mathbf{d} = \mathbf{I} + 2\mathbf{K}$. Find the coordinates of the points on the ray that correspond to $t = 0, 1, 2.5$, and 3, respectively.

SOLUTION

$$\mathbf{r}(0) = (2+0)\mathbf{I} + \mathbf{J} + (-3+0)\mathbf{K} = 2\mathbf{I} + \mathbf{J} - 3\mathbf{K} \rightarrow (2, 1, -3)$$
$$\mathbf{r}(1) = (2+1)\mathbf{I} + \mathbf{J} + (-3+2)\mathbf{K} = 3\mathbf{I} + \mathbf{J} - \mathbf{K} \rightarrow (3, 1, -1)$$
$$\mathbf{r}(2.5) = (2+2.5)\mathbf{I} + \mathbf{J} + (-3+5)\mathbf{K} = 4.5\mathbf{I} + \mathbf{J} + 2\mathbf{K} \rightarrow (4.5, 1, 2)$$
$$\mathbf{r}(3) = (2+3)\mathbf{I} + \mathbf{J} + (-3+6)\mathbf{K} = 5\mathbf{I} + \mathbf{J} + 3\mathbf{K} \rightarrow (5, 1, 3)$$

12.6 Let the viewpoint be at (a, b, c) and the center of a pixel at (x, y, z). Find vectors **s** and **d** to represent the corresponding primary ray.

SOLUTION

$$\mathbf{s} = a\mathbf{I} + b\mathbf{J} + c\mathbf{K}$$
$$\mathbf{d} = (x - a)\mathbf{I} + (y - b)\mathbf{J} + (z - c)\mathbf{K}$$

12.7 Lines in two-dimensional space can be represented by either the algebraic equation $y = mx + b$ or the parametric vector equation $\mathbf{L}(t) = \mathbf{s} + t\mathbf{d}$, where $-\infty < t < +\infty$. For $\mathbf{s} = \mathbf{I} + \mathbf{J}$ and $\mathbf{d} = \mathbf{I} - \mathbf{J}$, find the equivalent algebraic representation.

SOLUTION 1

Since $\mathbf{L}(t) = \mathbf{s} + t\mathbf{d} = (1 + t)\mathbf{I} + (1 - t)\mathbf{J}$, we have

$$x = 1 + t \qquad \text{and} \qquad y = 1 - t$$

Hence $x + y = 2$, or $y = -x + 2$.

SOLUTION 2

Find two points on the line

$$\mathbf{L}(0) = \mathbf{s} = \mathbf{I} + \mathbf{J} \rightarrow (1, 1)$$
$$\mathbf{L}(1) = \mathbf{s} + \mathbf{d} = 2\mathbf{I} \rightarrow (2, 0)$$

We have $(y - 1)/(x - 1) = (0 - 1)/(2 - 1)$, i.e., $y = -x + 2$.

12.8 Refer to Fig. 12-16(a), where **d** represents the direction of the primary ray, **t** the direction of the transmitted ray, and **n** the normal vector at the intersection point. Express **t** in terms of **d**, **n**, and the two angles α and β.

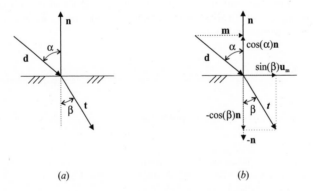

(a)   (b)

Fig. 12-16

SOLUTION

Let **d**, **t**, **n** be unit vectors [see Fig. 12-16(b)]. We have

$$\begin{cases} \mathbf{m} = \mathbf{d} + \cos(\alpha)\mathbf{n} \\ |\mathbf{m}| = \sin(\alpha) \end{cases}$$

and

$$\mathbf{t} = \sin(\beta)\mathbf{u_m} - \cos(\beta)\mathbf{n}$$
$$= \frac{\sin(\beta)}{\sin(\alpha)}(\mathbf{d} + \cos(\alpha)\mathbf{n}) - \cos(\beta)\mathbf{n}$$

12.9   Determine if a ray intersects a plane that is parallel to the xy plane.

SOLUTION

The equation for such a plane is $z = c$ where c is a constant. If a ray does intersect the plane, the intersection point is at (x_i, y_i, c). In order to find x_i and y_i we solve the following for t:

$$\mathbf{s} + t\mathbf{d} = x_i\mathbf{I} + y_i\mathbf{J} + c\mathbf{K}$$

With $\mathbf{s} = x_s\mathbf{I} + y_s\mathbf{J} + z_s\mathbf{K}$ and $\mathbf{d} = x_d\mathbf{I} + y_d\mathbf{J} + z_d\mathbf{K}$, we have

$$\begin{cases} x_s + tx_d = x_i \\ y_s + ty_d = y_i \\ z_s + tz_d = c \end{cases}$$

When $z_d = 0$, the ray is parallel to the plane (no intersection). When $z_s = c$, the ray originates from the plane (no intersection). Otherwise, we calculate t using the third equation

$$t = \frac{c - z_s}{z_d}$$

If $t < 0$, the negative extension of the ray intersects the plane. On the other hand, if $t > 0$, the ray itself intersects the plane and the coordinates x_i and y_i of the intersection point can be calculated from the first two equations.

12.10   Determine if a ray intersects a rectangular region defined by x_{min}, x_{max}, y_{min} and y_{max} in the xy plane.

SOLUTION

First determine if the ray intersects the xy plane (see Sect. 12.4 under "Coordinate System Plane"). If not, the ray does not intersect the region. Otherwise, find the coordinates x_i and y_i of the intersection point. If $x_{min} \leq x_i \leq x_{max}$ and $y_{min} \leq y_i \leq y_{max}$ the ray intersects the region; otherwise it does not.

12.11   Determine if a ray intersects a triangular (or convex polygonal) region in the xy plane.

SOLUTION

First determine if the ray intersects the xy plane (see Sect. 12.4 under "Coordinate System Plane"). If not, the ray does not intersect any region in the plane. Otherwise, find the coordinates x_i and y_i of the intersection point. The point is inside a triangular or convex polygonal region if it is on/inside all bounding edges of the region.

Now focus on just the xy plane (ignore z). To test if the intersection point (x_i, y_i) is inside or outside an edge in the plane, we choose a point on the edge (e.g., one of its endpoints) and define an outward normal vector $\mathbf{n}$ that points to the outside of the edge (see Fig. 12-17). We also use the chosen point to define vector $\mathbf{v}$, and the intersection point to define vector $\mathbf{v}_i$. We have

$$\mathbf{n} \cdot (\mathbf{v}_i - \mathbf{v}) \begin{cases} > 0 & (x_i, y_i) \text{ is outside the edge} & (\theta < 90°) \\ = 0 & (x_i, y_i) \text{ is on the edge} & (\theta = 90°) \\ < 0 & (x_i, y_i) \text{ is inside the edge} & (\theta > 90°) \end{cases}$$

12.12   A unit square is placed in the xy plane with one corner at the origin and the diagonal corner on the positive y axis [see Fig. 12-18(a)]. Determine if a ray emanating from $(0, 1, 2)$ going in the direction of the negative z axis intersects the square.

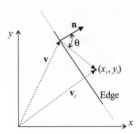

Fig. 12-17

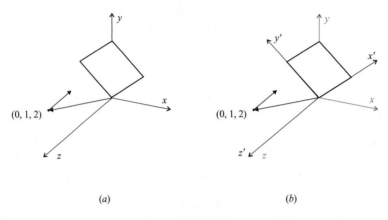

(a)   (b)

Fig. 12-18

SOLUTION

From the given condition we have

$$\mathbf{s} = \mathbf{J} + 2\mathbf{K} \qquad \text{and} \qquad \mathbf{d} = -\mathbf{K}$$

Since $z_s = 2 \neq 0$, $z_d = -1 \neq 0$, and $t = -z_s/z_d = 2 > 0$, the ray intersects the xy plane (see Sect. 12.4 under "Coordinate System Plane"). Using $x_s = 0$, $x_d = 0$, $y_s = 1$, and $y_d = 0$, we get

$$x_i = 0 + 2 \times 0 = 0 \qquad \text{and} \qquad y_i = 1 + 2 \times 0 = 1$$

To determine if the intersection point is inside the square, we may follow the solution for Prob. 12.10. Alternatively, we may perform a coordinate transformation from system xyz to $x'y'z'$ in order to align the x' and y' axes with the sides of the square [see Fig. 12-18(b)]. This requires a 45° rotation of the xyz system with respect to the z axis (or the origin if we ignore the z dimension). The square is now bounded by $x_{min} = 0$, $x_{max} = 1$, $y_{min} = 0$, and $y_{max} = 1$ in the new coordinate system, where the coordinate of the intersection point are (see Sect. 4.2)

$$x_i' = x_i \cos(45°) + y_i \sin(45°) = \frac{\sqrt{2}}{2}$$

$$y_i' = -x_i \sin(45°) + y_i \cos(45°) = \frac{\sqrt{2}}{2}$$

Since

$$x_{min} \leq x_i' \leq x_{max} \qquad \text{and} \qquad y_{min} \leq y_i' \leq y_{max}$$

the ray does intersect the square.

12.13 Let $\mathbf{n} = \mathbf{I} + \mathbf{J} + 2\mathbf{K}$ be the normal vector of a plane that passes through point P_0 $(1, 1, 0)$. Determine if a ray with $\mathbf{s} = -2\mathbf{I} + \mathbf{J} + 2\mathbf{K}$ and $\mathbf{d} = \mathbf{I} - \mathbf{K}$ intersects the plane.

SOLUTION

Refer to Sect. 12.4 under arbitrary plane. Since

$$\mathbf{n} \cdot \mathbf{d} = 1 \times 1 + 1 \times 0 + 2 \times (-1) = -1 < 0$$

the ray intersects the plane. We introduce

$$\begin{aligned}
\mathbf{p} &= (x_0 - x_s)\mathbf{I} + (y_0 - y_s)\mathbf{J} + (z_0 - z_s)\mathbf{K} \\
&= (1 - (-2))\mathbf{I} + (1 - 1)\mathbf{J} + (0 - 2)\mathbf{K} \\
&= 3\mathbf{I} - 2\mathbf{K}
\end{aligned}$$

and compute

$$t = \frac{\mathbf{n} \cdot \mathbf{p}}{\mathbf{n} \cdot \mathbf{d}} = \frac{1 \times 3 + 1 \times 0 + 2 \times (-2)}{-1} = 1$$

The intersection point is at $(x_s + x_d, y_s + y_d, z_s + z_d) = (-1, 1, 1)$.

12.14 Double check that the intersection point found in Prob. 12.13 is indeed on the given plane.

SOLUTION

The vector equation for the plane is

$$x_n(x - x_0) + y_n(y - y_0) + z_n(z - z_0) = 0$$

Since

$$1(-1 - 1) + 1(1 - 1) + 2(1 - 0) = 0$$

the intersection point $(-1, 1, 1)$ is indeed on the plane.

12.15 Let S_1 be a sphere of radius 8 centered at $(2, 4, 1)$ and S_2 a sphere of radius 10 centered at $(10, -2, -5)$. Determine if a ray with $\mathbf{s} = 2\mathbf{J} + 5\mathbf{K}$ and $\mathbf{d} = \mathbf{I} - 2\mathbf{K}$ intersects the spheres.

SOLUTION

First consider sphere S_1. We have

$$\begin{aligned}
A &= |\mathbf{d}|^2 = 1^2 + (-2)^2 = 5 \\
B &= (\mathbf{s} - \mathbf{c}) \cdot \mathbf{d} = [(0 - 2)\mathbf{I} + (2 - 4)\mathbf{J} + (5 - 1)\mathbf{K}] \cdot (\mathbf{I} - 2\mathbf{K}) = -10 \\
C &= |\mathbf{s} - \mathbf{c}|^2 - R^2 = (-2)^2 + (-2)^2 + 4^2 - 8^2 = -40
\end{aligned}$$

Since $B^2 - AC = (-10)^2 - 5(-40) = 300 > 0$, there are two t values:

$$t_1 = \frac{10 + \sqrt{300}}{5} = 2(1 + \sqrt{3}) > 0 \qquad \text{and} \qquad t_2 = \frac{10 - \sqrt{300}}{5} = 2(1 - \sqrt{3}) < 0$$

From these we know that the ray starts from inside S_1. Now considering sphere S_2, we have

$$\begin{aligned}
A &= |\mathbf{d}|^2 = 1^2 + (-2)^2 = 5 \\
B &= (\mathbf{s} - \mathbf{c}) \cdot \mathbf{d} = [(0 - 10)\mathbf{I} + (2 + 2)\mathbf{J} + (5 + 5)\mathbf{K}] \cdot (\mathbf{I} - 2\mathbf{K}) = -30 \\
C &= |\mathbf{s} - \mathbf{c}|^2 - R^2 = (-10)^2 + (4)^2 + 10^2 - 10^2 = 116
\end{aligned}$$

Since $B^2 - AC = (-30)^2 - 5 \times 116 = 320 > 0$, there are also two t values:

$$t_3 = \frac{30 + \sqrt{320}}{5} = 6 + 1.6\sqrt{5} > 0 \qquad \text{and} \qquad t_4 = \frac{30 - \sqrt{320}}{5} = 6 - 1.6\sqrt{5} > 0$$

From these we know that the ray intersects S_2 in two different places. By comparing $t_1 \approx 5.464$, $t_3 \approx 9.578$, and $t_4 \approx 2.422$, we see that the ray first enters S_2, then leaves S_1, and finally exits from S_2 (the two spheres overlap each other).

12.16 The (implicit) equation for a sphere of radius R centered at the origin is $x^2 + y^2 + z^2 - R^2 = 0$. Determine if a ray $\mathbf{s} + t\mathbf{d}$ intersects the sphere.

SOLUTION

Let $\mathbf{s} = x_s\mathbf{I} + y_s\mathbf{J} + z_s\mathbf{K}$ and $\mathbf{d} = x_d\mathbf{I} + y_d\mathbf{J} + z_d\mathbf{K}$. Substitute $x_s + tx_d$, $y_s + ty_d$, and $z_s + tz_d$ for x, y, and z, respectively:

$$(x_s + tx_d)^2 + (y_s + ty_d)^2 + (z_s + tz_d)^2 - R^2 = 0$$

Expand and regroup terms:

$$(x_d^2 + y_d^2 + z_d^2)t^2 + 2(x_s x_d + y_s y_d + z_s z_d)t + (x_s^2 + y_s^2 + z_s^2) - R^2 = 0$$

or

$$|\mathbf{d}|^2 t^2 + 2\mathbf{s} \cdot \mathbf{d}t + |\mathbf{s}|^2 - R^2 = 0$$

This matches the quadratic equation derived in the text (see Sect. 12.4 under "Sphere"), with the center of the sphere being set to $(0, 0, 0)$.

12.17 The (implicit) canonical equation for an elliptic paraboloid is $x^2 + y^2 - z = 0$ (see Chap. 9, Sect. 9.10, Fig. 9-19). Determine if a ray $\mathbf{s} + t\mathbf{d}$ intersects the paraboloid.

SOLUTION

Let $\mathbf{s} = x_s\mathbf{I} + y_s\mathbf{J} + z_s\mathbf{K}$ and $\mathbf{d} = x_d\mathbf{I} + y_d\mathbf{J} + z_d\mathbf{K}$. Substitute $x_s + tx_d$, $y_s + ty_d$, and $z_s + tz_d$ for x, y, and z, respectively:

$$(x_s + tx_d)^2 + (y_s + ty_d)^2 - (z_s + tz_d) = 0$$

Expand and regroup terms:

$$(x_d^2 + y_d^2)t^2 + (2x_s x_d + 2y_s y_d - z_d)t + (x_s^2 + y_s^2 - z_s) = 0$$

When the ray is parallel to the z axis (i.e., $x_d = 0$ and $y_d = 0$), the equation degenerates into

$$-z_d t + x_s^2 + y_s^2 - z_s = 0$$

From this we can find

$$t = \frac{x_s^2 + y_s^2 - z_s}{z_d}$$

where

$$t \begin{cases} < 0 & \text{ray's negative extension intersects paraboloid} \\ = 0 & \text{ray's starting point on paraboloid} \\ > 0 & \text{ray intersects paraboloid} \end{cases}$$

Otherwise, we can rewrite the quadratic equation as

$$At^2 + Bt + C = 0$$

where

$$A = x_d^2 + y_d^2 \qquad B = 2x_s x_d + 2y_s y_d - z_d \qquad C = x_s^2 + y_s^2 - z_s$$

and the solution for the equation is (note $A \neq 0$)

$$t = \frac{-B \pm \sqrt{B^2 - 4AC}}{2A}$$

If $B^2 - 4AC < 0$, the ray does not intersect (or touches) the paraboloid. If $B^2 - 4AC = 0$ and $t > 0$, the ray intersects (or touches) the paraboloid once. If $B^2 - 4AC > 0$, we get two t values; t_1 and t_2. If $t_1 < 0$ and $t_2 < 0$, the negative extension of the ray intersects the paraboloid (no intersection by the ray). If one of the two values is 0, the ray starts from a point on the paraboloid and intersects the paraboloid only if the other value is positive. If t_1 and t_2 differ in signs, the ray originates from inside the paraboloid (i.e., $x_s^2 + y_s^2 - z_s < 0$) and intersects the paraboloid once. If both values are positive, the ray intersects the paraboloid twice (first enters and then exits), and the smaller value corresponds to the intersection point that is closer to the starting point of the ray.

12.18 Figure 12-19 shows a ray $\mathbf{s} + t\mathbf{d}$ and a canonical paraboloid (see Prob. 12.17) that is defined in its own coordinate system $x'y'z'$. Describe how to make use of the result in Prob. 12.17 to determine if the ray intersects this paraboloid.

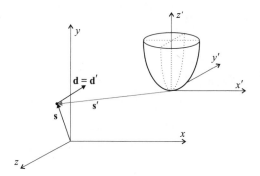

Fig. 12-19

SOLUTION

Find the coordinate transformation M from system xyz to $x'y'z'$. Apply M to transform (x_s, y_s, z_s) to (x'_s, y'_s, z'_s) and define $\mathbf{s}' = x'_s\mathbf{I} + y'_s\mathbf{J} + z'_s\mathbf{K}$. Apply M to transform the origin $(0, 0, 0)$ of xyz to (x'_0, y'_0, z'_0), and transform (x_d, y_d, z_d) to (x'_d, y'_d, z'_d). Define $\mathbf{d}' = (x'_d - x'_0)\mathbf{I} + (y'_d - y'_0)\mathbf{J} + (z'_d - z'_0)\mathbf{K}$, which describes the same vector as $\mathbf{d}$. Now represent the ray by $\mathbf{s}' + t\mathbf{d}'$ in the $x'y'z'$ coordinate system. Use the solution to Prob. 12.17 to determine if the ray intersects the paraboloid.

12.19 Refer to Fig. 12-12. If $k_{r1} = k_{r2} = k_{r3} = 0.3$, the threshold is 0.01, and the desired depth is 2, will the ray-tracer proceed to work on the third reflected ray?

SOLUTION

No, since the desired depth is 2. It would if the desired depth were 3 because $k_{r1}k_{r2}k_{r3} = 0.027 > 0.01$.

12.20 Describe a scene where the bounding volume techniques are definitely not applicable. Explain why.

SOLUTION

A number of spheres scattered across the scene. First of all, there is no simpler bounding volume for intersection testing. Furthermore, any bounding volume that encompasses several spheres is going to occupy a relatively large section of the scene. This brings about a relatively high probability for a ray to intersect the bounding volume, resulting in further testing against the enclosed spheres (something the bounding volume is supposed to help avoid in the first place).

12.21 In spatial subdivision we need to identify the regions along the ray's path. Since the ray exits from the current region and enters into the next region at the same point in space, a basic operation to guide the ray-tracer from one region to the next is: given the direction $\mathbf{d}$ of the ray and its entry point P_1 into the current region, find point P_2 through which the ray exits. Describe the operation for a parallelepiped region whose faces are parallel to the coordinate system planes.

SOLUTION

Such a region is bounded by the following planes:

$$x = x_{min} \qquad x = x_{max}$$
$$y = y_{min} \qquad y = y_{max}$$
$$z = z_{min} \qquad z = z_{max}$$

Since we are looking for the exit point, only planes that satisfy $\mathbf{n} \cdot \mathbf{d} > 0$, where $\mathbf{n}$ is the plane's normal vector, should be considered. The normal vectors of the planes listed above are simply $-\mathbf{I}$, $\mathbf{I}$, $-\mathbf{J}$, $\mathbf{J}$, $-\mathbf{K}$, and $\mathbf{K}$, respectively. Now we use P_1 to be the starting point of the ray. For each chosen plane, say, $z = z_{min}$, the t value that represents where the ray intersects the plane is (see Prob. 12.8)

$$t = \frac{z_{min} - z_s}{z_d}$$

(see Prob. 12.22 for similar formulae for the other planes). Once all eligible planes have been processed, the smallest t value from the calculation represents P_2.

12.22 Refer to Prob. 12.21, and write down the formulae for computing t for the other five planes.

SOLUTION

The formulae for planes $x = x_{min}$, $x = x_{max}$, $y = y_{min}$, $y = y_{max}$, and $z = z_{max}$ are

$$t = \frac{x_{min} - x_s}{x_d}, \qquad t = \frac{x_{max} - x_s}{x_d}, \qquad t = \frac{y_{min} - y_s}{y_d}, \qquad t = \frac{y_{max} - y_s}{y_d}, \qquad t = \frac{z_{max} - z_s}{z_d}$$

respectively.

12.23 Consider supersampling and adaptive supersampling. Which one is likely to perform better in reducing dropout?

SOLUTION

Supersampling is likely to perform better since the adaptive method will not subdivide a pixel if the center ray and corner rays return similar colors (but a small object may lie between those rays).

12.24 How to displace a ray from its normal position in the pixel grid?

SOLUTION

Let (x, y) be the ray's normal position in the grid. Define Δx and Δy such that $[x - \Delta x, x + \Delta x]$ and $[y - \Delta y, y + \Delta y]$ encompass the area for the new position (normally the area of the corresponding subpixel). Choose two random numbers δ_x and δ_y in the range of $[-\Delta x, \Delta x]$ and $[-\Delta y, \Delta y]$, respectively. The new/displaced position for the ray is $(x + \delta_x, y + \delta_y)$.

12.25 Illustrate why the relative size of an object affects the quality of environment mapping.

SOLUTION

The environment map is obtained by projecting the scene (a pyramid) from viewpoint C [see Fig. 12-20(a)]. When a small object is placed at C, the mapped reflection approximates the result of ray-tracing with the actual pyramid [see Fig. 12-20(b)]. On the other hand, if a relatively large object is placed at C, we may see a falsely reflected pyramid on the object when the pyramid is really behind the object [see Fig. 12-20(c)].

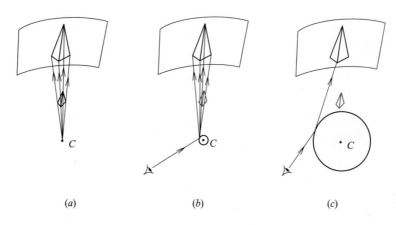

(a) (b) (c)

Fig. 12-20

12.26 Explain why the shape of an object affects the quality of environment mapping.

SOLUTION

A concave object may reflect part of itself. However, since the object is not depicted in the environment map, any self-reflection will be missing from the result of environment mapping.

Supplementary Problems

12.27 Snell's law is a consequence of Fermat's principle in optics: light travels from point A to point B along the path that takes the shortest time. Let A be in one medium where the speed of light is c_1, and B be in another medium where the speed of light is c_2 (see Fig. 12-21 where the x axis separates the two media). The path that takes the shortest time must be a straight line from A to a point P on the x axis followed by a straight line from P to B (since the light ray has to cross the x axis at some point and the shortest path within a medium is a straight line). Prove that the following holds for this path:

$$\frac{\sin(\alpha)}{\sin(\beta)} = \frac{c_1}{c_2}$$

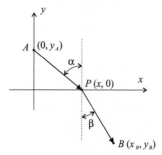

Fig. 12-21

12.28 The following pseudo-code procedure shows another way to describe the basic ray-tracing algorithm. The parameters are identical to those used in the procedure in Sect. 12.2, with the exception that the range for depth now includes value 0. Do these two procedures produce identical results when invoked with the same call? If yes, are they the same in terms of execution efficiency?

```
rayTrace(ray, depth, color)
{
  if (depth < 1) color = black;
  else {
    determine closest intersection of ray with an object;
    if (no intersection) color = background;
    else {
      color = local contribution;
      calculate reflected ray;
      rayTrace(reflected ray, depth-1, ref_color);
      calculate transmitted ray;
      rayTrace (transmitted ray, depth-1, trans_color);
      color = color + k_r · ref_color + k_t · trans_color;
    }
  }
}
```

12.29 Refer to Prob. 12.7, and convert $y = 2x - 6$ to parametric vector representation.

12.30 Determine if a ray intersects the yz plane.

12.31 The implicit equation for a cylinder of radius R along the z-axis is $x^2 + y^2 - R^2 = 0$. Determine if a ray $\mathbf{s} + t\mathbf{d}$ intersects the cylinder.

12.32 Show that the solution to equation $At^2 + 2Bt + C = 0$:

$$t = \frac{-B \pm \sqrt{B^2 - AC}}{A}$$

and the solution to equation $At^2 + Bt + C = 0$

$$t = \frac{-B \pm \sqrt{B^2 - 4AC}}{2A}$$

are essentially the same.

Mathematics for Two-Dimensional Computer Graphics

The key to understanding how geometric objects can be described and manipulated within a computer graphics system lies in understanding the interplay between geometry and numbers. While we have an innate geometric intuition which enables us to understand verbal descriptions such as *line*, *angle*, and *shape* and descriptions of the manipulation of objects (*rotating*, *shifting*, *distorting*, etc.), we also have the computer's ability to manipulate numbers. The problem then is to express our geometric ideas in numeric form so that the computer can do our bidding.

A *coordinate system* provides a framework for translating geometric ideas into numerical expressions. We start with our intuitive understanding of the concept of a two-dimensional plane.

A1.1 THE TWO-DIMENSIONAL CARTESIAN COORDINATE SYSTEM

In a two-dimensional plane, we can pick any point and single it out as a reference point called the *origin*. Through the origin we construct two perpendicular number lines called *axes*. These are traditionally labeled the x axis and the y axis. An orientation or sense of the plane is determined by the positions of the positive sides of the x and y axes. If a counterclockwise rotation of $90°$ about the origin aligns the positive x axis with the positive y axis, the coordinate system is said to have a *right-handed* orientation [see Fig. A1-1(*a*)]; otherwise, the coordinate system is called *left-handed* [see Fig. A1-1(*b*)].

The system of lines perpendicular to the x axis and perpendicular to the y axis forms a rectangular grid over the two-dimensional plane. Every point P in the plane lies at the intersection of exactly one line perpendicular to the x axis and one line perpendicular to the y axis. The number pair (x, y) associated with the point P is called the *Cartesian coordinates* of P. In this way every point in the plane is assigned a pair of coordinates (see Fig. A1-2).

Measuring Distances in Cartesian System

The distance between any two points P_1 and P_2 with coordinates (x_1, y_1) and (x_2, y_2) can be found with the formula

$$D = \sqrt{(x_2 - x_1)^2 + (y_2 - y_1)^2}$$

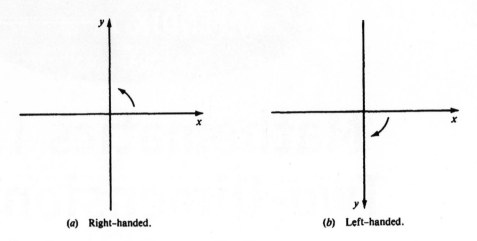

(a) Right-handed.   (b) Left-handed.

Fig. A1-1

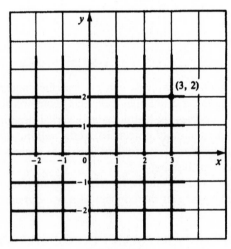

Fig. A1-2

The length of a line segment can be measured by finding the distance between the endpoints of the segment using the formula.

EXAMPLE 1.   The length of the line segment joining points $P_0(-1, 2)$ and $P_1(3, 5)$ can be found by

$$D = \sqrt{(5 - 2)^2 + [3 - (-1)]^2} = \sqrt{3^2 + 4^2} = 5$$

Measuring Angles in Cartesian System

The angles of a triangle can be measured in terms of the length of the sides of the triangle (see Fig. A1-3), by using the Law of Cosines, which is stated as

$$c^2 = a^2 + b^2 - 2ab(\cos \theta)$$

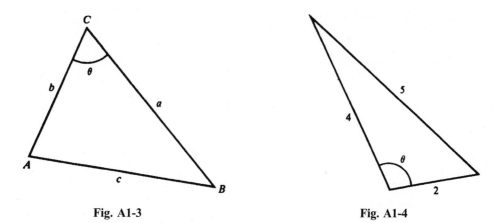

Fig. A1-3   Fig. A1-4

EXAMPLE 2.   Refer to Fig. A1-4. To find the angle θ, we use the Law of Cosines:

$$5^2 = 4^2 + 2^2 - 2(4)(2)\cos\theta \qquad \text{or} \qquad \cos\theta = \frac{-5}{16} \qquad \text{so} \qquad \theta = 108.21°$$

The angle formed by two intersecting lines can be measured by forming a triangle and applying the Law of Cosines.

Describing a Line in Cartesian System

The line is a basic concept of geometry. In a coordinate system, the description of a line involves an equation which enables us to find the coordinates of all those points which make up the line. The fact that a line is straight is incorporated in the quantity called the *slope m* of the line. Here $m = \tan\theta$, where θ is the angle formed by the line and the positive x axis.

From Fig. A1-5 we see that $\tan\theta = \Delta y/\Delta x$. This gives an alternate formula for the slope: $m = \Delta y/\Delta x$.

EXAMPLE 3.   The slope of the line passing through the points $P_0(-1, 2)$ and $P_1(3, 5)$ is found by

$$\Delta y = 5 - 2 = 3 \qquad \Delta x = 3 - (-1) = 4$$

so $m = \Delta y/\Delta x = \frac{3}{4}$. The angle θ is found by $\tan\theta = m = \frac{3}{4}$ or $\theta = 36.87°$.

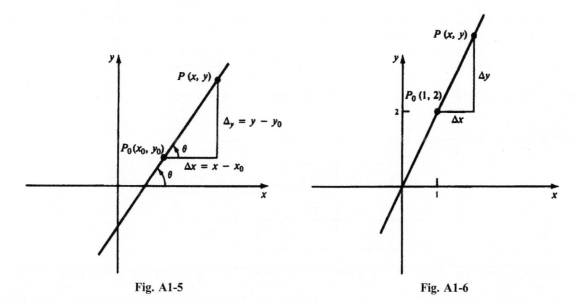

Fig. A1-5   Fig. A1-6

The straightness of a line is expressed by the fact that the slope of the line is the same regardless of which two points are used to calculate it. This enables us to find the equation of a line.

EXAMPLE 4. To find the equation of the line whose slope is 2 and passes through the point $P_0(1, 2)$, let $P(x, y)$ be any point on the line. The slope is the same regardless of which two points are used in calculating it. Using P and P_0, we obtain

$$\Delta y = y - 2 \qquad \Delta x = x - 1$$

so

$$m = \frac{\Delta y}{\Delta x} \qquad \text{or} \qquad 2 = \frac{y - 2}{x - 1}$$

Solving, we have $y = 2x$ (see Fig. A1-6).

Every line has an equation which can be put in the form $y = mx + b$, where m is the slope of the line and the point $(0, b)$ is the y intercept of the line (the point where the line intercepts the y axis).

Curves and Parametric Equations

The equation of a curve is a mathematical expression which enables us to determine the coordinates of the points that make up the curve.

The equation of a circle of radius r whose center lies at the point (h, k) is

$$(x - h)^2 + (y - k)^2 = r^2$$

It is often more convenient to write the equation of a curve in parametric form; that is

$$x = f(t) \qquad y = g(t)$$

where parameter t might be regarded as representing the "moment" at which the curve arrives at the point (x, y).

The parametric equations of a line can be written in the form (Probs. A1.21 and A1.23)

$$x = at + x_0 \qquad y = bt + y_0$$

EXAMPLE 5. The parametric equation of a circle of radius r and center at the origin $(0, 0)$ can be written as $x = r \cos t$ and $y = r \sin t$, where t lies in the interval $0 \leq t \leq 2\pi$.

A geometric curve consists of an infinite number of points. Thus any plot of such a curve can only approximate its real shape. Plotting a curve requires the calculation of the x and y coordinates of a certain number of the points of the curve and the placing of these points on the coordinate system. The more points plotted, the better the approximation to the actual shape.

EXAMPLE 6. Plot five points of the equations $x = t$, $y = t^2$ for t in the interval $[-1, 1]$.

t	-1	$-\frac{1}{2}$	0	$\frac{1}{2}$	1
x	-1	$-\frac{1}{2}$	0	$\frac{1}{2}$	1
y	1	$\frac{1}{4}$	0	$\frac{1}{4}$	1

Plotting (x, y) gives Fig. A1-7. We can approximate the actual curve by joining the plotted points by line segments.

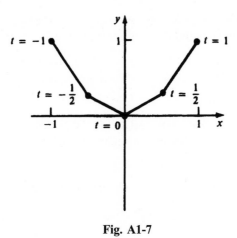

Fig. A1-7

A1.2   THE POLAR COORDINATE SYSTEM

The Cartesian coordinate system is only one of many schemes for attaching coordinates to the points of a plane. Another useful system is the *polar coordinate system*. To develop it, we pick any point in the plane and call it the origin. Through the origin we choose any *ray* (half-line) as the *polar axis*. Any point in the plane can be located at the intersection of a circle of radius r and a ray from the origin making an angle θ with the polar axis (see Fig. A1-8).

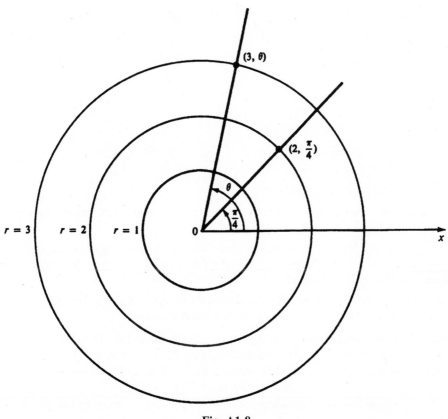

Fig. A1-8

The polar coordinates of a point are given by the pair (r, θ). The polar coordinates of a point are *not* unique. This is because the addition or subtraction of any multiple of 2π (360°) to θ describes the same ray as that described by θ.

Changing Coordinate Systems

How are the Cartesian coordinates of a point related to the polar coordinates of that point? If (r, θ) are the polar coordinates of point P, the Cartesian coordinates (x, y) are given by

$$x = r\cos\theta \qquad y = r\sin\theta$$

Conversely, the polar coordinates of a point whose Cartesian coordinates are known can be found by

$$r^2 = x^2 + y^2 \qquad \theta = \arctan\frac{y}{x}$$

A1.3   VECTORS

Vectors provide a link between geometric reasoning and arithmetic calculation. A vector is represented by a family of directed line segments that all have the same length or magnitude. That is, any two line segments pointing in the same direction and having the same lengths are considered to be the same vector, regardless of their location (see Fig. A1-9).

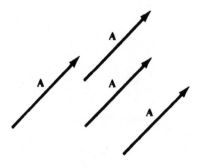

Fig. A1-9

Properties of Vectors

Vectors have special arithmetic properties:

1.   If **A** is a vector, then $-$**A** is a vector with the same length as **A** but pointing in the opposite direction.
2.   If **A** is a vector, then k**A** is a vector whose direction is the same as or opposite that of **A**, depending on the sign of the number k, and whose length is k times the length of **A**. This is an example of scalar multiplication.
3.   Two vectors can be added together to produce a third vector by using the *parallelogram method* or the *head-to-tail method*. This is an example of vector addition.

In the parallelogram method, vectors **A** and **B** are placed tail to tail. Their sum **A** + **B** is the vector determined by the diagonal of the parallelogram formed by the vectors **A** and **B** (see Fig. A1-10).

In the head-to-tail method, the tail of **B** is placed at the head of **A**. The vector **A** + **B** is determined by the line segment pointing from the tail of **A** to the head of **B** (see Fig. A1-11).

Both methods of addition are equivalent, but the head-to-tail is easier to use when adding several vectors.

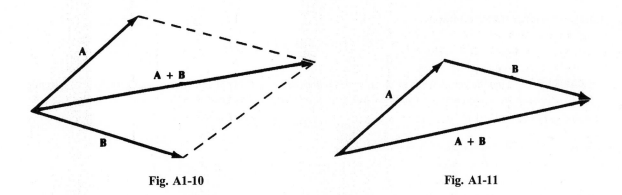

| Fig. A1-10 | Fig. A1-11 |

Coordinate Vectors and Components

In a Cartesian coordinate system, vectors having lengths equal to 1 and pointing in the positive direction along the x and y coordinate axes are called the *natural coordinate vectors* and are designated as **I** and **J** (see Fig. A1-12).

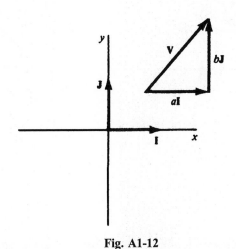

Fig. A1-12

By use of scalar multiplication and vector addition, any vector **V** can be written as a linear combination of the natural coordinate vectors. That is, we can find numbers a and b so that $\mathbf{V} = a\mathbf{I} + b\mathbf{J}$. The numbers $[a, b]$ are called the *components* of **V**. The components of a vector can be determined from the coordinates of the head and the coordinates of the tail of the vector. If (h_x, h_y) and (t_x, t_y) are the coordinates of the head and the tail, respectively, the components of **V** are given by

$$a = h_x - t_x \qquad b = h_y - t_y$$

Notice that if the tail of **V** is placed at the origin, the components of the vector are the coordinates of the head of **V**.

The introduction of components allows us to translate the geometric properties of vectors into computational properties. If the vector **A** has components $[x_1, y_1]$ and the vector **B** has components $[x_2, y_2]$, the length of **A**, denoted as $|\mathbf{A}|$, can be computed by

$$|\mathbf{A}| = \sqrt{x_1^2 + y_1^2}$$

To perform scalar multiplication by a number c, we have

$$c\mathbf{A} = cx_1\mathbf{I} + cy_1\mathbf{J}$$

and to perform vector addition

$$\mathbf{A} + \mathbf{B} = (x_1 + x_2)\mathbf{I} + (y_1 + y_2)\mathbf{J}$$

EXAMPLE 7.   Find the components of the vector **A** whose tail is at $P_1(1, 2)$ and whose head is at $P_2(3, 5)$ (see Fig. A1-13). To find the components, we shift the tail of **A** to the origin. The head is at

$$x = 3 - 1 = 2 \qquad y = 5 - 2 = 3$$

Thus $\mathbf{A} = 2\mathbf{I} + 3\mathbf{J}$. The length of **A** is

$$|\mathbf{A}| = \sqrt{2^2 + 3^2} = \sqrt{13}$$

If $\mathbf{B} = -3\mathbf{I} + 2\mathbf{J}$, then $\mathbf{A} + \mathbf{B} = (2 - 3)\mathbf{I} + (3 + 2)\mathbf{J} = -\mathbf{I} + 5\mathbf{J}$.

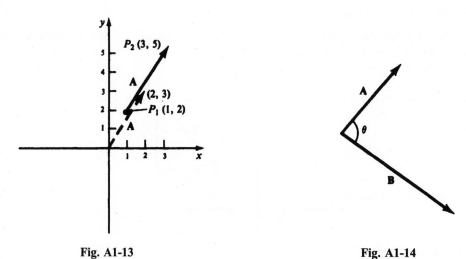

Fig. A1-13   Fig. A1-14

The Dot Product

The dot product $\mathbf{A} \cdot \mathbf{B}$ is the translation of the Law of Cosines into the language of vectors. It is defined as

$$\mathbf{A} \cdot \mathbf{B} = |\mathbf{A}||\mathbf{B}| \cos \theta$$

where θ is the smaller angle between the vectors **A** and **B** (see Fig. A1-14). If **A** has components $[x_1, y_1]$ and **B** has components $[x_2, y_2]$, then $\mathbf{A} \cdot \mathbf{B} = x_1 x_2 + y_1 y_2$ (componentwise multiplication). (*Note*: since $\cos 90° = 0$, two nonzero vectors **A** and **B** are perpendicular if and only if $\mathbf{A} \cdot \mathbf{B} = 0$.)

EXAMPLE 8.   To find the angle θ between the vectors $\mathbf{A} = 2\mathbf{I} + 3\mathbf{J}$ and $\mathbf{B} = \mathbf{J}$, we use the definition of the dot product to find

$$\cos \theta = \frac{\mathbf{A} \cdot \mathbf{B}}{|\mathbf{A}||\mathbf{B}|}$$

$$\mathbf{A} \cdot \mathbf{B} = (2\mathbf{I} + 3\mathbf{J}) \cdot (0\mathbf{I} + \mathbf{J}) = 2 \cdot 0 + 3 \cdot 1 = 3$$

$$|\mathbf{A}| = \sqrt{2^2 + 3^2} = \sqrt{13} \qquad |\mathbf{B}| = \sqrt{0^2 + 1^2} = 1$$

So

$$\cos \theta = \frac{3}{\sqrt{13}} \qquad \text{and} \qquad \theta = 33.69°$$

A1.4   MATRICES

A *matrix* is a rectangular array or table of numbers, arranged in rows and columns. The notation a_{ij} is used to designate the matrix entry at the intersection of row i with column j (see Fig. A1-15).

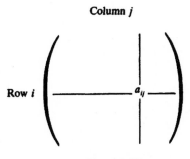

Fig. A1-15

The *size* or *dimension* of a matrix is indicated by the notation $m \times n$, where m is the number of rows in the matrix and n is the number of columns.

A matrix can be used as an organizational tool to represent the information content of data in tabular form. For example, a polygonal figure can be represented as an ordered array of the coordinates of its vertices. The geometric transformations used in computer graphics can also be represented by matrices.

Arithmetic Properties of Matrices

Examples of these properties are as follows.

1. *Scalar multiplication.* The matrix $k\mathbf{A}$ is the matrix obtained by multiplying every entry of $\mathbf{A}$ by the number k.

2. *Matrix addition.* Two $m \times n$ matrices $\mathbf{A}$ and $\mathbf{B}$ can be added together to form a new $m \times n$ matrix $\mathbf{C}$ whose entries are the sum of the corresponding entries of $\mathbf{A}$ and $\mathbf{B}$. That is,

$$c_{ij} = a_{ij} + b_{ij}$$

3. *Matrix multiplication.* An $m \times p$ matrix $\mathbf{A}$ can be multiplied by a $p \times n$ matrix $\mathbf{B}$ to form an $m \times n$ matrix $\mathbf{C}$. The entry c_{ij} is found by taking the dot product of the i row of $\mathbf{A}$ with the j column of $\mathbf{B}$ (see Fig. A1-16). So $c_{ij} = (\text{row } i) \cdot (\text{column } j) = a_{i1}b_{1j} + a_{i2}b_{2j} + \cdots + a_{im}b_{mj}$. Matrix multiplication is not commutative in general. So $\mathbf{AB} \neq \mathbf{BA}$. Matrix multiplication is also called *matrix concatenation.*

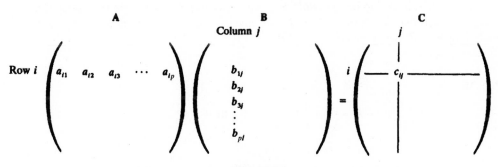

Fig. A1-16

4. *Matrix transpose.* The transpose of a matrix $\mathbf{A}$ is a matrix, denoted as $\mathbf{A}^T$, formed by exchanging the rows and columns of $\mathbf{A}$. If $\mathbf{A}$ is an $m \times n$ matrix, then $\mathbf{A}^T$ is an $n \times m$ matrix. A matrix is said to be symmetrical if $\mathbf{A} = \mathbf{A}^T$.

Two basic properties of the transpose operation are (1) $(\mathbf{A} + \mathbf{B})^T = \mathbf{A}^T + \mathbf{B}^T$ and (2) $(\mathbf{AB})^T = \mathbf{B}^T \mathbf{A}^T$.

EXAMPLE 9

$$\mathbf{A} = \begin{pmatrix} 3 & 2 & 5 \\ 1 & -1 & 2 \end{pmatrix} \quad \text{and} \quad \mathbf{B} = \begin{pmatrix} -1 & 0 \\ 2 & 3 \\ 1 & 2 \end{pmatrix}$$

$$-2\mathbf{A} = -2\begin{pmatrix} 3 & 2 & 5 \\ 1 & -1 & 2 \end{pmatrix} = \begin{pmatrix} -6 & -4 & -10 \\ -2 & 2 & -4 \end{pmatrix}$$

$$\mathbf{AB} = \begin{pmatrix} 3 & 2 & 5 \\ 1 & -1 & 2 \end{pmatrix}\begin{pmatrix} -1 & 0 \\ 2 & 3 \\ 1 & 2 \end{pmatrix} = \begin{pmatrix} [3 \cdot (-1)] + (2 \cdot 2) + (5 \cdot 1) & (3 \cdot 0) + (2 \cdot 3) + (5 \cdot 2) \\ [1 \cdot (-1)] + [(-1) \cdot 2] + (2 \cdot 1) & (1 \cdot 0) + [(-1) \cdot 3] + (2 \cdot 2) \end{pmatrix}$$

$$= \begin{pmatrix} 6 & 16 \\ -1 & 1 \end{pmatrix}$$

$$\mathbf{A}^T = \begin{pmatrix} 3 & 1 \\ 2 & -1 \\ 5 & 2 \end{pmatrix}$$

Matrix Inversion and the Identity Matrix

The $n \times n$ matrix whose entries along the main diagonal are all equal to 1 and all other entries are 0 is called the *identity matrix* and is denoted by $\mathbf{I}$ (Fig. A1-17).

$$\mathbf{I} = \begin{pmatrix} 1 & 0 & 0 & \cdots & 0 \\ 0 & 1 & 0 & \cdots & 0 \\ 0 & 0 & 1 & \cdots & 0 \\ \vdots & & & & \vdots \\ 0 & 0 & 0 & \cdots & 1 \end{pmatrix}$$

Fig. A1-17

If $\mathbf{A}$ is also an $n \times n$ matrix, then $\mathbf{AI} = \mathbf{IA} = \mathbf{A}$. That is, multiplication by the identity matrix $\mathbf{I}$ leaves the matrix $\mathbf{A}$ unchanged. Therefore, multiplication by the identity matrix is analogous to multiplication of a real number by 1.

An $n \times n$ matrix $\mathbf{A}$ is said to be *invertible* or to have an *inverse* if there can be found an $n \times n$ matrix, denoted by $\mathbf{A}^{-1}$, such that $\mathbf{A}^{-1}\mathbf{A} = \mathbf{AA}^{-1} = \mathbf{I}$. The inverse matrix, if there is one, will be unique.

A basic property of matrix inversion is $(\mathbf{AB})^{-1} = \mathbf{B}^{-1}\mathbf{A}^{-1}$.

EXAMPLE 10

$$\mathbf{A} = \begin{pmatrix} 1 & 0 \\ 2 & 1 \end{pmatrix} \quad \text{and} \quad \mathbf{M} = \begin{pmatrix} 1 & 0 \\ -2 & 1 \end{pmatrix}$$

Then

$$\mathbf{AM} = \begin{pmatrix} 1 & 0 \\ 2 & 1 \end{pmatrix} \cdot \begin{pmatrix} 1 & 0 \\ -2 & 1 \end{pmatrix} = \begin{pmatrix} 1 \cdot 1 + 0 \cdot (-2) & 1 \cdot 0 + 0 \cdot 1 \\ 2 \cdot 1 + 1 \cdot (-2) & 2 \cdot 0 + 1 \cdot 1 \end{pmatrix} = \begin{pmatrix} 1 & 0 \\ 0 & 1 \end{pmatrix}$$

and

$$\mathbf{MA} = \begin{pmatrix} 1 & 0 \\ -2 & 1 \end{pmatrix} \cdot \begin{pmatrix} 1 & 0 \\ 2 & 1 \end{pmatrix} = \begin{pmatrix} 1 \cdot 1 + 0 \cdot 2 & 1 \cdot 0 + 0 \cdot 1 \\ -2 \cdot 1 + 1 \cdot 2 & -2 \cdot 0 + 1 \cdot 1 \end{pmatrix} = \begin{pmatrix} 1 & 0 \\ 0 & 1 \end{pmatrix}$$

So $\mathbf{MA} = \mathbf{AM} = \mathbf{I}$. Thus $\mathbf{M}$ must be $\mathbf{A}^{-1}$.

A1.5   FUNCTIONS AND TRANSFORMATIONS

The concept of a *function* is at the very heart of mathematics and the application of mathematics as a tool for modeling the real world. Stated simply, a function is any process or program which accepts an input and produces a unique output according to a definite rule. Although a function is most often regarded in mathematical terms, this need not be the case. The concept can be usefully extended to include processes described in nonmathematical ways, such as a chemical formula, a recipe or a prescription, and such related concepts as a computer subroutine or a program module. All convey the idea of changing an input to an output. Some synonyms for the word function are *operator, mapping,* and *transformation.*

The quantities used as input to the function are collectively called the *domain* of the function. The outputs are called the *range* of the function. Various notations are used to denote functions.

EXAMPLE 11.   Some examples of functions are:

1.   The equation $f(x) = x^2 + 2x + 1$ is a numerical function whose domain consists of all real numbers and whose range consists of all real numbers greater than or equal to 0.

2.   The relationship $T(\mathbf{V}) = 2\mathbf{V}$ is a transformation between vectors. The domain of T is all real vectors, as is the range. This function transforms each vector into a new vector which is twice the original one.

3.   The expression $H(x, y) = (x, -y)$ represents a mapping between points of the plane. The domain consists of all points of the plane, as does the range. Each individual point is mapped to that point which is the reflection of the original point about the x axis.

4.   If $\mathbf{A}$ is a matrix and $\mathbf{X}$ is a column matrix, the column matrix $\mathbf{Y}$ found by multiplying $\mathbf{A}$ and $\mathbf{X}$ can be regarded as a function $\mathbf{Y} = \mathbf{AX}$.

Graphs of Functions

If x and y are real numbers (scalars), the graph of a function $y = f(x)$ consists of all points in the plane whose coordinates have the form $[x, f(x)]$, where x lies in the domain of f. The graph of a function is the curve associated with the function, and it consists of an infinite number of points. In practice, plotting the graph of a function is done by computing a table of values and plotting the results. This gives an approximation to the actual graph of f.

EXAMPLE 12.   Plot five points for the function $y = x^2$ over the interval $[-1, 1]$.

x	-1	$-\frac{1}{2}$	0	$\frac{1}{2}$	1
x^2	1	$\frac{1}{4}$	0	$\frac{1}{4}$	1

Plotting the points (x, x^2) calculated in the table and joining these points with line segments gives an approximation to the actual graph of $y = x^2$. See Fig. A1-7 for the plot of the graph.

The *plotting resolution* is determined by the number of x values used in plotting the graph. The higher the plotting resolution, the better the approximation.

Composing Functions

If the process performed by a function H can be described by the successive steps of first applying a function G and then applying a function F to the results of G, we say that H is the *composition* of F and G. We write $H = F \circ G$. If the input to the function is denoted by x, the output $H(x)$ is evaluated by

$$H(x) = F[G(x)]$$

That is, first G operates on x; then the result $G(x)$ is passed to F as input.

Composition of functions is not commutative in general; that is, $F \circ G \neq G \circ F$.

The concept of composition is not restricted to only two functions but extends to any number of functions. For functions that are represented by matrices, composition of functions is equivalent to matrix multiplication; that is, $\mathbf{A} \circ \mathbf{B} = \mathbf{AB}$.

EXAMPLE 13

1. If $f(x) = x^2 + 2$ and $g(x) = 2x + 1$, then $f[g(x)] = [g(x)]^2 + 2 = (2x + 1)^2 + 2 = 4x^2 + 4x + 3$.
2. If

$$\mathbf{A} = \begin{pmatrix} 1 & 3 \\ 0 & 2 \end{pmatrix} \quad \text{and} \quad \mathbf{B} = \begin{pmatrix} -5 & 4 \\ 2 & 2 \end{pmatrix}$$

then

$$\mathbf{A} \circ \mathbf{B} = \mathbf{AB} = \begin{pmatrix} 1 & 3 \\ 0 & 2 \end{pmatrix} \begin{pmatrix} -5 & 4 \\ 2 & 2 \end{pmatrix} = \begin{pmatrix} 1 & 10 \\ 4 & 4 \end{pmatrix}$$

The Inverse Function

The inverse of a function f (with respect to composition) is a function, denoted by f^{-1}, that satisfies the relationships $f^{-1} \circ f = i$ and $f \circ f^{-1} = i$, where i is the identity function $i(x) = x$. Applying the above compositions to an element x, we obtain the equivalent statements:

$$f^{-1}[f(x)] = x \qquad f[f^{-1}(x)] = x$$

The inverse operator thus "undoes" the work that f has performed.

Not every function has an inverse, and it is often very difficult to tell whether a given function has an inverse. One must often rely on geometric intuition to establish the inverse of an operator.

EXAMPLE 14. Let R be the transformation which rotates every point in the plane by an angle of $30°$ (in the positive or counterclockwise direction). Then it is clear that R^{-1} is the transformation that rotates every point by an angle of $-30°$ (a rotation of $30°$ in the clockwise direction).

Solved Problems

A1.1 Find the distance between the points whose coordinates are (*a*) $(5, 2)$ and $(7, 3)$, (*b*) $(-3, 1)$ and $(5, 2)$, (*c*) $(-3, -1)$ and $(-5, -2)$, and (*d*) $(0, 1)$ and $(2, 0)$.

SOLUTION

(*a*) $D = \sqrt{(7 - 5)^2 + (3 - 2)^2} = \sqrt{2^2 + 1^2} = \sqrt{5}$

(*b*) $D = \sqrt{[5 - (-3)]^2 + (2 - 1)^2} = \sqrt{(8)^2 + (1)^2} = \sqrt{65}$

(c) $D = \sqrt{[-5-(-3)]^2 + [-2-(-1)]^2} = \sqrt{(-2)^2 + (-1)^2} = \sqrt{5}$

(d) $D = \sqrt{(2-0)^2 + (0-1)^2} = \sqrt{2^2 + (-1)^2} = \sqrt{5}$

A1.2 Derive the equation for a straight line (see Fig. A1-5).

SOLUTION

A straight line never changes direction. We determine the direction of a line by the angle θ the line makes with the positive x axis. Then at any point P_0 on the line, the angle formed by the line and a segment through P parallel to the x axis is also equal to θ. Let $P_0(x_0, y_0)$ be a point on the line. Then if $P(x, y)$ represents any point on the line, drawing the right triangle with hypotenuse $\overline{P_0 P}$, we find

$$\tan\theta = \frac{y - y_0}{x - x_0}$$

The quantity $\tan\theta$ is called the slope of the line and its traditionally denoted by m.

We rewrite the equation as

$$m = \frac{y - y_0}{x - x_0} \qquad \text{or} \qquad m = \frac{\Delta y}{\Delta x}$$

(The term Δy is often called the "rise" and Δx, the "run.") This can be solved for y in terms of x.

A1.3 Write the equation of the line whose slope is 2 and which passes through the point $(-1, 2)$.

SOLUTION

Let $P(x, y)$ represent any point on the line. Then

$$\Delta y = y - 2 \qquad \Delta x = x - (-1) = x + 1$$

and $m = 2$. Using $\Delta y / \Delta x = m$, we find

$$\frac{y - 2}{x + 1} = 2 \qquad \text{or} \qquad y - 2 = 2(x + 1) = 2x + 2$$

thus $y = 2x + 4$.

A1.4 Write the equation of the line passing through $P_1(1, 2)$ and $P_2(3, -2)$.

SOLUTION

Let $P(x, y)$ represent any point on the line. Then using P_1, we compute

$$\Delta y = y - 2 \qquad \Delta x = x - 1$$

To find the slope m, we use P_1 and P_2 to find

$$\Delta y = -2 - 2 = -4 \qquad \Delta x = 3 - 1 = 2$$

Then

$$m = \frac{\Delta y}{\Delta x} = -2 \qquad \text{so} \qquad \frac{y - 2}{x - 1} = -2$$

Then

$$y - 2 = -2x + 2 \qquad \text{and} \qquad y = -2x + 4$$

A1.5 Show that lines are parallel if and only if their slopes are equal.

SOLUTION

Refer to Fig. A1-18. Suppose that lines l_1 and l_2 are parallel. Then the alternate interior angles θ_1 and θ_2 are equal, and so are the slopes $\tan\theta_1$ and $\tan\theta_2$.

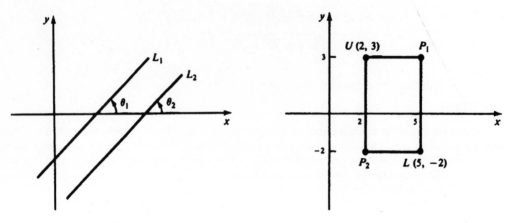

Fig. A1-18   Fig. A1-19

Conversely, if the slopes $\tan \theta_1$ and $\tan \theta_2$ are equal, so are the alternate interior angles θ_1 and θ_2. Consequently lines l_1 and l_2 are parallel.

A1.6 Let $U(2, 3)$ and $L(5, -2)$ be the upper left and lower right corners, respectively, of a rectangle whose sides are parallel to the x and y axes. Find the coordinates of the remaining two vertices.

SOLUTION

Referring to Fig. A1-19, we see that the x coordinate of P_1 is the same as that of L, namely 5, and the y coordinate that of U, namely 3. So $P_1 = (5, 3)$. Similarly, $P_2 = (2, -2)$.

A1.7 Plot the points $A(1, 1)$, $B(-1, 1)$, and $C(-4, 2)$. Then (*a*) show that ABC is a right triangle and (*b*) find a fourth point D such that $ABCD$ is a rectangle (see Fig. A1-20).

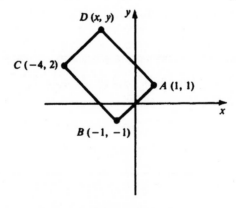

Fig. A1-20

SOLUTION

(*a*) Show that the Pythagorean theorem is satisfied:

$$\overline{AC}^2 = \overline{AB}^2 + \overline{BC}^2$$

Use the distance formula to compute the lengths of the sides of ABC:

$$\overline{AB} = \sqrt{[1-(-1)]^2 + [1-(-1)]^2} = \sqrt{2^2 + 2^2} = \sqrt{8}$$

$$\overline{BC} = \sqrt{[-1-(-4)]^2 + (-1-2)^2} = \sqrt{(3)^2 + (-3)^2} = \sqrt{18}$$

$$\overline{AC} = \sqrt{[1-(-4)]^2 + (1-2)^2} = \sqrt{5^2 + (-1)^2} = \sqrt{26}$$

So

$$\overline{AC}^2 = 26 = \overline{AB}^2 + \overline{BC}^2 = 8 + 18$$

(b) Let the unknown coordinates of D be denoted by (x, y). Use the fact that opposite sides of a rectangle are parallel to find x and y. Since parallel lines have equal slopes, compute the slopes of all four sides:

$$\text{Slope } \overline{AB} = \frac{-1-1}{-1-1} = \frac{-2}{-2} = 1 \qquad \text{Slope } \overline{CD} = \frac{y-2}{x-(-4)} = \frac{y-2}{x+4}$$

$$\text{Slope } \overline{BC} = \frac{-1-(2)}{-1-(-4)} = \frac{-3}{3} = -1 \qquad \text{Slope } \overline{DA} = \frac{y-1}{x-1}$$

Then, for $ABCD$ to be a rectangle

$$\text{Slope } \overline{CD} = \text{slope } \overline{AB} \qquad \text{Slope } \overline{DA} = \text{slope } \overline{BC}$$

or

$$\frac{y-2}{x+4} = 1 \qquad \text{and} \qquad \frac{y-1}{x-1} = -1$$

This leads to the equations

$$y - 2 = x + 4 \qquad \text{and} \qquad y - 1 = -x + 1$$

or

$$-x + y = 6 \qquad \text{and} \qquad x + y = 2$$

Solving, $x = -2$ and $y = 4$.

A1.8 Find the equation of a circle that has radius r and its center at the point (h, k).

SOLUTION

Refer to Fig. A1-21. If $P(x, y)$ is any point lying on the circle, its distance from the center of the circle must be equal to r. Using the distance formula to express this mathematically, we have

$$D = \sqrt{(x-h)^2 + (y-k)^2} = r$$

So $(x-h)^2 + (y-k)^2 = r^2$, which is the equation of the circle.

A1.9 Given any three points, not all lying on a line, find the equation of the circle determined by them.

SOLUTION

Refer to Fig. A1-22. Let $P_1(a_1, b_1)$, $P_2(a_2, b_2)$, and $P_3(a_3, b_3)$ be the coordinates of the points. Let r be the radius of the circle and (h, k) the center. Since each point is distance r from the center, then

$$(a_1 - h)^2 + (b_1 - k)^2 = r^2$$
$$(a_2 - h)^2 + (b_2 - k)^2 = r^2$$
$$(a_3 - h)^2 + (b_3 - k)^2 = r^2$$

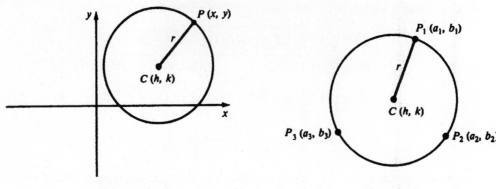

Fig. A1-21   **Fig. A1-22**

This yields, after multiplying and collecting like terms:

$$(a_2 - a_1)h + (b_2 - b_1)k = \frac{a_2^2 - a_1^2}{2} + \frac{b_2^2 - b_1^2}{2}$$

$$(a_3 - a_2)h + (b_3 - b_2)k = \frac{a_3^2 - a_2^2}{2} + \frac{b_3^2 - b_2^2}{2}$$

These equations can be solved for h and k to yield

$$h = \frac{1}{2} \frac{[d_1^2(b_2 - b_3) + d_2^2(b_3 - b_1) + d_3^2(b_1 - b_2)]}{d}$$

$$k = \frac{-1}{2} \frac{[d_1^2(a_2 - a_3) + d_2^2(a_3 - a_1) + d_3^2(a_1 - a_2)]}{d}$$

Here, $d_1^2 = a_1^2 + b_1^2$, $d_2^2 = a_2^2 + b_2^2$, $d_3^2 = a_3^2 + b_3^2$, and $d = a_1(b_2 - b_3) + a_2(b_3 - b_1) + a_3(b_1 - b_2)$. Finally, r can be found:

$$r = \sqrt{(a_1 - h)^2 + (b_1 - k)^2}$$

A1.10 Find the equation of the circle passing through the three points $P_1(1, 2)$, $P_2(3, 0)$, and $P_3(0, -4)$.

SOLUTION

As in Prob. A1.9, we find

$$
\begin{array}{lll}
d_1^2 = a_1^2 + b_1^2 = 5 & a_2 - a_3 = 3 & b_2 - b_3 = 4 \\
d_2^2 = a_2^2 + b_2^2 = 9 & a_3 - a_1 = -1 & b_3 - b_1 = -6 \\
d_3^2 = a_3^2 + b_3^2 = 16 & a_1 - a_2 = -2 & b_1 - b_2 = 2
\end{array}
$$

So

$$d = 1(4) + 3(-6) + 0(2) = -14$$

and

$$h = \frac{-1[5(4) + 9(-6) + 16(2)]}{28} = \frac{2}{28} = \frac{1}{14}$$

$$k = \frac{1[5(3) + 9(-1) + 16(-2)]}{28} = \frac{-26}{28} = \frac{-13}{14}$$

Therefore, the center of the circle is located at

$$\left(\frac{1}{14}, \ \frac{-13}{14} \right)$$

and the radius is calculated by

$$r = \sqrt{\left(1 - \frac{1}{14}\right)^2 + \left(2 + \frac{13}{14}\right)^2} = \frac{5}{14}\sqrt{74}$$

A1.11 Show that $x = r\cos t$, $y = r\sin t$ are the parametric equations of a circle of radius r whose center is at the origin.

SOLUTION

By Prob. A1.8 we must show that $x^2 + y^2 = r^2$. Using the trigonometric identity $\cos^2 t + \sin^2 t = 1$, we obtain

$$x^2 + y^2 = (r\cos t)^2 + (r\sin t)^2 = r^2\cos^2 t + r^2\sin^2 t = r^2(\cos^2 t + \sin^2 t) = r^2$$

A1.12 Show that the parametric equations

$$x = \frac{a + bt}{e + ft} \qquad y = \frac{c + dt}{e + ft}$$

are the equations of a line in the plane.

SOLUTION

We show that the slope

$$\frac{\Delta y}{\Delta x} = \frac{y_2 - y_1}{x_2 - x_1}$$

is a constant, independent of the parameter t. So

$$\frac{y_2 - y_1}{x_2 - x_1} = \frac{(c + dt_2)/(e + ft_2) - (c + dt_1)(e + ft_1)}{(a + bt_2)/(e + ft_2) - (a + bt_1)/(e + ft_1)}$$

$$= \frac{ce + det_2 + cft_1 + dft_2t_1 - ce - cft_2 - det_1 - dft_2t_1}{ae + aft_1 + bet_2 + bft_2t_1 - ae - aft_2 - ebt_1 - bft_2t_1}$$

$$= \frac{de(t_2 - t_1) - cf(t_2 - t_1)}{be(t_2 - t_1) - af(t_2 - t_1)} = \frac{de - cf}{be - af}$$

So if $be - af \neq 0$, the slope $\Delta y/\Delta x$ is constant, and so this is the equation of a line.

A1.13 Let the equations of a line be given by (Prob. A1.12)

$$x = \frac{1 + t}{1 - t} \qquad y = \frac{2 + t}{1 - t}$$

Then (a) plot the line for all values of t, (b) plot the line segment over the interval $[0, 2]$, and (c) find the slope of the line.

SOLUTION

Making a table of values, we have

t	-1	$-\frac{1}{2}$	0	$\frac{1}{2}$	2	3
x	0	$\frac{1}{3}$	1	3	-3	-2
y	$\frac{1}{2}$	1	2	5	-4	$-\frac{5}{2}$

The resulting line is shown in Fig. A1-23.

(a) We observe the following: (1) the line is undefined at $t = 1$, (2) $(x, y) \to (\infty, \infty)$ as $t \to 1^-$, (3) $(x, y) \to (-\infty, -\infty)$ as $t \to 1^+$, and (4) $(x, y) \to (-1, -1)$ as $t \to \pm\infty$ (see Fig. A1-23).

(b) The interval $[0, 2]$ includes the infinite point at $t = 1$. The corresponding region is the exterior line segment between points $P_1(1, 2)$ at $t = 0$ and $P_2(-3, -4)$ at $t = 2$ (see Fig. A1-24).

(c) From Prob. A1.12, the slope of the line is, with $a = 1$, $b = 1$, $c = 2$, $d = 1$, $e = 1$, and $f = -1$.

$$\frac{\Delta y}{\Delta x} = \frac{(1)(1) - (2)(-1)}{(1)(1) - (1)(-1)} = \frac{3}{2}$$

A1.14 Let $\mathbf{A} = 2\mathbf{I} + 7\mathbf{J}$, $\mathbf{B} = -3\mathbf{I} + \mathbf{J}$, and $\mathbf{C} = \mathbf{I} - 2\mathbf{J}$. Find (a) $2\mathbf{A} - \mathbf{B}$ and (b) $-3\mathbf{A} + 5\mathbf{B} - 2\mathbf{C}$.

SOLUTION

Perform the scalar multiplication and then the addition.

(a) $2\mathbf{A} - \mathbf{B} = 2(2\mathbf{I} + 7\mathbf{J}) - (-3\mathbf{I} + \mathbf{J}) = (4\mathbf{I} + 14\mathbf{J}) + (3\mathbf{I} - \mathbf{J})$

$\qquad = (4 + 3)\mathbf{I} + (14 - 1)\mathbf{J} = 7\mathbf{I} + 13\mathbf{J}$

(b) $-3\mathbf{A} + 5\mathbf{B} - 2\mathbf{C} = -3(2\mathbf{I} + 7\mathbf{J}) + 5(-3\mathbf{I} + \mathbf{J}) - 2(\mathbf{I} - 2\mathbf{J})$

$\qquad = (-6\mathbf{I} - 21\mathbf{J}) + (-15\mathbf{I} + 5\mathbf{J}) + (-2\mathbf{I} + 4\mathbf{J})$

$\qquad = (-6 - 15 - 2)\mathbf{I} + (-21 + 5 + 4)\mathbf{J} = -23\mathbf{I} - 12\mathbf{J}$

A1.15 Find x and y such that $2x\mathbf{I} + (y - 1)\mathbf{J} = y\mathbf{I} + (3x + 1)\mathbf{J}$.

SOLUTION

Since vectors are equal only if their corresponding components are equal, we solve the equations (1) $2x = y$ and (2) $y - 1 = 3x + 1$. Substituting into equation (2), we have $(2x) - 1 = 3x + 1$ and $-2 = x$ and finally $y = 2x = 2(-2) = -4$, so $x = -2$ and $y = -4$.

A1.16 The tail of vector $\mathbf{A}$ is located at $P(-1, 2)$, and the head is at $Q(5, -3)$. Find the components of $\mathbf{A}$.

SOLUTION

Translate vector $\mathbf{A}$ so that its tail is at the origin. In this position, the coordinates of the head will be the components of $\mathbf{A}$.

Translating P to the origin is the same as subtracting -1 from the x component and 2 from the y component. Thus the new head of $\mathbf{A}$ will be located at point Q_1, whose coordinates (x_1, y_1) can be found by

$$x_1 = 5 - (-1) = 6 \qquad y_1 = -3 - 2 = -5$$

Thus $\mathbf{A} = 6\mathbf{I} - 5\mathbf{J}$.

A1.17 Given the vectors $\mathbf{A} = \mathbf{I} + 2\mathbf{J}$ and $\mathbf{B} = 2\mathbf{I} - 3\mathbf{J}$, find (a) the length, (b) the dot product, and (c) the angle θ between the vectors.

SOLUTION

(a) $|\mathbf{A}| = \sqrt{1^2 + 2^2} = \sqrt{5} \qquad |\mathbf{B}| = \sqrt{2^2 + (-3)^2} = \sqrt{13}$

(b) $\mathbf{A} \cdot \mathbf{B} = (\mathbf{I} + 2\mathbf{J}) \cdot (2\mathbf{I} - 3\mathbf{J}) = (1 \cdot 2) + [2 \cdot (-3)] = 2 - 6 = -4$

(c) From the definition of the dot product, we can solve for $\cos\theta$:

$$\cos\theta = \frac{\mathbf{A} \cdot \mathbf{B}}{|\mathbf{A}||\mathbf{B}|} = \frac{-4}{\sqrt{5}\sqrt{13}}$$

So $\theta = 119.74°$.

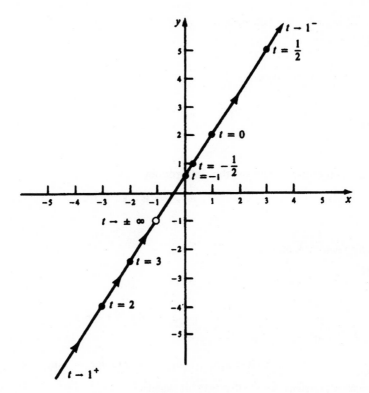

Fig. A1-23

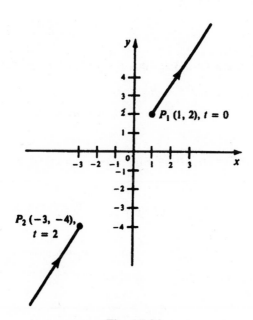

Fig. A1-24

A1.18 Find the unit vector $\mathbf{U_A}$ having the direction of $\mathbf{A} = 2\mathbf{I} - 3\mathbf{J}$.

SOLUTION

Since $\mathbf{U_A} = \dfrac{\mathbf{A}}{|\mathbf{A}|}$, it follows that

$$|\mathbf{A}| = \sqrt{2^2 + (-3)^2} = \sqrt{13} \quad \text{and} \quad \mathbf{U_A} = \frac{\mathbf{A}}{|\mathbf{A}|} = \frac{2\mathbf{I} - 3\mathbf{J}}{\sqrt{13}} = \frac{2}{\sqrt{13}}\mathbf{I} - \frac{3}{\sqrt{13}}\mathbf{J}$$

A1.19 Show that the commutative law for the dot product

$$\mathbf{A} \cdot \mathbf{B} = \mathbf{B} \cdot \mathbf{A}$$

holds for any vectors $\mathbf{A}$ and $\mathbf{B}$.

SOLUTION

Let

$$\mathbf{A} = a_1\mathbf{I} + a_2\mathbf{J} \qquad \mathbf{B} = b_1\mathbf{I} + b_2\mathbf{J}$$

So

$$\mathbf{A} \cdot \mathbf{B} = a_1b_1 + a_2b_2 \qquad \mathbf{B} \cdot \mathbf{A} = b_1a_1 + b_2a_2$$

Comparing both expressions, we see that they are equal.

A1.20 Show that the distributive law for the dot product

$$(\mathbf{A} + \mathbf{B}) \cdot \mathbf{C} = \mathbf{A} \cdot \mathbf{C} + \mathbf{B} \cdot \mathbf{C}$$

holds for any vectors $\mathbf{A}$, $\mathbf{B}$, and $\mathbf{C}$.

SOLUTION

Let

$$\mathbf{A} = a_1\mathbf{I} + a_2\mathbf{J} \qquad \mathbf{B} = b_1\mathbf{I} + b_2\mathbf{J} \qquad \mathbf{C} = c_1\mathbf{I} + c_2\mathbf{J}$$

So

$$\mathbf{A} + \mathbf{B} = (a_1 + b_1)\mathbf{I} + (a_2 + b_2)\mathbf{J}$$

and

$$(\mathbf{A} + \mathbf{B}) \cdot \mathbf{C} = (a_1 + b_1)c_1 + (a_2 + b_2)c_2 = a_1c_1 + b_1c_1 + a_2c_2 + b_2c_2$$

On the other hand,

$$\mathbf{A} \cdot \mathbf{C} = a_1c_1 + a_2c_2 \qquad \mathbf{B} \cdot \mathbf{C} = b_1c_1 + b_2c_2$$

so

$$\mathbf{A} \cdot \mathbf{C} + \mathbf{B} \cdot \mathbf{C} = a_1c_1 + a_2c_2 + b_1c_1 + b_2c_2$$

Comparing both expressions, we see that they are equal.

A1.21 Show that the equation of a line can be determined by specifying a vector $\mathbf{V}$ having the direction of the line and by a point on the line.

SOLUTION

Suppose that **V** has components $[a, b]$ and the point $P_0(x_0, y_0)$ is on the line (see Fig. A1-25). If $P(x, y)$ is any point on the line, the vector $\overline{P_0P}$ has the same direction as **V**, and so, by the definition of a vector, it must be a (scalar) multiple of **V**, that is $\overline{P_0P} = t\mathbf{V}$. The components of $\overline{P_0P}$ are $[x - x_0, y - y_0]$ and those of $t\mathbf{V}$ are $t[a, b]$. Equating components, we obtain the parametric equations of the line:

$$x - x_0 = ta \qquad y - y_0 = tb \qquad \text{or} \qquad x = at + x_0 \qquad y = bt + y_0$$

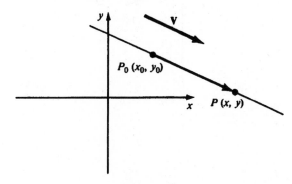

Fig. A1-25

The nonparametric form of the equation can be determined by eliminating the parameter t from both equations. So

$$\frac{x - x_0}{a} = t = \frac{y - y_0}{b}$$

Solving for y, we have

$$y = \frac{b}{a}x + \left(y_0 - \frac{b}{a}x_0\right)$$

A1.22 Find the (a) parametric and (b) nonparametric equation of the line passing through the point $P_0(1, 2)$ and parallel to the vector $\mathbf{V} = 2\mathbf{I} + \mathbf{J}$.

SOLUTION

As in Prob. A1.21, we find, with $a = 2$, $b = 1$, $x_0 = 1$, and $y_0 = 2$, that (a) $x = 2t + 1$, $y = t + 2$ and (b) with $b/a = \frac{1}{2}$, $y = \frac{1}{2}x + (2 - \frac{1}{2}) = \frac{1}{2}x + \frac{3}{2}$.

A1.23 Find the parametric equation of the line passing through points $P_1(1, 2)$ and $P_2(4, 1)$. What is the general form of the parametric equation of a line joining points $P_1(x_1, y_1)$ and $P_2(x_2, y_2)$?

SOLUTION

Refer to Fig. A1-26. Choosing $\mathbf{V} = \overline{P_1P_2} = (4 - 1)\mathbf{I} + (1 - 2)\mathbf{J} = 3\mathbf{I} - 1\mathbf{J}$. Then as in Prob. A1.21, $x = 3t - 1$ and $y = -t - 2$. In the general case, the direction vector **V** is chosen, as above, to be $\overline{P_1P_2} = (x_2 - x_1)\mathbf{I} + (y_2 - y_1)\mathbf{J}$. The equation of the line is then

$$x = x_1 + (x_2 - x_1)t \qquad y = y_1 + (y_2 - y_1)t$$

A1.24 Find the number c such that the vector $\mathbf{A} = \mathbf{I} + c\mathbf{J}$ is orthogonal to $\mathbf{B} = 2\mathbf{I} - \mathbf{J}$.

SOLUTION

Two nonzero vectors are orthogonal (perpendicular) if and only if their dot product is zero. So

$$\mathbf{A} \cdot \mathbf{B} = (\mathbf{I} + c\mathbf{J}) \cdot (2\mathbf{I} - \mathbf{J}) = (1 \cdot 2) + [c(-1)] = 2 - c$$

So **A** and **B** are orthogonal if $2 - c = 0$ or $c = 2$.

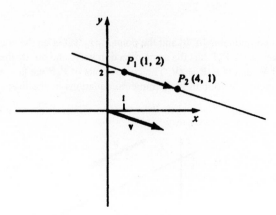

Fig. A1-26

A1.25 Compute:

(a) $\begin{pmatrix} 5 & 4 & 1 \\ 0 & -1 & 7 \end{pmatrix} + \begin{pmatrix} 2 & -1 & 3 \\ 2 & 0 & 1 \end{pmatrix}$

(b) $\begin{pmatrix} 5 & 3 & 1 \\ 1 & 2 & 3 \end{pmatrix} + \begin{pmatrix} 4 & 1 \\ 1 & 5 \end{pmatrix}$

(c) $3\begin{pmatrix} 5 & 4 & 1 \\ 0 & -1 & 7 \end{pmatrix}$

SOLUTION

(a) Adding corresponding entries, we obtain

$$\begin{pmatrix} 5 & 4 & 1 \\ 0 & -1 & 7 \end{pmatrix} + \begin{pmatrix} 2 & -1 & 3 \\ 2 & 0 & 1 \end{pmatrix} = \begin{pmatrix} 5+2 & 4-1 & 1+3 \\ 0+2 & -1+0 & 7+1 \end{pmatrix} = \begin{pmatrix} 7 & 3 & 4 \\ 2 & -1 & 8 \end{pmatrix}$$

(b) Since the matrices are of different sizes, we cannot add them.

(c) Multiplying each entry by 3, we have

$$3\begin{pmatrix} 5 & 4 & 1 \\ 0 & -1 & 7 \end{pmatrix} = \begin{pmatrix} 15 & 12 & 3 \\ 0 & -3 & 21 \end{pmatrix}$$

A1.26 Let

$$A = \begin{pmatrix} 3 & 2 \\ 0 & 1 \end{pmatrix} \qquad B = \begin{pmatrix} 5 & -7 \\ 3 & -2 \end{pmatrix}$$

Find $2A - 3B$.

SOLUTION

First multiply, and then add:

$$2A - 3B = 2\begin{pmatrix} 3 & 2 \\ 0 & 1 \end{pmatrix} - 3\begin{pmatrix} 5 & -7 \\ 3 & -2 \end{pmatrix} = \begin{pmatrix} 6 & 4 \\ 0 & 2 \end{pmatrix} + \begin{pmatrix} -15 & 21 \\ -9 & 6 \end{pmatrix} = \begin{pmatrix} 6-15 & 4+21 \\ 0-9 & 2+6 \end{pmatrix} = \begin{pmatrix} -9 & 25 \\ -9 & 8 \end{pmatrix}$$

A1.27 Determine the size of the following matrix multiplications $A \cdot B$, where the sizes of A and B are given as (a) (3×5), (5×2); (b) (1×2), (3×1); (c) (2×2), (2×1); and (d) (2×2), (2×2).

SOLUTION

(a) (3×2); (b) undefined, since the column size of **A** (2) and the row size of **B** (3) are not equal; (c) (2×1); (d) (2×2).

A1.28 Find the sizes of **A** and **B** so that **AB** and **BA** can both be computed. Show that, if both **A** and **B** are square matrices of the same size, both **AB** and **BA** are defined.

SOLUTION

Let the size of **A** be $(m \times n)$ and the size of **B** be $(r \times s)$. Then **AB** is defined only if $r = n$. Also, **BA** is defined only if $s = m$. Thus, if **A** is $(m \times n)$, then **B** must be $(n \times m)$. If **A** is square, say, $(n \times n)$, and **B** is also $(n \times n)$, then both **AB** and **BA** are defined.

A1.29 Given

$$\mathbf{A} = \begin{pmatrix} 1 & 2 \\ 5 & 1 \\ 6 & 3 \end{pmatrix}$$

find $\mathbf{A}^T$.

SOLUTION

Exchanging the rows and columns of **A**, we obtain

$$\mathbf{A}^T = \begin{pmatrix} 1 & 5 & 6 \\ 2 & 1 & 3 \end{pmatrix}$$

A1.30 Compute **AB** for

(a) $\mathbf{A} = \begin{pmatrix} 2 & 3 \\ 1 & 2 \end{pmatrix}$ and $\mathbf{B} = \begin{pmatrix} -4 \\ 7 \end{pmatrix}$

(b) $\mathbf{A} = \begin{pmatrix} 2 & 3 \\ 1 & 2 \end{pmatrix}$ and $\mathbf{B} = \begin{pmatrix} -4 & 5 \\ 7 & 6 \end{pmatrix}$

(c) $\mathbf{A} = \begin{pmatrix} 2 & 3 \\ 1 & 2 \end{pmatrix}$ and $\mathbf{B} = \begin{pmatrix} -4 & 5 & 9 \\ 7 & 6 & 10 \end{pmatrix}$

SOLUTION

(a) Since **A** is (2×2) and **B** is (2×1), then **AB** is (2×1):

$$\mathbf{AB} = \begin{pmatrix} 2 & 3 \\ 1 & 2 \end{pmatrix} \begin{pmatrix} -4 \\ 7 \end{pmatrix} = \begin{pmatrix} 2 \cdot (-4) + 3 \cdot 7 \\ 1 \cdot (-4) + 2 \cdot 7 \end{pmatrix} = \begin{pmatrix} 13 \\ 10 \end{pmatrix}$$

(b) $\mathbf{AB} = \begin{pmatrix} 2 & 3 \\ 1 & 2 \end{pmatrix} \begin{pmatrix} -4 & 5 \\ 7 & 6 \end{pmatrix} = \begin{pmatrix} 2 \cdot (-4) + 3 \cdot 7 & 2 \cdot 5 + 3 \cdot 6 \\ 1 \cdot (-4) + 2 \cdot 7 & 1 \cdot 5 + 2 \cdot 6 \end{pmatrix} = \begin{pmatrix} 13 & 28 \\ 10 & 17 \end{pmatrix}$

(c) $\mathbf{A} \cdot \mathbf{B} = \begin{pmatrix} 2 & 3 \\ 1 & 2 \end{pmatrix} \begin{pmatrix} -4 & 5 & 9 \\ 7 & 6 & 10 \end{pmatrix} = \begin{pmatrix} 2 \cdot (-4) + 3 \cdot 7 & 2 \cdot 5 + 3 \cdot 6 & 2 \cdot 9 + 3 \cdot 10 \\ 1 \cdot (-4) + 2 \cdot 7 & 1 \cdot 5 + 2 \cdot 6 & 1 \cdot 9 + 2 \cdot 10 \end{pmatrix}$

$$= \begin{pmatrix} 13 & 28 & 48 \\ 10 & 17 & 29 \end{pmatrix}$$

A1.31 Let

$$\mathbf{A} = \begin{pmatrix} 3 & 2 \\ 5 & 6 \\ 2 & 1 \end{pmatrix} \quad \text{and} \quad \mathbf{B} = \begin{pmatrix} 6 & 2 & 1 \\ 3 & 5 & 8 \end{pmatrix}$$

Find (a) **AB** and (b) **BA**.

SOLUTION

(a) $\mathbf{AB} = \begin{pmatrix} 3 & 2 \\ 5 & 6 \\ 2 & 1 \end{pmatrix} \begin{pmatrix} 6 & 2 & 1 \\ 3 & 5 & 8 \end{pmatrix} = \begin{pmatrix} 3\cdot6+2\cdot3 & 3\cdot2+2\cdot5 & 3\cdot1+2\cdot8 \\ 5\cdot6+6\cdot3 & 5\cdot2+6\cdot5 & 5\cdot1+6\cdot8 \\ 2\cdot6+1\cdot3 & 2\cdot2+1\cdot5 & 2\cdot1+1\cdot8 \end{pmatrix} = \begin{pmatrix} 24 & 16 & 19 \\ 48 & 40 & 53 \\ 15 & 9 & 10 \end{pmatrix}$

(b) $\mathbf{BA} = \begin{pmatrix} 6 & 2 & 1 \\ 3 & 5 & 8 \end{pmatrix} \begin{pmatrix} 3 & 2 \\ 5 & 6 \\ 2 & 1 \end{pmatrix} = \begin{pmatrix} 6\cdot3+2\cdot5+1\cdot2 & 6\cdot2+2\cdot6+1\cdot1 \\ 3\cdot3+5\cdot5+8\cdot2 & 3\cdot2+5\cdot6+8\cdot1 \end{pmatrix} = \begin{pmatrix} 30 & 25 \\ 50 & 44 \end{pmatrix}$

A1.32 Find the inverse of $\mathbf{A} = \begin{pmatrix} 1 & 2 \\ 3 & 4 \end{pmatrix}$.

SOLUTION

We wish to find a matrix $\begin{pmatrix} p & q \\ r & s \end{pmatrix}$ so that

$$\begin{pmatrix} 1 & 2 \\ 3 & 4 \end{pmatrix} \begin{pmatrix} p & q \\ r & s \end{pmatrix} = \begin{pmatrix} 1 & 0 \\ 0 & 1 \end{pmatrix}$$

Multiplying, we have

$$\begin{pmatrix} p+2r & q+2s \\ 3p+4r & 3q+4s \end{pmatrix} = \begin{pmatrix} 1 & 0 \\ 0 & 1 \end{pmatrix}$$

So $p + 2r = 1$, $q + 2s = 0$, $3p + 4r = 0$, and $3q + 4s = 1$. Solving the first and third equations we find $p = -2$, $r = \frac{3}{2}$. Solving the second and fourth equations gives $q = 1$ and $s = -\frac{1}{2}$. So

$$\mathbf{A}^{-1} = \begin{pmatrix} -2 & 1 \\ \frac{3}{2} & -\frac{1}{2} \end{pmatrix}$$

A1.33 Let G be the function which multiplies a given vector by 2 and F be the function that adds the vector **b** to a given vector. Find (a) $F + G$, (b) $F \circ G$, (c) $G \circ F$, (d) F^{-1}, and (e) G^{-1}.

SOLUTION

If **v** is any vector, the functions F and G operate on **v** as $F(\mathbf{v}) = 2\mathbf{v}$ and $G(\mathbf{v}) = \mathbf{v} + \mathbf{b}$.

1. $(F + G)(\mathbf{v}) = F(\mathbf{v}) + G(\mathbf{v}) = (2\mathbf{v}) + (\mathbf{v} + \mathbf{b}) = 3\mathbf{v} + \mathbf{b}$.
2. $(F \circ G)(\mathbf{v}) = F[G(\mathbf{v})] = 2[G(\mathbf{v})] = 2[\mathbf{v} + \mathbf{b}] = 2\mathbf{v} + 2\mathbf{b}$.
3. $(G \circ F)(\mathbf{v}) = G[F(\mathbf{v})] = [F(\mathbf{v})] + \mathbf{b} = 2\mathbf{v} + \mathbf{b}$.
4. We can guess that $F^{-1}(\mathbf{v}) = \frac{1}{2}\mathbf{v}$. To check this, we set $F^{-1}[F(\mathbf{v})] = \frac{1}{2}[F(\mathbf{v})] = \frac{1}{2}[2\mathbf{v}] = \mathbf{v}$ and $F[F^{-1}(\mathbf{v})] = 2[F^{-1}(\mathbf{v})] = 2[(\frac{1}{2})\mathbf{v}] = \mathbf{v}$.
5. We can verify that $G^{-1}(\mathbf{v}) = \mathbf{v} - \mathbf{b}$: $G^{-1}[G(\mathbf{v})] = G^{-1}(\mathbf{v} + \mathbf{b}) = (\mathbf{v} + \mathbf{b}) - \mathbf{b} = \mathbf{v}$ and $G[G^{-1}(\mathbf{v})] = G^{-1}(\mathbf{v}) + \mathbf{b} = (\mathbf{v} - \mathbf{b}) + \mathbf{b} = \mathbf{v}$.

A1.34 Show that $\mathbf{A} \circ \mathbf{B} = \mathbf{AB}$ for any two matrices (that can be multiplied together).

SOLUTION

The terms $\mathbf{A} \circ \mathbf{B}$ and $\mathbf{AB}$ produce the same effect on any column matrix **X**, i.e., $(\mathbf{A} \circ \mathbf{B})(\mathbf{X}) = \mathbf{ABX}$.

Recall that any matrix function $\mathbf{A}(\mathbf{X})$ is defined by $\mathbf{A}(\mathbf{X}) = \mathbf{AX}$. So

$$(\mathbf{A} \circ \mathbf{B})(\mathbf{X}) = \mathbf{A}[\mathbf{B}(\mathbf{X})] = \mathbf{A}(\mathbf{BX}) = \mathbf{ABX}$$

A1.35 Given that $\mathbf{A}$ is a 2×2 matrix and $\mathbf{b}$ is a vector, show that the function $F(\mathbf{X}) = \mathbf{AX} + \mathbf{b}$, called an affine transformation, can be considered as either a transformation between vectors or as a mapping between points of the plane.

SOLUTION

Suppose that

$$\mathbf{A} = \begin{pmatrix} a_{11} & a_{12} \\ a_{21} & a_{22} \end{pmatrix}$$

and $\mathbf{b}$ has components $[b_1, b_2]$. If $\mathbf{X}$ is a vector with components $[x_1, x_2]$, then

$$\mathbf{AX} = \begin{pmatrix} a_{11} & a_{12} \\ a_{21} & a_{22} \end{pmatrix} \begin{pmatrix} x_1 \\ x_2 \end{pmatrix}$$

can be identified with the vector having components $[a_{11}x_1 + a_{12}x_2, a_{21}x_1 + a_{22}x_2]$. And so $\mathbf{AX} + \mathbf{b}$ is a vector.

If $X = (x_1, x_2)$ is a point of the plane, then as a point mapping, $F(X) = [f_1(X), f_2(X)]$, where the coordinate functions f_1 and f_2 are

$$f_1(X) = a_{11}x_1 + a_{12}x_2 + b_1 \qquad \text{and} \qquad f_2(X) = a_{21}x_1 + a_{22}x_2 + b_2$$

A1.36 Show that for any 2×2 matrix $\mathbf{A}$ and any vector $\mathbf{b}$ the transformation $F(\mathbf{X}) = \mathbf{AX} + \mathbf{b}$ transforms lines into lines.

SOLUTION

Let $x = at + x_0$ and $y = bt + y_0$ be the parametric equations of a line. With $\mathbf{X} = (x, y)$ then

$$\mathbf{AX} = \begin{pmatrix} a_{11} & a_{12} \\ a_{21} & a_{22} \end{pmatrix} \begin{pmatrix} at + x_0 \\ bt + y_0 \end{pmatrix} = \begin{pmatrix} a_{11}at + a_{11}x_0 + a_{12}bt + a_{12}y_0 \\ a_{21}at + a_{21}x_0 + a_{22}bt + a_{22}y_0 \end{pmatrix}$$

So

$$F(\mathbf{X}) = \mathbf{AX} + \mathbf{b} = \begin{pmatrix} t(a_{11}a + a_{12}b) + (a_{11}x_0 + a_{12}y_0 + b_1) \\ t(a_{21}a + a_{22}b) + (a_{21}x_0 + a_{22}y_0 + b_2) \end{pmatrix}$$

This can be recognized as the parametric equation of a line (Prob. A1.21) passing through the point with coordinates $(a_{11}x_0 + a_{12}y_0 + b_1, a_{21}x_0 + a_{22}y_0 + b_2)$ and having the direction of the vector $\mathbf{v}$ with components $[a_{11}a + a_{12}b, a_{21}a + a_{22}b]$.

A1.37 Show that the transformation $F(\mathbf{X}) = \mathbf{AX} + \mathbf{b}$ transforms a line passing through points P_1 and P_2 into a line passing through $F(P_1)$ and $F(P_2)$.

SOLUTION

As in Prob. A1.23, the parametric equation of the line passing through P_1 and P_2 can be written as

$$x = x_1 + (x_2 - x_1)t \qquad y = y_1 + (y_2 - y_1)t$$

As in Prob. A1.36 with $a = x_2 - x_1$ and $b = y_2 - y_1$, we find that F transforms this line into another line.
Now when $t = 0$, this line passes through the point

$$(a_{11}x_1 + a_{12}y_1 + b_1, a_{21}x_1 + a_{22}y_1 + b_2) = F(P_1)$$

and when $t = 1$, it passes through the point

$$(a_{11}a + a_{12}b + a_{11}x_1 + a_{12}y_1 + b_1, a_{21}a + a_{22}b + a_{21}x_1 + a_{22}y_1 + b_2) = F(P_2)$$

Mathematics for Three-Dimensional Computer Graphics

A2.1 THREE-DIMENSIONAL CARTESIAN COORDINATES

The three-dimensional Cartesian (rectangular) coordinate system consists of a reference point, called the *origin*, and three mutually perpendicular lines passing through the origin. These mutually perpendicular lines are taken to be number lines and are labeled the x, y, and z coordinate axes. The labels are placed on the positive ends of the axes (see Fig. A2-1).

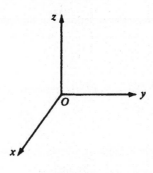

Fig. A2-1

Orientation

The labeling of the x, y, and z axes is arbitrary. However, any labeling falls into one of two classifications, called *right-* and *left-handed orientation*. The orientation is determined by the *right-hand rule*.

298

The Right-Hand Rule

A labeling of the axes is a *right-handed orientation* if whenever the fingers of the right hand are aligned with the positive x axis and are then rotated (through the smaller angle) toward the positive y axis, then the thumb of the right-hand points in the direction of the positive z axis. Otherwise, the orientation is a *left-handed orientation* (see Fig. A2-2).

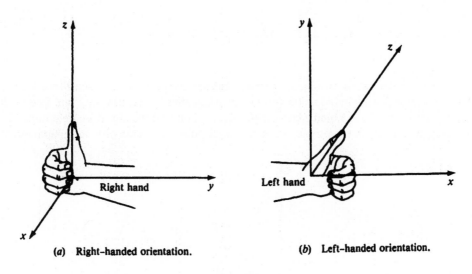

(*a*) **Right–handed orientation.**   (*b*) **Left–handed orientation.**

Fig. A2-2

Cartesian Coordinates of Points in Three-dimensional Space

Any point P in three-dimensional space can have coordinates (x, y, z) associated with it as follows:

1. Let the x coordinate be the directed distance that P is above or below the yz plane.
2. Let the y coordinate be the directed distance that P is above or below the xz plane.
3. Let the z coordinate be the directed distance that P is above or below the xy plane.

See Fig. A2-3.

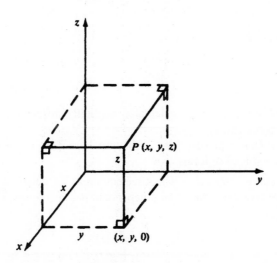

Fig. A2-3

Distance Formula

If $P_0(x_0, y_0, z_0)$ and $P_1(x_1, y_1, z_1)$ are any two points in space, the distance D between these points is given by the distance formula:

$$D = \sqrt{(x_1 - x_0)^2 + (y_1 - y_0)^2 + (z_1 - z_0)^2}$$

A2.2   CURVES AND SURFACES IN THREE-DIMENSIONS

Curves

A three-dimensional curve is an object in space that has direction only, much like a thread (see Fig. A2-4). A curve is specified by an equation (or group of equations) that has only one free (independent) variable or parameter, and the x, y, and z coordinates of any point on the curve are determined by this free variable or parameter. There are two types of curve description, nonparametric and parametric.

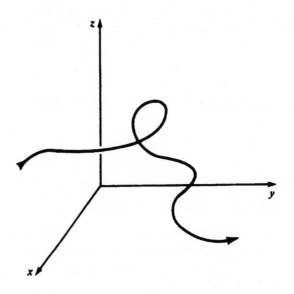

Fig. A2-4

1. *Nonparametric curve description.*

   (*a*) *Explicit form.* The equation for curve C are given in terms of a variable, say, x, as

   $$C: \quad y = f(x) \qquad z = g(x)$$

   That is, y and z can be calculated explicitly in terms of x. Any point P on the curve has coordinates $P[x, f(x), g(x)]$.

   (*b*) *Implicit form.* The equations of the curve are $F(x, y, z) = 0$ and $G(x, y, z) = 0$. Here, y and z must be solved in terms of x.

2. *Parametric curve description.* The three equations for determining the coordinates of any point on the curve are given in terms of an independent parameter, say, t, in a parameter range $[a, b]$, which may be infinite:

   $$C: \quad \begin{aligned} x &= f(t) \\ y &= g(t), \qquad a \le t \le b \\ z &= h(t) \end{aligned}$$

Any point P on the curve has coordinates $[f(t), g(t), h(t)]$.

- *Equations of a straight line.* The equations of a line L determined by two points $P_0(x_0, y_0, z_0)$ and $P_1(x_1, y_1, z_1)$ are given by:

  nonparametric form

  $$L: \quad \begin{aligned} y &= m_1 x + b_1 = \left(\frac{y_1 - y_0}{x_1 - x_0}\right) x + \left(\frac{y_0 x_1 - y_1 x_0}{x_1 - x_0}\right) \\[2mm] z &= m_2 x + b_2 = \left(\frac{z_1 - z_0}{x_1 - x_0}\right) x + \left(\frac{z_0 x_1 - z_1 x_0}{x_1 - x_0}\right) \end{aligned}$$

  parametric form

  $$x = x_0 + (x_1 - x_0)t \qquad y = y_0 + (y_1 - y_0)t \qquad z = z_0 + (z_1 - z_0)t$$

  Note that when $t = 0$, then $x = x_0$, $y = y_0$, and $z = z_0$. When $t = 1$, then $x = x_1$, $y = y_1$, and $z = z_1$. Thus, when the parameter t is restricted to the range $0 \le t \le 1$, the parametric equations describe the line segment $\overline{P_0 P_1}$.

Surfaces

A surface in three-dimensional space is an object that has breadth and width, much like a piece of cloth (see Fig. A2-5).

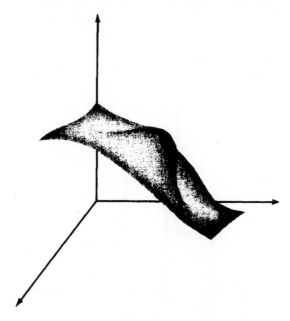

Fig. A2-5

A surface is specified by an equation (or group of equations) that has two free (or independent) variables or parameters. There are two types of surface description, nonparametric and parametrics.

1. *Nonparametric surface description*

    (a) *Explicit form.* The z coordinate of any point on the surface S is given in terms of two free variables x and y, that is, $z = f(x, y)$. Any point P on the surface has coordinates $[x, y, f(x, y)]$.

(b) *Implicit form*. The equation of the surface is given in the form $F(x, y, z) = 0$. Here, z is to be solved in terms of x and y. There is no restriction as to which variables are free. The convention is to represent z in terms of x and y, but nothing disallows a representation of x in terms of y and z or y in terms of x and z.

2. *Parametric description*. The three equations for determining the coordinates of any point on the surface S are described in terms of parameters, say, s and t, and in parameter ranges $[a, b]$ and $[c, d]$, which may be infinite:

$$S: \quad \begin{aligned} x &= f(s, t), & a \le s \le b \\ y &= g(s, t), & c \le t \le d \\ z &= h(s, t) \end{aligned}$$

The coordinates of any point P on the surface have the form $[f(s, t), g(s, t), h(s, t)]$.

- *Equations of a plane*. The equation of a plane can be written in explicit form as $z = ax + by + c$ or in implicit form as $Ax + By + Cz + D = 0$ (see Prob. A2.8). The equation of a plane is linear in the variables x, y, and z. A plane divides three-dimensional space into two separate regions. The implicit form of the equation of a plane can be used to determine whether two points are on the same or opposite sides of the plane. Given the implicit equation of the plane $Ax + By + Cz + D = 0$, let $f(x, y, z) = Ax + By + Cz + D$. The two sides of the plane R^+, R^- are determined by the sign of $f(x, y, z)$; that is, point $P(x_0, y_0, z_0)$ lies in region R^+ if $f(x_0, y_0, z_0) > 0$ and in region R^- if $f(x_0, y_0, z_0) < 0$. If $f(x_0, y_0, z_0) = 0$, the point lies on the plane. The equations $x = 0$, $y = 0$, and $z = 0$ represent the yz, xz, and xy planes, respectively.

- *Quadric surfaces*. Quadric surfaces have the (implicit) form $Ax^2 + By^2 + Cz^2 + Dxy + Exz + Fyz + Gx + Hy + Iz + J = 0$. The basic quadric surfaces are described in Chap. 9.

- *Cylinder surfaces*. In two dimensions, the equation $y = f(x)$ represents a (planar) curve in the xy plane. In three dimensions, the equation $y = f(x)$ is a surface. That is, the variables x and z are free. This type of surface is called a *cylinder surface* (see Fig. A2- 6).

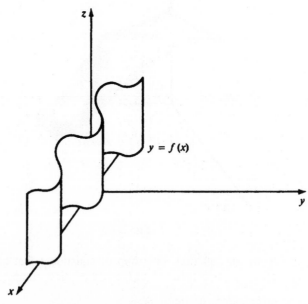

Fig. A2-6

EXAMPLE 1.   The equation $x^2 + y^2 = 1$ is a circle in the xy plane. However, in three dimensions, it represents a cylinder (see Fig. A2-7).

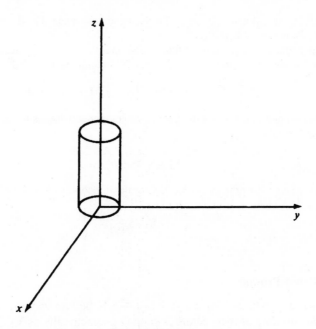

Fig. A2-7

A2.3 VECTORS IN THREE-DIMENSIONS

The definition of a vector and the concepts of magnitude, scalar multiplication, and vector addition are completely analogous to the two-dimensional case in App. 1.

In three-dimensions, there are three natural coordinate vectors **I**, **J**, and **K**. These vectors are unit vectors (magnitude 1) having the direction of the positive x, y, and z axes, respectively. Any vector **V** can be resolved into components in terms of **I**, **J**, and **K**: $\mathbf{V} = a\mathbf{I} + b\mathbf{J} + c\mathbf{K}$.

The components $[a, b, c]$ of vectors **V** are also the Cartesian coordinates of the head of the vector **V** when the tail of **V** is placed at the origin of the Cartesian coordinate system (see Fig. A2-8).

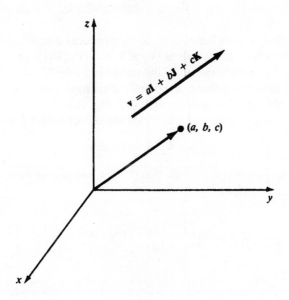

Fig. A2-8

EXAMPLE 2. Let $P_0(x_0, y_0, z_0)$ and $P_1(x_1, y_1, z_1)$ be two points in space. The directed line segment $\overline{P_0P_1}$ defines a vector whose tail is at P_0 and head is at P_1.

To find the components of $\overline{P_0P_1}$, we must translate so that the tail P_0 is placed at the origin. The head of the vector will then be at the point $(x_1 - x_0, y_1 - y_0, z_1 - z_0)$. The components of $\overline{P_0P_1}$ are then

$$\overline{P_0P_1} = (x_1 - x_0)\mathbf{I} + (y_1 - y_0)\mathbf{J} + (z_1 - z_0)\mathbf{K}$$

Vector addition and scalar multiplication can be performed componentwise, as in App. 1. The magnitude of a vector $\mathbf{V}$, $|\mathbf{V}|$, is given by the formula

$$|\mathbf{V}| = \sqrt{a^2 + b^2 + c^2}$$

For any vector $\mathbf{V}$, a *unit vector* (magnitude 1) $\mathbf{U_V}$ having the direction of $\mathbf{V}$ can be written as

$$\mathbf{U_V} = \frac{\mathbf{V}}{|\mathbf{V}|}$$

The Dot and the Cross Product

Let $\mathbf{V}_1 = a_1\mathbf{I} + b_1\mathbf{J} + c_1\mathbf{K}$ and $\mathbf{V}_2 = a_2\mathbf{I} + b_2\mathbf{J} + c_2\mathbf{K}$ be two vectors.

The *dot* or *scalar product* of two vectors is defined geometrically as $\mathbf{V}_1 \cdot \mathbf{V}_2 = |\mathbf{V}_1||\mathbf{V}_2| \cos \theta$, where θ is the smaller angle between $\mathbf{V}_1$ and $\mathbf{V}_2$ (when the vectors are placed tail to tail). The component form of the dot product can be shown to be

$$\mathbf{V}_1 \cdot \mathbf{V}_2 = a_1a_2 + b_1b_2 + c_1c_2$$

Note that the dot product of two vectors is a number and the order of the dot product is immaterial: $\mathbf{V}_1 \cdot \mathbf{V}_2 = \mathbf{V}_2 \cdot \mathbf{V}_1$. This formula enables us to calculate the angle θ between two vectors from the formula

$$\cos \theta = \frac{\mathbf{V}_1 \cdot \mathbf{V}_2}{|\mathbf{V}_1||\mathbf{V}_2|} = \frac{a_1a_2 + b_1b_2 + c_1c_2}{\sqrt{a_1^2 + b_1^2 + c_1^2}\sqrt{a_2^2 + b_2^2 + c_2^2}}$$

Note that two vectors are *perpendicular* (*orthogonal*) (i.e., $\theta = 90°$) if and only if their dot product $\mathbf{V}_1 \cdot \mathbf{V}_2 = 0$. This provides a rapid test for determining whether two vectors are perpendicular. (Equivalently, we say that two vectors are *parallel* if they are scalar multiples of each other, i.e, $\mathbf{V}_1 = k\mathbf{V}_2$ for some number k.)

The *cross product* of two vectors, denoted $\mathbf{V}_1 \times \mathbf{V}_2$, produces a new vector defined geometrically as follows: $\mathbf{V}_1 \times \mathbf{V}_2$ is a vector whose magnitude is $|\mathbf{V}_1 \times \mathbf{V}_2| = |\mathbf{V}_1||\mathbf{V}_2| \sin \theta$, where θ is the angle between $\mathbf{V}_1$ and $\mathbf{V}_2$ and whose direction is determined by the right-hand rule: $\mathbf{V}_1 \times \mathbf{V}_2$ is a vector perpendicular to both $\mathbf{V}_1$ and $\mathbf{V}_2$ and whose direction is that of the thumb of the right hand when the fingers are aligned with $\mathbf{V}_1$ and rotated toward $\mathbf{V}_2$ through the smaller angle (see Fig. A2-9).

From this definition, we see that the order in which the cross product is performed is relevant. In fact:

$$\mathbf{V}_1 \times \mathbf{V}_2 = -(\mathbf{V}_2 \times \mathbf{V}_1)$$

Note also that $\mathbf{V} \times \mathbf{V} = \mathbf{0}$ for any vector $\mathbf{V}$, since $\theta = 0°$. The component form for the cross product can be calculated as a determinant as follows:

$$\mathbf{V}_1 \times \mathbf{V}_2 = \begin{vmatrix} \mathbf{I} & \mathbf{J} & \mathbf{K} \\ a_1 & b_1 & c_1 \\ a_2 & b_2 & c_2 \end{vmatrix} = \begin{vmatrix} b_1 & c_1 \\ b_2 & c_2 \end{vmatrix}\mathbf{I} - \begin{vmatrix} a_1 & c_1 \\ a_2 & c_2 \end{vmatrix}\mathbf{J} + \begin{vmatrix} a_1 & b_1 \\ a_2 & b_2 \end{vmatrix}\mathbf{K}$$

$$= (b_1c_2 - b_2c_1)\mathbf{I} + (c_1a_2 - c_2a_1)\mathbf{J} + (a_1b_2 - a_2b_1)\mathbf{K}$$

EXAMPLE 3. For a right-handed Cartesian coordinate system, we have $\mathbf{I} \times \mathbf{J} = \mathbf{K}$, $\mathbf{J} \times \mathbf{K} = \mathbf{I}$, $\mathbf{I} \times \mathbf{K} = -\mathbf{J}$.

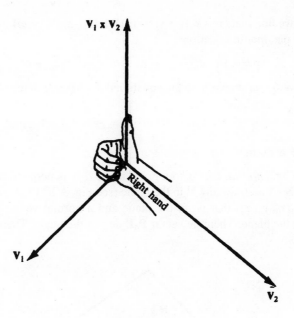

Fig. A2-9

The Vector Equation of a Line

A line L in space is determined by its direction and a point $P_0(x_0, y_0, z_0)$ that the line passes through. If the direction is specified by a vector $\mathbf{V} = a\mathbf{I} + b\mathbf{J} + c\mathbf{K}$ and if $P(x, y, z)$ is any point on the line, the direction of the vector $\overline{P_0P}$ determined by the points P_0, and P is parallel to the vector $\mathbf{V}$ (see Fig. A2-10). Thus, $\overline{P_0P} = t\mathbf{V}$ for some number t.

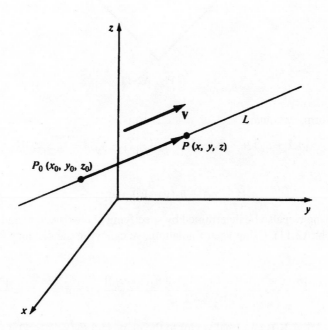

Fig. A2-10

In component form, we find that $(x - x_0)\mathbf{I} + (y - y_0)\mathbf{J} + (z - z_0)\mathbf{K} = ta\mathbf{I} + tb\mathbf{J} + tc\mathbf{K}$. Comparison of components leads to the parametric equations:

$$x = x_0 + at \qquad y = y_0 + bt \qquad z = z_0 + ct$$

In Probs. A2.5 and A2.6 it is shown how the equations of a line are determined when given two points on the line.

The Vector Equation of a Plane

A vector $\mathbf{N}$ is said to be a *normal vector* to a given plane if $\mathbf{N}$ is perpendicular to any vector $\mathbf{V}$ which lies on the plane; that is, $\mathbf{N} \cdot \mathbf{V} = 0$ for any $\mathbf{V}$ in the plane (see Fig. A2-11). A plane is uniquely determined by specifying a point $P_0(x_0, y_0, z_0)$ that is on the plane and a normal vector $\mathbf{N} = n_1\mathbf{I} + n_2\mathbf{J} + n_3\mathbf{K}$. Let $P(x, y, z)$ be any point on the plane. Then the vector $\overline{\mathbf{P_0P}}$ lies on the plane. Therefore, $\mathbf{N}$ is perpendicular to it. So $\mathbf{N} \cdot \overline{\mathbf{P_0P}} = 0$.

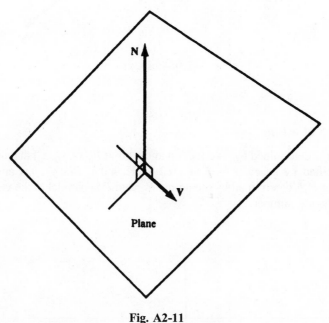

Fig. A2-11

In component form, we obtain

$$[n_1\mathbf{I} + n_2\mathbf{J} + n_3\mathbf{K}] \cdot [(x - x_0)\mathbf{I} + (y - y_0)\mathbf{J} + (z - z_0)\mathbf{K}] = 0$$

or

$$n_1(x - x_0) + n_2(y - y_0) + n_3(z - z_0) = 0$$

The equation of a plane can also be determined by specifying (1) two vectors and a point (Prob. A2.10) and (2) three points (Prob. A2.11). Using vector notation, we can write the distance D from a point $\bar{P}(\bar{x}, \bar{y}, \bar{z})$ to a plane as

$$D = \frac{[n_1(\bar{x} - x_0) + n_2(\bar{y} - y_0) + n_3(\bar{z} - z_0)]}{\sqrt{n_1^2 + n_2^2 + n_3^2}} \qquad \text{or} \qquad D = \frac{|\mathbf{N} \cdot \overline{\mathbf{P_0\bar{P}}}|}{|\mathbf{N}|}$$

where $\mathbf{N} = n_1\mathbf{I} + n_2\mathbf{J} + n_3\mathbf{K}$ is a normal vector to the plane and $P_0(x_0, y_0, z_0)$ is a point on the plane (Prob. A2.13).

A2.4   HOMOGENEOUS COORDINATES

The Two-dimensional Projective Plane

The *projective plane* was introduced by geometers in order to study the geometric relationships of figures under perspective transformations.

The two-dimensional projective plane $\mathbf{P}_3$ is defined as follows.

In three-dimensional Cartesian space, consider the set of all lines through the origin and the set of all planes through the origin. In the projective plane, a line through the origin is called a *point* of the projective plane, while a plane through the origin is called a *line* of the projective plane.

To see why this is "natural" from the point of view of a perspective projection, consider the perspective projection onto the plane $z = 1$ using the origin as the center of projection. Then a line through the origin projects onto a point of the plane $z = 1$, while a plane through the origin projects onto a line in the plane $z = 1$ (Fig. A2-12).

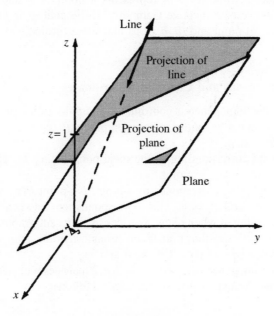

Fig. A2-12

In this projection, lines through points $(x, y, 0)$ in the plane project to infinity. This leads to the notion of ideal points, discussed later.

Homogeneous Coordinates of Points and Lines of the Projective Plane

If (a, b, c) is any point in Cartesian three-dimensional space, this point determines a line through the origin whose equations are

$$x = at$$
$$y = bt \qquad \text{(where } t \text{ is a number)}$$
$$z = ct$$

That is, any other point (at, bt, ct) determines the same line. So two points (a_1, b_1, c_1) and (a_2, b_2, c_2), are on the same line through the origin if there is a number t so that

$$a_2 = a_1 t \qquad b_2 = b_1 t \qquad c_2 = c_1 t \qquad\qquad (A2.1)$$

We say that two triples, (a_1, b_1, c_1) and (a_2, b_2, c_2), are equivalent (i.e., define the same line through the origin) if there is some number t so that the equations ($A2.1$) hold. We write $(a_1, b_1, c_1) \sim (a_2, b_2, c_2)$. The equivalence classes of all triples equivalent to (a, b, c), written as $[a, b, c]$, are the points of the projective plane. Any representative (a_1, b_1, c_1) equivalent to (a, b, c) is called the *homogeneous coordinate* of the point $[a, b, c]$ in the projective plane.

The points of the form $(a, b, 0)$ are called *ideal points* of the projective plane. This arises from the fact that lines in the plane $z = 0$ project to infinity. In a similar manner, any plane through the origin has an equation $n_1 x + n_2 y + n_3 z = 0$. Note that any multiple $k n_1 x + k n_2 y + k n_3 z = 0$ defines the same plane.

Any triple of numbers (n_1, n_2, n_3) defines a plane through the origin. Two triples are equivalent, $(n_1, n_2, n_3) \sim (d_1, d_2, d_3)$ (i.e., define the same plane), if there is a number k so that $d_1 = k n_1$, $d_2 = k n_2$, and $d_3 = k n_3$. The equivalence classes of all triples, $[n_1, n_2, n_3]$, are the lines of the projective plane. Any representative (d_1, d_2, d_3) of the equivalence class $[n_1, n_2, n_3]$ is called the *homogeneous line coordinate* of this line in the projective plane.

The ambiguity of whether a triple (a, b, c) represents a point or a line of the projection plane is exploited as the Duality Principle of Projective Geometry. If the context is not clear, one usually writes (a, b, c) to indicate a (projective) point and $[a, b, c]$ to indicate a (projective) line.

Correlation between Homogeneous and Cartesian Coordinates

If (x_1, y_1, z_1), $z_1 \neq 0$ are the homogeneous coordinates of a point of the projective plane, the equations $x = x_1/z_1$ and $y = y_1/z_1$ define a correspondence between points $P_1(x_1, y_1, z_1)$ of the projective plane and points $P(x, y)$ of the Cartesian plane.

There is no Cartesian point corresponding to the ideal point $(x_1, y_1, 0)$. However, it is convenient to consider it as defining an infinitely distant point.

Also, any Cartesian point $P(x, y)$ corresponds to a projective point $P(x_1, y_1, z_1)$ whose homogeneous coordinates are $x_1 = x$, $y_1 = y$, and $z_1 = 1$. This correspondence between Cartesian coordinates and homogeneous coordinates is exploited when using matrices to represent graphics transformations. The use of homogeneous coordinates allows the translation transformation and the perspective projection transformation to be represented by matrices (Chaps. 6 and 7).

To conform to the use of homogeneous coordinates, 2×2 matrices representing transformations of the plane can be augmented to use homogeneous coordinates as follows:

$$\mathbf{AX} = \left(\begin{pmatrix} a & b \\ c & d \end{pmatrix} \begin{matrix} 0 \\ 0 \end{matrix} \\ \begin{matrix} 0 & 0 & 1 \end{matrix} \right) \begin{pmatrix} x \\ y \\ 1 \end{pmatrix}$$

Finally, note that even though we have a correspondence between the points of the projective plane and those of the Cartesian plane, the projective plane and the Cartesian plane have different topological properties which must be taken into account in work with homogeneous coordinates in advanced applications.

Three-dimensional Projective Plane and Homogeneous Coordinates

Everything stated about the two-dimensional projective plane and homogeneous coordinates may be generalized to the three-dimensional case. For example, if $P_1(x_1, y_1, z_1, w_1)$ are the homogeneous coordinates of a point in the three-dimensional projective plane, the corresponding three-dimensional Cartesian point $P(x, y, z)$ is, for $w_1 \neq 0$,

$$x = \frac{x_1}{w_1} \qquad y = \frac{y_1}{w_1} \qquad z = \frac{z_1}{w_1}$$

In addition, if $P(x, y, z)$ is a Cartesian point, it corresponds to the projective point $P(x, y, z, 1)$. Finally, 3×3 matrices can be augmented to use homogeneous coordinates:

$$\begin{pmatrix} \begin{pmatrix} 3 \times 3 \end{pmatrix} & \begin{matrix} 0 \\ 0 \\ 0 \end{matrix} \\ \begin{matrix} 0 & 0 & 0 \end{matrix} & 1 \end{pmatrix}$$

Solved Problems

A2.1 Describe the space curve whose parametric equations are $x = \cos t$, $y = \sin t$, and $z = t$.

SOLUTION

Noting that $x^2 + y^2 = \cos^2 t + \sin^2 t = 1$ (see Fig. A2-13), we find that the x, y variables lie on a unit circle, while the z coordinate varies. The curve is a (cylindrical) spiral.

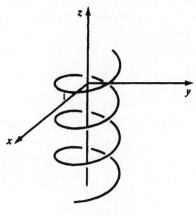

Fig. A2-13

A2.2 Find the equation of a sphere of radius r centered at the origin $(0, 0, 0)$.

SOLUTION

Let $P(x, y, z)$ be any point on the sphere. Then the distance D between this point and the center of the sphere is equal to the length of the radius r. The distance formula yields

$$\sqrt{(x - 0)^2 + (y - 0)^2 + (z - 0)^2} = r \qquad \text{or} \qquad x^2 + y^2 + z^2 = r^2$$

This is the (implicit) equation of the sphere.

A2.3 Show that $\mathbf{V} \cdot \mathbf{V} = |\mathbf{V}|^2$ for any vector $\mathbf{V}$.

SOLUTION

If $\mathbf{V} = a\mathbf{I} + b\mathbf{J} + c\mathbf{K}$, then

$$\mathbf{V} \cdot \mathbf{V} = (a\mathbf{I} + b\mathbf{J} + c\mathbf{K}) \cdot (a\mathbf{I} + b\mathbf{J} + c\mathbf{K}) = a^2 + b^2 + c^2 = |\mathbf{V}|^2$$

A2.4 Let $\mathbf{V}_1 = 2\mathbf{I} - \mathbf{J} + \mathbf{K}$ and $\mathbf{V}_2 = \mathbf{I} + \mathbf{J} - \mathbf{K}$. Find (a) the angle between $\mathbf{V}_1$ and $\mathbf{V}_2$, (b) a vector perpendicular to both $\mathbf{V}_1$ and $\mathbf{V}_2$, and (c) a unit vector perpendicular to both $\mathbf{V}_1$ and $\mathbf{V}_2$.

SOLUTION

(a)   We use the formula

$$\cos \theta = \frac{\mathbf{V_1} \cdot \mathbf{V_2}}{|\mathbf{V_1}||\mathbf{V_2}|}$$

Now

$$|\mathbf{V_1}| = \sqrt{2^2 + (-1)^2 + (1)^2} = \sqrt{6} \qquad |\mathbf{V_2}| = \sqrt{1^2 + 1^2 + (-1)^2} = \sqrt{3}$$

and

$$\mathbf{V_1} \cdot \mathbf{V_2} = (2)(1) + (-1)(1) + (1)(-1) = 0$$

Thus $\cos \theta = 0$, and so $\theta = 90°$. So the vectors are perpendicular.

(b)   The vector $\mathbf{V_1} \times \mathbf{V_2}$ is perpendicular to both $\mathbf{V_1}$ and $\mathbf{V_2}$. So

$$\mathbf{V_1} \times \mathbf{V_2} = \begin{vmatrix} \mathbf{I} & \mathbf{J} & \mathbf{K} \\ 2 & -1 & 1 \\ 1 & 1 & 1 \end{vmatrix} = \begin{vmatrix} -1 & 1 \\ 1 & 1 \end{vmatrix}\mathbf{I} - \begin{vmatrix} 2 & 1 \\ 1 & 1 \end{vmatrix}\mathbf{J} + \begin{vmatrix} 2 & -1 \\ 1 & 1 \end{vmatrix}\mathbf{K} = -2\mathbf{I} - \mathbf{J} + 3\mathbf{K}$$

(c)   Since $\mathbf{V_1} \times \mathbf{V_2}$ is perpendicular to both $\mathbf{V_1}$ and $\mathbf{V_2}$, we find a unit vector having the direction of $\mathbf{V_1} \times \mathbf{V_2}$. This is

$$\mathbf{U}_{v_1 \times v_2} = \frac{\mathbf{V_1} \times \mathbf{V_2}}{|\mathbf{V_1} \times \mathbf{V_2}|}$$

From part (b), we have

$$|\mathbf{V_1} \times \mathbf{V_2}| = \sqrt{(-2)^2 + (-1)^2 + (3)^2} = \sqrt{14}$$

So

$$\mathbf{U}_{v_1 \times v_2} = \frac{-2}{\sqrt{14}}\mathbf{I} - \frac{1}{\sqrt{14}}\mathbf{J} + \frac{3}{\sqrt{14}}\mathbf{K}$$

A2.5   Find the equation of the line passing through two points $P_0(x_0, y_0, z_0)$ and $P_1(x_1, y_1, z_1)$.

SOLUTION

To find the equation of a line, we need to know a point on the line and a vector having the direction of the line. The vector determined by P_0 and P_1, $\overline{P_0 P_1}$ clearly has the direction of the line (see Fig. A2-14), and point P_0 lies on the line, so with direction vector

$$\overline{P_0 P_1} = (x_1 - x_0)\mathbf{I} + (y_1 - y_0)\mathbf{J} + (z_1 - z_0)\mathbf{K}$$

and point $P_0(x_0, y_0, z_0)$, the equation is

$$x = x_0 + (x_1 - x_0)t \qquad y = y_0 + (y_1 - y_0)t \qquad z = z_0 + (z_1 - z_0)t$$

A2.6   Find the equation of the line passing through $P_0(1, -5, 2)$ and $P_1(6, 7, -3)$.

SOLUTION

From Prob. A2.5, the direction vector is

$$\overline{P_0 P_1} = (6 - 1)\mathbf{I} + [7 - (-5)]\mathbf{J} + (-3 - 2)\mathbf{K} = 5\mathbf{I} + 12\mathbf{J} - 5\mathbf{K}.$$

Using point $P_0(1, -5, 2)$, we have $x = 1 + 5t$, $y = -5 + 12t$, and $z = 2 - 5t$.

A2.7   Let line segment L_1 be determined by points $P_1(a_1, b_1, c_1)$ and $P_2(a_2, b_2, c_2)$. Let line segment L_2

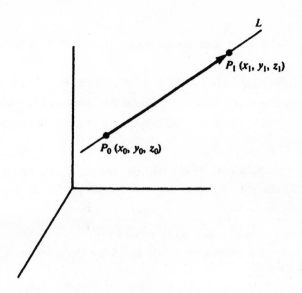

Fig. A2-14

be determined by points $Q_1(u_1, v_1, w_1)$ and $Q_2(u_2, v_2, w_2)$. How can we determine whether the line segments intersect?

SOLUTION

The parametric equations of L_1 are (Prob. A2.5)

$$x = a_1 + (a_2 - a_1)s$$
$$y = b_1 + (b_2 - b_1)s$$
$$z = c_1 + (c_2 - c_1)s$$

The equations of L_2 are

$$x = u_1 + (u_2 - u_1)t$$
$$y = v_1 + (v_2 - v_1)t$$
$$z = w_1 + (w_2 - w_1)t$$

Equating, we find

$$(u_2 - u_1)t - (a_2 - a_1)s = a_1 - u_1$$
$$(v_2 - v_1)t - (b_2 - b_1)s = b_1 - v_1$$
$$(w_2 - w_1)t - (c_2 - c_1)s = c_1 - w_1$$

Using the first two equations, we solve for s and t:

$$t = \frac{(b_1 - v_1)(a_2 - a_1) - (a_1 - u_1)(b_2 - b_1)}{(a_2 - a_1)(v_2 - v_1) - (b_2 - b_1)(u_2 - u_1)}$$

$$s = \frac{(b_1 - v_1)(u_2 - u_1) - (a_1 - u_1)(v_2 - v_1)}{(a_2 - a_1)(v_2 - v_1) - (b_2 - b_1)(u_2 - u_1)}$$

We now substitute the s value into equation L_1 and the t value into equation L_2. If all three corresponding numbers x, y, and z are the same, the lines intersect; if not, the lines do not intersect. Next, if both $0 \le s \le 1$ and $0 \le t \le 1$, the intersection point is on the line segments L_1 and L_2, between P_1 and P_2 and Q_1 and Q_2.

A2.8 Show that the equation of a plane has the implicit form $Ax + By + Cz + D = 0$, where A, B, and C are the components of the normal vector.

SOLUTION

The equation of a plane with normal vector $N = AI + BJ + CK$ and passing through a point $P_0(x_0, y_0, z_0)$ is

$$A(x - x_0) + B(y - y_0) + C(z - z_0) = 0 \quad \text{or} \quad Ax + By + Cz + (-Ax_0 - By_0 - Cz_0) = 0$$

Calling the quantity $D = (-Ax_0 - By_0 - Cz_0)$ yields the equation of the plane:

$$Ax + By + Cz + D = 0$$

A2.9 Given the plane $5x - 3y + 6z = 7$: (a) find the normal vector to the plane, and (b) determine whether $P_1(1, 5, 2)$ and $P_2(-3, -1, 2)$ are on the same side of the plane.

SOLUTION

Write the equation in implicit form as $5x - 3y + 6z - 7 = 0$.

(a) From Prob. A2.8, the coefficients 5, −3, and 6 are the components of a normal vector, that is, $N = 5I - 3J + 6K$.

(b) Let $f(x, y, z) = 5x - 3y + 6z - 7$. The plane has two sides, R^+ where $f(x, y, z)$ is positive and R^- where $f(x, y, z)$ is negative. Now for point $P_1(1, 5, 2)$, we have

$$f(1, 5, 2) = 5(1) - 3(5) + 6(2) - 7 = -5$$

and for point $P_2(-3, -1, 2)$,

$$f(-3, -1, 2) = 5(-3) - 3(-1) + 6(2) - 7 = -7$$

Since both $f(1, 5, 2)$ and $f(-3, -1, 2)$ are negative, P_1 and P_2 are on the same side of the plane.

A2.10 Find the equation of a plane passing through the point $P_0(1, -1, 1)$ and containing the vectors $V_1 = I - J + K$ and $V_2 = -I + J + 2K$ (see Fig. A2-15).

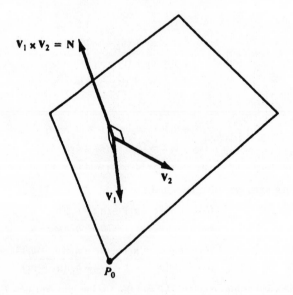

Fig. A2-15

SOLUTION

To find the equation of a plane, we need to find a normal vector perpendicular to the plane. Since V_1 and V_2 are to lie on the plane, the cross product $V_1 \times V_2$ perpendicular to both V_1 and V_2 can be chosen to be the normal vector $\mathbf{N}$ (see Fig. A2-15). So

$$\mathbf{N} = \mathbf{V}_1 \times \mathbf{V}_2 = \begin{vmatrix} \mathbf{I} & \mathbf{J} & \mathbf{K} \\ 1 & -1 & 1 \\ -1 & 1 & 2 \end{vmatrix} = \begin{vmatrix} -1 & 1 \\ 1 & 2 \end{vmatrix} \mathbf{I} - \begin{vmatrix} 1 & 1 \\ -1 & 2 \end{vmatrix} \mathbf{J} + \begin{vmatrix} 1 & -1 \\ -1 & 1 \end{vmatrix} \mathbf{K} = -3\mathbf{I} - 3\mathbf{J} + 0\mathbf{K}$$

So with $\mathbf{N} = -3\mathbf{I} - 3\mathbf{J}$ and the point $P_0(1, -1, 1)$, the equation of the plane is

$$-3(x - 1) - 3[y - (-1)] + 0(z - 1) = 0 \qquad \text{or} \qquad -3x - 3y = 0$$

Finally, $x + y = 0$ is the equation of the plane. This is an example of a cylinder surface, since z is a free variable and $y = -x$.

A2.11 Find the equation of the plane determined by the three points $P_0(1, 5, -7)$, $P_1(2, 6, 1)$, and $P_2(0, 1, 2)$ (see Fig. A2-16).

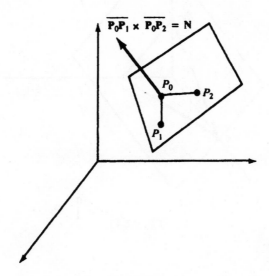

Fig. A2-16

SOLUTION

To find the equation of a plane, we must know a point on the plane and a normal vector perpendicular to the plane.

To find the normal vector, we observe that the vectors $\overline{P_0P_1}$ and $\overline{P_0P_2}$ lie on the plane, and so the cross product will be a vector perpendicular to both these vectors and so would be our choice for the normal vector; that is,

$$\mathbf{N} = \overline{P_0P_1} \times \overline{P_0P_2}$$

Now

$$\overline{P_0P_1} = (2 - 1)\mathbf{I} + (6 - 5)\mathbf{J} + (1 - (-7))\mathbf{K} = \mathbf{I} + \mathbf{J} + 8\mathbf{K}$$

and

$$\overline{P_0P_2} = (0 - 1)\mathbf{I} + (1 - 5)\mathbf{J} + (2 - (-7))\mathbf{K} = -\mathbf{I} - 4\mathbf{J} + 9\mathbf{K}$$

So

$$\overline{P_0P_1} \times \overline{P_0P_2} = \begin{vmatrix} \mathbf{I} & \mathbf{J} & \mathbf{K} \\ 1 & 1 & 8 \\ -1 & -4 & 9 \end{vmatrix} = \begin{vmatrix} 1 & 8 \\ -4 & 9 \end{vmatrix} \mathbf{I} - \begin{vmatrix} 1 & 8 \\ -1 & 9 \end{vmatrix} \mathbf{J} + \begin{vmatrix} 1 & 1 \\ -1 & -4 \end{vmatrix} \mathbf{K} = 41\mathbf{I} - 17\mathbf{J} - 3\mathbf{K}$$

So $\mathbf{N} = 41\mathbf{I} - 17\mathbf{J} - 3\mathbf{K}$, and with point $P_0(1, 5, -7)$, the equation of the plane is

$$41(x - 1) - 17(y - 5) - 3[z - (-7)] = 0 \qquad \text{or} \qquad 41x - 17y - 3z + 23 = 0$$

A2.12 Show that the equation of the plane that has x, y, and z intercepts $A(a, 0, 0)$, $B(0, b, 0)$, and $C(0, 0, c)$, respectively, is (see Fig. A2-17) $x/a + y/b + z/c = 1$.

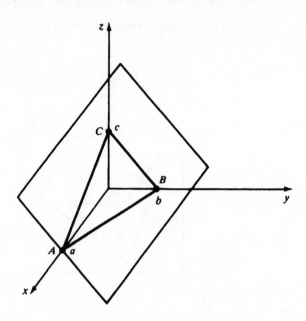

Fig. A2-17

SOLUTION

As in Prob. A2.11, we form the vectors $\overline{\mathbf{AB}} = -a\mathbf{I} + b\mathbf{J}$ and $\overline{\mathbf{AC}} = -a\mathbf{I} + c\mathbf{K}$. The normal vector to the plane is then

$$\mathbf{N} = \overline{\mathbf{AB}} \times \overline{\mathbf{AC}} = \begin{vmatrix} \mathbf{I} & \mathbf{J} & \mathbf{K} \\ -a & b & 0 \\ -a & 0 & c \end{vmatrix} = \begin{vmatrix} b & 0 \\ 0 & c \end{vmatrix}\mathbf{I} - \begin{vmatrix} -a & 0 \\ -a & c \end{vmatrix}\mathbf{J} + \begin{vmatrix} -a & b \\ -a & 0 \end{vmatrix}\mathbf{K} = bc\mathbf{I} + ac\mathbf{J} + ab\mathbf{K}$$

The equation of the plane with this normal vector and passing through $A(a, 0, 0)$ is

$$bc(x - a) + ac(y - 0) + ab(z - 0) = 0 \qquad \text{or} \qquad bcx + acy + abz = abc$$

Dividing both sides by abc, we have $x/a + y/b + z/c = 1$.

A2.13 Find the distance from a point $P_1(x_1, y_1, z_1)$ to a given plane (see Fig. A2-18).

SOLUTION

Let $\mathbf{N} = n_1\mathbf{I} + n_2\mathbf{J} + n_3\mathbf{K}$ be the normal vector to the plane, and let $P_0(x_0, y_0, z_0)$ be any point on the plane. The equation of the plane is

$$n_1(x - x_0) + n_2(y - y_0) + n_3(z - z_0) = 0$$

The distance D from $P_1(x_1, y_1, z_1)$ to the plane is measured along the perpendicular or normal to the plane. Let L_N be the line through $P_1(x_1, y_1, z_1)$ and having the direction of the normal vector $\mathbf{N}$. The equation of

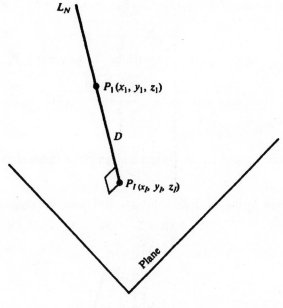

Fig. A2-18

L_N is

$$
L_N: \quad \begin{aligned} x &= x_1 + n_1 t \\ y &= y_1 + n_2 t \\ z &= z_1 + n_3 t \end{aligned}
$$

We first find the intersection point $P_I(x_I, y_I, z_I)$ of the line L_N with the plane. The distance from the point $P_1(x_1, y_1, z_1)$ to the plane will be the same as the distance from the point $P_1(x_1, y_1, z_1)$ to the intersection point $P_I(x_I, y_I, z_I)$.

Substituting the equations of the line L_N into the equation of the plane, we find

$$
n_1(x_1 + n_1 t - x_0) + n_2(y_1 + n_2 t - y_0) + n_3(z_1 + n_3 t - z_0) = 0
$$

Solving for t, we have

$$
t = -\frac{n_1(x_1 - x_0) + n_2(y_1 - y_0) + n_3(z_1 - z_0)}{n_1^2 + n_2^2 + n_3^2}
$$

Calling this number t_I, we find that the coordinates of P_I are

$$
x_I = x_1 + n_1 t_I \qquad y_I = y_1 + n_2 t_I \qquad z_I = z_1 + n_3 t_I \tag{A2.2}
$$

The distance D from $P(x_1, y_1, z_1)$ to $P_I(x_I, y_I, z_I)$ is

$$
D = \sqrt{(x_I - x_1)^2 + (y_I - y_1)^2 + (z_I - z_1)^2}
$$

From equation $(A2.2)$, we obtain

$$
x_I - x_1 = n_1 t_I \qquad y_I - y_1 = n_2 t_I \qquad z_I - z_1 = n_3 t_I
$$

Substitution into the formula for D yields

$$
D = \sqrt{(n_1 t_I)^2 + (n_2 t_I)^2 + (n_3 t_I)^2} = |t_I|\sqrt{n_1^2 + n_2^2 + n_3^2}
$$

or, substituting for t_I

$$
D = \frac{|n_1(x_1 - x_0) + n_2(y_1 - y_0) + n_3(z_1 - z_0)|}{\sqrt{n_1^2 + n_2^2 + n_3^2}}
$$

We can rewrite this in vector form by observing that

$$|\mathbf{N}| = \sqrt{n_1^2 + n_2^2 + n_3^2}$$

and that $(x_1 - x_0, y_1 - y_0, z_1 - z_0)$ are the components of the vector $\overline{\mathbf{P_0P_1}}$. So

$$D = \frac{|\mathbf{N} \cdot \overline{\mathbf{P_0P_1}}|}{|\mathbf{N}|} = \frac{d}{|\mathbf{N}|}$$

where $d = |\mathbf{N} \cdot \overline{\mathbf{P_0P_1}}|$.

A2.14 Find the projection $\mathbf{V_p}$ of a vector $\mathbf{V}$ onto a given plane in the direction of the normal vector $\mathbf{N}$.

SOLUTION

From Fig. A2-19, by the definition of (head-to-tail) vector addition (see App. 1), we have

$$\mathbf{V_p} + k\mathbf{N} = \mathbf{V} \qquad \text{or} \qquad \mathbf{V_p} = \mathbf{V} - k\mathbf{N}$$

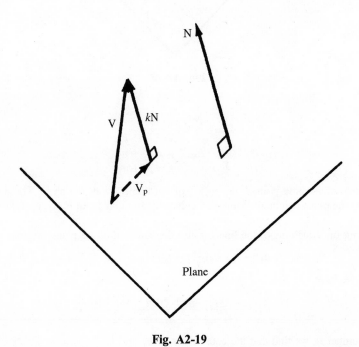

Fig. A2-19

To find the number k, we use the fact that $\mathbf{V_p}$ lies on the plane, so $\mathbf{N}$ is perpendicular to $\mathbf{V_p}$, i.e., $\mathbf{V_p} \cdot \mathbf{N} = 0$. So

$$0 = \mathbf{V_p} \cdot \mathbf{N} = \mathbf{V} \cdot \mathbf{N} - k(\mathbf{N} \cdot \mathbf{N}) \qquad \text{or} \qquad k = \frac{\mathbf{V} \cdot \mathbf{N}}{\mathbf{N} \cdot \mathbf{N}} = \frac{\mathbf{V} \cdot \mathbf{N}}{|\mathbf{N}|^2} \qquad (\text{since } \mathbf{N} \cdot \mathbf{N} = |\mathbf{N}|^2)$$

Then

$$\mathbf{V_p} = \mathbf{V} - \left(\frac{\mathbf{V} \cdot \mathbf{N}}{|\mathbf{N}|^2}\right)\mathbf{N} \tag{A2.3}$$

A2.15 Let a plane be determined by the normal vector $\mathbf{N} = \mathbf{I} - \mathbf{J} + \mathbf{K}$ and a point $P_0(2, 3 - 1)$.

(a) Find the distance from point $P_1(5, 2, 7)$ to the plane.

(b) Let $\mathbf{V} = 2\mathbf{I} + 3\mathbf{J} - \mathbf{K}$ be a vector. Find the projection of $\mathbf{V_p}$ (in the direction of the normal) onto the plane.

SOLUTION

(a) The vector $\overline{\mathbf{P_0P_1}} = 3\mathbf{I} - \mathbf{J} + 8\mathbf{K}$. From Prob. A2.13 we have

$$D = \frac{|\mathbf{N} \cdot \overline{\mathbf{P_0P_1}}|}{|\mathbf{N}|} = \frac{|(1)(3) + (-1)(-1) + (1)(8)|}{\sqrt{(1)^2 + (-1)^2 + (1)^2}} = \frac{12}{\sqrt{3}} = 4\sqrt{3}$$

(b) From Prob. A2.14, the projection vector $\mathbf{V_p}$ is given by

$$\mathbf{V_p} = \mathbf{V} - \left(\frac{\mathbf{V} \cdot \mathbf{N}}{|\mathbf{N}|^2}\right)\mathbf{N}$$

Now

$$\frac{\mathbf{V} \cdot \mathbf{N}}{|\mathbf{N}|^2} = \frac{(2)(1) + (3)(-1) + (-1)(1)}{(1)^2 + (-1)^2 + (1)^2} = \frac{-2}{3}$$

So

$$\mathbf{V_p} = (2\mathbf{I} + 3\mathbf{J} - \mathbf{K}) - (-\tfrac{2}{3})(\mathbf{I} - \mathbf{J} + \mathbf{K})$$
$$= (2\mathbf{I} + 3\mathbf{J} - \mathbf{K}) - (-\tfrac{2}{3}\mathbf{I} + \tfrac{2}{3}\mathbf{J} - \tfrac{2}{3}\mathbf{K}) = \tfrac{8}{3}\mathbf{I} + \tfrac{7}{3}\mathbf{J} - \tfrac{1}{3}\mathbf{K}$$

A2.16 Given vectors $\mathbf{A}$ and $\mathbf{B}$ that are placed tail to tail we define the perpendicular projection of $\mathbf{A}$ onto $\mathbf{B}$ to be the vector $\mathbf{V}$ shown in Fig. A2-20. Find a formula for computing $\mathbf{V}$ from $\mathbf{A}$ and $\mathbf{B}$.

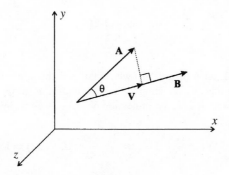

Fig. A2-20

SOLUTION

We first find (see Fig. A2-20)

$$|\mathbf{V}| = |\mathbf{A}| \cos(\theta) = |\mathbf{A}| \frac{\mathbf{A} \cdot \mathbf{B}}{|\mathbf{A}||\mathbf{B}|} = \frac{\mathbf{A} \cdot \mathbf{B}}{|\mathbf{B}|}$$

Using the unit vector

$$\mathbf{V} = |\mathbf{V}|\mathbf{U_V}$$

Since $\mathbf{V}$ and $\mathbf{B}$ have the same direction, we have $\mathbf{U_V} = \mathbf{U_B}$. Hence

$$\mathbf{V} = |\mathbf{V}|\mathbf{U_B} = \frac{\mathbf{A} \cdot \mathbf{B}}{|\mathbf{B}|} \frac{\mathbf{B}}{|\mathbf{B}|} = \frac{\mathbf{A} \cdot \mathbf{B}}{|\mathbf{B}|^2}\mathbf{B}$$

A2.17 Let $(3, 1, -3)$ be the coordinate of point A. Find a point B on the line $y = 2x$ in the xy plane such that the line connecting A and B is perpendicular to $y = 2x$.

SOLUTION 1

Since point B is on $y = 2x$, it has coordinates $(x, 2x, 0)$. We introduce two vectors $\mathbf{V_1}$ and $\mathbf{V_2}$ (see Fig. A2-21):

$$\mathbf{V_1} = x\mathbf{I} + 2x\mathbf{J}$$
$$\mathbf{V_2} = (3 - x)\mathbf{I} + (1 - 2x)\mathbf{J} - 3\mathbf{K}$$

The line connecting A and B is perpendicular to $y = 2x$ if

$$\mathbf{V_1} \cdot \mathbf{V_2} = 0$$

or

$$x(3 - x) + 2x(1 - 2x) = 0$$

This yields $x(1 - x) = 0$. Since the angle between the line $y = 2x$ and the line from the origin to point A is verifiably not $90°$, we have $x \neq 0$. Hence $x = 1$, and the coordinates of point B are $(1, 2, 0)$.

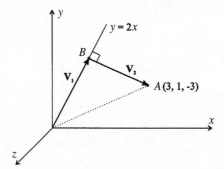

Fig. A2-21

SOLUTION 2

Referring to Fig. A2-21, let $\mathbf{A}$ be a vector whose tail is at the origin and whose head is at point A. From Prob. A2.16, we can see that $\mathbf{V_1}$ is simply the perpendicular projection of $\mathbf{A}$ onto $\mathbf{V_1}$ itself. Since $\mathbf{A} = 3\mathbf{I} + \mathbf{J} - 3\mathbf{K}$ and $\mathbf{V_1} = x\mathbf{I} + 2x\mathbf{J}$, the projection $\mathbf{V} = \mathbf{V_1}$ is given by

$$\mathbf{V_1} = \frac{\mathbf{A} \cdot \mathbf{V_1}}{|\mathbf{V_1}|^2} \mathbf{V_1} = \frac{3x + 2x}{x^2 + 4x^2}(x\mathbf{I} + 2x\mathbf{J}) = \mathbf{I} + 2\mathbf{J}$$

This means that the coordinates of point B are $(1, 2, 0)$.

A2.18 Let $a = |\mathbf{A}|$ and $b = |\mathbf{B}|$. Show that the vector

$$\mathbf{C} = \frac{a\mathbf{B} + b\mathbf{A}}{a + b}$$

bisects the angle between $\mathbf{A}$ and $\mathbf{B}$.

SOLUTION 1

$$\mathbf{C} = \frac{a\mathbf{B} + b\mathbf{A}}{a + b} = \frac{ab\mathbf{U_B} + ba\mathbf{U_A}}{a + b} = \frac{ab}{a + b}(\mathbf{U_B} + \mathbf{U_A})$$

Since vector $\mathbf{C}$ is in the direction of the diagonal line of the diamond figure formed by the two unit vectors $\mathbf{U_A}$ and $\mathbf{U_B}$ (see Fig. A2-22), it bisects the angle between $\mathbf{U_A}$ and $\mathbf{U_B}$, which is also the angle between $\mathbf{A}$ and $\mathbf{B}$.

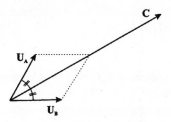

Fig. A2-22

SOLUTION 2

Let α be the angle between **A** and **C**, β be the angle between **B** and **C**, and $c = |\mathbf{C}|$. We have

$$\cos(\alpha) = \frac{\mathbf{A} \cdot \mathbf{C}}{ac} = \frac{\mathbf{A} \cdot \dfrac{a\mathbf{B} + b\mathbf{A}}{a+b}}{ac} = \frac{a\mathbf{A} \cdot \mathbf{B} + b\mathbf{A} \cdot \mathbf{A}}{ac(a+b)} = \frac{\mathbf{A} \cdot \mathbf{B} + ba}{c(a+b)}$$

and

$$\cos(\beta) = \frac{\mathbf{B} \cdot \mathbf{C}}{bc} = \frac{\mathbf{B} \cdot \dfrac{a\mathbf{B} + b\mathbf{A}}{a+b}}{bc} = \frac{a\mathbf{B} \cdot \mathbf{B} + b\mathbf{A} \cdot \mathbf{B}}{bc(a+b)} = \frac{ab + \mathbf{A} \cdot \mathbf{B}}{c(a+b)}$$

Comparing the two expressions we get $\cos(\alpha) = \cos(\beta)$, or $\alpha = \beta$.

A2.19 Prove the formula $\mathbf{V}_1 \cdot \mathbf{V}_2 = |\mathbf{V}_1||\mathbf{V}_2| \cos(\theta)$, where $\mathbf{V}_1$ and $\mathbf{V}_2$ are two vectors and θ is the smaller angle between $\mathbf{V}_1$ and $\mathbf{V}_2$ (when the vectors are placed tail to tail).

SOLUTION

Since $\mathbf{V} \cdot \mathbf{V} = |\mathbf{V}|^2$ for any vector **V** (see Prob. A2.3), we have (see Fig. A2- 23):

$$
\begin{aligned}
|\mathbf{V}_1 - \mathbf{V}_2|^2 &= (\mathbf{V}_1 - \mathbf{V}_2) \cdot (\mathbf{V}_1 - \mathbf{V}_2) \\
&= \mathbf{V}_1 \cdot (\mathbf{V}_1 - \mathbf{V}_2) - \mathbf{V}_2 \cdot (\mathbf{V}_1 - \mathbf{V}_2) \qquad \text{(Prob. A1.20)} \\
&= \mathbf{V}_1 \cdot \mathbf{V}_1 - 2\mathbf{V}_1 \cdot \mathbf{V}_2 + \mathbf{V}_2 \cdot \mathbf{V}_2 \qquad \text{(Prob. A1.19)} \\
&= |\mathbf{V}_1|^2 - 2\mathbf{V}_1 \cdot \mathbf{V}_2 + |\mathbf{V}_2|^2
\end{aligned}
$$

On the other hand, using the Law of Cosines (see Sect. A1.1), we have

$$|\mathbf{V}_1 - \mathbf{V}_2|^2 = |\mathbf{V}_1|^2 + |\mathbf{V}_2|^2 - 2|\mathbf{V}_1||\mathbf{V}_2| \cos(\theta)$$

Comparing the two expressions we get $\mathbf{V}_1 \cdot \mathbf{V}_2 = |\mathbf{V}_1||\mathbf{V}_2| \cos(\theta)$.

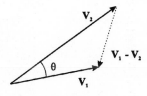

Fig. A2-23

A2.20 Use vectors to show that, if the two diagonals of a rectangle area perpendicular to each other, the rectangle is a square.

SOLUTION

Let the lower left corner of the rectangle be at the origin and the upper right corner be at (x, y) or $(x, y, 0)$. The two diagonals of the rectangle can be expressed as $\mathbf{V}_1 = x\mathbf{I} + y\mathbf{J}$ and $\mathbf{V}_2 = x\mathbf{I} - y\mathbf{J}$. When the two diagonals are perpendicular to each other, we have $xx - yy = 0$, or $x = y$. Hence the rectangle is a square.

A2.21 (*a*) What three-dimensional line determines the homogeneous coordinate point $(1, 5, -1)$? (*b*) Do the homogeneous coordinates $(1, 5, -1)$ and $(-2, -10, -3)$ represent the same projective point?

SOLUTION

(*a*) The line passes through the origin $(0, 0, 0)$ and the Cartesian point $(1, 5, -1)$. So $x = t$, $y = 5t$, and $z = -t$ is the equation of the line.

(*b*) The homogeneous coordinates represent the same projective point if and only if the coordinates are proportional, i.e., there is some number t so that $-2 = (1)t$, $-10 = (5)t$, and $-3 = (-1)t$. Since there is no such number, these coordinates represent different projective points.

Answers to Supplementary Problems

Chapter 2

2.42 No, since there is a change in aspect ratio ($5/3.5 \neq 6/4$).

2.43 Yes, since $5.25/3.5 = 6/4 = 1.5$.

2.44 Present the image at an aspect ratio that is lower than the original.

2.45
```
int i, j, c, rgb[3];
for ( j = 0; j < height; j++)
    for (i = 0; i < width; i++) {
        getPixel(i, j, rgb);
        c = 0.299*rgb[0] + 0.587*rgb[1] + 0.144*rgb[2];
        setPixel(i, j, c);
    }
```

Chapter 3

3.35

(a)

$y = 4x + 3$	x
11	2
31	7
7	1

(b)

$y = 1x + 0$	x
2	2
7	7
1	1

(c)

$y = -3x - 4$	x
-10	2
-25	7
-7	1

(d)

$y = -2x + 1$	x
-3	2
-13	7
-1	1

3.36
1. Compute the initial values. Prior to passing the variables to the line plotting routine, we exhange x and y coordinates, (x, y) giving (y, x).

$$dx = y_1 - y_2 \quad Inc_1 = 2dy$$
$$dy = x_1 - x_2 \quad Inc_2 = 2(dy - dx)$$
$$d = Inc_1 - dx$$

2. Set (x, y) equal to the lower left-hand endpoint and x_{end} equal to the largest value of x. If $dx < 0$, then $y = x_2$, $x = y_2$, $x_{\text{end}} = y_1$. If $dx > 0$, then $y = x_1$, $x = y_1$, $x_{\text{end}} = y_2$.
3. Plot a point at the current (y, x) coordinates. Note the coordinate values are exchanged before they are passed to the plot routine.
4. Test to determine whether the entire line has been drawn. If $x = x_{\text{end}}$, stop.
5. Compute the location of the next pixel. If $d < 0$, then $d = d + Inc_1$. If $d \geq 0$, then $d = d + Inc_2$, $y = y + 1$.
6. Increment x: $x = x + 1$.
7. Prior to plotting, the (x, y) coordinates are again exchanged. Plot a point at the current (x, y) coordinates.
8. Go to step 4.

3.37
1. Set the initial values: $(x_1, y_1) = $ start of line; $(x_3, y_3) = $ end of line; $\alpha = \tan^{-1}((y_3 - y_1)/(x_3 - x_1))$; $d = $ length of dash; $c = $ length of blank.
2. Test to see whether the entire line has been drawn. If $x_1 \geq x_3$, stop.

3. Compute end of dash:

$$x_2 = x_1 + d\cos(\alpha)$$
$$y_2 = y_1 + d\sin(\alpha)$$

4. Send (x_1, y_1) and (x_2, y_2) to the line routine and plot dash.
5. Compute the starting point of the next dash:

$$x_1 = x_2 + c\cos(\alpha)$$
$$y_1 = y_2 + c\sin(\alpha)$$

6. Go to step 2.

3.38 See Fig. S-1. Solving for $\theta = \pi/4$:

$$x = 2\cos(\pi/4) + 0 = 1.414 \qquad y = 1\sin(\pi/4) + 0 = 0.7071$$

Solving for $\theta = 3\pi/4$:

$$x = 2\cos(3\pi/4) + 0 = -1.414 \qquad y = 1\sin(3\pi/4) + 0 = 0.7071$$

Solving for $\theta = 5\pi/4$:

$$x = 2\cos(5\pi/4) + 0 = -1.414 \qquad y = 1\sin(5\pi/4) + 0 = -0.7071$$

Solving for $\theta = 7\pi/4$:

$$x = 2\cos(7\pi/4) + 0 = 1.414 \qquad y = 1\sin(7\pi/4) + 0 = -0.7071$$

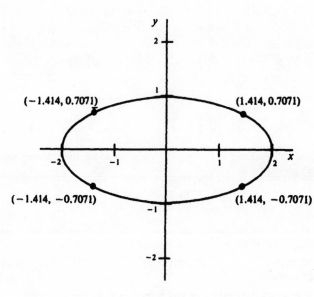

Fig. S-1

3.39 (*a*) Step 3 should be changed to read

$$x = a\cos(\theta) - b\sin\left(\theta + \frac{\pi}{4}\right) + h$$
$$y = b\sin(\theta) + a\cos\left(\theta + \frac{\pi}{4}\right) + k$$

(b)   Step 3 should be changed to read

$$x = a\cos(\theta) - b\sin\left(\theta + \frac{\pi}{9}\right) + h$$

$$y = b\sin(\theta) + a\cos\left(\theta + \frac{\pi}{9}\right) + k$$

(c)   Step 3 should be changed to read

$$x = a\cos(\theta) - b\sin\left(\theta + \frac{\pi}{2}\right) + h$$

$$y = b\sin(\theta) + a\cos\left(\theta + \frac{\pi}{2}\right) + k$$

Note that rotating an ellipse $\pi/2$ requires only that the major and minor axes be interchanged. Therefore, the rotation could also be accomplished by changing step 3 to read

$$x = b\cos\theta \qquad y = a\sin(\theta)$$

3.40   1.   Set initial variables: a = radius, (h, k) = coordinates of sector center, θ_1 = starting angle, θ_2 = ending angle, and i = step size.

2.   Plot line from sector center to coordinates of start of arc: plot (h, k) to $(a\cos(\theta_1) + h, a\sin(\theta_1) + k)$.

3.   Plot line from sector center to coordinates of end of arc: plot (h, k) to $(a\cos(\theta_2) + h, a\sin(\theta_2) + h)$.

4.   Plot arc.

3.41   When a region is to be filled with a pattern, the fill algorithm must look at a table containing the pattern before filling each pixel. The correct value for the pixel is taken from the table and placed in the pixel examined by the fill algorithm.

3.42   The human brain tends to compensate for deficiencies in models. For example, although the cube shown in Fig. S-2 is lacking the visual cue, convergence, it is perceived as a cube. When the choice of aliasing is inconsistent, the brain either cannot decode the model or can decode it only with difficulty because there is no one rule that can be learned to compensate for the inconsistencies of the models.

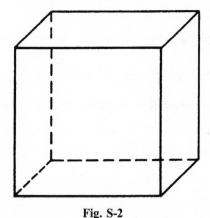

Fig. S-2

3.43   1.   Initialize the edge list. For each nonhorizontal edge, find $1/m (= \Delta x/\Delta y)$, y_{max}, y_{min}, and the x coordinate of the edge's lower endpoint.

2.   Begin with the first scan line y.

3.   If y is beyond the last scan line, stop.

4.   Activate all edges with $y_{min} = y$ and delete all edges for which $y > y_{max}$.

5.   Sort the intersection points by x value.

6.   Fill the pixels between and including each pair of intersection points.

7.   Increment x by $1/m$ for each active edge.

8.   Increment y by 1 and go to step 3.

3.44 Overstrike can be eliminated by checking each pixel before writing to it. If the pixel has already been written to, no point will be written. Or better yet, design scan-conversion algorithms that do not result in overstrike.

Chapter 4

4.19

$$R_\theta = \begin{pmatrix} \cos\theta & -\sin\theta \\ \sin\theta & \cos\theta \end{pmatrix} \quad \text{and} \quad R_{-\theta} = \begin{pmatrix} \cos(-\theta) & -\sin(-\theta) \\ \sin(-\theta) & \cos(-\theta) \end{pmatrix} = \begin{pmatrix} \cos\theta & \sin\theta \\ -\sin\theta & \cos\theta \end{pmatrix}$$

Also

$$\begin{aligned} R_\theta \cdot R_{-\theta} &= \begin{pmatrix} \cos\theta & -\sin\theta \\ \sin\theta & \cos\theta \end{pmatrix}\begin{pmatrix} \cos\theta & \sin\theta \\ -\sin\theta & \cos\theta \end{pmatrix} \\ &= \begin{pmatrix} (\cos^2\theta + \sin^2\theta) & (\cos\theta\sin\theta - \sin\theta\cos\theta) \\ (\sin\theta\cos\theta - \cos\theta\sin\theta) & (\sin^2\theta + \cos^2\theta) \end{pmatrix} = \begin{pmatrix} 1 & 0 \\ 0 & 1 \end{pmatrix} \end{aligned}$$

Therefore, R_θ and $R_{-\theta}$ are inverse, so $R_{-\theta} = R_\theta^{-1}$. In other words, the inverse of a rotation by θ degrees is a rotation in the opposite direction.

4.20 Magnification and reduction can be achieved by a uniform scaling of s units in both the X and Y directions. If $s > 1$, the scaling produces magnification. If $s < 1$, the result is a reduction. The transformation can be written as

$$(x, y) \longmapsto (sx, sy)$$

In matrix form, this becomes

$$\begin{pmatrix} s & 0 \\ 0 & s \end{pmatrix}\begin{pmatrix} x \\ y \end{pmatrix} = \begin{pmatrix} sx \\ sy \end{pmatrix}$$

(a) Choosing $s = 2$ and applying the transformation to the coordinates of the points A, B, C yields the new coordinates $A'(0, 0), B'(2, 2), C'(10, 4)$.

(b) Here, $s = \frac{1}{2}$ and the new coordinates are $A''(0, 0), B''(\frac{1}{2}, \frac{1}{2}), C''(\frac{5}{2}, 1)$.

4.21 The line $y = x$ has slope 1 and y intercept $(0, 0)$. If point P has coordinates (x, y), then following Prob. 4.10 we have

$$M_L \cdot P = \begin{pmatrix} 0 & 1 \\ 1 & 0 \end{pmatrix}\begin{pmatrix} x \\ y \end{pmatrix} = \begin{pmatrix} y \\ x \end{pmatrix} \quad \text{or} \quad M_L(x, y) = (y, x)$$

4.22 The rotation matrix is

$$R_{45°} = \begin{pmatrix} \dfrac{\sqrt{2}}{2} & -\dfrac{\sqrt{2}}{2} & 0 \\ \dfrac{\sqrt{2}}{2} & \dfrac{\sqrt{2}}{2} & 0 \\ 0 & 0 & 1 \end{pmatrix}$$

The translation matrix is

$$T_{\mathbf{I}} = \begin{pmatrix} 1 & 0 & 1 \\ 0 & 1 & 0 \\ 0 & 0 & 1 \end{pmatrix}$$

The matrix of vertices $[A \quad B \quad C]$ is

$$V = \begin{pmatrix} 1 & 0 & 1 \\ 0 & 1 & 1 \\ 1 & 1 & 1 \end{pmatrix}$$

(a)

$$T_{\mathbf{I}} \cdot R_{45^\circ} = \begin{pmatrix} \dfrac{\sqrt{2}}{2} & -\dfrac{\sqrt{2}}{2} & 1 \\ \dfrac{\sqrt{2}}{2} & \dfrac{\sqrt{2}}{2} & 0 \\ 0 & 0 & 1 \end{pmatrix} \quad \text{and} \quad T_{\mathbf{I}} \cdot R_{45^\circ} \cdot V = \begin{pmatrix} \left(\dfrac{\sqrt{2}}{2}+1\right) & \left(-\dfrac{\sqrt{2}}{2}+1\right) & 1 \\ \dfrac{\sqrt{2}}{2} & \dfrac{\sqrt{2}}{2} & \sqrt{2} \\ 1 & 1 & 1 \end{pmatrix}$$

So the transformed vertices are $A'\left(\dfrac{\sqrt{2}}{2}+1, \dfrac{\sqrt{2}}{2}\right)$, $B'\left(-\dfrac{\sqrt{2}}{2}+1, \dfrac{\sqrt{2}}{2}\right)$, and $C'(1, \sqrt{2})$.

(b)

$$R_{45^\circ} \cdot T_{\mathbf{I}} = \begin{pmatrix} \dfrac{\sqrt{2}}{2} & -\dfrac{\sqrt{2}}{2} & \dfrac{\sqrt{2}}{2} \\ \dfrac{\sqrt{2}}{2} & \dfrac{\sqrt{2}}{2} & \dfrac{\sqrt{2}}{2} \\ 0 & 0 & 1 \end{pmatrix} \quad \text{and} \quad R_{45^\circ} \cdot T_{\mathbf{I}} \cdot V = \begin{pmatrix} \sqrt{2} & 0 & \dfrac{\sqrt{2}}{2} \\ \sqrt{2} & \sqrt{2} & \dfrac{3\sqrt{2}}{2} \\ 1 & 1 & 1 \end{pmatrix}$$

The transformed coordinates are $A''(\sqrt{2}, \sqrt{2})$, $B''(0, \sqrt{2})$, and $C''(\sqrt{2}/2, 3\sqrt{2}/2)$. From this we see that the order in which the transformations are applied is important in the formation of composed or concatenated transformations (see Fig. S-3). Figure S-3(b) represents the triangle of Fig. S-3(a) after application of the transformation $T_{\mathbf{I}} \cdot R_{45^\circ}$; Fig. S-3(c) represents the same triangle after the transformation $R_{45^\circ} \cdot T_{\mathbf{I}}$.

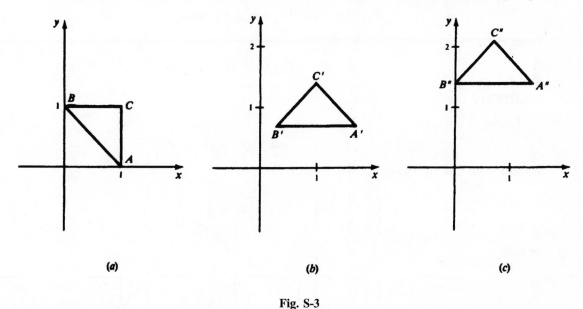

(a)   (b)   (c)

Fig. S-3

4.23   To determine the coordinates of the displaced object from the observer's point of view, we must find the coordinates of the object with respect to the observer's coordinate system. In our case we have performed an object translation $T_{\mathbf{v}}$ and a coordinate system translation $\bar{T}_{\mathbf{v}}$. The result is found by the composition $\bar{T}_{\mathbf{v}} \cdot T_{\mathbf{v}}$ (or $T_{\mathbf{v}} \cdot \bar{T}_{\mathbf{v}}$):

$$\begin{pmatrix} x \\ y \end{pmatrix} \mapsto \begin{pmatrix} x+a \\ y+b \end{pmatrix} \mapsto \begin{pmatrix} x+a-a \\ y+b-b \end{pmatrix} = \begin{pmatrix} x \\ y \end{pmatrix}$$

So the coordinates have remained the same.

4.24   We express the general form of an equation in the $x'y'$ coordinate system as $F(x', y') = 0$. Writing the coordinate transformation in equation form as

$$x' = q(x, y) \qquad y' = r(x, y)$$

and substituting this into the expression for F, we get

$$F(q(x, y), r(x, y)) = 0$$

which is an equation in xy coordinates.

4.25

SOLUTION 1

Let

$$V_1 = t_{x_1}\mathbf{I} + t_{y_1}\mathbf{J} \qquad \text{and} \qquad V_2 = t_{x_2}\mathbf{I} + t_{y_2}\mathbf{J}$$

We have

$$T_{V_1} \cdot T_{V_2}(x, y) = T_{V_1}(x + t_{x_2}, y + t_{y_2}) = (x + t_{x_2} + t_{x_1}, y + t_{y_2} + t_{y_1})$$

and

$$T_{V_2} \cdot T_{V_1}(x, y) = T_{v_2}(x + t_{x_1}, y + t_{y_1}) = (x + t_{x_1} + t_{x_2}, y + t_{y_1} + t_{y_2})$$

Since

$$V_1 + V_2 = (t_{x_1} + t_{x_2})\mathbf{I} + (t_{y_1} + t_{y_2})\mathbf{J}$$

we also have

$$T_{V_1 + V_2}(x, y) = (x + t_{x_1} + t_{x_2}, y + t_{y_1} + t_{y_2})$$

Therefore

$$T_{V_1} \cdot T_{V_2} = T_{V_2} \cdot T_{V_1} = T_{V_1 + V_2}$$

SOLUTION 2

Let

$$V_1 = t_{x_1}\mathbf{I} + t_{y_1}\mathbf{J} \qquad \text{and} \qquad V_2 = t_{x_2}\mathbf{I} + t_{y_2}\mathbf{J}$$

and express the translation transformations in matrix form

$$T_{V_1} = \begin{pmatrix} 1 & 0 & t_{x_1} \\ 0 & 1 & t_{y_1} \\ 0 & 0 & 1 \end{pmatrix} \qquad \text{and} \qquad T_{V_2} = \begin{pmatrix} 1 & 0 & t_{x_2} \\ 0 & 1 & t_{y_2} \\ 0 & 0 & 1 \end{pmatrix}$$

we have

$$T_{V_1} \cdot T_{V_2} = \begin{pmatrix} 1 & 0 & t_{x_1} \\ 0 & 1 & t_{y_1} \\ 0 & 0 & 1 \end{pmatrix} \cdot \begin{pmatrix} 1 & 0 & t_{x_2} \\ 0 & 1 & t_{y_2} \\ 0 & 0 & 1 \end{pmatrix} = \begin{pmatrix} 1 & 0 & t_{x_2} + t_{x_1} \\ 0 & 1 & t_{y_2} + t_{y_1} \\ 0 & 0 & 1 \end{pmatrix}$$

and

$$T_{V_2} \cdot T_{V_1} = \begin{pmatrix} 1 & 0 & t_{x_2} \\ 0 & 1 & t_{y_2} \\ 0 & 0 & 1 \end{pmatrix} \cdot \begin{pmatrix} 1 & 0 & t_{x_1} \\ 0 & 1 & t_{y_1} \\ 0 & 0 & 1 \end{pmatrix} = \begin{pmatrix} 1 & 0 & t_{x_1} + t_{x_2} \\ 0 & 1 & t_{y_1} + t_{y_2} \\ 0 & 0 & 1 \end{pmatrix}$$

Also since

$$V_1 + V_2 = (t_{x_1} + t_{x_2})\mathbf{I} + (t_{y_1} + t_{y_2})\mathbf{J}$$

we have

$$T_{V_1+V_2} = \begin{pmatrix} 1 & 0 & t_{x_1}+t_{x_2} \\ 0 & 1 & t_{y_1}+t_{y_2} \\ 0 & 0 & 1 \end{pmatrix}$$

Therefore

$$T_{V_1} \cdot T_{V_2} = T_{V_2} \cdot T_{V_1} = T_{V_1+V_2}$$

4.26

SOLUTION 1

Since

$$S_{a,b} \cdot S_{c,d}(x,y) = S_{a,b}(cx, dy) = (acx, bdy)$$
$$S_{c,d} \cdot S_{a,b}(x,y) = S_{c,d}(ax, by) = (cax, dby)$$
$$S_{ac,bd}(x,y) = (acx, bdy)$$

we have $S_{a,b} \cdot S_{c,d} = S_{c,d} \cdot S_{a,b} = S_{ac,bd}$.

SOLUTION 2

Express the scaling transformations in matrix form

$$S_{a,b} = \begin{pmatrix} a & 0 \\ 0 & b \end{pmatrix}, \qquad S_{c,d} = \begin{pmatrix} c & 0 \\ 0 & d \end{pmatrix}, \qquad \text{and} \qquad S_{ac,bd} = \begin{pmatrix} ac & 0 \\ 0 & bd \end{pmatrix}$$

Since

$$S_{a,b} \cdot S_{c,d} = \begin{pmatrix} a & 0 \\ 0 & b \end{pmatrix} \cdot \begin{pmatrix} c & 0 \\ 0 & d \end{pmatrix} = \begin{pmatrix} ac & 0 \\ 0 & bd \end{pmatrix}$$

and

$$S_{c,d} \cdot S_{a,b} = \begin{pmatrix} c & 0 \\ 0 & d \end{pmatrix} \cdot \begin{pmatrix} a & 0 \\ 0 & b \end{pmatrix} = \begin{pmatrix} ca & 0 \\ 0 & db \end{pmatrix}$$

we have $S_{a,b} \cdot S_{c,d} = S_{c,d} \cdot S_{a,b} = S_{ac,bd}$.

4.27 Express the rotation transformations in matrix form

$$R_\alpha = \begin{pmatrix} \cos(\alpha) & -\sin(\alpha) \\ \sin(\alpha) & \cos(\alpha) \end{pmatrix} \qquad \text{and} \qquad R_\beta = \begin{pmatrix} \cos(\beta) & -\sin(\beta) \\ \sin(\beta) & \cos(\beta) \end{pmatrix}$$

we have

$$R_\alpha \cdot R_\beta = \begin{pmatrix} \cos(\alpha) & -\sin(\alpha) \\ \sin(\alpha) & \cos(\alpha) \end{pmatrix} \cdot \begin{pmatrix} \cos(\beta) & -\sin(\beta) \\ \sin(\beta) & \cos(\beta) \end{pmatrix}$$
$$= \begin{pmatrix} \cos(\alpha)\cos(\beta) - \sin(\alpha)\sin(\beta) & -\cos(\alpha)\sin(\beta) - \sin(\alpha)\cos(\beta) \\ \sin(\alpha)\cos(\beta) + \cos(\alpha)\sin(\beta) & -\sin(\alpha)\sin(\beta) + \cos(\alpha)\cos(\beta) \end{pmatrix}$$

and

$$R_\beta \cdot R_\alpha = \begin{pmatrix} \cos(\beta) & -\sin(\beta) \\ \sin(\beta) & \cos(\beta) \end{pmatrix} \cdot \begin{pmatrix} \cos(\alpha) & -\sin(\alpha) \\ \sin(\alpha) & \cos(\alpha) \end{pmatrix}$$
$$= \begin{pmatrix} \cos(\beta)\cos(\alpha) - \sin(\beta)\sin(\alpha) & -\cos(\beta)\sin(\alpha) - \sin(\beta)\cos(\alpha) \\ \sin(\beta)\cos(\alpha) + \cos(\beta)\sin(\alpha) & -\sin(\beta)\sin(\alpha) + \cos(\beta)\cos(\alpha) \end{pmatrix}$$

Using trigonometric identities

$$\cos(\alpha + \beta) = \cos(\alpha)\cos(\beta) - \sin(\alpha)\sin(\beta)$$

and

$$\sin(\alpha + \beta) = \sin(\alpha)\cos(\beta) + \cos(\alpha)\sin(\beta)$$

we have

$$R_\alpha \cdot R_\beta = R_\beta \cdot R_\alpha = \begin{pmatrix} \cos(\alpha + \beta) & -\sin(\alpha + \beta) \\ \sin(\alpha + \beta) & \cos(\alpha + \beta) \end{pmatrix} = R_{\alpha+\beta}$$

4.28 First express scaling and rotation in matrix form

$$S_{s_x,s_y} = \begin{pmatrix} s_x & 0 \\ 0 & s_y \end{pmatrix} \quad \text{and} \quad R_\theta = \begin{pmatrix} \cos(\theta) & -\sin(\theta) \\ \sin(\theta) & \cos(\theta) \end{pmatrix}$$

we have

$$S_{s_x,s_y} \cdot R_\theta = \begin{pmatrix} s_x & 0 \\ 0 & s_y \end{pmatrix} \cdot \begin{pmatrix} \cos(\theta) & -\sin(\theta) \\ \sin(\theta) & \cos(\theta) \end{pmatrix} = \begin{pmatrix} s_x\cos(\theta) & -s_x\sin(\theta) \\ s_y\sin(\theta) & s_y\cos(\theta) \end{pmatrix}$$

and

$$R_\theta \cdot S_{s_x,s_y} = \begin{pmatrix} \cos(\theta) & -\sin(\theta) \\ \sin(\theta) & \cos(\theta) \end{pmatrix} \cdot \begin{pmatrix} s_x & 0 \\ 0 & s_y \end{pmatrix} = \begin{pmatrix} \cos(\theta)s_x & -\sin(\theta)s_y \\ \sin(\theta)s_x & \cos(\theta)s_y \end{pmatrix}$$

In order to satisfy

$$S_{s_x,s_y} \cdot R_\theta = R_\theta \cdot S_{s_x,s_y}$$

we need

$$s_y\sin(\theta) = \sin(\theta)s_x$$

This yields $\theta = n\pi$, where n is an integer, or $s_y = s_x$, which means that the scaling transformation is uniform.

4.29 No, since

$$\begin{pmatrix} 1 & a \\ 0 & 1 \end{pmatrix} \cdot \begin{pmatrix} 1 & 0 \\ b & 1 \end{pmatrix} = \begin{pmatrix} 1+ab & a \\ b & 1 \end{pmatrix} \neq \begin{pmatrix} 1 & a \\ b & 1 \end{pmatrix}$$

and

$$\begin{pmatrix} 1 & 0 \\ b & 1 \end{pmatrix} \cdot \begin{pmatrix} 1 & a \\ 0 & 1 \end{pmatrix} = \begin{pmatrix} 1 & a \\ b & ba+1 \end{pmatrix} \neq \begin{pmatrix} 1 & a \\ b & 1 \end{pmatrix}$$

4.30 A rotation followed by a simultaneous shearing can be expressed as

$$\begin{pmatrix} \cos(\theta) & -\sin(\theta) \\ \sin(\theta) & \cos(\theta) \end{pmatrix} \cdot \begin{pmatrix} 1 & a \\ b & 1 \end{pmatrix} = \begin{pmatrix} \cos(\theta) - b \cdot \sin(\theta) & a \cdot \cos(\theta) - \sin(\theta) \\ \sin(\theta) + b \cdot \cos(\theta) & a \cdot \sin(\theta) + \cos(\theta) \end{pmatrix}$$

On the other hand, a simultaneous shearing followed by a rotation can be expressed as

$$\begin{pmatrix} 1 & a \\ b & 1 \end{pmatrix} \cdot \begin{pmatrix} \cos(\theta) & -\sin(\theta) \\ \sin(\theta) & \cos(\theta) \end{pmatrix} = \begin{pmatrix} \cos(\theta) + a \cdot \sin(\theta) & -\sin(\theta) + a \cdot \cos(\theta) \\ b \cdot \cos(\theta) + \sin(\theta) & -b \cdot \sin(\theta) + \cos(\theta) \end{pmatrix}$$

In order for the two composite transformation matrices to be the same, we need

$$\cos(\theta) - b \cdot \sin(\theta) = \cos(\theta) + a \cdot \sin(\theta)$$

or

$$-b \cdot \sin(\theta) = a \cdot \sin(\theta)$$

which means $\theta = n\pi$, where n is an integer, or $a = -b$.

4.31 Consider the following sequence of rotate–scale–rotate transformations

$$R_\alpha \cdot S_{s_x,s_y} \cdot R_\beta = \begin{pmatrix} \cos(\alpha) & -\sin(\alpha) \\ \sin(\alpha) & \cos(\alpha) \end{pmatrix} \cdot \begin{pmatrix} s_x & 0 \\ 0 & s_y \end{pmatrix} \cdot \begin{pmatrix} \cos(\beta) & -\sin(\beta) \\ \sin(\beta) & \cos(\beta) \end{pmatrix}$$

$$= \begin{pmatrix} \cos(\alpha)\cos(\beta)s_x - \sin(\alpha)\sin(\beta)s_y & -\cos(\alpha)\sin(\beta)s_x - \sin(\alpha)\cos(\beta)s_y \\ \sin(\alpha)\cos(\beta)s_x + \cos(\alpha)\sin(\beta)s_y & -\sin(\alpha)\sin(\beta)s_x + \cos(\alpha)\cos(\beta)s_y \end{pmatrix}$$

By equating the composite transformation matrix on the right-hand side to the matrix for a simultaneous shearing transformation

$$\begin{pmatrix} 1 & a \\ b & 1 \end{pmatrix}$$

we have four equations that can be solved for parameters α, β, s_x and s_y.

4.32 Consider the following sequence of shearing and scaling transformations:

$$\begin{pmatrix} 1 & a \\ 0 & 1 \end{pmatrix} \cdot \begin{pmatrix} s_x & 0 \\ 0 & s_y \end{pmatrix} \cdot \begin{pmatrix} 1 & 0 \\ b & 1 \end{pmatrix} = \begin{pmatrix} s_x + a \cdot b \cdot s_y & a \cdot s_y \\ b \cdot s_y & s_y \end{pmatrix}$$

By equating the composite transformation matrix on the right to

$$R_\theta = \begin{pmatrix} \cos(\theta) & -\sin(\theta) \\ \sin(\theta) & \cos(\theta) \end{pmatrix}$$

we have

$$a = -\frac{\sin(\theta)}{\cos(\theta)}, \qquad b = \frac{\sin(\theta)}{\cos(\theta)}, \qquad s_x = \frac{1}{\cos(\theta)}, \qquad s_y = \cos(\theta).$$

4.33 Consider the following sequence of shearing transformations:

$$\begin{pmatrix} 1 & a_1 \\ 0 & 1 \end{pmatrix} \cdot \begin{pmatrix} 1 & 0 \\ b & 1 \end{pmatrix} \cdot \begin{pmatrix} 1 & a_2 \\ 0 & 1 \end{pmatrix} = \begin{pmatrix} 1 + a_1 b & (1 + a_1 b)a_2 + a_1 \\ b & ba_2 + 1 \end{pmatrix}$$

By equating the composite transformation matrix on the right to

$$R_\theta = \begin{pmatrix} \cos(\theta) & -\sin(\theta) \\ \sin(\theta) & \cos(\theta) \end{pmatrix}$$

we have

$$a_1 = a_2 = \frac{\cos(\theta) - 1}{\sin(\theta)} \qquad \text{and} \qquad b = \sin(\theta)$$

4.34 Let CTM_n be the composite transformation matrix representing the concatenation of n basic transformation matrices. We prove, by mathematical induction on n, that CTM_n is always in the following form

$$\begin{pmatrix} a & b & c \\ d & e & f \\ 0 & 0 & 1 \end{pmatrix}$$

$n = 1$: The basis case is true since CTM_1 is simply a basic transformation matrix, which fits into the given template.

$n = k$: Suppose that CTM_k is indeed in the specified form.

$$\text{CTM}_k = \begin{pmatrix} a_k & b_k & c_k \\ d_k & e_k & f_k \\ 0 & 0 & 1 \end{pmatrix}$$

ANSWERS TO SUPPLEMENTARY PROBLEMS

$n = k + 1$: We now show that CTM_{k+1} is in the same form:

$$\text{CTM}_{k+1} = \begin{pmatrix} a & b & c \\ d & e & f \\ 0 & 0 & 1 \end{pmatrix} \cdot \text{CTM}_k = \begin{pmatrix} a & b & c \\ d & e & f \\ 0 & 0 & 1 \end{pmatrix} \cdot \begin{pmatrix} a_k & b_k & c_k \\ d_k & e_k & f_k \\ 0 & 0 & 1 \end{pmatrix}$$

$$= \begin{pmatrix} a \cdot a_k + b \cdot d_k & a \cdot b_k + b \cdot e_k & a \cdot c_k + b \cdot f_k + c \\ d \cdot a_k + e \cdot d_k & d \cdot b_k + e \cdot e_k & d \cdot c_k + e \cdot f_k + f \\ 0 & 0 & 1 \end{pmatrix}$$

4.35 Let $P_1'(x_1', y_1')$ be the transformation of $P_1(x_1, y_1)$ and $P_2'(x_2', y_2')$ be the transformation of $P_2(x_2, y_2)$. Also let the composite transformation be expressed as

$$\begin{pmatrix} a & b & c \\ d & e & f \\ 0 & 0 & 1 \end{pmatrix}$$

we have

$$x_1' = ax_1 + by_1 + c \qquad y_1' = dx_1 + ey_1 + f$$

and

$$x_2' = ax_2 + by_2 + c \qquad y_2' = dx_2 + ey_2 + f$$

Now consider an arbitrary point $P(x, y)$ on the line from P_1 to P_2. We want to show that the transformed P, denoted by $P'(x', y')$, where $x' = ax + by + c$ and $y' = dx + ey + f$, is on the line between P_1' and P_2'. In other words, we want to show

$$\frac{y_2' - y_1'}{x_2' - x_1'} = \frac{y_2' - y'}{x_2' - x'}$$

which is

$$\frac{dx_2 + ey_2 + f - dx_1 - ey_1 - f}{ax_2 + by_2 + c - ax_1 - by_1 - c} = \frac{dx_2 + ey_2 + f - dx - ey - f}{ax_2 + by_2 + c - ax - by - c}$$

and is

$$\frac{d + e\dfrac{y_2 - y_1}{x_2 - x_1}}{a + b\dfrac{y_2 - y_1}{x_2 - x_1}} = \frac{d + e\dfrac{y_2 - y}{x_2 - x}}{a + b\dfrac{y_2 - y}{x_2 - x}}$$

Since (x, y) satisfies

$$\frac{y_2 - y_1}{x_2 - x_1} = \frac{y_2 - y}{x_2 - x}$$

we have established the equality that shows P' being on the line between P_1' and P_2'.

Chapter 5

5.20 From Prob. 5.1 we need only identify the appropriate parameters.

(a) The window parameters are $wx_{\min} = 0$, $wx_{\max} = 1$, $wy_{\min} = 0$, and $wy_{\max} = 1$. The viewport parameters are $vx_{\min} = 0$, $vx_{\max} = 199$, $vy_{\min} = 0$, and $vy_{\max} = 639$. Then $s_x = 199$, $s_y = 639$, and

$$W = \begin{pmatrix} 199 & 0 & 0 \\ 0 & 639 & 0 \\ 0 & 0 & 1 \end{pmatrix}$$

(b) The parameters are the same, but the device y coordinate is now $639 - y$ (see Prob. 2.8) instead of the y

value computed by W in (a)

$$W = \begin{pmatrix} 199 & 0 & 0 \\ 0 & -639 & 639 \\ 0 & 0 & 1 \end{pmatrix}$$

5.21 If $s_x = s_y$, then

$$\frac{vx_{\max} - vx_{\min}}{wx_{\max} - wx_{\min}} = \frac{vy_{\max} - vy_{\min}}{wy_{\max} - wy_{\min}} \qquad \text{or} \qquad \frac{wy_{\max} - wy_{\min}}{wx_{\max} - wx_{\min}} = \frac{vy_{\max} - vy_{\min}}{vx_{\max} - vx_{\min}}$$

Inverting, we have $a_w = a_v$.

A similar argument shows that if the aspect ratios are equal, $a_w = a_v$, the scale factors are equal, $s_x = s_y$.

5.22 We form N by composing (1) a translation mapping the center $(1, 1)$ to the center $(\frac{1}{2}, \frac{1}{2})$ and (2) a scaling about $C(\frac{1}{2}, \frac{1}{2})$ with uniform scaling factor $s = \frac{1}{10}$, so

$$N = S_{1/10, 1/10, C} \cdot T_{\mathbf{v}}, \qquad \text{where} \qquad \mathbf{v} = -\tfrac{1}{2}\mathbf{I} - \tfrac{1}{2}\mathbf{J}$$

$$= \begin{pmatrix} \frac{1}{10} & 0 & \frac{9}{20} \\ 0 & \frac{1}{10} & \frac{9}{20} \\ 0 & 0 & 1 \end{pmatrix} \begin{pmatrix} 1 & 0 & -\frac{1}{2} \\ 0 & 1 & -\frac{1}{2} \\ 0 & 0 & 1 \end{pmatrix} = \begin{pmatrix} \frac{1}{10} & 0 & \frac{2}{5} \\ 0 & \frac{1}{10} & \frac{2}{5} \\ 0 & 0 & 1 \end{pmatrix}$$

5.23 Let the clipping region be a circle with center at $O(h, k)$ and radius r. We reduce the number of candidates for clipping by assigning region codes as in the Cohen–Sutherland algorithm. To do this, we use the circumscribed square with lower left corner at $(h - r, k - r)$ and upper right corner at $(h + r, k + r)$ to preprocess the line segments. However, we now have only two clipping categories—not displayed and candidates for clipping. Next, we decide which line segments are to be displayed. Since the (nonparametric) equation of the circle is $(x - h)^2 + (y - k)^2 = r^2$, the quantity $K(x, y) = (x - h)^2 + (y - k)^2 - r^2$ determines whether a point $P(x, y)$ is inside, on, or outside the circle. So, if $K \le 0$ for both endpoints P_1 and P_2 of a line segment, both points are inside or on the circle and so the line segment is displayed. If $K > 0$ for either P_1 or P_2 or both, we calculate the intersection(s) of the line segment and the circle. Using parametric representations, we find (App. 1, Prob. A1.24) that the intersection parameter is

$$t_I = \frac{-S \pm \sqrt{S^2 - L^2 C}}{L^2}$$

where

$$L^2 = (x_2 - x_1)^2 + (y_2 - y_1)^2$$
$$S = (x_1 - h)(x_2 - x_1) + (y_1 - k)(y_2 - y_1)$$
$$C = (x_1 - h)^2 + (y_1 - k)^2 - r^2$$

If $0 \le t_I \le 1$, the actual intersection point(s) $I(\bar{x}, \bar{y})$ is (are)

$$\bar{x} = x_1 + t_I(x_2 - x_1) \qquad \bar{y} = y_1 + t_I(y_2 - y_1)$$

So, if $K > 0$ for either P_1 or P_2 (or both), we first relabel the endpoints so that P_1 satisfies $K > 0$. Next we calculate t_I. The following situations arise:

1. $S^2 - L^2 C < 0$. Then t_I is undefined and no intersection takes place. The line segment is not displayed.
2. $S^2 - L^2 C = 0$. There is exactly one intersection. If $t_I > 1$ or $t_I < 0$, the intersection point is on the extended line, and so there is no actual intersection. The line is not displayed. If $0 < t_I \le 1$, $\overline{P_1 P_2}$ is tangent to the circle at point I, so only I is displayed.
3. $S^2 - L^2 C > 0$. Then there are two values for t_I, t_I^+, and t_I^-. If $0 < t_I^-$, $t_I^+ \le 1$, the line segment $\overline{I^- I^+}$ is displayed and the segments (assuming $t_I^+ > t_I^-$) $\overline{P_1 I^-}$ and $\overline{I^+ P_2}$ are clipped. If only one value, say, t_I^+, satisfies $0 < t_I^+ \le 1$, there is one actual intersection and one apparent intersection. Since in this case P_2 is either point I^+ or inside the circle, $\overline{P_1 I^+}$ is clipped and $\overline{I^+ P_2}$ is displayed. If t_I^+, $t_I^- > 1$ or t_I^+, $t_I^- < 0$, then $\overline{P_1 P_2}$ is not displayed.

5.24 Following the logic of the Sutherland–Hodgman algorithm as described in Prob. 5.14, we first clip the "polygon" P_1P_2 against edge $\overline{AB}$ of the window:

1. $\overline{AB}$. We first determine which side of $\overline{AB}$ the points P_1 and P_2 lie. Calculating the quantity (see Prob. 5.13), we have

$$\bar{C} = (x_2 - x_1)(y - y_1) - (y_2 - y_1)(x - x_1)$$

With point $A = (x_1, y_1)$ and point $B = (x_2, y_2)$, we find $\bar{C} = 8$ for point P_1 and $\bar{C} = 2$ for point P_2. So both points lie on the left of $\overline{AB}$. Consequently, the algorithm will output both P_1 and P_2.

2. $\overline{BC}$. Setting point $B = (x_1, y_1)$ and $\bar{C} = (x_2, y_2)$, we calculate $\bar{C} = 13$ for point P_1 and $\bar{C} = -3$ for point P_2. Thus P_1 is to the left of $\overline{BC}$ and P_2 is to right of $\overline{BC}$. We now find the intersection point I_1 of $\overline{P_1P_2}$ with the extended line $\overline{BC}$. From Prob. A2.7 in App. 2, we have $I_1 = (4\frac{11}{16}, 3\frac{5}{8})$. Following the algorithm, points P_1 and I_1 are passed on to be clipped.

3. $\overline{CD}$. Proceedings as before, we find that $\bar{C} = 2$ for point P_1 and $\bar{C} = 6\frac{7}{8}$ for point I_1. So both points lie to the left of $\overline{CD}$ and consequently are passed on.

4. $\overline{DA}$. Setting point $D = (x_1, y_1)$ and $A = (x_2, y_2)$, we find $\bar{C} = -3$ for P_1 and $\bar{C} = 10$ for I_1. Then P_1 lies to the right of $\overline{DA}$ and I_1 to the left. The intersection point of $\overline{P_1I_1}$ with the extended edge $\overline{DA}$ is $I_2 = (\frac{5}{16}, 2\frac{3}{8})$. The clipped line is the segment $\overline{I_1I_2}$.

Chapter 6

6.9 From Prob. 6.2, we identify the parameters

$$\mathbf{V} = a\mathbf{I} + b\mathbf{J} + c\mathbf{K} = \mathbf{I} + \mathbf{J} + \mathbf{K}$$
$$|\mathbf{V}| = \sqrt{a^2 + b^2 + c^2} = \sqrt{1^2 + 1^2 + 1^2} = \sqrt{3}$$
$$\lambda = \sqrt{b^2 + c^2} = \sqrt{1^2 + 1^2} = \sqrt{2}$$

Then

$$A_{\mathbf{V}} = \begin{pmatrix} \dfrac{\sqrt{2}}{\sqrt{3}} & \dfrac{-1}{\sqrt{2}\sqrt{3}} & \dfrac{-1}{\sqrt{2}\sqrt{3}} & 0 \\ 0 & \dfrac{1}{\sqrt{2}} & \dfrac{-1}{\sqrt{2}} & 0 \\ \dfrac{1}{\sqrt{3}} & \dfrac{1}{\sqrt{3}} & \dfrac{1}{\sqrt{3}} & 0 \\ 0 & 0 & 0 & 1 \end{pmatrix}$$

6.10 From Prob. 6.5, $A_{\mathbf{V},\mathbf{N}} = A_{\mathbf{N}}^{-1} \cdot A_{\mathbf{V}}$. We find $A_{\mathbf{V}}$ first. From Prob. 6.2 we identify the parameters $|\mathbf{V}| = \sqrt{3}$, $\lambda = \sqrt{2}$, $a = 1$, $b = 1$, $c = 1$. So

$$A_{\mathbf{V}} = \begin{pmatrix} \dfrac{\sqrt{2}}{\sqrt{3}} & \dfrac{-1}{\sqrt{2}\sqrt{3}} & \dfrac{-1}{\sqrt{2}\sqrt{3}} & 0 \\ 0 & \dfrac{1}{\sqrt{2}} & \dfrac{-1}{\sqrt{2}} & 0 \\ \dfrac{1}{\sqrt{3}} & \dfrac{1}{\sqrt{3}} & \dfrac{1}{\sqrt{3}} & 0 \\ 0 & 0 & 0 & 1 \end{pmatrix}$$

For $A_{\mathbf{N}}^{-1}$, we have $|\mathbf{N}| = \sqrt{6}$, $\lambda = \sqrt{2}$, $a = 2$, $b = -1$, and $c = -1$. So

$$A_{\mathbf{N}}^{-1} = \begin{pmatrix} \dfrac{\sqrt{2}}{\sqrt{6}} & 0 & \dfrac{2}{\sqrt{6}} & 0 \\[2mm] \dfrac{2}{\sqrt{2}\sqrt{6}} & \dfrac{-1}{\sqrt{2}} & \dfrac{-1}{\sqrt{6}} & 0 \\[2mm] \dfrac{2}{\sqrt{2}\sqrt{6}} & \dfrac{1}{\sqrt{2}} & \dfrac{-1}{\sqrt{6}} & 0 \\[2mm] 0 & 0 & 0 & 1 \end{pmatrix}$$

Note that $\mathbf{V}' = A_{\mathbf{V},\mathbf{N}} \cdot \mathbf{V} = A_{\mathbf{N}}^{-1} \cdot A_{\mathbf{V}} \cdot \mathbf{V} = \sqrt{2}\mathbf{I} - \dfrac{\sqrt{2}}{2}\mathbf{J} - \dfrac{\sqrt{2}}{2}\mathbf{K}$ so that $\mathbf{V}' = \dfrac{\sqrt{2}}{2}\mathbf{N}$. In other words, the image of $\mathbf{V}$ under $A_{\mathbf{V},\mathbf{N}}$ is not the vector $\mathbf{N}$, but a vector that has the direction of $\mathbf{N}$.

6.11 This follows from comparing the matrices $A_{\mathbf{V}}^{-1}$ with $A_{\mathbf{V}}^{T}$ from Prob. 6.2.

6.12 If we place vectors $\mathbf{V}$ and $\mathbf{N}$ at the origin, then from App. 2, $\mathbf{V} \times \mathbf{N}$ is perpendicular to both $\mathbf{V}$ and $\mathbf{N}$. If θ is the angle between $\mathbf{V}$ and $\mathbf{N}$, then a rotation of $\theta°$ about the axis L whose direction is that of $\mathbf{V} \times \mathbf{N}$ and which passes through the origin will align $\mathbf{V}$ with $\mathbf{N}$. So $A_{\mathbf{V},\mathbf{N}} = R_{\theta,L}$.

6.13 As in the two-dimensional case in Chap. 4, we reduce the problem of scaling with respect to an arbitrary point P_0 to scaling with respect to the origin by translating P_0 to the origin, performing the scaling about the origin and then translating back to P_0. So

$$S_{s_x, s_y, s_z, P_0} = T_{-P_0}^{-1} \cdot S_{s_x, s_y, s_z} \cdot T_{-P_0}$$

Chapter 7

7.16 From Prob. 7.5, we need to evaluate the parameters (a, b, c), (n_1, n_2, n_3), (d, d_0, d_1) to construct the transformation. From the equations in Prob. 7.6, part (b) [denoting the principal vanishing points as $P_1(x_1, y_1, z_1)$, $P_2(x_2, y_2, z_2)$, and $P_3(x_3, y_3, z_3)$], we find $a = x_2$ (or x_3), $b = y_1$ (or y_3), and $c = z_1$ (or z_2). Also

$$n_1 = \frac{d}{x_1 - a} \qquad n_2 = \frac{d}{y_2 - b} \qquad n_3 = \frac{d}{z_3 - c}$$

To find d, d_0, and d_1, we note (App. 2, Prob. A2.13) that the distance D from the point $C(a, b, c)$ to the plane can be expressed as $D = |d|/|\mathbf{N}|$, where $|\mathbf{N}|$ is the magnitude of $\mathbf{N}$. Since we need only find the direction of the normal $\mathbf{N}$, we can assume $|\mathbf{N}| = 1$. Then $d = \pm D$. The choice $\pm$, based on the definition of d in Prob. 7.5, is dependent on the direction of the normal vector $\mathbf{N}$, the reference point R_0, and the center of projection C. Since these are not all specified, we are free to choose, and we shall choose the $+$ sign, that is, $d = D$. Finally

$$d_1 = n_1 a + n_2 b + n_3 c \qquad \text{and} \qquad d_0 = d + d_1$$

7.17 We use the coordinate matrix $\mathbf{V}$ constructed in Prob. 7.1 to represent the unit cube.

(a) From Problem 7.14, the isometric projection matrix Par is applied to the coordinate matrix $\mathbf{V}$:

$$Par \cdot \mathbf{V} = \begin{pmatrix} 0 & \sqrt{\dfrac{2}{3}} & \dfrac{3}{2}\sqrt{\dfrac{2}{3}} & \dfrac{1}{2}\sqrt{\dfrac{2}{3}} & \sqrt{\dfrac{2}{3}} & \dfrac{1}{2}\sqrt{\dfrac{2}{3}} & \dfrac{3}{2}\sqrt{\dfrac{2}{3}} & 2\sqrt{\dfrac{2}{3}} \\[2mm] 0 & 0 & \dfrac{\sqrt{2}}{2} & \dfrac{\sqrt{2}}{2} & 0 & \dfrac{-\sqrt{2}}{2} & \dfrac{-\sqrt{2}}{2} & 0 \\[2mm] 0 & 0 & 0 & 0 & 0 & 0 & 0 & 0 \\[2mm] 1 & 1 & 1 & 1 & 1 & 1 & 1 & 1 \end{pmatrix}$$

This is the matrix of the projected vertices, which can now be read off (see also Fig. S-4).

$$A' = (0, 0, 0) \qquad E' = \left(\sqrt{\frac{2}{3}}, 0, 0\right)$$

$$B' = \left(\sqrt{\frac{2}{3}}, 0, 0\right) \qquad F' = \left(\frac{1}{2}\sqrt{\frac{2}{3}}, -\frac{\sqrt{2}}{2}, 0\right)$$

$$C' = \left(\frac{3}{2}\sqrt{\frac{2}{3}}, \frac{\sqrt{2}}{2}, 0\right) \qquad G' = \left(\frac{3}{2}\sqrt{\frac{2}{3}}, -\frac{\sqrt{2}}{2}, 0\right)$$

$$D' = \left(\frac{1}{2}\sqrt{\frac{2}{3}}, \frac{\sqrt{2}}{2}, 0\right) \qquad H' = \left(2\sqrt{\frac{2}{3}}, 0, 0\right)$$

(b) To produce a dimetric drawing, we proceed, as in part (a), by using the dimetric transformation *Par* from Prob. 7.15. Choosing the projection ratio of $\frac{1}{2}$:1:1 (i.e., $l = \frac{1}{2}$), we have

$$Par = \begin{pmatrix} \dfrac{\sqrt{2}}{3} & \dfrac{\sqrt{14}}{6} & \dfrac{\sqrt{14}}{6} & 0 \\ 0 & \dfrac{\sqrt{2}}{2} & \dfrac{-\sqrt{2}}{2} & 0 \\ 0 & 0 & 0 & 0 \\ 0 & 0 & 0 & 1 \end{pmatrix}$$

The projected image coordinates are found by multiplying the matrices *Par* and **V**:

$$Par \cdot \mathbf{V} = \begin{pmatrix} 0 & \dfrac{\sqrt{2}}{3} & \dfrac{2\sqrt{2}+\sqrt{14}}{6} & \dfrac{\sqrt{14}}{6} & \dfrac{\sqrt{14}}{3} & \dfrac{\sqrt{14}}{6} & \dfrac{2\sqrt{2}+\sqrt{14}}{6} & \dfrac{\sqrt{2}+\sqrt{14}}{3} \\ 0 & 0 & \dfrac{\sqrt{2}}{2} & \dfrac{\sqrt{2}}{2} & 0 & \dfrac{-\sqrt{2}}{2} & \dfrac{-\sqrt{2}}{2} & 0 \\ 0 & 0 & 0 & 0 & 0 & 0 & 0 & 0 \\ 1 & 1 & 1 & 1 & 1 & 1 & 1 & 1 \end{pmatrix}$$

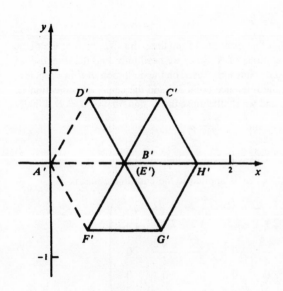

Fig. S-4

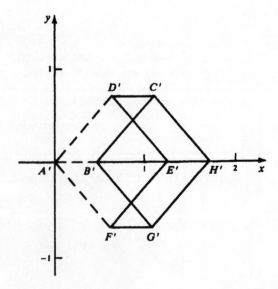

Fig. S-5

The image coordinates are (see Fig. S-5)

$$A' = (0, 0, 0) \qquad\qquad E' = \left(\frac{\sqrt{14}}{3}, 0, 0\right)$$

$$B' = \left(\frac{\sqrt{2}}{3}, 0, 0\right) \qquad\qquad F' = \left(\frac{\sqrt{14}}{6}, \frac{-\sqrt{2}}{2}, 0\right)$$

$$C' = \left(\frac{2\sqrt{2} + \sqrt{14}}{6}, \frac{\sqrt{2}}{2}, 0\right) \qquad G' = \left(\frac{2\sqrt{2} + \sqrt{14}}{6}, \frac{-\sqrt{2}}{2}, 0\right)$$

$$D' = \left(\frac{\sqrt{14}}{6}, \frac{\sqrt{2}}{2}, 0\right) \qquad\qquad H' = \left(\frac{\sqrt{2} + \sqrt{14}}{3}, 0, 0\right)$$

7.18 Since the planes we seek are to be located at the origin, we need only find the normal vectors of these planes so that orthographic projections onto these planes produce isometric projections. In Prob. 7.14, we rotated the *xyz* triad first about the *x* axis and then about the *y* axis to produce an isometric projection onto the *xy* plane. Equivalently, we could have tilted the *xy* plane (and its normal vector **K**) to a new position, thus yielding a new view plane which produces an isometric projection with respect to the (unrotated) *xyz* triad. Using this approach to find all possible view planes, we shall use the equations from Prob. 7.14 to find the appropriate rotation angles. From the equations

$$\sin^2 \theta_x - \cos^2 \theta_x = 0 \qquad \cos^2 \theta_y = \tfrac{1}{2}[\sin^2 \theta_y + 1]$$

we find the solutions

$$\sin \theta_x = \pm \frac{\sqrt{2}}{2}, \qquad \cos \theta_x = \pm \frac{\sqrt{2}}{2} \qquad \text{and} \qquad \sin \theta_y = \pm \sqrt{\frac{1}{3}}, \qquad \cos \theta_y = \pm \sqrt{\frac{2}{3}}$$

From Chap. 6, Prob. 6.1, part (*b*), the matrix that produces the tilting is

$$R_{\theta_{x,I}} \cdot R_{\theta_{y,J}} = \begin{pmatrix} \cos \theta_y & 0 & \sin \theta_y \\ \sin \theta_x \sin \theta_y & \cos \theta_x & -\sin \theta_x \cos \theta_y \\ -\cos \theta_x \sin \theta_y & \sin \theta_x & \cos \theta_x \cos \theta_y \end{pmatrix}$$

Applying this to the vector **K** = (0, 0, 1), we find the components of the tilted vector to be

$$x = \sin \theta_y \qquad y = -\sin \theta_x \cos \theta_y \qquad z = \cos \theta_x \cos \theta_y$$

Substituting the values found above, we have eight candidates for the normal vector $\mathbf{N} = x\mathbf{I} + y\mathbf{J} + z\mathbf{K}$, where

$$x = \pm \sqrt{\frac{1}{3}} \qquad y = \pm \sqrt{\frac{1}{3}} \qquad z = \pm \sqrt{\frac{1}{3}}$$

However, both **N** and −**N** define normals to the same plane. So we finally have four solutions. These are the view planes (through the origin) with normals

$$\mathbf{N}_1 = \sqrt{\frac{1}{3}} \, (\mathbf{I} + \mathbf{J} + \mathbf{K}) \qquad \mathbf{N}_3 = \sqrt{\frac{1}{3}} \, (\mathbf{I} - \mathbf{J} + \mathbf{K})$$

$$\mathbf{N}_2 = \sqrt{\frac{1}{3}} \, (-\mathbf{I} + \mathbf{J} + \mathbf{K}) \qquad \mathbf{N}_4 = \sqrt{\frac{1}{3}} \, (\mathbf{I} + \mathbf{J} - \mathbf{K})$$

Chapter 8

8.11 Referring to Fig. 8-7 (and Prob. 8.4) we call $\overline{\mathbf{CR}}$ the vector having the direction of the line from the center of projection C to the window corner R. Similarly, we call $\overline{\mathbf{CL}}$ the vector to the window corner L. Then:

1. *Top plane*—determined by the vectors $\mathbf{I_p}$ and $\overline{\mathbf{CR}}$ and the reference point R_f
2. *Bottom plane*—determined by the vectors $\mathbf{I_p}$ and $\overline{\mathbf{CL}}$ and the reference point L_f
3. *Right side plane*—determined by the vectors $\mathbf{J_q}$ and $\overline{\mathbf{CR}}$ and the reference point R_f

4. *Left side plane*—determined by the vectors $\mathbf{J_q}$ and $\overline{\mathbf{CL}}$ and the reference point L_f
5. *Front (near) plane*—determined by the (view plane) normal vector $\mathbf{N}$ and the reference point P_f
6. *Back (far) plane*—determined by the normal vector $\mathbf{N}$ and the reference point P_b

8.12   Suppose that the plane passes through point $R_0(x_0, y_0, z_0)$ and has a normal vector $\mathbf{N} = n_1\mathbf{I} + n_2\mathbf{J} + n_3\mathbf{K}$. Let the points $P_1(x_1, y_1, z_1)$ and $P_2(x_2, y_2, z_2)$ determine a line segment. From App. 2, the equation of the plane is

$$n_1(x - x_0) + n_2(y - y_0) + n_3(z - z_0) = 0$$

and the parametric equation of the line is

$$x = x_1 + (x_2 - x_1)t \qquad y = y_1 + (y_2 - y_1)t \qquad z = z_1 + (z_2 - z_1)t$$

Substituting these equations into the equations of the plane, we obtain

$$n_1[x_1 + (x_2 - x_1)t - x_0] + n_2[y_1 + (y_2 - y_1)t - y_0] + n_3[z_1 + (z_2 - z_1)t - z_0] = 0$$

Solving this for t yields the parameter value t_I at the time of intersection:

$$t_I = -\frac{n_1(x_1 - x_0) + n_2(y_1 - y_0) + n_3(z_1 - z_0)}{n_1(x_2 - x_1) + n_2(y_2 - y_1) + n_3(z_2 - z_1)}$$

We can rewrite this using vector notation as

$$t_I = -\frac{\mathbf{N} \cdot \overline{R_0P_1}}{\mathbf{N} \cdot \overline{P_1P_2}}$$

The intersection points $I(x_I, y_I, z_I)$ can be found from the parametric equations of the line:

$$x_I = x_1 + (x_2 - x_1)t_I \qquad y_I = y_1 + (y_2 - y_1)t_I \qquad z_I = z_1 + (z_2 - z_1)t_I$$

If $0 \le t_I \le 1$, the intersection point I is on the line segment from P_1 to P_2; if not, the intersection point is on the extended line.

Chapter 9

9.9   Referring to Fig. 7-12 in Chap. 7, we define a vertex list as

$$V = \{ABCDEFGH\}$$

and an explicit edge list is:

$$E = \{\overline{AB}, \overline{AD}, \overline{AF}, \overline{BC}, \overline{BG}, \overline{CD}, \overline{CH}, \overline{DE}, \overline{EF}, \overline{EH}, \overline{FG}, \overline{GH}\}$$

The cube can be drawn by drawing the edges in list E. Referring to Prob. 9.2, we note that a typical polygon, say, P_1, can be represented in terms of its edges as

$$P_1 = \{\overline{AB}, \overline{AD}, \overline{BC}, \overline{CD}\}$$

The polygons sharing a specific edge can be identified by extending the edge's representation to include pointers to those polygons. For example:

$$\overline{AB} \rightarrow P_1, P_4 \qquad \overline{AD} \rightarrow P_1, P_3$$

9.10   The knot set can be represented as $t_0, t_0 + L, t_0 + 2L, \ldots$. On the interval $t_i = t_0 + (i - 1)L$ to $t_{i+2} = t_0 + (i + 1)L$, we have

$$B_{i,1}(x) = \frac{x - [t_0 + (i - 1)L]}{(t_0 + iL) - [t_0 + (i - 1)L]} B_{i,0}(x) + \frac{[t_0 + (i + 1)L] - x}{[t_0 + (i + 1)L] - (t_0 + iL)} B_{i+1,0}(x)$$

On the interval $[t_i, t_{i+1}]$, that is, $t_0 + (i - 1)L \le x \le t_0 + iL$, we have $B_{i,0}(x) = 1$ and $B_{i+1,0}(x) = 0$. On the interval $[t_{i+1}, t_{i+2}]$, that is, $t_0 + iL \le x \le t_0 + (i + 1)L$, we have $B_{i,0}(x) = 0$ and $B_{i+1,0}(x) = 1$. Elsewhere both

$B_{i,0}(x) = 0$ and $B_{i+1,0}(x) = 0$. So

$$B_{i,1}(x) = \begin{cases} \dfrac{x - t_0 + (i-1)L}{L} & \text{on} & t_0 + (i-1)L \le x \le t_0 + iL \\[2ex] \dfrac{t_0 + (i+1)L - x}{L} & \text{on} & t_0 + iL \le x \le t_0 + (i+1)L \\[2ex] 0 & & \text{elsewhere} \end{cases}$$

9.11 From the definition of a B-spline, $B_{i,3}(x)$ is nonzero only if $t_i \le x \le t_{i+4}$. In terms of the given knot set, this equates to $i \le x \le i+4$. With $x = 5.5$, $B_{i,3}(5.5)$ is nonzero for $i = 2, 3, 4,$ and 5. Now

$$B_{i,3}(5.5) = \frac{(5.5) - i}{(i+3) - i} B_{i,2}(5.5) + \frac{(i+4) - (5.5)}{(i+4) - (i+1)} B_{i+1,2}(5.5)$$

or

$$B_{i,2}(5.5) = \frac{(5.5) - i}{3} B_{i,2}(5.5) + \frac{i - (1.5)}{3} B_{i+1,2}(5.5)$$

Starting with $i = 2$,

$$B_{2,3}(5.5) = \frac{3.5}{3} B_{2,2}(5.5) + \frac{0.5}{3} B_{3,2}(5.5)$$

Now $B_{2,2}(x)$ is nonzero if $2 \le x \le 5$. Thus $B_{2,2}(5.5) = 0$, and so $B_{2,3}(5.5) = (0.5/3) B_{3,2}(5.5)$. Because $B_{3,2}(x)$ is nonzero for $3 \le x \le 6$, we find that

$$B_{3,2}(5.5) = \frac{(5.5) - 3}{5 - 3} B_{3,1}(5.5) + \frac{6 - (5.5)}{6 - 4} B_{4,1}(5.5)$$

Now $B_{3,1}(x)$ is nonzero if $3 \le x \le 5$. So $B_{3,1}(5.5) = 0$. Now $B_{4,1}(x)$ is nonzero if $4 \le x \le 6$. Thus

$$B_{3,2}(5.5) = \frac{0.5}{2} B_{4,1}(5.5)$$

Now

$$B_{4,1}(5.5) = \frac{(5.5) - 4}{5 - 4} B_{4,0}(5.5) + \frac{6 - (5.5)}{6 - 5} B_{5,0}(5.5)$$

Since $B_{4,0}(x)$ is nonzero if $4 \le x \le 5$, we find that $B_{4,0}(5.5) = 0$. So

$$B_{4,1}(5.5) = \frac{0.5}{1} B_{5,0}(5.5)$$

However, $B_{5,0}(x) = 1$ if $5 \le x \le 6$. So $B_{5,0}(5.5) = 1$, $B_{4,1}(5.5) = 0.5(1) = 0.5$, and $B_{3,2}(5.5) = (0.5/2)(0.5) = 0.25/2$, and finally

$$B_{2,3}(5.5) = \frac{0.5}{3} \left(\frac{0.25}{2} \right) = \frac{0.125}{6} = 0.0208333$$

The computations for $B_{3,3}(5.5)$, $B_{4,3}(5.5)$, and $B_{5,3}(5.5)$ are carried out in the same way.

Chapter 10

10.25 The properties of parallel projection can be used to simplify calculations if the objects to be projected are transformed into "new objects" whose parallel projection results in the same image as the perspective projection of the original object.

10.26 Since the Z-buffer algorithm changes colors at a pixel only if $Z(x, y) < Z_{buf}(x, y)$, the first polygon written will determine the color of the pixel (see Prob. 10.7).

10.27 A priority flag could be assigned to break the tie resulting in applying the Z-buffer algorithm.

10.28 A system that distinguishes 2^{24} depth values would require three bytes of memory to represent each z value. Thus $3 \times 1024 \times 768 = 2304\,\text{K}$ of memory would be needed.

10.29 The scan-line method can take advantage of (*a*) scan-line coherence, (*b*) edge coherence, (*c*) area coherence, and (*d*) spatial coherence.

10.30 Scan-line coherence is based on the assumption that if a pixel belongs to the scan-converted image of an object, the pixels next to it will (most likely) also belong to this object.

10.31 Since this figure is a polygon, we need only find the maximum and minimum coordinate values of the vertices A, B, and C. Then

$$
\begin{aligned}
x_{\min} &= 0 & x_{\max} &= 2 \\
y_{\min} &= 0 & y_{\max} &= 2 \\
z_{\min} &= 1 & z_{\max} &= 2
\end{aligned}
$$

The bounding box is shown in Fig. 10-26.

10.32 Horizontal line segments ($y_{\min} = y_{\max}$) lie on only one scan line; they are automatically displayed when nonhorizontal edges are used in the scan-conversion process.

10.33 We search the z coordinates of the vertices of the polygon for the largest value, $z_{\max}$. The depth of the polygon is then $z_{\max}$.

10.34 Area coherence is exploited by classifying polygons with respect to a given screen area as either a surrounding polygon, an intersecting polygon, a contained polygon, or a disjoint polygon. The key fact is that a polygon is not visible if it is in back of a surrounding polygon.

10.35 When using a hidden-surface algorithm to eliminate hidden lines, we set the fill color of the polygons, determined by the lines, to the background color.

Chapter 11

11.25 Let W, H, D, and P be defined in the same way as in Prob. 11.3. We can calculate saturation using $D \times P/(W \times H + D \times P)$.

11.26 The color-sensitive cones in our eyes do not respond well to low intensity light. On the other hand, the rods that are sensitive to low intensity light are color blind.

11.27 Yes. We can use

$$
X = \frac{x}{1 - x - y} Z, \qquad Y = \frac{y}{1 - x - y} Z, \qquad Z = Z
$$

11.28 The Y in *CMY* means yellow, whereas the Y in *YIQ* represents luminance.

11.29

$$
\mathbf{N} = \frac{x - x_c}{R}\mathbf{I} + \frac{y - y_c}{R}\mathbf{J} + \frac{z - z_c}{R}\mathbf{K}
$$

11.30   The parametric representation for the target area is

$$\begin{cases} x = \theta \\ y = 1.2\cos(\varphi) \\ z = 1.2\sin(\varphi) \end{cases} \qquad \begin{aligned} 0 \le \theta \le 3.0 \\ 0 \le \varphi \le \pi/2 \end{aligned}$$

Note the relationship between the corner points:

$$\begin{aligned} u = 0, & \quad w = 0 \to \theta = 0, & \quad \varphi = \pi/2 \\ u = 1, & \quad w = 0 \to \theta = 3, & \quad \varphi = \pi/2 \\ u = 0, & \quad w = 2 \to \theta = 0, & \quad \varphi = 0 \\ u = 1, & \quad w = 2 \to \theta = 3, & \quad \varphi = 0 \end{aligned}$$

Substitute these into $\theta = Au + B$ and $\varphi = Cw + D$, we get

$$A = 3, \qquad B = 0, \qquad C = -\pi/4, \qquad D = \pi/2$$

Hence the mapping functions are

$$\theta = 3u \qquad \text{and} \qquad \varphi = \frac{\pi}{2} - \frac{\pi}{4}w$$

The inverse mapping functions are

$$u = \frac{\theta}{3} \qquad \text{and} \qquad w = \frac{\pi/2 - \varphi}{\pi/4}$$

Chapter 12

12.27   Let t_1 be the time required for the light ray to travel from A to P, and t_2 be the time required for the light ray to travel from P to B (see Fig. 12-21). We have

$$t_1 = \frac{\sqrt{x^2 + y_A^2}}{c_1} \qquad t_2 = \frac{\sqrt{(x_B - x)^2 + y_B^2}}{c_2}$$

To locate P (i.e., to determine x) such that the total travel time $t = t_1 + t_2$ is minimal, we find

$$\frac{dt}{dx} = \frac{x}{c_1\sqrt{x^2 + y_A^2}} - \frac{x_B - x}{c_2\sqrt{(x_B - x)^2 + y_B^2}}$$

or

$$\frac{dt}{dx} = \frac{\sin(\alpha)}{c_1} - \frac{\sin(\beta)}{c_2}$$

Notice that $0 \le x \le x_B$ and

$$\left(\frac{dt}{dx}\right)_0 < 0 \qquad \left(\frac{dt}{dx}\right)_{x_B} > 0$$

These suggest that t reaches a minimum when

$$\frac{\sin(\alpha)}{c_1} - \frac{\sin(\beta)}{c_2} = 0$$

Hence

$$\frac{\sin(\alpha)}{\sin(\beta)} = \frac{c_1}{c_2}$$

12.28 Yes, these two procedures produce identical results when invoked with the same call. However, for a given depth value the procedure in this question involves one more level of recursion than the one in the text. Hence the procedure in Sect. 12.2 has better execution efficiency.

12.29 Find two points on the line

$$x = 0 \rightarrow y = 0 - 6 = -6$$
$$x = 1 \rightarrow y = 2 - 6 = -4$$

Use $(0, -6)$ to be the starting point, we have

$$\mathbf{s} = -6\mathbf{J}$$
$$\mathbf{d} = (1 - 0)\mathbf{I} + (-4 - (-6))\mathbf{J} = \mathbf{I} + 2\mathbf{J}$$

and the parametric vector equation for the line is

$$\mathbf{L}(t) = \mathbf{s} + t\mathbf{d} \qquad \text{where } -\infty < t < +\infty$$

12.30 Intersection of a ray with the yz plane can be determined by solving the following for t:

$$\mathbf{s} + t\mathbf{d} = y_i\mathbf{J} + z_i\mathbf{K}$$

With $\mathbf{s} = x_\mathbf{s}\mathbf{I} + y_\mathbf{s}\mathbf{J} + z_\mathbf{s}\mathbf{K}$ and $\mathbf{d} = x_\mathbf{d}\mathbf{I} + y_\mathbf{d}\mathbf{J} + z_\mathbf{d}\mathbf{K}$, we have

$$\begin{cases} x_\mathbf{s} + tx_\mathbf{d} = 0 \\ y_\mathbf{s} + ty_\mathbf{d} = y_i \\ z_\mathbf{s} + tz_\mathbf{d} = z_i \end{cases}$$

When $x_\mathbf{d} = 0$, the ray is parallel to the plane (no intersection). When $x_\mathbf{s} = 0$, the ray originates from the plane (no intersection). Otherwise, we calculate t using the first equation

$$t = -\frac{x_\mathbf{s}}{x_\mathbf{d}}$$

If $t < 0$, the negative extension of the ray intersects the plane. On the other hand, if $t > 0$, the ray itself intersects the plane and the coordinates y_i and z_i of the intersection point can be calculated from the second and third equations.

12.31 Let $\mathbf{s} = x_\mathbf{s}\mathbf{I} + y_\mathbf{s}\mathbf{J} + z_\mathbf{s}\mathbf{K}$ and $\mathbf{d} = x_\mathbf{d}\mathbf{I} + y_\mathbf{d}\mathbf{J} + z_\mathbf{d}\mathbf{K}$. Substitute $x_\mathbf{s} + tx_\mathbf{d}$ and $y_\mathbf{s} + ty_\mathbf{d}$ for x and y, respectively

$$(x_\mathbf{s} + tx_\mathbf{d})^2 + (y_\mathbf{s} + ty_\mathbf{d})^2 - R^2 = 0$$

Expand and regroup terms

$$(x_\mathbf{d}^2 + y_\mathbf{d}^2)t^2 + 2(x_\mathbf{s}x_\mathbf{d} + y_\mathbf{s}y_\mathbf{d})t + (x_\mathbf{s}^2 + y_\mathbf{s}^2) - R^2 = 0$$

or

$$At^2 + 2Bt + C = 0$$

where

$$A = x_\mathbf{d}^2 + y_\mathbf{d}^2 \qquad B = x_\mathbf{s}x_\mathbf{d} + y_\mathbf{s}y_\mathbf{d} \qquad C = x_\mathbf{s}^2 + y_\mathbf{s}^2 - R^2$$

When $A = 0$, the ray is parallel to the z axis and does not intersect the cylinder (the entire ray is on the cylinder if the starting point is on the cylinder). Otherwise, the solution for the quadratic equation is

$$t = \frac{-B \pm \sqrt{B^2 - AC}}{A}$$

with

$$B^2 - AC \begin{cases} < 0 & \text{no intersection} \\ = 0 & \text{ray (or its negative extension) touching cylinder} \\ > 0 & \text{two (possible) intersection points} \end{cases}$$

The last case ($B^2 - AC > 0$) produces two t values: t_1 and t_2. If $t_1 < 0$ and $t_2 < 0$, the negative extension of the ray intersects the cylinder (no intersection by the ray). If one of the two values is 0, the ray starts from a point on the cylinder and intersects the cylinder only if the other value is positive. If t_1 and t_2 differ in signs, the ray originates from inside the cylinder and intersects the cylinder once. If both values are positive, the ray intersects the cylinder twice (first enters and then exits), and the smaller value corresponds to the intersection point that is closer to the starting point of the ray.

12.32 Substitute B in $At^2 + Bt + C = 0$ with D we have

$$At^2 + Dt + C = 0$$

and the solution is

$$t = \frac{-D \pm \sqrt{D^2 - 4AC}}{2A}$$

Now let $D = 2B$, the above equation becomes

$$At^2 + 2Bt + C = 0$$

and the solution is

$$t = \frac{-2B \pm \sqrt{(2B)^2 - 4AC}}{2A} = \frac{-2B \pm 2\sqrt{B^2 - AC}}{2A} = \frac{-B \pm \sqrt{B^2 - AC}}{A}$$

INDEX